# PREVAILING OVER TIME

# PREVAILING

Ethnic Adjustment on the
Kansas Prairies,
1875–1925

University of Nebraska Press

# OVER TIME

D. Aidan McQuillan

Lincoln and London

F
690
AI
M37
1990

*Publication of this book was assisted by a grant from*
*The Andrew W. Mellon Foundation*

Manufactured in the United States of America
The paper in this book meets the minimum requirements of
American National Standard for Information Sciences—Permanence
of Paper for Printed Library Materials, ANSI Z39.48–1984.

Library of Congress Cataloging-in-Publication Data
McQuillan, D. Aidan.
     Prevailing over time : ethnic adjustment on the Kansas prairies,
  1875–1925 / D. Aidan McQuillan.
        p.   cm.
     Includes bibliographical references.
     ISBN 0-8032-3143-1
     1. Minorities—Kansas—History.   2. Immigrants—Kansas—History.
  3. Kansas—Ethnic relations.   4. Kansas—Emigration and immigration—
  History.   I. Title.
  F690.AIM37   1990
  305.8'009781—dc20                                    89-28957
                                                          CIP

# CONTENTS

# FIGURES

# TABLES

Still let thy voice, prevailing over time,
Redress the rigours of th' inclement clime;
Aid slighted truth; with thy persuasive strain
Teach erring man to spurn the rage of gain;
Teach him, that states of native strength possess'd,
Though very poor, may still be very bless'd. . . .

Oliver Goldsmith, "The Deserted Village"

# PREFACE

This book is an attempt to understand the process whereby Europeans become Americans. The subject is not new, but the aim of the study is to take a fresh look at the issue by examining the adaptation that immigrant farmers made to a demanding environment whose constraints were poorly understood in the first decades of settlement. Both European immigrants and American farmers faced the same difficulties: no one fully appreciated the nature of the drought problem and subtleties of moisture supply for at least several decades after initial settlement.

As the agricultural frontier pushed westward from the Atlantic seaboard into the heart of the continent, the pioneer phase grew shorter and shorter. In the eastern woodland frontier, decades might pass between the arrival of the first pioneers and the completion of a transportation link that facilitated a commercial grain economy. But as the frontier moved from the Mississippi lowlands toward the high plains in the 1860s and 1870s, the pioneer phase lasted little longer than ten years. In central Kansas, railroad branch lines crisscrossed the countryside less than fifteen years after the first farm families had arrived. Farmers adjusted rapidly to new commercial opportunities even while the constraints of environment were not yet mastered. On this fast-changing frontier social simplification was short-lived.

A new culture, a new way of life, was established immediately on the western prairies. For example, the rectangular survey system precluded the possibility of reestablishing Old World nucleated villages and the community life associated with them. The rectangular grid of farmsteads, designed for Jefferson's nation of yeoman farmers, underscored an ethos of liberal individualism. It was a powerful mold for the assimilation of immigrants. While the newcomers fitted into the pattern of rectangular fields and dispersed homesteads, they simultaneously created areas of homogeneous settlement that became sharply distinctive communities. Immigrants became ethnics: the impulse of ethnogenesis overrode the pull of assimilation. The early arrival of railroad branch lines and the penetration of American cultural influences did not check the ethnic impulse.

Community life was critical in the next step of Americanization. Expansion or contraction of an ethnic settlement over the years depended on a variety of factors. Population turnover had always been high on the frontier, although it was believed that ethnic farmers were less mobile than American farmers. But the ethnics proved remarkably mobile too. Population loss in a community could be overcome over the long term in part through high fertility rates and natural regeneration. In the short term, immigration from sister communities in the Midwest could make a critical difference. And indeed, a communications network did develop, linking ethnic communities across the country and promoting the infusion of new blood into weakening rural enclaves. But more than anything else, financial security and community stability were essential conditions for the success of an ethnic community, its distinctive way of life, and its distinctive identity.

Security and stability could be achieved if the community adapted successfully to the environment. The problem along the prairie-plains ecotone was that climatic difficulties were very imperfectly understood. Drought was an elusive and subtle phenomenon that could vary in intensity, duration, and areal extent. Not surprisingly, farmers were baffled by it until they had experienced its most severe impact. The great drought of 1893–96 marked a turning point in central Kansas, and an enduring environmental lesson was learned. The lesson was not lost on the next generation of farmers, who, shortly after 1900, increasingly took over management of their parents' farms. And so a new generation assumed leadership in the ethnic communities, nurturing the ties of ethnic loyalty and seeking out new opportunities in American commercial life. They became American farmers.

In the course of preparing this book, I have received invaluable help from many Kansans. The late Nyle Miller, then director of the Kansas State Historical Society, and his staff, especially Joseph Snell and Robert Richmond, facilitated my work in the Topeka archives. Larry Wilson of the U.S. Weather Bureau in Kansas City searched for hidden sources of nineteenth-century weather data. Finally, Nyle and Esther Miller took me into their home during the many months of research in Topeka and in their quiet, unspoken way revealed to me the great kindness of Kansans.

I have been most fortunate in the scholarly support I have received during the preparation of this study. Professors David Ward, Allan Bogue, and Morton Rothstein sharpened concepts and methods of analysis when I prepared an early stage of the work as a doctoral dissertation at the University of Wisconsin. Professor George Dury, in his characteristic manner, gave generously of his time and unsparingly of his incisive comments in the final stages of dissertation preparation. My greatest debt, however, is to the late Andrew H. Clark, who supervised my work at the University of Wisconsin; his criticism and advice helped to formulate and develop this piece of research.

Geoffrey Matthews and his staff in the cartography laboratory at the University of Toronto prepared the maps and graphs. Mrs. Anne McMaster typed various drafts of the manuscript and throughout them all exercised a keen editorial eye above and beyond the call of duty. My colleagues Bill Callahan, David Higgs, and Jock Galloway at the University of Toronto have given me constant encouragement over the years. Royce La Nier provided not only support but a quiet environment in which much of the writing was done. For all this I am deeply grateful.

The book is dedicated to the memory of two men who guided the first and final steps of my formal education.

# THE AMERICANIZATION OF IMMIGRANTS AND ETHNICITY

1

The American republic was barely six years old when Crèvecoeur remarked on the diversity of the ethnic origins of its population. Throughout the course of American history ethnicity has been an inescapable fact of the country's social organization and a factor of considerable importance in its political development. "What then is an American, this new man? He is either a European, or the descendant of a European, hence that strange mixture of blood which you will find in no other country. I could point out to you a family whose grandfather was an Englishman, whose wife was Dutch, whose son married a French woman, and whose present four sons now have four wives of different nations." Crèvecoeur visualized the new American as having diverse origins, shaking off the prejudices and constrictions of his European peasant past and thus producing a new order of society. "Here individuals of all nations are melted into a new race of men, whose labors and posterity will one day cause great changes in the world." [1]

Crèvecoeur's comments on the diversity of American origins were perhaps more a statement of ideals than an observation of reality. Implicit within his statement is the notion that the ethnicity or identity that distinguished one European from another would quickly disappear in North America. However, the amalgamation of European groups into American society has been neither a complete nor a uniform process. Successive waves of immigration during the nineteenth and early twentieth centuries added new blood to old communities. Sharp distinctions developed between more recent arrivals and older immigrant groups. With the ending of large-scale immigration in the 1920s, the imminent disappearance of ethnicity has been heralded many times.[2] Nevertheless, the "Little Italys," Greek quarters, Polish sections, and Ukrainian districts are still realities.

As an immigrant to North America more than two decades ago I was fascinated by the persistence of ethnic communities and by two questions that they raised: How and why do immigrants retain certain traits that set them apart from the general population? and How do these immigrants eventually become Americans? The two questions are concerned with the process of Americanization and with the nature of ethnicity.

## The Process of Americanization

While European immigrants continued to pour into the United States throughout the nineteenth century, there was a major problem, notwithstanding Crèvecoeur's idealistic comments, of fusing these diverse elements into a new nation, a new national group with a strong, cohesive identity. The persistence of European traditions and languages or affiliations with the European homeland, together with the development of segregated settlements in North America, hindered the process of Americanization. To be sure, throughout the nineteenth century there were surges of American nationalism, which attacked the residual European traits: the best-known examples are the Nativist and Know-Nothing movements of the 1850s and 1860s.[3] Often the effect of these nationalist impulses was to produce a backlash within the immigrant groups, causing a reinforcement of their identity as distinctive groups and so postponing their assimilation into American society. The Americanization of immigrants was not a simple historical progression. There were periods of rapid change and regression and as settlement eventually penetrated the farthest corners of the continent and a mature, urban system emerged.

Historians and sociologists have formulated three models to explain the development of American society that encompass these changes in national direction. They are Anglo-conformity, identified with the period of British colonial rule, particularly in New England and the southern colonies, where it persisted long after the colonial period had ended; the melting-pot thesis, first identified with the Middle Atlantic states and later with the rural Midwest in the nineteenth century; and finally cultural pluralism, the realization in twentieth-century urban America that diversity rather than cultural homogeneity is the most attractive format and an ideal vital to the life of a nation.

Anglo-conformity was the dominant concept for the development of American society throughout the eighteenth and into the nineteenth century, at least up to the beginning of Andrew Jackson's presidency. In the territories of the former British colonies aesthetic tastes and style of living, systems of local government and judicial administration, and social organization survived the American Revolution. In the newly settled backwoods communities, social life was characterized by isolation and roughness. Nevertheless, it was hoped that they too would eventually develop a refined lifestyle based on the British model and similar to that of the older communities along the eastern seaboard. Frederick Jackson Turner recognized that the impact of Anglo-conformity was greatest in New England and in the South:

> The tidewater part of the South represented typical Englishmen, modified by a warm climate and servile labor, and living in a baronial fashion on great plantations; New England stood for a special English movement— Puritanism. The Middle region was less English than the other sections. It had a wide mixture of nationalities, a varied society, the mixed town and country system of local government, a varied economic way of life, many religious sects. In short it was a region mediating between New England and the South, and the East and the West.[4]

When Turner presented his "frontier thesis" in 1893, he was unhappy with the emphasis on European antecedents in American social development. The late nineteenth century was a period of rapid change in the United States, when a new effort was needed to strengthen American national identity. The divisions between North and South wrought during the Civil War had not healed. The hegemony of the North was confirmed by rapid industrial expansion and urban growth. Growth in the northern states was fueled by an influx of labor from eastern Europe and by heavy capital investment, particularly from Britain and Germany. Turner sought to focus attention on the growth of another part of the United States, which was more truly American in character and less reliant on European contribution: the Midwest.[5]

Turner argued that those characteristics which truly reflected American society were developed on the frontier as it moved westward beyond the Appalachians. On the frontier, where population density was low and preexisting community structures were absent, the Europeans threw off their cultural baggage, embraced American democracy, and were thus transformed into a new type, Americans. The frontier was not only the mainspring of American democracy but also the origin of those traits that characterized the American—rugged individuality, inquisitiveness, inventiveness, ambition, fearlessness, and a zest for getting things done efficiently. On the frontier the inhibitions and strictures imposed by European society were thrown aside, and in the land of equal opportunity ethnic distinctiveness quickly disappeared with biological assimilation. As one writer has observed, "The frontier promoted the formation of a composite nationality for the American people. The coast was preponderantly English, but the later tides of continental immigration flowed across to the free lands. . . . In the crucible of the frontier the immigrants were Americanized, liberated, and fused into a mixed race, English in neither nationality nor characteristics."[6]

The melting-pot concept was not a purely rural midwestern phenomenon. There were many who regarded it as more typical of cities on the eastern seaboard, particularly with the onset of another great wave of immigration in the 1890s and early 1900s. In fact, Turner never used the term "melting pot"; it was the title of a play written by Israel Zangwill, an immigrant Jewish playwright, and produced in 1908. In the period immediately before World War I, American nationalist feelings began to run high, and many crash programs in American civics and much instruction in the English language were instituted in an attempt to assimilate and Americanize the new immigrants. The concept of the melting pot was an attractive ideal, but despite the pressure-cooker tactics of American nationalists in the eastern cities, the immigrant ghettos persisted.

In 1915 and 1916 a number of intellectuals began to question the desirability of the cultural homogeneity implied in the melting pot thesis. John Dewey, in an address to the National Education Association in 1916, suggested that in the teaching of American history emphasis should be given to immigration and to the tremendously varied contributions of ethnic groups to American life.[7] Horace Kallen, who introduced the term cultural pluralism, wrote several articles on democracy versus the melting pot in which he argued that the accommodation of distinct subcultures in America represented a challenge to American democracy. He accepted that linguistic, economic, and political integration were desirable, but he also argued that the maintenance of separate aesthetic and intellectual forms would contribute tremendous vitality to American life. Randolph Bourne developed a similar theme in his essay on America as a transnational state, written in 1916. He noted that attempts to homogenize the immigrants into a new American type had failed and pointed out that America had a splendid opportunity to show the world that national groups could live alongside one another, maintaining their cultural heritage and contributing to the variety and richness of cultural life.

These three concepts—Anglo-conformity, the melting pot, and cultural pluralism—are used in a general way to characterize the ideal form toward which society in the United States has evolved over the past two hundred years. They are key to understanding the challenge that European immigrants faced in becoming Americans. To understand the immigrants' response to that challenge, however, it is necessary to outline the basic elements of their ethnic identity that had to be modified before they could participate fully in American life.

## The Elements of Ethnicity

Ethnicity in the 1980s is a slightly different phenomenon from what it was in the 1920s, 1840s, or 1770s. The component characteristics of ethnicity have continuously taken on new connotations, and the relative importance of these components has shifted with changes in the general social climate. For example, the Roman Catholic religion of Irish immigrants, a source of ridicule and discrimination during the Nativist and Know-Nothing movements of the 1860s, became a source of particular pride during the 1960s because of the internationally popular figures of President Kennedy and Pope John XXIII. Although various manifestations of ethnicity have changed or even faded away with the passage of time, at least five essential elements are of such importance that they have survived over a long period.[8] These elements are language, religion, race, culture, and a sense of territorial identification.

The function of language is easily understood. A common language is necessary for communication in any group, but it can also be used to exclude outsiders from participation in the activities of the group. The role of language in preserving ethnic identity has not been widely studied.[9] This may be due to the fact that English was generally adopted by second-generation Americans even though their parents continued to use the European mother tongue. The public school played a critical role in the linguistic assimilation of immigrants. The flip side of the coin, however, was the church. Through church services, Sunday school, and summer school programs, the churches worked toward retention of the European languages, thereby retarding linguistic assimilation. Nevertheless, the adoption of English marked an important step in the Americanization of immigrant groups. J. N. Carman made one of the few attempts to establish when that transition took place; he defined a "critical year" when the European language ceased to be spoken in a majority of homes within various ethnic communities in Kansas.[10]

The use of racial characteristics in the definition of an ethnic group has declined since the turn of the century, when it was widely used in America to distinguish not only the African and Asian groups from the Europeans but also the light-haired, fair-complexioned north Europeans from the dark-haired, sallow-skinned immigrants from southern and eastern Europe. Endogamy and intermarriage continue to attract the attention of sociologists because they are such important indices of interpersonal and intergroup relations, knowledge of which is vital to understanding structural assimilation.[11] Although such traits as color, hair type, and facial features are extremely important in the identity of those ethnic groups that have not been fully assimilated in American society—blacks, Puerto Ricans, Japanese, Chinese, and American Indians—they are still studiously ignored by sociologists commenting on ethnicity. Because the use of physical traits to define a group has been tinged with the opprobrium of racism, there seems to be a silent agreement not to discuss them. The result is that ignorance largely persists of their role in the formation of prejudices toward and in the persistent identity of a given ethnic group, and so the embers of racism continue to smolder.

The culture of immigrants finds external expression in a multitude of different ways. Geographers and historians have described rural immigrant culture in terms of the distribution of the various immigrant groups, their farming practices and farming systems, and their architectural tastes, all of which have combined to produce distinctive cultural landscapes. Several authors have attempted to explain cultural landscapes by suggesting that the immigrants sought out a habitat similar to the one they had left behind in Europe. For example, the Finns in western Canada settled in wooded locations where the physical landscape closely resembled their Finnish homeland.[12] However, one cannot overlook the fact that Finnish settlements in Ontario were in the relatively inhospitable areas of Sudbury-Timmins and Thunder Bay, areas with industries, such as lumbering and mining, that provided occupations in which the Finns had prior experience.

Much attention also has been given to the supposed preference of ethnic groups for areas having distinctive soil and vegetation patterns. It seemed that the Germans of Pennsylvania and North Carolina preferred the heavy-textured, loam soils of wooded lowlands, whereas the Scotch-Irish, at least in Pennsylvania, selected thin, inferior, hilly soils, to which they had been accustomed in Ulster. In Wisconsin, the Germans were joined by Norwegians and Irish in selecting wooded lands, while the English and the Yankee settlers from New England and New York preferred to farm in prairie openings.[13] Few of these statements on the preference of various ethnic groups for different soils (or vegetation) have been verified by a careful or complete examination of the historical record, and so they are little more than hypotheses that remain to be tested.

The preferences in land selection by the German immigrants, however, have been subjected to some critical reevaluation. A methodical examination of settlement in southeastern Pennsylvania in the late eighteenth century revealed that the Germans settled on all types of soils, not exclusively the better-quality loam ones. In fact, J. T. Lemon concluded that there was no clear relation between soils and the settlements of national groups. Furthermore, J. Schafer noted that the Germans arrived in southern Wisconsin at a time when the better-quality lands near Milwaukee were already taken. However, their desire to be close to the urban market was so strong that they took up the remaining wooded lands. Similarly, accessibility was important in accounting for the distribution of Germans in Minnesota.[14] Proximity to a navigable waterway was very important for German farmers, and these locations often coincided with areas of woodland.

Teutonic superiority in farming practices, as well as the outward tidiness of barns and farmhouses, is another theme in the writings on the cultural landscape developed by German immigrant farmers. These cultural traits were ascribed to the German farmers of Illinois and Missouri and those of Pennsylvania and North Carolina. The German farmers in Illinois and Missouri were said to be the only ones concerned with soil conservation. This concern accounted for their continuing success in farming and helped to explain the greater stability of their communities in contrast to those in the surrounding, non-German areas. P. W. Gates suggested that the superior performance of German farmers in soil management was due to the technical agricultural education available in German schools in the mid-nineteenth century. Whatever the reasons were for the superior farming of different immigrant groups, the alleged sharp differences in farming practices and crop preferences produced anomalous agricultural islands, which in turn could be closely correlated with a highly segregated rural settlement pattern.[15]

It was the distinctive cropping patterns of each ethnic group that produced these agricultural islands. Cropping patterns, however, were only one element in the cultural landscape; other elements, such as land subdivision patterns, architectural styles, and the distribution of folk artifacts, could also be used to distinguish one area from another.[16] Studies of the distribution of house types, dairy barns, saunas, and placenames bear witness to the immigrant contribution to a varied cultural landscape.[17] The problem with many such studies of the cultural landscape is that they were not organized in a systematic way. It is often the unique and the unusual that attracts attention, and the various indices have not yet been organized in such a way as to cast more light on the processes of assimilation or accommodation of the immigrant group to the larger American community.[18]

The final attribute of an ethnic group that helps to reinforce its ethnicity is a sense of territorial identity.[19] The struggle of European nationalism during the nineteenth century resulted in a strong emotional tie between the immigrant and the homeland for which his forebears had shed their blood. On a personal level, an individual felt a strong affection for the particular place where he was born, where his forebears had lived for decades (or even centuries), and where they were buried. This gave another dimension to the individual's identity. There were many bonds between the individual and his homeland. In a few immigrants the bonds were weak; in others they were strong.[20]

When one considers the strength of the political and economic upheavals during the nineteenth century, the time many immigrants left Europe, it is not surprising that several foreign groups should have developed territorial ambitions in North America. The first attempt to acquire territory was made in 1818, when a request was submitted to the U.S. government for a tract of land on which to settle impoverished Irish immigrants.[21] The request was rejected. In doing so the government established a principle that no assistance would ever be given for the creation of ethnic enclaves within the United States. Such communities would have to be voluntary, the result of decisions by a large number of individuals who wished to settle together. The government, while it would not actively support the creation of large, homogeneous settlements, would not actively prevent them from developing, either. Nevertheless, such settlements on a large scale were considered suspect—an internal threat to the territorial integrity of the American republic. The Germans in particular were suspect. They had settled in large numbers in Wisconsin and in Texas; they had ambitions of creating a new German state, and in Wisconsin it was feared that they might succeed.[22]

For reasons quite different from nationalist aspirations, it was not entirely unexpected that as immigrant groups arrived in North America they would cluster together, forming homogeneous communities, not only in the cities of the eastern seaboard but also in the rural townships of the Midwest. Such homogeneous communities provided a buffer for the immigrant in transition from the tightly knit, stable communities of Europe to the turbulent and highly atomistic society of North America. By forming homogeneous communities the immigrant could find shelter and employment alongside people who shared the same language, values, and cultural heritage as himself. The ethnic communities provided security, stability, and identity for the uprooted European in the bewildering, mobile American society.

## Aims of the Study

Language, religion, race, culture, and territoriality are the major components of ethnicity that have been examined by sociologists, anthropologists, historians, and geographers. The rubric *ethnicity* is more than the sum of the components listed above. There is yet another element that cannot be separated easily from them: the *value system* of an ethnic group. For example, the differences among Germans, Chinese, French Canadians, and Ukrainians are more than skin color, cultural heritage, language, or religion. In some groups the work ethic combined with economic individualism is believed to be strong, and to be a major factor in their social and economic hegemony, whereas in others the work ethic varies in importance within their system of values. It is difficult to isolate the values and priorities of ethnic groups from the major components of ethnicity outlined above because a set of values has its origin in the groups' cultural history and may find indirect expression not only in the material culture of ethnic settlements but also in the social structure of their communities.

The major difficulty at this point is to obtain *direct* access to the system of values and priorities. One could, of course, read the cultural histories, where available, of each ethnic group, because they are important sources for information on how specific groups thought about themselves. However, in writing their own histories members of ethnic groups have always been tempted to show their best face to the outside world—to idealize and to develop flattering images that would counteract negative stereotypes. One should go beyond these sources for an independent view of the groups' set of values.

A way to resolve this particular problem is to examine the basic decisions that members of an ethnic group make in everyday life. If one accepts the axiom that individuals reveal a great deal about themselves (what makes them tick) through the decisions that they make, then it is reasonable to assume that one has direct access to the value system of a group by examining their basic decisions in life. By examining the farming decisions of immigrant groups in the American Midwest over the first fifty years of settlement, it is possible to monitor adaptations in the priorities of each group as it adjusted to the opportunities of American life. It is hoped through this approach to provide new insight into the Americanization of immigrants in a rural setting.

This study draws on two traditional themes in geographical inquiry: it focuses on the adaptation of human groups to a new physical environment and on the spatial organization of the communities that they created. The three immigrant groups chosen for this study are Swedes, Mennonites, and French Canadians. Samples of farm operators were drawn from six townships in central Kansas for each census year between 1875 and 1925. Two townships were selected for each immigrant group: one township from a highly segregated part of the ethnic community and a second representing a heterogeneous mix of the population at the outer edge of the ethnic community (appendix A).

Swedes, Mennonites, and French Canadians were selected because they have been ranked at different points along a work ethic continuum by historians. The Mennonites were considered prime examples of the Protestant work ethic in operation because they emphasized hard work, frugal living, thriftiness, and the reinvestment of earned capital in farming. The French Canadians, by contrast, enjoyed a poor reputation in farming and represented the opposite end of the work ethic continuum from the Mennonites. French-Canadian values emphasized the importance of family solidarity and isolation, even at the expense of increased commercial agriculture and improved standards of living. They had even been described by some visitors to Quebec as indolent, inefficient, and spendthrift. Swedes represented an intermediate position on the continuum between Mennonites and French Canadians. They characterized many of the traits of the northern and western Europeans who flooded into the American Midwest during the second half of the nineteenth century. They were Protestant and hardworking, although they lacked the tight cohesion and cooperation that marked the Mennonite communities.

The Swedes, Mennonites, and French Canadians settled in central Kansas along the outer edge of the settlement frontier in the late 1860s and early 1870s. Central Kansas represents a narrow transition zone between the humid Mississippi lowlands to the east and the subhumid Great Plains to the west. Farther west on the plains the problems of moisture shortage were clearly evident and accounted for a new approach in the utilization of this major resource region. But in the transition zone the problems of moisture shortage were not so apparent, especially during the first decades of farming. Despite great year-to-year variability in rainfall there were enough good years, or months within years, to lead farmers into the gamble of planting in almost any year. Drought was a hazard that could strike at any time, and the transition zone affords an opportunity to study the farmers' decisions in the face of hazards imperfectly perceived. Under conditions of uncertainty and environmental stress the value system is revealed more sharply in the farming decisions of each ethnic group.

A block of thirty-two counties in central Kansas, where average annual rainfall varied between twenty-five and thirty inches, was chosen as the locus for the study (fig. 1). The reason for selecting the Kansas segment of the transition zone was the availability of a detailed data source. The state of Kansas took a full census every ten years from 1865 through 1925, and the manuscripts of the population and agricultural schedules of these censuses are available for research.[23] This very detailed data source was used in conjunction with local taxation records, federal homestead records, land-sales documents of the major railroad companies, county atlases, and local newspapers in order to study the distribution of ethnic groups, population turnover, economic improvement, and agricultural decision making.

Before beginning the analysis of agricultural achievement and decision making, it is necessary to provide some background information. Before migrating to Kansas some of the immigrant groups were involved in the world of commercial agriculture to a significantly greater degree. At the other extreme were ethnic groups that reflected their rural European past more sharply: they were strongly community oriented, less individualistic in outlook, and more inclined to some degree of self-sufficiency in agriculture rather than commercial production. Some of the Swedes and French Canadians had farmed in Illinois before coming to Kansas. The Mennonites, however, had farmed in southern Russia, in an environment of recurring droughts similar to that of Kansas. These variations in farming experience and market orientation, in community cohesion and social organization, are explored in Chapter 2.

The challenge facing immigrants after they arrived in central Kansas was

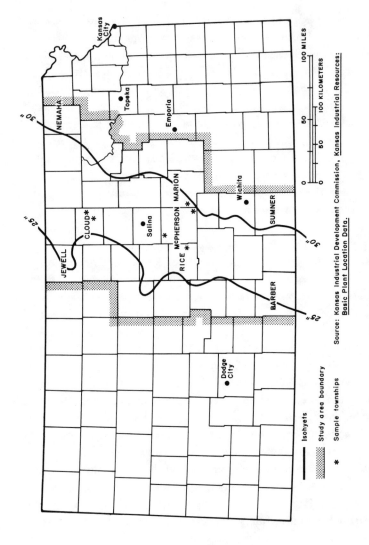

FIG. 1. Location of the study area in central Kansas

SOURCE: Kansas Industrial Development Commission, *Kansas Industrial Resources: Basic Plant Location Data.*

to *establish* a community. Pioneer farmers had to endure numerous hardships in order to create a viable farm out of the untamed Kansas prairie. Droughts, grasshopper plagues, prairie fires, and isolation tested their will. The loneliness of pioneer life was mitigated by the development of a community around the local church. Chapter 3 examines not only the efforts to develop a social life but also the difficulties in establishing an economic basis for the community. Thus the chapter investigates how they obtained their land, the quality of it, and differences in the price they paid for it. Within a short time railroad branch lines extended across the prairie, reducing the haulage distance to market for farm produce, especially grain. Entrepreneurial eagerness as well as a persevering spirit were very important during the first fifteen years of settlement in creating viable ethnic communities.

Beyond the pioneer stage of settlement the immigrants and their descendants adjusted to the long-term needs of *sustaining* an ethnic community. Adjustments were made, some more slowly than others, in the cultural practices of the community. English replaced the ethnic's mother tongue in everyday life, and community members became involved in politics. The stability of the population was also important. In a highly mobile community economic costs in moving from one farm to another could act as an impediment to capital accumulation and the development of farming know-how. For example, the more farmers who persisted in a given area, the better their understanding of recurring drought probabilities in that area. Finally, the rate of farm turnover played an important role in the efforts made by an ethnic group to consolidate and retain the community's territorial base. These are the themes explored in Chapter 4.

Ethnic success can be measured in two ways. The most obvious, of course, is in economic terms. But successful adaptation to one's geographical environment can also be measured, in terms of risk minimization. Chapter 5 examines the levels of economic success achieved by each ethnic group. The several measures of economic success include increases in personal property, the value of real estate, farm acreage, the value of farm equipment and machinery, and the degree to which farms were rented, mortgaged, or owned debt-free.

The farming decisions of immigrants provide the focus for examining environmental adaptation in Chapter 6. Each farmer had to decide how he would allocate the labor resources of his farm, and his decision was reflected in the acreage under various crops and the number of livestock he kept. The crop acreages and livestock numbers for each farm were recorded by the census enumerator in the manuscripts of the censuses. Facing market uncertainty and drought hazards, the farmer had to decide whether to specialize his farm operation in one or two major enterprises, such as wheat and corn production, or to diversify with a variety of crops and livestock. In making his decision the farmer revealed something of his priorities. One has an opportunity to judge the degree to which his decision was that of a conservative or a gambler. By looking at the distribution of high-risk and low-risk decisions for an ethnic group, one is afforded an opportunity of discovering the changing value system of the group from a relatively unbiased source.

A recurring theme throughout this study is the importance of rural segregation in the persistence of Old World behavior patterns or, conversely, how segregation acts as a barrier to the adoption of a New World way of life. As noted above, two sample townships were selected for each ethnic group: one township in which the group was highly dominant, and another in which the group was interspersed with nongroup farmers or outsiders. These samples represent segregated and nonsegregated parts of each ethnic community. The local nongroup farmers in the nonsegregated township, mostly American farmers from the East but also a few other European immigrants, are used as a control group for that particular ethnic group.

The performance of each ethnic group is measured against the standards achieved by their American neighbors. The Americanization of immigrants in this case implies, first, the adoption and realization of the goals of American farmers in the Midwest. Those particular goals, characterized in the American Dream, include the accumulation of wealth, the achievement of financial independence through hard work, and the successful management of capital. Americanization also implies successful adaptation to the particular North American physical environment in which the immigrants found themselves. It implies the degree to which ethnic farmers understood the limitations and challenges of that environment, and that environmental constraints influenced the development of a communal spirit, of community cooperation during periods of stress, around which the ethnic community would be built. The underlying questions in this study are: To what extent were these goals adopted by the immigrants? and To what extent were wealth and financial security attained as immigrants confronted climatic hazards in central Kansas and market uncertainties in the years between 1875 and 1925?

# THE SOCIAL AND ECONOMIC BACKGROUND OF THE IMMIGRANTS

## 2

The facility with which immigrants adjusted to life in North America depended in part on their premigration condition in the old country. In the two centuries preceding large-scale migration to the American Midwest, rural life witnessed the gradual breakdown of the last constricting institutions of medieval life and the feudal organization of agriculture. These changes were to produce greater *individual* freedom than before. In northern Europe the culmination of this process of change came in the late eighteenth and early nineteenth centuries with the enclosure movements, which brought to an end the old open-field system of agriculture. Concomitant with enclosure came improvements in farming technology and transportation, the development of distant markets, and a quickening in the change from subsistence to commercial agriculture.

Social conditions also changed. As towns and cities grew in number and size, industrialization and the factory system created a new way of life. Expanding urban markets not only created an impetus to develop commercial agriculture but also absorbed the surplus rural population no longer engaged in farming. The population of Europe was shaken loose from its traditions as the rural unemployed migrated to towns and cities, and across the Atlantic to North America. With the disruption of local communities came a restructuring of social order. The out-migrants had an opportunity to break the ties of kinship, tradition, authority, and obedience to local church leaders. The bonds of village life were shattered for those who embraced the new ethic of competition, contract, and economic individualism. But they soon discovered the flip side of the coin— rootlessness, anomie, and an absence of social identity. Others, however, retained the bonds of family and community life through the migration and resettlement phases.

Scholars have given increased attention to the premigration experience of immigrants and how it contributed to the development of a new ethnic identity among immigrants to the American Midwest. R. Ostergren demonstrated that variations in economic conditions within different communities in Dalarna, Sweden, explained the degree to which tightly knit communities were formed in Minnesota and South Dakota. J. Gjerde illustrated the survival of social patterns in the chain migration of Norwegians from the Sogne fjord region to western Wisconsin and Iowa. And W. D. Kamphoefner examined the significance of social class and economic conditions among emigrants from northwestern Germany who settled in eastern Missouri. The importance of premigration conditions has been underscored in these detailed studies of chain migrations from select areas in northern Europe to communities in the American Midwest.[1]

Such meticulous examinations cannot be duplicated in this study for several reasons. Quite apart from the fact that this study examines three groups rather than one group and that the demands of space do not permit such an exhaustive inquiry, many immigrants analyzed here did not come from a single localized source in the old country. For example, some of the Swedes came from Småland, some from Värmland, and others from different provinces in southern Sweden. The precise origins of French Canadians from the St. Lawrence valley who migrated to Kankakee and then to Kansas are not clear either. Consequently, the examination of premigration conditions is general in nature in order to determine the potential adaptability among the three groups prior to their setting out for the American Midwest.

The survey of the agricultural and social history of Swedes, Mennonites, and French Canadians that follows focuses on the themes of social reorganization and agricultural change in Europe and Quebec in order to determine the social cohesion and agricultural experience of each group. The themes include efforts made to retain stable communities based on kinship and family ties in contrast to the increasing prevalence of nuclear families and economic individualism; survival of subsistent agriculture against the pressure to commercialize farming that accompanied agricultural innovation; and provision of farmland for each new generation of farmers as seen through inheritance practices, farm subdivision, and the clearing of unimproved land. Finally, an examination of the decision to emigrate to Kansas reveals something of each group's willingness to accept change and ultimately is a measure of their potential assimilability in Kansas.

# Swedes

The changes in Swedish society during the latter part of the eighteenth century and much of the nineteenth century were typical of what was happening throughout northern Europe. The structure and authority of the Teutonic villages were gradually broken down, and the agricultural system was reorganized. In the mideighteenth century the medieval village system was still characterized by much of the settlement pattern and organization of agriculture in Sweden.[2] Farmhouses were grouped together, forming a compact unit surrounded by one or several large open fields, and within these fields farmers held scattered strips of land that they cultivated. All livestock in the village were grazed together in a common pasture, which made up the remainder of the so-called village enclosure. This agricultural system engendered interdependence as farmers coordinated planting and harvesting schedules, but there was little room for individual enterprise in improving the quality of livestock and crops through selective breeding. Rural isolation was great, and farming patterns reflected the subsistent nature of rural communities.

In the late eighteenth century a series of agricultural reforms destroyed the old village system. The Storskifte Act of 1757 was the first attempt to consolidate farm strips, but it met with limited success because of its rigid regulations.[3] The Enskifte Act of 1807 had widespread success: the enclosure movement begun in Denmark and Skåne spread fairly rapidly northward across the broad lowlands of southern Sweden, where new farms were easily created for farmers who had been dispossessed by the reforms (fig. 2).

In upland and hilly areas where good agricultural soils existed only in isolated pockets, the progress of enclosure was usually slow. And so a new law was introduced in 1827, the Lagaskifte Act, which relaxed some of the requirements for consolidation. This allowed farm consolidation to continue in central Sweden, although progress remained slow in the northern provinces of Dalarna and Norland, where it was not enforced by law until later in the nineteenth century. The one area in southern Sweden that resisted reforms until well after 1850 was Småland. In this upland area the old villages remained intact and the conservatism of the peasants entrenched; the traditional way of life persisted well into the latter part of the nineteenth century.

The agrarian reforms in Sweden were accompanied by an increase in population and an expansion in agricultural land.[4] The growth in popula-

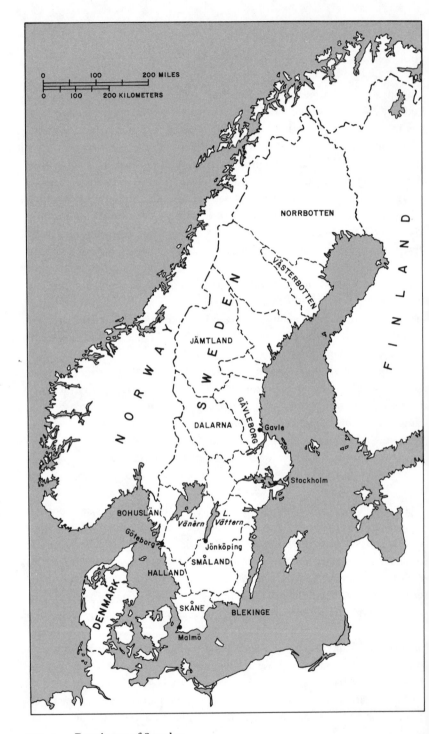

FIG. 2. Provinces of Sweden

tion was much greater in the agricultural laboring class than in the *bonde* (yeoman farmer, landowning) class. Furthermore, the extension of agricultural land resulted in a significant increase in the size of existing farms rather than a dramatic increase in the number of new farms. In rural Sweden the economic gap widened between the *bonde* class, who were becoming wealthier, and the lower agricultural class, who were not benefiting to the same extent from economic growth. With increased efficiency in farm operations and increased market opportunities, the old bonds of obligation that tied the laboring class to the *bonde* were loosened and replaced by an open, competitive labor-market system. Within rural communities contract, rather than the traditional bonds of personal obligation, became the basis of social relations as fewer and fewer people shared in the expanding wealth generated by the increase in agricultural land.

Changes in Swedish agriculture picked up momentum after 1850. The opening of an agricultural college at Ultuna in 1848 heralded a new era combining scientific research with agricultural education. New cultivation techniques and new strains of crops were introduced.[5] Horses replaced oxen as the major source of animal power on farms, and the area of oats production expanded rapidly (fig. 3). The major crops were oats, rye, barley, and potatoes. Wheat was a relatively minor crop because Sweden is on the northern margin of the wheat-growing areas in Europe, due to climatic constraints. The most important new advance was the development of commercial dairy farming, especially in southwestern Sweden (Skåne and Halland) and in the central provinces between Stockholm and Göteborg. The expansion of dairying was indicative of some regional specialization in Swedish agriculture as a result of improved transportation.

This trend toward farm specialization was also indicative of growing commercialization on Swedish farms and the gradual disappearance of the old subsistent pattern of farming. More and more capital was being invested as farm credit became increasingly available. Prior to 1800 agricultural credit was largely unknown in Sweden, and even during the agrarian enclosure program the *bonde* had to go no farther than the local large landowner to obtain a personal note for capital. However, throughout the early decades of the nineteenth century, with the opening up of agriculture to commercial outlets there was an increase in mortgaging. The increase in farm mechanization (the replacement of hand tools with new farm machinery) and changes in the laws of inheritance in 1863 contributed to the expansion of mortgaging. Under the new law all children in the family were entitled to an equal share of the father's property. Consequently,

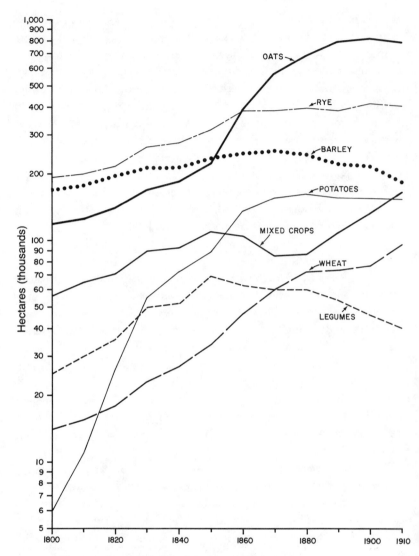

FIG. 3.   Changes in cropland in Sweden, 1800–1910

SOURCE: *Emigrationsutredningen Betänkande,* p. 92.

that member of the family who retained the family farm had to take out a mortgage in order to pay off the shares bequeathed to his brothers and sisters.

By the 1870s agriculture in Sweden had undergone a revolution. The old subsistent patterns of farming had by and large disappeared, except from some of the isolated upland areas, particularly in northern Sweden and in Småland. Throughout lowland Sweden, however, agriculture became capitalized, commercialized, and, to a degree, specialized. Significant improvements in agricultural education, agricultural credit facilities, and an internal transportation network had brought Sweden into a competitive position with other European states.

*Factors Contributing to Emigration*

With the growth in agriculture and employment opportunities during the first half of the nineteenth century, there was very little emigration from Sweden to North America. But during the later decades, as rural unemployment became widespread, the flood of emigration became so great that there were fears of rural depopulation and a shortage of agricultural labor. A wide range of factors produced this emigration, and in order to appreciate the relative importance of these, J. S. Lindberg has argued that it is necessary to distinguish between the early migrations and those that came after 1860.

Before 1860 much of the Swedish emigration was the product of political and religious persecution, and most of the emigrants came from the *bonde* and wealthier classes. Earlier in the century, following the Napoleonic Wars, the political climate in Sweden was conservative and repressive: political freedom was curtailed and restrictions were imposed on dissenters. Particularly important from the point of emigration was the increasing pressure for religious conformity. The authority of the Lutheran state church was challenged by the independence of the Pietists, who believed in personal interpretation of the Scriptures and organized Bible readings in private homes. It was the classic challenge of liberal individualism to the authority of the church. The church had sufficient influence in the Rijksdag to have these meetings outlawed, and so Pietists who could afford the cost decided to emigrate to America. Consequently, the early emigrants were often men of some financial means who were motivated to emigrate by the desire for greater freedom of religious belief. Among those emigrants in the 1840s was a group of Pietists who developed a community around Galesburg in western Illinois, which subsequently produced a new generation of Swedish pioneers for the settling of Kansas in the 1870s.

In contrast, the emigrations following 1860 came overwhelmingly from the small landowner and agricultural laborer classes and were motivated primarily by factors of economic hardship. Very few members of the *bonde* class participated in the later migration; more often than not they joined with the local church leaders in condemning the trend.[6] For the *bonde* and large landowners, increased emigration would bring a decline in available labor and a corresponding increase in farm wages, which they were reluctant to pay. Despite the opposition of the authorities, emigration continued among the lower classes. The decision to emigrate to America was not an easy one; the economic factors, however, were compelling. Rural unemployment, farm mechanization, a tightening in the flow of credit, and a combination of declining farm prices with a series of poor harvests all contributed directly to emigration.

Although the area of agricultural land increased dramatically during the first half of the nineteenth century, as shown above, the rapid rate of growth began to taper off after 1860.[7] During the same period the rate of population growth developed a momentum of its own that could not be halted. Eventually, by 1870, the land being added to the existing inventory of agricultural land was not keeping abreast of population growth. The problem was compounded by the fact that farm mechanization was contributing to rural unemployment. Since industrialization had barely begun in Sweden by 1860, emigration represented a major solution to the growing problem of rural unemployment. In these conditions the pressure to emigrate was continuous and, one by one, sons and daughters decided to leave home for a new life in America.

The credit squeeze also took its toll and contributed heavily to emigration. So long as credit was easily available, mortgaging did not contribute to farm failures, foreclosure, and rural depopulation. However, during the early 1860s, and particularly after 1870, the prices of agricultural commodities declined in Sweden. The farmer's income was dropping, and he was required to maintain his interest payments from a declining income. Caught within this squeeze the financially insecure farmers had no option but to abandon the family farm on foreclosure and emigrate.

The farmer's difficulties were exacerbated by a series of drought years and severe crop failures in 1861, 1865, 1867, 1868, and 1869, which had a disastrous effect. One of the hardest hit areas was Småland, in south-central Sweden. It was a hilly upland area of thin soils, isolated from the remainder of southern Sweden because of poor transportation links. Agrarian reforms and enclosure had made very slow progress; in Småland the old, traditional way of life persisted well into the late nineteenth century. Rural isolation, however, was no protection against the droughts of the 1860s. The historian G. M. Stephenson gives a vivid image of conditions:

> From April to September 1868, rain fell only two or three times, and then for only two or three hours. Everything was scorched by the sizzling heat; trees were burned black and died. Nobody remembered such a drought. The lean cows roamed at large; houses and farms were deserted.
>
> At every station, says an eyewitness, crowds were gathered begging for money and bread. The unripe rye was chopped up, dried in ovens, ground into flour, and made into bread. When even this scanty fare was denied, grass was eaten. In desperation, those who were able stampeded to America, Germany, Mecklenberg, and Hanover, many abandoning farms and sacrificing everything of value they possessed.[8]

Against this background of environmental stress and economic hardship a number of Småland families, led by the Reverend C. Olson, crossed the Atlantic and joined their fellow countrymen from Illinois in migrating to the Smoky River valley in central Kansas.

In addition to the "push" factors, a number of "pull" factors tended to moderate the traumatic experience of upheaval and emigration. Emigration agents, employed by the large North American railroad companies, disseminated information about employment opportunities and living conditions in the New World. But more important than the railroad advertisements in mitigating the terror of leaving home for an unknown land were the "America letters," written by expatriates who had settled in Chicago or in the rural areas of Illinois and Minnesota. The letters brought news of success (but rarely of failures) from those in America and were read aloud in the evenings to family and neighbors gathered in the old home. The correspondence contained not only news and information but also money and steamship tickets for those who would follow. Personal contacts of this kind were extremely important in the chain migration that contributed to the growth and success of many Swedish communities in the American Midwest.

## Mennonites

The Mennonites originated as a religious sect in the Netherlands during the post-Reformation period. They were followers of a former Dutch priest, Menno Simmons, a leader of the Anabaptist movement in the lower Rhine and northern Germany. Members of the new sect adopted a rigid and un-compromising attitude in their religious beliefs and were at loggerheads with Catholics, Lutherans, and Calvinists alike. As a result, when the first edict against heretics was issued in the Netherlands in 1521, Sim-mons's followers migrated to Poland. It was the first of many Mennonite migrations: each successive move served to reinforce the group's separate identity. Migration became a means of escaping real or imagined persecu-tion, rekindled the zeal of flagging members, and also served to isolate the group by removing it to new, uninhabited areas where they would not be distracted by the temptations of secular civilization.[9]

Over two centuries the Mennonites developed distinctive settlements and a reputation for agricultural pioneering in Poland. They were experts in dyking the coastal marshes of the Baltic, which they converted into excellent dairy pastures.[10] The Mennonite settlements produced enough food and clothing to meet their own modest needs; they sold their surplus locally but seldom bought goods in return. Over time as the settlements became wealthy their success aroused the jealousy of their neighbors. The wealth, the religious unorthodoxy, and the freedom from military service of the Mennonites were all sources of friction with the host society. During the eighteenth century the Mennonites' freedom to expand was curtailed and their taxes increased to compensate for military service. But when their religious identity was challenged, they responded by emigrating once again.

The opportunity to emigrate from Prussia came in 1786 with an invita-tion from Catherine the Great to participate in the colonization of southern Russia. The Russians were actively recruiting Europeans to colonize the unsettled grasslands of the south, the southern Ukraine, the Crimea, and the Volga district. Mennonites decided to investigate the possibility of a Russian colony and sent a delegation to visit several sites in the region to the north of the Crimea. The locations seemed suitable for colonization, and they received guarantees from the empress that they would have free-dom of religious observance, freedom from military service and billeting, and a loan of five hundred rubles per family. In 1789 the first Mennonite families arrived and settled in the southern Ukraine.[11]

The environmental conditions in the new colonies were quite different from anything the Mennonites had known before. The great expanse of un-dulating steppes presented little variation in relief apart from the narrow, incised valleys of the rivers, which meandered southward to the Black Sea. It was a fertile agricultural region, with soils ranging from rich black chernozems to the brown and light brown chernozem soils of the grasslands. The annual temperature range was greater than in northern Europe: the average January temperature of 20°F contrasted sharply with the average July temperature of over 70°F. The most unpredictable element of the climate was precipitation. The total annual rainfall was between fourteen and sixteen inches, most of it in the form of heavy showers during the months of May, June, and July. Because of high temperatures during these months, high rates of evapotranspiration caused much of the moisture to be lost to plant growth. To make matters worse for the maturing crops, the high temperatures of July were sometimes accompanied by warm, dry winds, which desiccated the plants.

The earliest Mennonite colony in southern Russia was founded at Khortitsa on the Dnieper River (fig. 4). The first fifteen years were especially difficult, as several of the winters were very severe and livestock losses were heavy. In addition, the crop harvests of 1798 and 1799 were destroyed by summer droughts and plagues of grasshoppers. The colonists became increasingly pessimistic about the ability of their colonies to survive, and even the imperial government in St. Petersburg began to wonder if the Mennonites would ever prosper.[12]

Despite these early setbacks, more Mennonites arrived from Prussia and new sites were selected for colonization. In 1797 two new colonies were created at Ekaterinoslav, some eighty miles north of Khortitsa on the Dnieper. A third and much larger Mennonite settlement was begun in 1803 along the Molochnaia River on 332,000 acres of land set aside by the Russian government. Additional Mennonite colonists came from Prussia year after year despite the reluctance of the Prussian authorities to grant them emigrant visas. By 1840, when immigration came to an end, forty-five Mennonite colonies had been established in southern Russia.

In the early years of the nineteenth century Mennonite farmers concentrated on subsistence cropping and livestock breeding. Isolation of the settlements from markets severely limited the development of commercial agriculture, although the demand for fibers had stimulated silk and wool production in the 1810s. The Mennonites imported merino sheep from western Europe to improve their sheep herds. They had also successfully crossbred their Frisian dairy cattle with the local gray Ukrainian stock to produce the famous Molotschna dairy cow. Some butter and cheese were sold in the distant towns of Berdiansk, Sebastopol, Evpatoria, and Ekaterinoslav, but the dominant pattern of Mennonite agriculture was subsistent, with a small income from the sale of wool.

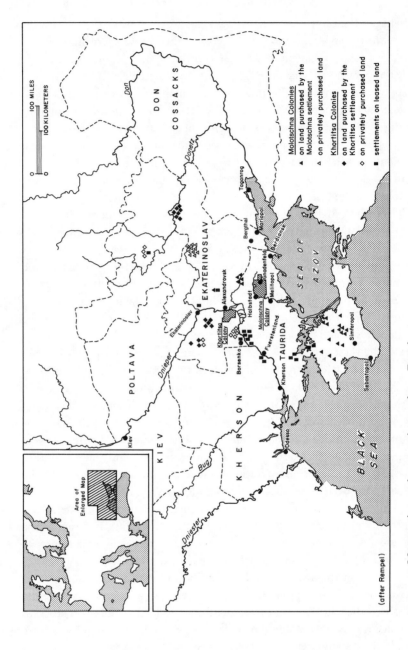

FIG. 4. Mennonite settlements in southern Russia

This pattern changed rapidly in the 1840s as the Mennonites established new commercial outlets for their farm produce; the agricultural economy switched from sheep rearing to commercial grain production. The new emphasis on arable farming was a result of several factors: declining wool prices in the 1840s; the lowering and removal of grain tariffs in Britain, Holland, Belgium, and other European countries in 1846; and effective leadership in the introduction of new, efficient methods of farming within the Mennonite colonies.[13] Much of the change, however, was due to a significant improvement in the internal communications system in southern Russia after 1840, which facilitated the transport of surplus grain to Black Sea ports. The leadership provided by the Agricultural Union also contributed to the revolution in Mennonite agriculture.

The Russian authorities created the Agricultural Union in the 1820s to foster agricultural improvements and to increase commercial production in the Mennonite settlements. Union officers appointed by the Russians were usually the most enterprising farmers in the district and set an excellent example for their fellow Mennonites. One of the leaders in the union was Johann Cornies, a pioneer in livestock breeding, reforestation, and the introduction of new cultivation techniques such as black fallowing. Cornies and other leaders in the union oversaw the conversion of agriculture into grain farming. This required breaking up the large common pasture lands in each village and redistributing them to all who held pasture rights. But the reorganization of farming did not extend to agrarian enclosures and the consolidation of farm strips, as it had in other parts of Europe. Instead, Cornies increased the efficiency of Mennonite agriculture by concentrating on the development of new technology—new strains of crops, improved livestock breeds, agricultural mechanization, and new cultivation techniques—which enabled the Mennonites to overcome the limitations of their semiarid environment.[14]

Despite the technical advances in agriculture, an ingrained conservatism to social change persisted in the Mennonite communities, and this eventually produced a crisis. By 1860 the distribution of wealth had become unbalanced: a small percentage of farmers had acquired large quantities of land that they had built up over the years, and an increasingly high percentage of Mennonites (estimated at about 65 percent) could not obtain even a small farm on which to make a beginning.[15] Leaders in the Mennonite villages had failed to survey and distribute the surplus village lands, which were intended for the creation of new farms. Instead, the wealthiest farmers had leased the surplus lands and were now unwilling to give them up. Consequently, landless Mennonites, or Anwohners, as they were known, rented lands from neighboring herdsmen and nomads.

The crisis came to a head in 1860 when the nomadic Nogai herdsmen migrated en masse to Turkey and the Russian government settled the Nogai lands with Bulgarian colonists, thereby displacing the Anwohner Mennonites. Throughout the 1860s the Anwohners petitioned for a subdivision of the village surplus lands, but they were powerless: the poor could not vote in local elections. To complicate matters, the religious views of poorer Mennonites had been tainted by a strong Pietist influence from the neighboring German colonies, alienating them somewhat from the religious establishment in the Mennonite villages. It was only through the intervention of the Russian authorities that the land problem was resolved in favor of the landless Anwohners.

The image of Mennonite society in southern Russia during the 1860s is of strong, centralized control within the old village settlement pattern. The civic leaders in the communities were conservative, usually wealthy, and worked closely with the religious leaders. As a result there was increasing alienation between the governing and governed.[16] As the rich became richer they were concerned with maintaining the patriarchal farmland and farm home.[17] As they became concerned primarily with maintaining the economic standards of their own families, they were reluctant to concern themselves with the problems of the poor. Besides, the Anwohners, or landless Mennonites, provided a pool of cheap labor on which the wealthy farmers depended to maintain their large farms. The large landowners found willing allies among the church leaders in the community but resented the challenge to their authority from the independent Anwohners. (The community leaders ignored the fact that religious unorthodoxy resulted from these poorer Mennonites having to seek land beyond the Mennonite communities.) But once the crisis had passed, all Mennonites resolved not to permit such conditions to develop again.

That the Mennonites survived as a cohesive group at all in spite of internal dissension must also have been due to lingering feelings of alienation, hostility, and perhaps even jealousy in the local host society. The religious differences between the Mennonites and their neighbors were so marked that the internal dissensions within the Mennonite religion seemed to pale in comparison. Furthermore, the Mennonites had been very successful in farming and had achieved their success without help from outsiders. For example, they were reluctant to seek credit from non-Mennonite sources. The Mennonite communities were also regarded as a state within the state:

they retained their German language, their own educational system, and they did not participate in or contribute to military service. It was their tendency to form homogeneous settlements, not to compromise their cultural heritage and religious beliefs, that accounted for the social gap between Mennonites and the remainder of society.[18] Once threatened by any action on the part of the host society, Mennonites reacted by closing ranks and reaffirming their cohesion.

*Factors Contributing to Emigration*

As the crisis within the Mennonite colonies was resolved toward the end of the 1860s, a new threat to their survival as a group appeared. In 1871 the imperial government introduced a new Russianization program that would affect all German colonies in southern Russia. The program included, among other things, compulsory military service and the use of the Russian language in all schools. The proposals represented a complete abrogation of the guarantees given to the Mennonites by Catherine the Great a century earlier. This threat to the cultural identity of the Mennonites, and in particular to their basic principle of pacifism, brought forth the institutionalized response—withdrawal and flight to a new homeland, preferably in some isolated, unsettled part of the world.

The Russian authorities, for their part, were anxious to prevent a mass exodus. They went so far as to curtail the emigration agents' activities among the Mennonites and even expelled the American agent C. B. Schmidt from Russia in 1875. In a further effort to forestall emigration, the Russians suggested that the Mennonites could perform forestry service in lieu of military service, and although the language question was not resolved, the more compromising and wealthier Mennonites decided not to emigrate. The most intractable attitudes were found in the poorest Mennonite settlements among those who had suffered because of the land problem and who had adopted a strong evangelical fervor from the Pietist movement. Emigration was heavy from such communities as Bergthal, Fuerstenland, Borsenko, and Alexanderwohl.[19] Of the eight hundred in Alexanderwohl only seven families remained in 1874, so adamant were they against any compromise.

Leaders in the Mennonite communities began to organize for the migration. First they contacted the British and American consuls at Berdiansk and Odessa; the British in turn referred them to a visiting Canadian immigration agent, William Hespeler, who arranged for a group of leaders to visit Canada and inspect potential areas of settlement. The group was also to visit the United States for the same purpose, and their instructions were simple: They would request the right to freedom from military service and

> the right to live in closed settlements with the privilege of autonomous local administration and the use of the German language, which also involved, as they thought, their own German schools. . . . The future of every aspect of their social life depended upon the right to settle in the same way as they had settled three generations before when their grandfathers came to Russia.[20]

The Mennonite leaders who investigated opportunities in North America encountered a mixed reception from government officials and enthusiastic encouragement from coreligionists in Ontario and Pennsylvania. The U.S. Congress refused the Mennonites, as it had refused all immigrant groups, assistance in forming large homogeneous settlements on the grounds that such settlements would retard the inevitable Americanization of immigrants.[21] The American president had already informed other pacifist groups that the power to grant freedom from military service was not a federal one, but belonged to the individual states. This particular hurdle was quickly overcome when state legislatures in Minnesota, Kansas, and Nebraska passed appropriate laws granting this freedom in 1873 and 1874. American and Canadian Mennonites formed a Mennonite Board of Guardians and subscribed thousands of dollars to assist in the migration of Russian Mennonites to North America.

## French Canadians

The spread of settlement in the St. Lawrence lowlands took place within a system of land granting and land subdivision that was patterned on the French feudal framework. The small farms represented elongated strips of land that fronted on the St. Lawrence River. Once all the riverfront lands had been allocated, a second range or "rang" of farms was begun behind the first line of settlement. Rivers and streams were so important as lines of communication and transportation that they formed the baseline for farm surveys: each farm had a narrow frontage on the water. But where tributary streams were not available, a road was built along the inland boundary line, forming the baseline for the second "rang" of farms.[22]

The settlement pattern that this form of land subdivision produced was quite unlike the nucleated agricultural villages of Sweden, Prussia, or southern Russia in the eighteenth century. The *habitant*, or farmer, located his home on the farm close to the main line of communication—either the river or the road. Consequently, the distances between farmhouses depended on the width of the farm, and since farms were of irregular width, the pattern of settlement that developed was a straggling line of homes spaced at irregular intervals. The pattern of elongated linear settlement at first hindered the development of a close-knit community spirit and identity since there was no effective way of determining where one community might end and another begin.[23]

Rural life in Quebec in the eighteenth century was characterized neither by a rigid hierarchical class structure nor by the same strong sense of community control associated with rural life in Europe. The *habitant* knew little of common lands, grazing rights, or other features of communal life, and the seigneury provided a weak focus for the community. R. C. Harris has argued convincingly that the seigneury was neither an economic nor a social unit. The *seigneur* exercised little control over the economy of his territory. His leadership was limited to the construction of an occasional grist mill or conducting a seigneurial court. In a recent appraisal of the seigneurial system, A. Greer has argued that the *censitaire*'s financial obligations to the seigneur and parish priest were a major drain on his farm surplus, thereby limiting capital accumulation and economic advance.[24]

The British conquest of French Canada in 1763 did not significantly alter the existing settlement pattern or social structure in the colony. The seigneurial system of land subdivision and land tenure was to continue where it already existed. But in the new, unsettled areas the British imposed a township survey that was being used in Upper Canada (later Ontario). The new system dominated the southeastern part of the colony, especially between the Richelieu and Chaudière rivers, an area that became known as the Eastern Townships and included the counties of Drummond, Mégantic, Shefford, Sherbrooke, Missisquoi, and Stanstead (fig. 5). French Canadians, unfamiliar with the new system of land tenure and the dispersed farmstead settlement pattern and unable to raise the money to purchase land from speculative land companies, avoided settling in the Eastern Townships, creating overcrowded conditions in the old seigneurial lands of the St. Lawrence lowlands.[25]

The effect of the British conquest was to make French Canada increasingly conscious of its distinctive identity. The chief characteristics of Quebec society were isolationism, a rural way of life centered on the family

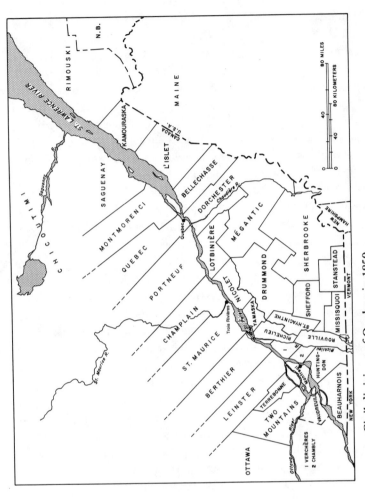

FIG. 5.   Civil divisions of Quebec in 1850

SOURCE: R. D. Vicero, "Immigration of French-Canadians to New England, 1840–1900: A Geographical Analysis," unpublished Ph.D. diss., University of Wisconsin, 1968, p. 21.

farm, organized by parishes and dominated by the Catholic church. The isolationism of Quebec was not simply the inability or unwillingness of the French Canadians to identify and cooperate with the new British authority. It was part of a French-Canadian desire to avoid foreign entanglements. Led by their bishops, French Canadians recoiled from the antitheistic and antimonarchical sentiments emanating from the American and French revolutions. French-Canadian society was overwhelmingly rural—beyond the three urban centers on the St. Lawrence (Montreal, Trois Rivières, and Quebec City, all small) few settlements rose much above the level of villages. There was little commercial intercourse between Lower Canada and the remainder of North America. The normative image of French-Canadian society was of the family operating its small, long-lot farm within sight of the village church, where family members had been baptized, married, and buried for generations.

The family represented the basic unit of social organization, and the influence of the patriarchal family was pervasive. Unlike the stem family, which apparently prevailed in Anglo America, the French-Canadian pattern was of interrelated extended families that incorporated widowed and orphaned relatives. If, for example, a farmer had no sons to help him with his farm, he called on nephews and cousins as supplementary sources to his own labor. The family farm was the basic unit of production. Despite the dangers of increasing population pressure on a limited resource base, families clung to the farm as it was.[26]

Coupled with the image of the cohesive French-Canadian family is the idea that agriculture was of a subsistent nature. Indeed, many items for the family's needs, from bread and vegetables to the rough homespun clothing, were produced on the family farm, and commercial agriculture was generally limited to the proximities of Montreal, Trois Rivières, and Quebec. The generally subsistent image of farming reinforced the idea that the French-Canadian farmer was conservative in habits and very slow to accept changes or technological innovation. By the early decades of the nineteenth century, however, increasing population pressure on a limited agricultural resource base created great difficulties for the development of efficient farming. The French-Canadian farmer began to produce an inferior wheat for export to the British market. As Quebec was drawn increasingly into Britain's market system after 1895, French-Canadian farmers had few competitive advantages over other farmers in the United States and Upper Canada.[27]

Beginning in the early years of the nineteenth century, the agricultural economy of Quebec went into a tailspin that lurched into a severe economic depression in the 1830s and 1840s. A major historiographic debate has raged over the onset of the "agricultural crisis" and the causes responsible for it, but as M. McInnis notes in a review of the debate, virtually everyone agrees that the agricultural situation had become very serious by midcentury. Some, like M. Séguin, argue that French Canadians were inefficient peasant farmers trapped in their *esprit payson* by the lack of strong market forces. Others, like F. Ouellet, contended that the basic problem was overpopulation. Soil exhaustion and a short growing season have also been recognized as important factors contributing to the crisis.[28]

French-Canadian farmers were indeed conservative in their habits and did not respond readily to new commercial opportunities. Farmers had been unable to improve the efficiency of agriculture because they were unwilling to adapt to the changing conditions of population pressure. They went deeper into debt in order to retain the family farm; relatively few of them moved to new areas of land clearing and pioneer settlement. They had not increased the commercial nature of their farming enterprise to the point where they could compete successfully with American producers for the local markets associated with lumbering in the St. Lawrence and Ottawa valleys. They were unable to capture for themselves a share of the commercial world in North America owing to a basic antipathy toward external interference in their lives. The Anglophone element in Canada did not appreciate fully the isolationism in French-Canadian society; their attitude was reflected in Lord Durham's arrogant comment that French Canadians adhered "to ancient prejudices, ancient customs, and ancient laws, not from any strong sense of their beneficial effects, but with the unreasoning tenacity of uneducated and unprogressive people."[29]

An important product of that "unreasoning tenacity" was the subdivision of farms in lower Canada, which had a serious impact on agricultural performance. The population of the colony had increased from 65,000 in 1763 to 669,528 in 1851 without a comparable tenfold increase in the area of agricultural land. The result was increased population pressure in rural areas, since there was little urban-industrial development to absorb the surplus population and emigration was still on a very modest scale. Consequently, although the proportion of landless laborers in the population continued to increase, the subdivision of farms also continued apace. The small average size of farms in the old seigneurial districts contrasted sharply with the larger farms of the Eastern Townships. In some areas along the St. Lawrence River farm holdings of fewer than eight acres accounted for more than 25 percent of all holdings. A member of the Assembly of Lower Canada testified in 1823 that "almost all the old concessions have been cut into narrow strips of land, some of which are no wider than an ordinary large road and sometimes longer than a mile." [30] With each subdivision of the farm, the resulting strips of land became extremely elongated, as each strip had to have river frontage. The result was a pattern of land subdivision that defied efficient organization of the farm's resources.

The major crops grown in the St. Lawrence valley in the early nineteenth century continued to be wheat, peas, oats, barley, potatoes, and buckwheat. Despite its poor quality, wheat was the most important crop, not only because it could be sold on the British market but also because it was a major staple in the French-Canadian diet. But the British market provided very limited opportunities for expansion because the quality of French-Canadian grains was so poor they could not compete with grains of American or Upper Canadian farmers. Part of the problem was due to differences in soil quality and the length of the growing season, which favored western producers, rather than lack of market opportunities. Lumber camps in Quebec were supplied by American farmers in Vermont and Ohio.

Livestock on French-Canadian farms were also of poor quality and held little prospect for the development of a marketable surplus. A few oxen and dairy cattle provided farm power, plus limited quantities of milk, butter, cheese, and meat for the family. Some sheep were kept for their wool, but the scarcity of winter feed limited their numbers. Horses were also few in number, being kept for personal travel rather than as work animals. The number of pigs kept on farms is difficult to estimate, since many were turned out to forage in the forest and no accurate records were kept. In general, the livestock element in French-Canadian farming produced very little marketable surplus.

The pattern of agriculture in lower Canada changed dramatically in the 1830s and 1840s on account of several environmental disasters. During the 1830s the preeminence of wheat cultivation collapsed with the appearance of a wheat midge that destroyed large portions of the harvest year after year. [31] In the districts of Kamaska, Islet, Quebec, Portneuf, and Champlain wheat acreages declined by more than 90 percent between the census years of 1827 and 1844. The only areas where wheat cultivation managed to expand was in the pioneer settlements among the Anglophone farmers of the Eastern Townships.

Before the collapse of wheat farming, potatoes had increased in importance on French-Canadian farms, and when wheat production collapsed in the 1830s, potatoes assumed an important place in the French-Canadian diet. The potato, however, was not a reliable substitute crop. In the early 1840s a blight appeared on the crop (and later spread to Europe), greatly reducing yields and acreages. Despite the fact that the acreage of all other crops, except barley, continued to increase during these disastrous decades, the ravages caused by the wheat midge and the potato blight were sufficient to plunge Quebec into a severe agricultural depression and even famine during the latter part of the 1830s and 1840s.

Few of the *habitants* found their salvation by expanding into livestock farming because a conversion of their farm economy would have required considerable capital investment, which they could not undertake. Nevertheless, what cattle they raised continued to produce small amounts of milk and very inferior beef.[32] There was little or no commercial dairying, as the butter and cheese were poorly made and there were no ready outlets for fresh milk. Horses were becoming more important as sources of power on the farm, but sheep and pig rearing were still of relatively minor importance. In livestock farming, the *habitant* had not made any significant improvements in breeding animals since the days of the French regime.

Not only did the French Canadian not improve his livestock—horses always excepted—he was also impervious to all appeals to improve the efficiency of his farming methods. Plowing was shallow, farm implements were long outdated, and despite a considerable input of labor, yields were depressingly low. Travelers in Lower Canada in the early nineteenth century remarked on the weed-infested state of the fields. With little or no concern for crop rotation and fallow, soil exhaustion was inevitable. A special investigation by the legislative assembly into the state of agriculture in 1830 reported that "independently of all other defects, there are three capital vices generally followed in lower Canada: one relates to manure, another to the rotation of crops, and the third to the raising of cattle."[33] Manure was not used on the fields but dumped on the frozen river in winter to be swept away in the spring flood. There was no organized rotation system, and in many cases the crops, especially wheat, were planted in the same fields year after year. Furthermore, little attention was given to the selection of clean seed for sowing, not to mention improvement of the varieties of wheat grown. "The habitants were notorious for the defective manner in which they fed and sheltered their cattle, sheep, and pigs. Their pastures were deficient, except for a few valuable ones along the riverfronts, and even these were probably entirely composed of wild grasses."[34]

The agricultural depression lifted in the late 1840s, and the general condition of the economy improved as the opportunities for export increased throughout the 1850s and early 1860s. In 1848 the export of horses to the United States picked up considerably as a result of demand created by booming railroad construction and shortages brought on by the Mexican War. The increased demand for food in eastern seaboard cities was reflected in the dramatic increase in beef prices in New York. Lower Canada became a beef-exporting region. The Reciprocity Treaty of 1855 further boosted the trade of lower Canada to the United States as coarse grains were added to the list of exports. Finally, the outbreak of the American Civil War sustained the demand for Canadian horses, beef, and dairy produce while creating new demand for barley and wool.[35]

Despite the expanding market opportunities in the United States, the impact on French-Canadian farming was slight. Those who had benefited largely from the expansion of American markets were Anglophone farmers in the Eastern Townships. Only in the export of horses and some coarse grains had French-Canadian farmers achieved significant success, and the effect of the horse trade was not entirely beneficial either: by the 1860s the best of French-Canadian breeding stock was gone. French Canadians, with their large families, subdivided long lots, and limited access to capital for the improvement of farming, eventually resolved the problem of overcrowding along the St. Lawrence lowlands by emigrating to the United States.

*Factors Contributing to Emigration*

The process of emigration of French Canadians from the seigneurial districts along the St. Lawrence developed slowly. There was some movement to the United States as early as the 1780s, but the total number involved was small. As population increased during the first decades of the nineteenth century and as the old long lots were subdivided, the need for new areas of settlement became apparent. That need became even more critical as soil exhaustion and crop failure plagued the St. Lawrence communities in the 1830s. The stress was partly alleviated by migrations of families into the northern tributary valleys, particularly the Ottawa and Saguenay valleys and on to the margin of the Canadian Shield. Migration southward was stalled by the alien system of land tenure in the Eastern Townships. However, after the crop failures of the 1830s and the political unrest of 1837–38, which was followed by a deepening agricultural depression in the

1840s, the first small groups of emigrants made their way into the Eastern Townships and to New England.[36]

After 1850, despite the return of relative prosperity to some parts of Lower Canada, emigration continued from the older, overcrowded areas. By this time migration routes were being formed that led to the mill towns of southern New England. The leaders in the Catholic church, anxious to curtail emigration to the United States, feared for the spiritual welfare of the migrant souls. The bishops tried to redirect the flow into the townships where the migrants would remain under their pastoral care. Those who finally decided to settle in the Eastern Townships were few compared with those emigrating to New England; the reason for avoiding the townships "included the high price of land, the lack of roads, and the speculating activities of large landowners" in southeastern Quebec.[37]

Although New England attracted the great majority of French-Canadian émigrés during the second half of the nineteenth century, there was a time during the 1850s when the midwestern states of Illinois, Michigan, Wisconsin, and Minnesota attracted almost as many. One of the largest settlements was at Kankakee in Bourbonnais County in northeastern Illinois, founded by the Reverend Charles Chiniquy, a French-Canadian priest. Father Chiniquy, appalled by the poverty he saw during his travels through rural Quebec, planned to find new farmlands for the émigrés where they could still remain together and form new communities. When the difficulties in raising cash to cover the costs of transportation and setting up farms in Illinois had been overcome, Chiniquy led the first group westward through the Great Lakes to Illinois in 1852. Within a few years, as new immigrants continued to arrive, the priest fell out of favor with his bishop in Montreal because he was directing emigrants to the United States rather than to some other part of eastern Canada. Chiniquy also quarreled with the bishop of Chicago, in whose diocese Kankakee was located, over control of the French-Canadian parish. Chiniquy's abrasive personality, combined with personal ambition and a desire to preserve a distinctive French-Canadian character in the Illinois settlement, led to difficulties with the bishop in Chicago, his new superior. An open break developed in 1858 when Chiniquy established a schismatic church in the Illinois settlement. The schism had the effect of discouraging further emigration from Quebec to the Midwest. However, by 1860 the French-Canadian population in Illinois was approximately twenty thousand, an increase of over twelve thousand since 1850.[38] It was from this colony in Illinois that French-Canadian farmers established new communities in Kansas.

## Summary

The adaptability of Swedes, Mennonites, and French Canadians to farming life in Kansas depended in large part on their social and economic conditions prior to their migration to the American Midwest. Those social and economic conditions varied widely. Each group had developed different social systems, agricultural economies, and responses to their environmental conditions. Social systems were often reflected in distinctive settlement patterns: a decline of the old village system was often accompanied by a rise in economic individualism within the farming community. The manner in which a community might restrain individualistic behavior and the influence of the church in community affairs, especially in the preservation of social mores and cultural identity, all varied from group to group. In addition, major differences emerged in the way each group responded to the crisis of increasing population pressure. As the nature of the crisis varied, so also did the response in terms of emigration, intensification of agriculture, increased capital investment, adoption of agricultural innovations, farm specialization, and the development of external markets. In short, the degree to which each group developed commercial forms of agriculture varied considerably and would affect their ability to adapt to commercial farming opportunities in Kansas. Similarly, their environmental experience was important. In the short term, familiarity with crops that could be grown in Kansas would affect their initial success, but broad experience in an environment with major difficulties in the moisture regime would affect their ability to succeed over the long term.

The degree to which community obligations might restrain the development of economic individualism declined as the old village system was dismantled in nineteenth-century Sweden. The consolidation of multiple strips of land into compact farm units and the emergence of an isolated homestead settlement pattern in some parts of the country symbolized the development of a new social order. The mutual interdependence of village life gradually disappeared. Relations between the *bonde* and the agricultural laboring classes were now based on contract rather than tradition and obligation. As a result of increased economic individualism the gap between landowning and landless widened. But in the Mennonite settlements of southern Russia the agricultural village had persisted, and with it a degree of community restraint. This restraint did not entirely prevent competition and the emergence of a powerful landowning class with strong entrepreneurial instincts when market opportunities appeared. In sharp contrast, village life and community constraints had never been strong along the lower St. Lawrence valley. Although there had been a long tradition of economic individualism (from the earliest fur-trading days), its development was limited by the absence of export opportunities in agriculture until the early nineteenth century and by obligations to the extended family, the *seigneur*, and the church.

The church played an important role in the social and cultural life of all three groups throughout the nineteenth century. Although the Pietist movement had challenged the authority of the state Lutheran church, Swedish emigrants affiliated with evangelical branches of Lutheranism and the church continued to set the standard in community mores and behavior. The role of the church was even more powerful in Mennonite communities. Church leaders not only mediated in social dissensions but also provided leadership in the preservation of Mennonite values and culture, and in maintaining an isolationist position toward the rest of society. The Catholic church in Quebec played a similar role in the identification and preservation of French-Canadian culture after the British conquest. Consequently, religious affiliation continued to be a powerful factor in the development of an ethnic identity among all three immigrant groups in the American Midwest, although it became somewhat weaker for French Canadians than for the others because of the polyglot nature of their church in both Illinois and Kansas.

Swedes, Mennonites, and French Canadians all faced a crisis of excessive population pressure in the midnineteenth century prior to their arrival in the Midwest. In Sweden and southern Russia the crisis came to a head suddenly; along the St. Lawrence it continued to deepen for decades. During the first fifty years of the century the development of new agricultural land in Sweden barely kept pace with population growth until about 1860, when the supply of new agricultural land ran out. As a result rural unemployment had become serious even before the crises of drought and crop failures of the late 1860s. In Russia the Mennonites had been restricted to Crown lands originally allocated to them, but they were able to cope with population expansion by renting land from neighboring nomads. When the nomads moved away entirely and their lands were granted to others, the Mennonite tenants became landless; this precipitated a crisis that had been simmering for some time. In contrast, the French-Canadian crisis had persisted over a much longer period of time and deepened with each decade as a result of continued population growth, crop failures, and impoverished farm technology during the 1820s, 1830s, and 1840s. For each of the three groups no new agricultural lands were available, and only two responses were possible: emigration and/or intensified agricultural production. Resolution of the crisis revealed something not only of the priorities of each group but also of their ability to develop efficient forms of commercial agriculture.

In emigrating to the New World, Swedish emigrants followed a series of chain migrations that revealed a deep desire to settle among their own kind, especially those from their own parish and neighborhood. The Mennonites, on the other hand, sought an internal solution to the crisis, thereby reasserting their desire to remain apart from society. Rather than let the conflict spill over into public dissension, which might have required Russian interference, the Mennonites managed an internal resolution of the crisis through partial redistribution of land. French Canadians, for their part, refused to emigrate to new agricultural lands beyond the St. Lawrence valley even as the crisis worsened. They clung with tenacity to the family farm and parish, thereby revealing a deeply ingrained isolationism from the Anglophone world around them, at least for a time. These varying degrees of social isolationism among the three groups would assert themselves again as each group established a new community in Kansas.

The second response to increased population pressure was to intensify agricultural production. Efficiency would have to be improved: horses would replace oxen, new machinery would replace hand tools, and farmers would introduce new strains of crops and livestock. To achieve all of this capital was required, which could be generated by selling surplus produce in local and distant markets. Intensification, specialization, commercialization, and capitalization went hand in hand. Mortgages were the means whereby capital investment was initiated to purchase new machinery, livestock, and crops. But mortgages had also been used in attempts to preserve the economic viability of the family farm; as partible inheritance practices spread, the inheriting offspring needed cash to pay off his coinheriting siblings if he wished to prevent continued subdivision of the farm. Swedish farmers were increasingly accustomed to mortgages after midcentury and experienced the bitter taste of foreclosure after crop failures in the late 1860s and early 1870s. Mennonites tended to raise mortgages among themselves and so avoided external dependency. Likewise, French Canadians borrowed from the local landowner or storekeeper, but the burden of debt that built up seemed to overwhelm any hope of farm improvement.

Agricultural innovation became key to success. Swedes demonstrated their ability by midcentury to mechanize, try new grain crops, and specialize in dairying in selected areas of south-central Sweden. The creation of an agricultural research facility at Ultuna confirmed their growing commitment to agricultural innovation. Mennonites had proved even more daring. They experimented in the production of silk and fine wool in the first half of the century and later embraced dairying and wheat production with enthusiasm. They pioneered in crop and livestock breeding, developed new cultivation techniques, and invented new equipment and machinery in their drive to increase the efficiency of farm production. They were innovators par excellence. French Canadians lagged far behind. Their farming was infamous for its weak strains of grain crops and livestock breeds, and their farm technology, by general agreement, was backward and outdated.

Access to markets was also an important determinant in the development of commercial agriculture. The improvement in transportation facilities and the growth of domestic urban markets in southern Sweden came later than in other parts of northwestern Europe. The Mennonites were even more isolated when they first settled the steppes of southern Russia. But they overcame the problems of transportation by producing high-quality goods for distant markets. By midcentury, Mennonites were among the leading producers in the thriving Crimean wheat trade, which supplied markets in western Europe through Black Sea ports. Mennonites successfully sought out and developed their markets. While Swedes and Mennonites had to struggle to overcome the difficulties of transportation and market access, French Canadians lay astride one of the major routeways from the North American continent to Europe—the St. Lawrence River. As a member of the British imperial trading system they enjoyed slightly preferential access to the British market for grain before the repeal of the Corn Laws in 1845. But French Canadians could not compete, so poor was the quality and efficiency of their production; they even failed in the competition to supply the lumber camps in the Ottawa valley, which lay at their own back door.

Prior to their arrival in the American Midwest, each of the three groups had achieved different rates of success with commercial farming. Swedes slowly embraced commercial agriculture as domestic urban markets expanded and transportation facilities improved. Mennonites clearly led the way in the development of commercial farming. They had not only overcome the obstacles of distance to market but also come successfully to terms with what seemed in the beginning to be a hostile environment. French Canadians, however, burdened with debt and committed to remaining on the ancestral seigneurial lands, were far less successful in developing a commercial agrarian economy. Only with hindsight was it realized that their resource base represented a major constraint.

Just as the commercial experience of each group varied widely, so did their environmental experience, and only the Mennonites had adequate preparation for the conditions they would encounter in Kansas. Swedes from south-central Sweden came from a part of Europe that lay beyond the realm of successful wheat cultivation. The short growing season permitted the cultivation of oats, barley, and rye, but not wheat or corn. Mennonites, however, had successfully developed a commercial wheat economy on the steppes of southern Russia. Despite the problems of an uncertain moisture supply and hot, desiccating summer conditions, the winter wheat crop proved highly successful on the rich soils of these southern grasslands. The Mennonites were coming from an environment that was remarkably similar to what they would encounter in central Kansas. French Canadians occupied an ecumene that was not ideal for wheat production. Summers could be cool and moist, favoring the development of wheat rust. The combined attacks of rust and midge devastated the wheat economy in the 1830s. The growing season was also too short for the production of corn in the lower St. Lawrence valley in the nineteenth century.

One might argue that the Mennonite advantage in terms of environmental experience was lessened by the fact that some Swedes and French Canadians had farmed for ten or twenty years in Illinois before coming to Kansas and had thus developed some familiarity with the prairie environment. In the end, this Illinois experience may have been a disadvantage rather than an advantage. It took several decades in Kansas for farmers from Illinois, Iowa, and Indiana to realize that they must forget the farming strategies they had employed in the eastern Midwest. In Kansas, environmental conditions, especially the moisture regime, were subtly but so substantially different that farmers had to develop entirely new strategies for successful farming. If anything, the Mennonites from southern Russia may have been slightly better off in having escaped this environmental experience before coming to Kansas.

# 3

## FORMATION OF ETHNIC COMMUNITIES IN KANSAS

When the Swedes, Mennonites, and French Canadians arrived in central Kansas in the late 1860s and early 1870s, they were not far removed in time and space from some of the most colorful and infamous scenes in American history. Memories of bloody clashes between proslavery and abolitionist groups in Kansas had not been obliterated during the Civil War. The ruthless removal of Indians to new reservations farther to the south and west of Kansas was not quite complete before the immigrants arrived.[1] Sporadic Indian attacks on pioneer farmsteads continued through 1868 and 1869, but the attacks did not deter the flood of farmers from Europe (Germany, Sweden, Denmark, and Bohemia) and from the eastern Midwest (Indiana, Illinois, Wisconsin, Iowa, and Missouri), who poured into Kansas in the late 1860s. The railroads had pushed the cattle-town frontier into western Kansas. Abilene, Wichita, Ellsworth, and Dodge City each enjoyed a very brief spell as the center of cattle shipping and hell raising between 1867 and 1872—so that conflicts between cattlemen and farmers seldom disturbed immigrant settlements. The newcomers were absorbed in the work of selecting land and breaking in new farms close to the valley bottomlands and were little affected by recent events around them.

An important factor in the location of new communities was the railroad. The resumption of railroad construction after 1865 pumped new life into an agricultural frontier that had stagnated in eastern Kansas during the Civil War years, although the economic recession of 1872 effectively slowed the rate of railroad expansion for almost five years. Railroad building went through two phases: first construction from east to west of the transcontinental trunk lines, which were vitally important for the cattle towns; then the creation of a network of branch lines, which were very important for the farming communities and fed into the trunk-line system.

The first major trunk line across Kansas, the Union Pacific (later known as the Kansas Pacific), began westward from Kansas City in 1863 but had reached only as far as Topeka in 1866. In the next four years it was built all the way across the state, eventually reaching Denver, Colorado, in 1870. The second major trunk line, the Atchison, Topeka and Santa Fe (often known simply as the Santa Fe), also got off to a halting start during the 1860s. However, in 1870, with renewed impetus, the transcontinental Santa Fe line was built through Emporia and on to Newton by 1871; with a final frantic push in 1872 the railroad passed through Dodge City to the western boundary of the state. The Kansas Pacific and the Santa Fe were the two major trunk lines built across Kansas in the post–Civil War years (fig. 6).

The second phase of railroad development in Kansas involved the creation of small railroad companies that built a network of feeder lines connecting rural areas, distant from the trunk lines, with the continental railroad system. This phase began in the late 1870s and continued through the 1880s. Gradually, more and more frontier communities were linked directly with regional market centers such as Kansas City, and ultimately with the larger national and international markets of St. Louis, Chicago, and New York. The expansion of the railroad network is reflected in the statistics of railroad construction. Whereas in 1865 only 71 miles of railroad had been laid in Kansas, by 1870 there were 1,234 miles, in 1880 some 3,104 miles, and in 1890 8,763 miles of track.[2]

Railroads played a critical role in the success of agricultural settlement for two reasons. In the first place, the pioneer farmer needed cash as quickly as possible. Subsistence agriculture could not support a family for very long on the western prairies.[3] Cash was needed to buy land, to hire labor for breaking in the new farm, and for implements and seeds. Hence the farmer had to produce a cash crop as quickly as possible. The railroad provided a critical link between the farmer and the market for his cash crop. Second, railroad companies were actively involved in settling the lands of central and western Kansas since railroad construction had been underwritten by large grants of land from the federal government. Although some companies may have behaved as unconscionable land speculators, others were anxious to sell blocks of land to bring in new farmers and generate traffic for their transportation business. The large railroad companies, such as the Kansas Pacific and the Santa Fe, advertised Kansas lands throughout Europe and eastern North America, attracting large numbers of settlers. Among the settlers were immigrants from Sweden, Mennonites

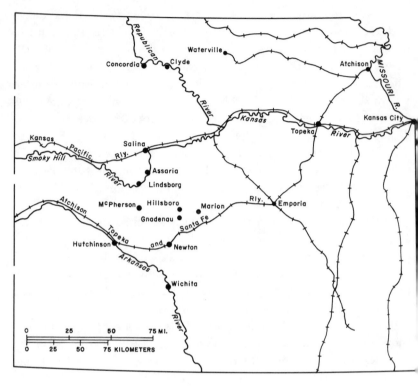

FIG. 6.    Major railroads in eastern Kansas, 1875

from Russia, and other Swedish, French-Canadian, and American farmers from communities in Illinois, all of them contributing to the swelling population along the frontier of central Kansas in the early 1870s.

The experience of each immigrant group in locating a settlement, obtaining farms, and developing a viable ethnic community varied. The success of immigrant farmers depended on a number of factors: quality of farmland selected, cost of acquiring land, development of transportation links to markets, and stability of market prices for their farm produce. The immigrants also faced personal problems in adjusting to the prairie environment and forming a network of neighborly friendships in the developing frontier society. A review of the first fifteen years of settlement reveals how each immigrant group adjusted to the environmental shocks, seized economic opportunities, and developed a community spirit on the Kansas frontier.

## Swedish Settlements

The broad swath of Swedish settlements in central Kansas originated as a daughter colony of Swedish colonies in Illinois but was soon enlarged with fresh immigration direct from Sweden. The very first Swedish settlers in central Kansas were several footloose bachelors from Illinois and Iowa who took up land in the Smoky Hill River valley in the mid-1860s; they created the nucleus around which the settlement grew.[4] Fellow countrymen flooded into the valley in 1869 under the banner of two Illinois colonization companies, one from Galesburg, the other from Chicago. The Galesburg Colonization Company, led by Rev. A. W. Dahlsten, directed its members into the Smoky Hill valley ten miles west of Lindsborg.[5] The Chicago-based First Swedish Colonization Society took up land immediately north of Lindsborg. These settlers were joined in May 1869 by another stream of migrants coming directly from Sweden under the leadership of the Rev. Olof Olsson. Thus, the axes were established that would direct a chain migration of Swedish families from the overcrowded settlements in Illinois and Sweden into the open spaces of central Kansas.

The immigrant leaders hoped to create homogeneous communities in a broad band of Swedish settlement along the Smoky Hill valley (fig. 7). Pioneers would, of course, claim homesteads on the even-numbered sections of federal land, and in order to prevent non-Swedes from buying odd-numbered sections from the railroads, the two colonization companies contracted to purchase these lands and so preserve the homogeneity of their settlements. Everyone understood the potential benefits that derived from such settlements in terms of community spirit that mitigated the loneliness of the frontier, fostered a spirit of cooperation, and facilitated the development of church and school services. The importance of the church is underscored by the fact that clergymen organized and led the migrations; even the Chicago company, which was organized by laymen, required that its members belong to the Evangelical Lutheran Church. As one historian explained simply, they "were by no means clannish, but desirous of unity and order. Within the colony they naturally favored people of their own nationality and belief."[6]

Union Township, a few miles west of Lindsborg, lay in the heart of

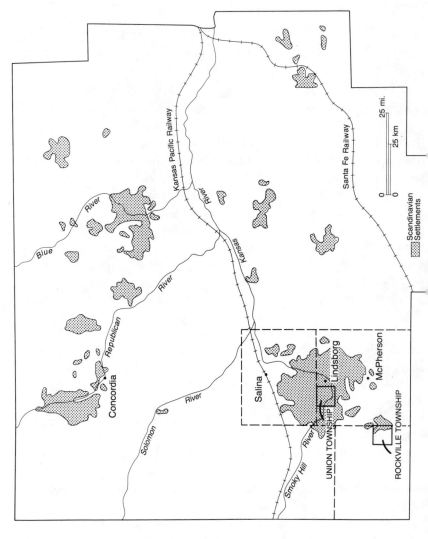

FIG. 7. **Distribution of Swedish settlements in central Kansas**

SOURCE: After J. N., Carman, *Foreign Language Units of Kansas: Historical Atlas and Statistics.*

this broad band of rural Swedish settlement and contained more Swedish farmers than in any other township in central Kansas. Most of them had lived at one time in Galesburg, Illinois. Although the earliest Swedish settlers had taken up farms in the southernmost tier of sections close to the river, where the alluvial soils of the bottomlands are fertile, the core of the Swedish colony developed in the second and third tier of sections north of the river, in the so-called second bottom lands. Here, on an old river terrace, the soils were the best in the township, predominantly alluvial and fertile but less liable to river flooding than the lowest bottomlands. The founding members of the Union Township colony built the Fremount Church on the river terrace in 1869, and they located their eighty-acre homesteads around the church.[7] The northern half of the township was not settled, however, until the late 1870s;[8] these lands rise to a height of four hundred feet above the floodplain, where outcrops of Dakota sandstones survive to form the Smoky Hill Buttes. The soils are thin and dry, have a low water table, and are among the least productive in the township. The northern uplands are better suited to livestock grazing than to crop production and did not attract many settlers in the first rush of settlement during the early 1870s.[9]

Rockville Township, some twenty miles southwest of Lindsborg, represented an outlier from the main band of Swedish settlement, and the township contains some of the best farmland in Kansas. The topography is generally undulating, although there are a few level areas in eastern parts, where drainage is a problem. Rockville is located in that portion of the Arkansas River valley known as the Great Bend lowland, where local variations in relief are slight and the outcrops of sandstone disappear under a mantle of alluvium and a few eolian deposits of sand and loess.[10] The suitability of the rich, fertile soils and gentle topography for crop production attracted Swedish leaders from the Smoky Hill valley as early as 1870. Because much of the best land around Lindsborg was quickly occupied, sites for new colonies had to be found. As one historian noted:

> More Swedes kept coming who wanted land. Therefore it was necessary to find land farther away. Old man Rodell and Peter Dahlsten, with a score of others, made a trip, during January of 1870, to the Little Arkansas River and surrounding territory in McPherson and Rice counties in search of land.[11]

It was clear that these Swedes set a higher priority on homesteading productive farmland than on establishing their families within a solidly

Swedish community. They claimed 160-acre homesteads along the eastern margins of Rice and western margins of McPherson counties and named the settlement New Andover in honor of the Illinois community from which many of them had come.

These early Swedish settlers in Union and Rockville townships had only brief contact with the Indian and cattleman frontiers. The massacre of fourteen settlers in May 1868, only forty miles northwest of Lindsborg, temporarily discouraged a band of Swedes on their way from New York to Kansas but did not prevent their eventually reaching the Smoky Hill valley. One of the last encounters with the Indians was related in December 1869. A Swedish farmer from Union Township, on his way to Lindsborg, was frightened when he suddenly came upon ten or twelve Indian families in the Smoky Hill Buttes north of Fremount, and was greatly relieved to discover that the Indians would not harm him if they were unmolested.[12] Contact with and fear of the Indians diminished as the natives were moved to new reserves farther west and south of Kansas. Likewise, the conflict with cattlemen was short-lived. Swedish farmers supported the demands for a herd law, and within eighteen months of his arrival in Lindsborg, Pastor Olsson, newly elected to the Kansas legislature, was active in the adoption of the herd law. As late as June 1871, Mrs. Olsson wrote to her friends in Sweden: "Almost every day they go past here with thousands of cattle from Texas. I wish you were here and could see the line that we saw an hour ago, when there was such a long stretch of cattle that it was more than an English mile in length and wider than the main road in Sunnemo."[13] But within a year the cattle herds were gone, the railroad pushed farther west, and the Smoky Hill valley no longer lay astride one of the major Texas trails.

In the early 1870s, nature's capricious destruction was far more disconcerting to the Swedish farmers of central Kansas than the damage wrought by cattle herds. Settlers were awestruck by the sudden and arbitrary nature of these "acts of God," which brought general catastrophe and personal loss. In June 1870 a violent hailstorm destroyed much of the wheat, rye, and oat crop, in addition to some young corn, in the Smoky Hill valley. Six months later, young Peter Nilsson lost his life in another freakish accident. He left home on a pleasant, balmy December morning to buy groceries in Lindsborg. A snowstorm struck without warning, and the farmer's frozen body was discovered two weeks later where he had sought shelter in a haystack less than two miles from his home. Several other farmers were lucky to escape with their lives in June 1876 when a tornado touched down as they hauled grain to Salina. They took refuge in a nearby ditch, but the horses were killed and the grain scattered wastefully about the trail. But perhaps the greatest single catastrophe occurred in August 1874. A cloud of millions of grasshoppers descended from a clear blue sky on a Sunday afternoon, wreaking havoc among the terrified farm families. Orchards were stripped of their leaves, crops disappeared on the stalk, window curtains were eaten to shreds, and even wooden implements, especially those with a trace of grease, were attacked by the marauding insects.[14] The damage to crops and morale was enormous. Throughout all of these travails constant terror of prairie fire added to the unsettled feeling among new immigrants, who wondered if these bottomlands and plains would ever become home for them.

Swedish families turned to the Almighty in all these hardships, and their deep Pietistic faith helped them to persevere in Kansas. Lutheran pastors taught their parishioners the spiritual merit in sustaining hardship and privation. The dugout or sod cabin with its earthen floor and primitive water supply could test the endurance of women who were accustomed to the relative comfort of a stone or frame house in Sweden or in Illinois. Infant mortality was high, and typhoid fever took a heavy toll in the primitive frontier homes. But the long work day began and ended with family prayers. The rough labor that was required to convert prairie sod into bountiful farmland could be turned to spiritual advantage if it was accepted as a means of self-discipline to check one's emotions. An ascetic ethos pervaded the immigrant church. According to Harold Millar from Skåne, "Emotions were, indeed, heavenly implantings, but to be curbed and kept in subjection, not to froth and slop over like milk from a top full bucket."[15]

The influence of church leaders was powerful in the development of Swedish community spirit, as pastors kept a tight rein on the observance of public morals. Reverend Olsson was determined that drunkenness, unchastity, cursing, and card playing, which he had fought in Sweden, would not be tolerated in Kansas. But there was less opportunity in rural areas than in a small town like Lindsborg to indulge these social passions. Leisure time was limited on frontier farms, and social contacts were limited to Sunday church service. Occasionally the womenfolk gathered to make butter and gossip—a fairly harmless social diversion, from the pastor's viewpoint. But the young folk, especially the young men, needed close supervision. In 1874, Pastor Olsson came out from Lindsborg to establish a Young Men's Society in Union Township.

A fine library was assembled for use by members. The entire program was to be based on the confessions of the Lutheran Church. Members were not to use alcohol, they should not dance, and they were expected to avoid unwholesome associations. Discipline was to be enforced upon the members.[16]

Despite the pastor's efforts, tensions developed between those who sought personal freedom and those who sought to impose a code of behavior in the frontier community. The Swedes of central Kansas did not escape this pattern, and the tensions sometimes created schisms in the community. A conflict developed between Rev. Olsson and his old friend C. W. Carlson, a founder of the First Swedish Agricultural Company, who had invited Olsson from Sweden. The two men clashed openly over the doctrine of atonement—a contentious theological issue that had split other Swedish Lutheran congregations in Iowa and Illinois. A contributing factor to this social division may have been the increasing political and economic leadership that Olsson provided, thereby superseding original lay community leaders such as Carlson, Andors Johan Nilson, and John Ferm.[17]

The dissension that afflicted Lindsborg did not seriously affect the Fremount congregation of Union Township or the New Andover congregation in Rockville Township. One explanation offered is that the Fremount congregation was composed of immigrants who originally came from Småland, some from Dalarna, and a few from Östergötland and Skåne. These farmers did not have the volatile, discursive temperament, combined with a heady individualism, characteristic of the Värmlanders, who predominated in Lindsborg. Furthermore, the Pietist influence was not as strong in the Fremount or New Andover congregations as it was among the newly arrived Swedish immigrants in Lindsborg. Fremount, according to E. K. Lindquist, "represented to a greater degree than Lindsborg a settlement one step removed from Sweden."[18] The farmers in Union and Rockville followed the leadership of their pastor from Illinois, Rev. Dahlsten, a less taxing critic of public morality than his close friend, Rev. Olsson.

The clergy became community leaders whose influence extended far beyond the local village or town. The bonds of friendship among them served as useful links among Swedish communities throughout the Midwest. For example, when the grasshopper plague of 1874 destroyed the unharvested crops and threatened the fledgling communities with ruin, the Lutheran pastor of Swedesburg, Iowa, invited Olsson to come and raise funds for the stricken Kansas communities. As noted earlier, Olsson became a U.S. citizen and was elected to the Kansas legislature within eighteen months of his arrival in the state. He was not only a spokesman for the Swedish community in the legislature but also became a leader in the economic affairs of the settlements. In November 1874 he tried to have a branch line of the Kansas Pacific railroad constructed to Lindsborg, writing to the president of the railroad company extolling the productivity of Kansas settlements and the railroad traffic being generated there. Enough broomcorn to fill 120 cars had been exported from Lindsborg alone in 1874, and 400,000 bushels of wheat had been threshed—crops that must have escaped the grasshopper plague. Olsson's confidence fairly brimmed as he wrote that "the amount of grain will double or triple next year, since greater acreage has been sown and the fields are in excellent condition." [19]

The influence of Illinois rather than Sweden seemed to overshadow pioneer agriculture. The principal crop grown by Swedish farmers during the first years was winter wheat, although corn was a good sod-busting crop that prepared the soil for other small grains, such as oats and rye. Buckwheat, potatoes, and turnips were also widely grown. The Chicago-based directors of the First Swedish Agricultural Society instructed their Lindsborg members to plant twenty acres of wheat and twenty acres of oats and to provide ample space for buckwheat and potatoes. In 1870 new instructions from Chicago added broomcorn to the list. Although some farmers in Union and Rockville did not belong to the company and so were not bound by its directives, they nevertheless planted broomcorn, and it became an important cash crop. A few dairy cows were kept to supply the family with fresh milk and butter. Olsson estimated that the Lindsborg area would ship some three hundred beef cattle and three hundred hogs by rail from Salina in 1875. [20]

The cash obtained from the sale of crops and livestock was very important to the pioneer farmer, who needed to construct outbuildings, buy farm machinery, and replace oxen with horses if his cropland was to be extended. Even the technology introduced by the Swedish farmers in Kansas reflected their brief Illinois farming experience. The earliest investments included a Moline breaking plow, a Buckeye reaper, and a farm wagon. This farm machinery facilitated the expansion of small-grain cultivation, whereas corn cultivation continued to rely on manual implements such as hoes. Potatoes and turnips were also sown and harvested by hand; they were stored in shallow pits with a layer of straw and earth to protect them from the frost. The first farm buildings to appear after the dwelling was completed included, according to Peter Henry Pearson, "a box-like granary, a corn crib with open-ribbed walls and no roof, a chicken coop, perhaps a smoke house, a stable of sod and straw." [21]

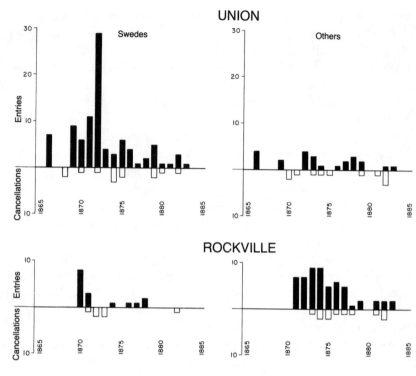

FIG. 8. Homestead entries and cancellations in Union and Rockville townships

Many Swedish farmers in Kansas found that their cash outlay for land was a good deal less than it had been in Illinois. When the Swedes first arrived in Union and Rockville townships, they took advantage of provisions of the Homestead Act and obtained land with no more expense than the ten-dollar filing fee. The data presented in figure 8 suggest that settlement progressed slowly and that 1872 was the most active year of homesteading for Swedes in Union Township, with 1870 as the most active year in Rockville Township. Accounts in local histories clarify the picture. Land was occupied rapidly, but homestead applications were not filed immediately. Many Swedish farmers "squatted" on government land for as many as five years before they decided to apply for their homestead rights. In Union Township the most active years of actual land settlement were 1868 and 1869, several years earlier than the government records suggest (fig. 9).

In addition to homestead land the settler could also obtain land from the railroads. The Swedish colonization companies arranged the sale of this land to their members. The price paid for railroad land varied according to its suitability for farming. For example, the Swedish settlers from Galesburg paid from $1.50 to $5.00 per acre of land in the central areas of Union Township. In the northeastern corner of Union, where a few members of the First Swedish Agricultural Society obtained land along the flanks of the Smoky Hill Buttes, the average price varied from only $1.25 to $2.12 per acre. In Rockville Township, however, where the soil was more fertile than in Union, the average price of land ran as high as $7.00 per acre.

A major difference between Union and Rockville townships was the size of the homestead land grants: in Union many early applications were for eighty-acre lots, whereas in Rockville they were for 160-acre lots. The reason is that Union Township lay within a belt of land adjoining the major railroads, where homesteads were restricted in size to eighty acres, and these regulations were not changed until 1878, after the first wave of settlement. Another major difference between Union and Rockville townships was the amount of railroad land purchased by settlers. In Union, approximately half the land occupied by Swedes was purchased from the railroad company, and half came from the government through homestead and timber culture claims. In Rockville, the amount of railroad land purchased by Swedes was very small: most of the farmland there was obtained from government sources (fig. 10). In fact, large areas of railroad land in Rockville were purchased by non-Swedish speculators and large landowning companies such as the Kentucky, Kansas, and Texas Cattle Company, and the Snider Land and Stock Company.

Despite the advantages of large tracts of fertile land, the Swedish migration to Rockville Township faltered in the 1870s, probably because of land speculation. In any case, there were not enough Swedes in the New Andover colony to form a permanent church congregation until 1879, and the high cost of land resulting from speculation seems the most obvious culprit. But other contributing factors were the uncertain condition of the national economy and the low price for farm produce after the crash of 1872. Certainly, isolation from markets would not have been a major factor in retarding settlement, as Rockville farmers were within easier reach of a railroad throughout the 1870s than their counterparts in Union Township.

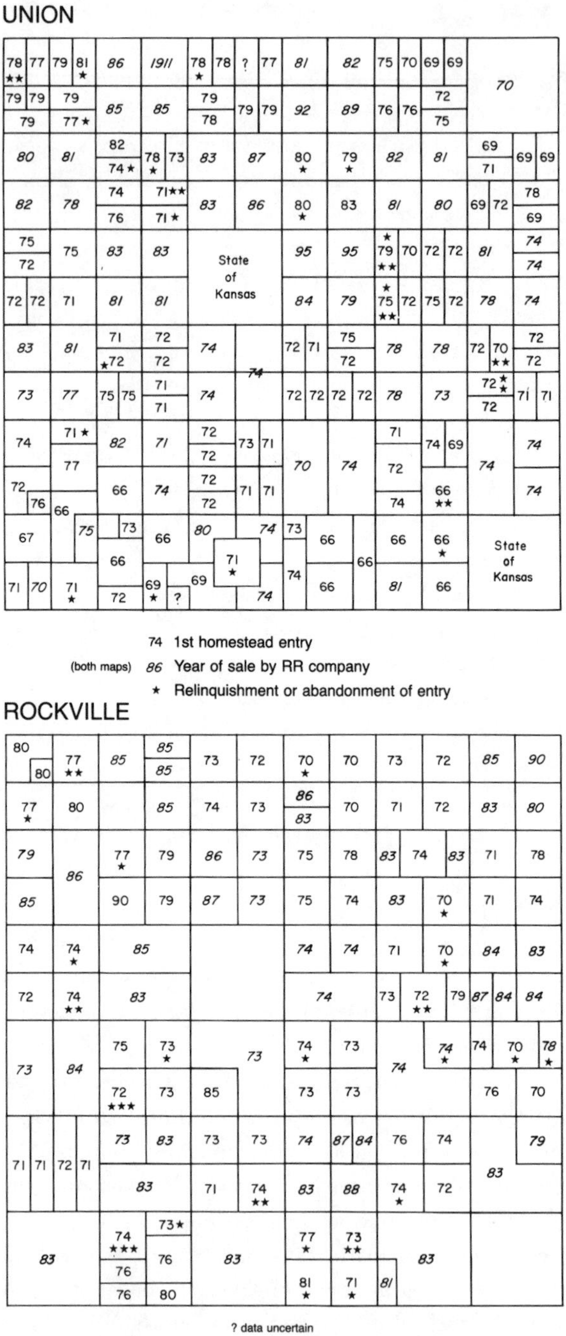

**UNION**

*(grid map of Union township with year values in cells — see figure)*

74  1st homestead entry

(both maps)  86  Year of sale by RR company

★  Relinquishment or abandonment of entry

**ROCKVILLE**

*(grid map of Rockville township with year values in cells — see figure)*

? data uncertain

FIG. 9.  Year of initial land entry and purchase from the railroad in Union and Rockville townships

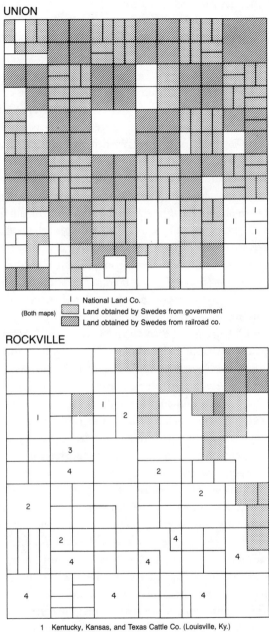

UNION

ROCKVILLE

| National Land Co.
(Both maps) | Land obtained by Swedes from government
| Land obtained by Swedes from railroad co.

1 Kentucky, Kansas, and Texas Cattle Co. (Louisville, Ky.)
2 Walter and Daniel Irwin
3 J. M. Allen
4 Snider Land and Stock Co. (Louisville, Ky.)

FIG. 10. Lands obtained by Swedes in Union and Rockville townships

SOURCE: *Mennonite Life* 4 (1949): 21.

Farmers in the Smoky Hill valley had to haul their grain more than twenty miles north to Salina for shipment to eastern markets on the Kansas Pacific railroad. The journey to Salina with slow-moving oxen could take two days, although with horse teams the journey could be completed in one long day. Access to the railroad, and thus to market outlets, was a major constraint during the 1870s in the development of commercial agriculture in Union Township and other Swedish settlements in the Smoky Hill valley. For the farmers in Rockville Township the problem of railroad accessibility was not quite as serious. The Santa Fe Railroad had been operating its main transcontinental line just south of Rockville since 1871, and farmers in the township had only a twelve-mile haul to the nearest railroad stop at Sterling.

Railroad accessibility greatly improved for farmers in both Union and Rockville townships in 1879. Construction in 1879 of the Salina and Southwestern Railroad from Salina through Lindsborg south to McPherson reduced haulage distances for farmers in Union Township to five or six miles. In the same year another railroad was built westward linking the county seats of Marion, McPherson, and, farther west, Lyons in Rice County. Railroad stations at Windom and Little River on this line were within a few miles of the Swedish farms in the northern parts of Rockville Township. Consequently, by the time the census of 1885 was taken, most of the farmers in both Union and Rockville were within a few miles of the railroad, and with the construction of branch lines these communities passed beyond the pioneer stage of frontier development.

In the process Lindsborg became increasingly important as the commercial and cultural center for Swedish settlements in Kansas. Swedish farmers now came to Lindsborg for provisions, flour milling, mail delivery, and other services. The construction of several flour mills on the Smoky Hill River in the early 1870s reduced the farmers' dependence on Salina, and Lindsborg's importance also increased when the First Swedish Agricultural Company opened a general trading store there.[22] The manager, J. H. Johnson, became postmaster and land agent in the town. Mail delivery from Salina continued on a once-weekly basis throughout the 1870s, and Lindsborg served briefly as the county seat from 1870 until 1873, in large part because of the numerical strength of the Swedes in the northern part of the county. But when it came to banking, the county seats of Salina, McPherson, and Lyons continued to overshadow Lindsborg. In fact, the Merchants Bank of McPherson had many young Swedish employees who were willing to help their compatriots from the northern parts of the county apply for mortgages. A few Swedish farmers in the Smoky Hill valley, however, continued to draw credit on the Skandinaviska Banken in Chicago.

Although the Swedish language was universal among the settlements in 1870, by the end of the pioneer phase in 1885 English was making strong inroads. Chicago produced a Swedish-language weekly newspaper that circulated widely in central Kansas during the 1870s. In 1879 two local Swedish newspapers appeared: the short-lived *Kansas Stats Tidning*, published in Lindsborg, and the Salina *Svenska Heralden*. The *Pedagogen Tidskrift*, a Swedish educational newspaper published by Bethany Normal, had a limited local audience in the late 1870s. But by this time English was gaining ground, and the English-language *Lindsborg Localist* carried news of interest to the Swedish community. English was taught in the newly established Bethany College for higher education, and when the college gave the first of its famous *Messiah* performances in March 1882, the text was sung in English.[23]

The rapid cultural attainments and improved living standards in Lindsborg accentuated the contrast in the Swedish settlement between town and country. Lindsborg developed social stratification and a starchy community leadership, which sought to impose strict standards of behavior. In rural areas, where the refinements of town living were still a long way off, a simple, rugged lifestyle prevailed. Farm work began at five in the morning and continued until well after dark. Farm families piously observed morning and evening prayers. The upwardly mobile and the leaders jockeying for social position in Lindsborg were far removed from the farmers, who were concerned with spring frosts and summer fires, grasshoppers, mortgages, markets, and droughts.

## Mennonite Settlements

The first Mennonites to settle in central Kansas came in 1870 from Pennsylvania, creating a nucleus for the thousands who came from eastern and central Europe during the remainder of the decade. This great immigration wave included Mennonite groups from Russia, Poland, Germany, and Switzerland. Those from southern Russia began arriving in 1874 under the guidance of the Santa Fe Railroad. Over five thousand families settled on lands owned by the railroad in a wide arc stretching from Marion County south and west to include portions of McPherson, Butler, Harvey, and Reno counties (fig. 11). Distinctive among the Russian immigrants was a

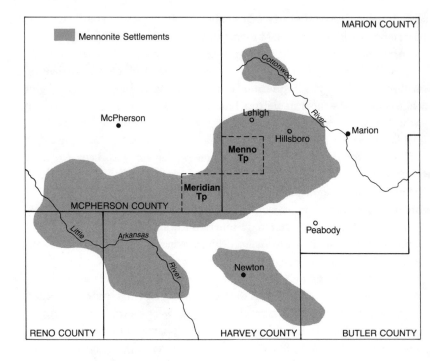

FIG. 11. **Distribution of Mennonite settlements in central Kansas**

SOURCE: After Janzen, A Study of the Mennonite Settlement in the Counties of Marion, McPherson, Harvey, Reno, and Bulter, Kansas, unpublished Ph.D. diss., University of Chicago, 1926.

large group of Alexanderwohlers—virtually the entire village of Alexander-wohl in the Molotschna district migrated to central Kansas led by their elder, Jacob Buller. The community clung together throughout the migration process, and the village leadership remained intact after the new community was established in Kansas.[24]

The area these Mennonites selected included some of the best farmland in central Kansas. Menno Township, which has a gently rolling topography, is situated where the Flint Hills upland imperceptibly merges into the Great Bend lowlands of the Arkansas River valley. The high-quality clay soils are drained by the eastward-lowing tributary streams of South Cottonwood Creek. Meridian Township, an almost flat plain farther west, lies within the Great Bend lowlands. The alluvial soils and sands produce a fertile silt loam ranging in depth from twelve to sixteen inches that is lighter in texture than the soils in Menno Township. The beauty and potential of these prairies, however, were not appreciated by everyone in 1874, as one historian has recorded:

> At that time it [the rolling prairie] was covered with grass three feet high. There were no roads, no trees except a fringe along the creek banks, and no sign of habitation except an occasional settler's shanty. Many of these were deserted because of the drought and grasshopper invasion of the preceding weeks. The hot, dry winds sweeping over the prairies and the parched grass made the countryside seem even more desolate and uninviting than it would have been in a normal season. Mrs. Wiebe burst into tears when she saw where they were to live.[25]

The Mennonites were very anxious to create homogeneous communities and went much further in their efforts to obtain that goal than the Swedish immigrants. The Alexanderwohlers attempted to reconstruct the morphology and social life of Russian villages. They established a total of eight villages in southern Menno, northern Meridian, and the adjacent sections of West Branch township, situating them on slight ridges along the section roads (fig. 12). They pooled their lands to create farm strips and common pastures around the villages. Within two years, however, the village system collapsed as farmers withdrew their land from the project; the principal explanations given were a desire for independence, confusion over taxation, and uncertainty of tenure with inheritance.[26] Despite the collapse of the communal system, some of the villages survived and families continued to live in the small *strassendorfer,* which, with their churches and schools, formed a focus for the community.

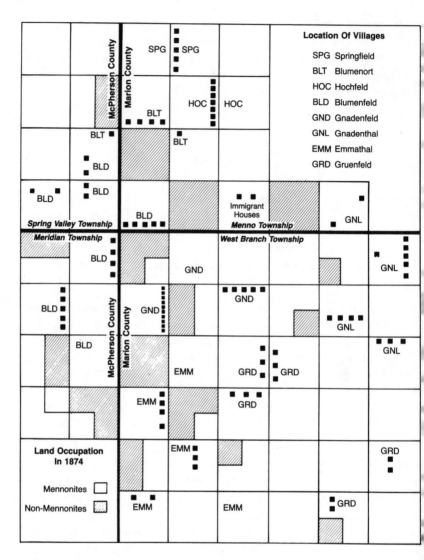

FIG. 12.  Alexanderwohl villages in western Marion and eastern McPherson counties

SOURCE: *Mennonite Life*, April 1970.

The original houses in the village were unmistakably Russian in design. Some were A-frames built with sod and timber; a dominant house feature was a brick Russian oven, with a chamber for cooking and apertures in the chimney for smoking meats. The fire could be sustained with only four armfuls of straw per day and obviated the use of either coal, which was imported and expensive, or wood, which was scarce and badly needed for other uses. The Russian oven was even incorporated into houses that were not built in the Russian manner. Some sixty-five families in the Alexanderwohl settlements eventually contracted with a Halstead businessman to build frame houses of American design in the late fall of 1874. The houses cost several hundred dollars, and within a few months of their arrival some moderately well-off Mennonites had already begun to adopt American styles.[27]

As the Mennonites built homes and laid out their farms, they had even less contact with the cattlemen and Indian frontiers than the Swedish farmers in McPherson County—the cattle trails did not pass through the Cottonwood valley. Newton, ten miles south of Menno and Meridian townships, had been a cattle town briefly before the major Mennonite influx. Although western Marion County had been part of the Kaw Indian Reservation until 1873, the Indians had been relocated in Indian Territory (Oklahoma) before the Mennonites arrived. A few Indians returned each year to visit their old hunting grounds, but they never interfered with the Mennonite farmers.

The Mennonites did face the trials of drought, prairie fires, and grasshopper plagues that other pioneers endured. The summer of 1875 was one of intense heat and searing winds, which discouraged many Mennonite Kansas farmers. They had come to terms with the *sukhovey,* similar desiccating winds in southern Russia. They were not familiar, however, with controlling prairie fires. In the fall of 1874 a great fire sweeping south for over fifty miles encroached on the village of Gnadenau, five miles east of Menno Township. John Risley, an American farmer, saved the village by showing immigrants the value of plowing protective furrows around the village. The Mennonites were more fortunate than their American neighbors with grasshopper plagues: the worst plague struck central Kansas in August 1874, barely a week before they arrived. When the grasshoppers struck again in 1876 and 1877 the damage to crops was much less severe than in 1874, and the Mennonites knew from their experience in southern Russia that grasshopper plagues were a temporary problem. A visitor to the settlements, admiring their perseverance, exclaimed: "They have encountered the same seasons, the same grasshoppers, the same drouths, the same hot winds that other settlers have contended with, and yet they have remained on their farms while thousands of gifted Americans have fled."[28]

The Mennonites' tenacity was due not only to their Russian grassland experience but also to their religious faith, the most powerful molding force of the Mennonite temperament.[29] Religious values permeated every aspect of their daily life, emphasizing the importance of frugal consumption, hard work, perseverance, and a cheerful acceptance of stinging environmental setbacks as the will of God. The mores of the church regulated public behavior, encouraged economic cooperation, and enforced community discipline to a greater degree than in the Swedish or French-Canadian communities.

To be sure, sectarian differences existed within the settlements. The majority of farmers in Menno and Meridian townships belonged to the broad mainstream of the Mennonite faith—the General Conference Mennonite group. Although many Alexanderwohlers were a little more conservative than most General Conference Mennonites, they were not quite as conservative in matters of dress and behavior as the Mennonite Brethren sect, which predominated in the village of Gnadenau, some five miles east of Menno Township. Church elders and ministers continuously emphasized differences among the sects and exercised a powerful role as community leaders. However, during the pioneer years the leaders emphasized helping their less fortunate brothers; during times of hardship sectarian differences tended to diminish, and they were never allowed to become divisive forces threatening the stability or survival of the Mennonite settlements.[30]

During the early years of pioneering almost all family members worked in the fields and contributed directly to the development of the community. Men and women worked side by side during periods of peak labor demand, and even young girls operated threshing machines. The Mennonite historian C. C. Janzen recorded that there was very little money in the settlement and so labor was the article of exchange. The need for help in breaking the prairie sod, raising barns and building fences, and butchering hogs and hauling grain was so great that families frequently pooled labor resources until the economy of the Mennonite settlements was on a firm footing.[31]

In Kansas the Mennonites established a mixed-farming pattern of agriculture and grew many of the crops they had in Russia. The principal grains (wheat, oats, rye, and barley) were grown in varying quantities on many farms. Although the Mennonites were especially familiar with the cultivation of winter wheat, they have received exaggerated credit for introducing this crop. Census returns from the immigrant farmers confirmed that winter wheat was not widely cultivated during the pioneer years; the really distinctive crops on Mennonite farms included flax, sunflowers, and sorghums. Sorghum molasses was a staple of their diet, and in the early 1880s sorghum mills dotted the landscape of southwestern Marion County. Large quantities of watermelons were also grown, and the Mennonites' reputation for producing apricots and peaches, in addition to apples, pears, and plums, was soon established in the Newton market. In a short-lived attempt to establish a silk industry, mulberry trees were planted in the orchards.[32] Each family acquired one or two dairy cows when they could afford to; produce was retained for family use. The main thrust in livestock farming was sheep rather than cattle, and Mennonite women wove and tailored clothes for the family during these pioneer years.

A few tools and pieces of farm equipment had been brought from Russia, but large equipment could not be transported; several farmers ordered custom-made, heavy cylindrical roller stones made of limestone for their grain mills soon after arriving in Marion County. Within a short time these rollers and other Russian equipment were discarded in favor of American machinery. As early as 1875 one visitor to the Mennonite farms observed "ample evidence of progress. One of the stone rollers which were procured to thresh grain was lying in the yard, while a short distance away an American threshing machine was in full blast."[33] One reason for the ready adoption of American machinery was that some Mennonites bought it at greatly reduced prices from American farmers who had abandoned their homesteads following the drought and grasshopper invasion of 1874–75.

Exaggerated reports appeared in the Kansas press about the wealth of the new immigrants. The *Marion County Record* reported in 1876: "These people are an industrious, honest class of citizens and many of them are immensely wealthy." One claim estimated that the combined wealth of some 1,900 of the immigrants in 1876 was $2.25 million. If such wealth had been evenly distributed among the Mennonites who settled in Menno and Meridian townships, it would have been quickly absorbed in the purchase of land.[34] Obtaining farmland was a much more expensive enterprise for the Mennonites than it was for Swedes or French Canadians.

In the 1870s none of the Mennonites who came to Menno and only a few of those who settled in Meridian were able to find government land for homesteading. The federal government had already sold many even-numbered sections, which would otherwise have been available for homesteading, in July 1870 at a public auction in Junction City. Speculators such as T. J. Peter, H. H. Wilcox, and N. A. Miles bought many of these sections and sold them in 1874 and 1875 to the Mennonites at inflated prices. The only Mennonites in Meridian Township to obtain homesteads were a few families from Illinois who had come west in the first years of the decade. They provided a nucleus for the European Mennonite migrations of 1874 and 1875 (fig. 13).[35]

The majority of Mennonites in Menno and Meridian townships obtained their land from the Santa Fe Railroad at prices ranging from $2.50 to $7.50 per acre. The company agreed to graduated payments, with terms varying from one individual to another. The most common agreement was that the Mennonite purchaser would repay the price of the land over ten years. In practice, many immigrants repaid their debts sooner than that. For example, Peter Pankratz undertook to purchase 160 acres of section 7 in October 1874. He agreed to repay on a monthly basis $45.60 toward the principal and $28.73 interest, with the final due date in 1884. He made his final payment on April 5, 1881. The amount of land each Mennonite bought also varied according to his financial resources. Peter Harms, who purchased all 640 acres of section 13 in August 1875 (and completed his payments in August 1882), became one of the largest landowners in Menno Township. The majority of Mennonite farm lots, however, were eighty- or one hundred-acre units (fig. 14).

The Santa Fe Railroad took an active role in settling the Mennonites in central Kansas. The company housed newly arrived immigrants in Topeka for a short time and built two large immigration halls in the southwestern part of Menno Township to shelter families until they had built their own homes. Railroad authorities also donated two sections of land in the township to support schools and churches. One commentator noted, "For several years freight rates were reduced by 10 percent or more, a reduction which the company said wiped out all profit. In some cases, freight was carried for a time without any cost to the settler."[36]

Notwithstanding the close cooperation between Mennonite leaders and railroad officials, many farmers faced transportation difficulties in the 1870s. The residents of Menno and Meridian townships hauled their grain fifteen to twenty miles south to the Santa Fe line at Peabody, Newton, and Halstead; farmers in the northern part of the township had the longest haul. When the Santa Fe proposed building a branch line west from Marion to McPherson, the conservative community of Gnadenau at first opposed it, fearing the railroad would bring American influences into their commu-

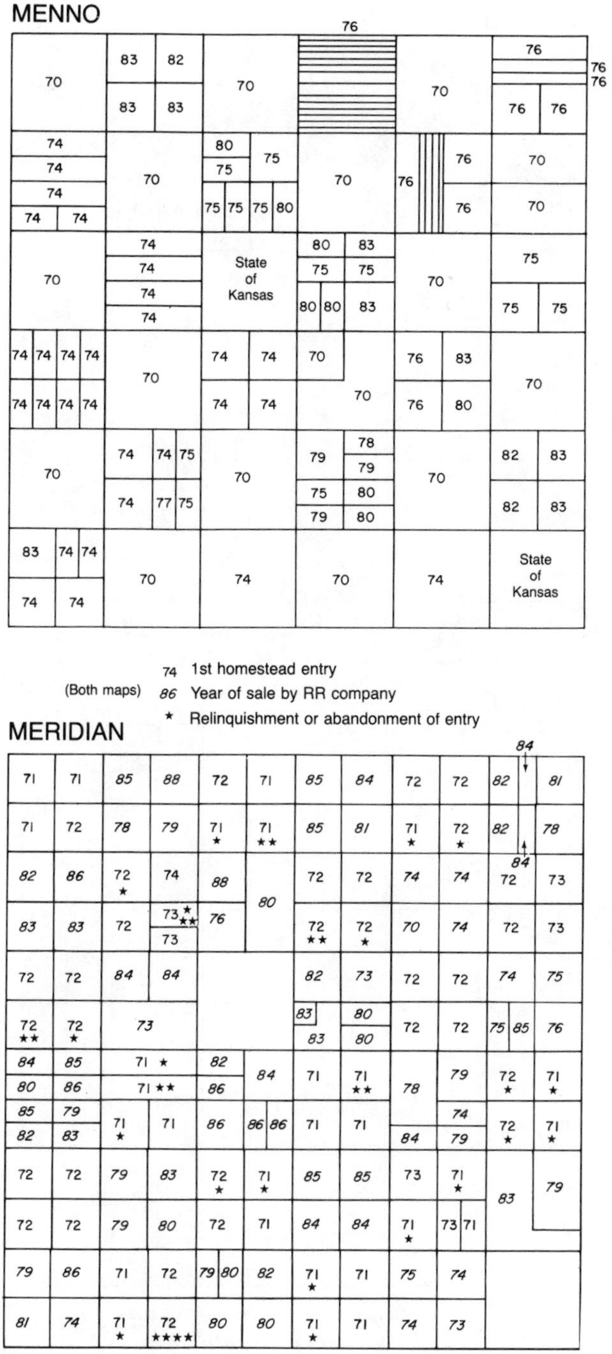

**MENNO**

76

| 70 | 83 | 82 | 70 | | 76 | 76 | 76 |
| | 83 | 83 | | | | 70 | 76 76 |

(Menno map grid with values: 83, 82, 83, 83, 70, 70, 70, 76, 76, 76, 76, 76, 76)

74
74
74
74  74
70

80  75
75
75 75 75 80
70
70
76 76
76 76
70
70

74
74
74
74
70

State
of
Kansas
80 83
75 75
80 80 83
70
75
75 75

74 74 74 74
74 74 74 74
70

74 74 70
74 74 70
76 83
76 80
70

70
74 74 75
74 77 75
70

78
79
79
75 80
79 80
70

82 83
82 83

83 74 74
74 74
70
74
70
74

State
of
Kansas

| | 1st homestead entry |
| 74 | |
| (Both maps) | 86 Year of sale by RR company |
| | * Relinquishment or abandonment of entry |

**MERIDIAN**

84

| 71 | 71 | 85 | 88 | 72 | 71 | 85 | 84 | 72 | 72 | 82 | 81 |
| 71 | 72 | 78 | 79 | 71 ★ | 71 ★★ | 85 | 81 | 71 ★ | 72 ★ | 82 | 78 |
| 82 | 86 | 72 ★ | 74 | 88 | 80 | 72 | 72 | 74 | 74 | 84 72 | 73 |
| 83 | 83 | 72 | 73 ★ ★★ 73 | 76 | | 72 ★★ | 72 ★ | 70 | 74 | 72 | 73 |
| 72 | 72 | 84 | 84 | | | 82 | 73 | 72 | 72 | 74 | 75 |
| 72 ★★ | 72 ★ | 73 | | | | 83 83 | 80 80 | 72 | 72 | 75 85 | 76 |
| 84 80 | 85 86 | 71 ★ 71 ★★ | 82 86 | 84 | 71 | 71 ★★ | 78 | 79 | 72 ★ | 71 ★ |
| 85 82 | 79 83 | 71 ★ | 71 | 86 | 86 86 | 71 | 71 | 84 | 74 79 | 72 ★ | 71 ★ |
| 72 | 72 | 79 | 83 | 72 ★ | 71 ★ | 85 | 85 | 73 | 71 ★ | 83 | 79 |
| 72 | 72 | 79 | 80 | 72 | 71 | 84 | 84 | 71 ★ | 73 71 | | |
| 79 | 86 | 71 | 72 | 79 80 | 82 | 71 ★ | 71 | 75 | 74 | | |
| 81 | 74 | 71 ★ | 72 ★★★★ | 80 | 80 | 71 ★ | 71 | 74 | 73 | | |

FIG. 13. Year of initial land entry and purchase from the railroad in Menno and Meridian townships

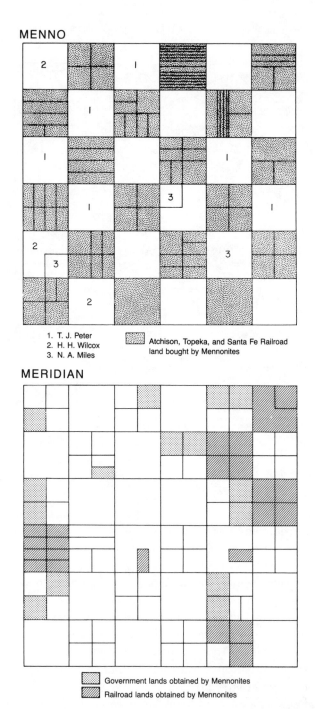

MENNO

1. T. J. Peter
2. H. H. Wilcox
3. N. A. Miles

Atchison, Topeka, and Santa Fe Railroad
land bought by Mennonites

MERIDIAN

Government lands obtained by Mennonites
Railroad lands obtained by Mennonites

FIG. 14. Lands obtained by Mennonites in Menno and Meridian townships

nity. But when the railroad was built in 1879, the Mennonites proved to be more aggressive than the American entrepreneurs who had, according to Janzen, "settled in considerable numbers in Hillsboro and hoped to split the large 'Rooshian' settlement. In this they failed. Within four years time Hillsboro was completely German and almost entirely Mennonite." [37] The farmers of northern Menno now had railroad outlets at Lehigh and Hillsboro, a few miles from their farms. For the farmers in Meridian Township the nearest outlets remained at Newton and Halstead.

Although Newton, Halstead, and Peabody had all been disembarkation points and market centers for the early Mennonite settlers, Newton was the principal center and Halstead a rapidly growing competitor. By 1878, Halstead had become an important railroad stop on the Santa Fe route, complete with a telegraph office and two large hotels, one German operated. Mennonite farmers came to Halstead to use the flour mill built by Bernard Warkentin, a leader in the Russian emigration. His close friend David Goerz established a publishing firm that produced the semi-monthly Mennonite newspaper *Zur Heimath*. Newton continued to attract Mennonite farmers with its opportunities for marketing grain and livestock. The banks in Newton employed Mennonite clerks, who could handle any Mennonite business from the broad swath of settlement north of town.

Hillsboro, to the north, also became a business and cultural center for Mennonites after the construction of the Marion and McPherson railroad in 1879. The *Phonograph* newspaper, which appeared in 1881, listed "Four dry goods and grocery stores, two drug stores, two lumber yards, three grain elevators, four notary publics [sic], one land and loan office, two blacksmith shops, two livery stables, one bank, postmaster, two hotels, two physicians, and one tinner." [38] The *Phonograph* was the first of several German-language newspapers that served the district. Although Hillsboro became a convenient market outlet and later an educational center, the town did not seriously threaten the hegemony of Halstead and Newton as a major religious and cultural center for the Mennonite settlements.

By 1885 the Mennonites had rapidly passed through the pioneer phase of prairie life. They had learned to cultivate new crops and adopted American farm equipment and housing. They had borrowed heavily to finance their farms and paid off their loans within a very short time by frugal living and neighborly cooperation. The Mennonites impressed their American neighbors by their hard work, careful tilling of the soil, and tenacity in the face of drought, hot winds, and grasshoppers. Their closely knit religious communities encouraged the virtues of simple living, cooperation, and perseverance. They tamed the prairie landscape, planted orchards around their farmsteads and street villages, and built fences around their quarter-section and eighty-acre farms. Although they still kept largely to themselves, they welcomed the improvement in railroad connections that improved market accessibility and opportunities for commercial agriculture.

## French-Canadian Settlements

The immigration of French Canadians to Kansas is not as well documented as that of the Swedes and Mennonites, probably because the French Canadians did not organize colonization companies, bargain for tracts of land from the railroad companies, or have religious leaders to organize their migration. The French Canadians arrived in a series of chain migrations from Kankakee, Illinois, and Quebec. Groups of families migrated to Kansas, urged their relatives back east to join them, and quickly developed an area of French-Canadian settlement extending from eastern and central Cloud County into western Clay County (fig. 15).

The decision to establish a new colony in this section of the Republican River valley was primarily a function of the railroad's location in the late 1860s and early 1870s. The immigrants traveled westward from Illinois to Atchison, where they took the Atchison and Pike's Peak railroad for the last leg of the journey to the agricultural frontier. The Atchison and Pike's Peak had been intended as one of the major trunk lines to cross Kansas, but after three years of construction only one hundred miles of track had been laid to Waterville in Marshall County. Construction came to a halt in 1868 because the new railroad could not compete with the Kansas Pacific line, which ran parallel but farther south along the Smoky Hill valley. Ten years later, the line was extended westward to the Republican River valley and eventually to Beloit. But during the construction hiatus many settlers, including the French Canadians, disembarked at Waterville and took up farmland wherever possible. They settled along the Republican valley in Clay and Cloud counties, some thirty to forty miles west of the railhead, where land was available for homesteading in the late 1860s.

The land the French Canadians first obtained was by no means the best farmland in the Republican valley. The well-watered sandy loam soils of the bottomlands, which marked the northern boundary of Shirley Township, had been taken in the early 1860s by American settlers. These deep, fertile soils with an adequate groundwater supply were ideally suited for

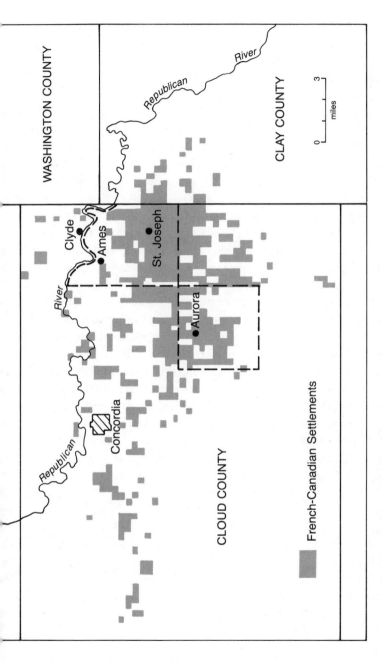

FIG. 15. Distribution of French-Canadian settlements in central Kansas

the production of corn.[39] In the central parts of Shirley Township the allu
vial soils on the old river terraces, or "second bottoms," were not as deep
nor was the water table as close to the surface, as in the true bottomland
to the north. Farther from the river, along the southern margins of Shirley
Township and throughout Aurora Township, the prairie upland soils wer
shallower and drier than the second-bottom soils. The prairie soils, how
ever, contained a rich humus layer and were reputed to be among the bes
for wheat cultivation. The majority of French Canadians settled on th
second bottoms and on the prairie uplands.

The farmers who settled in the southern part of Shirley Township and
in Aurora Township found they had to contend with a treeless, rolling
landscape. The upland soils did not support the woodlands of elm, cotton
wood, walnut, and ash that clothed the bottomlands at the northern edge
of Shirley; native timber was almost unknown on the French Canadians
land. The topography, on the other hand, presented no special problem fo
farming. In Shirley Township the old river terraces were barely discernibl
in the gentle northward slope of the land toward the river. But in Aurora
the undulating landscape had a broken appearance in places, particularly i
sections 28 and 29 in the southwestern part of the township. Although th
soils and topography of Shirley and Aurora had developed from the same
Dakota sandstone of Union Township, the land in the French-Canadian
settlement was nowhere as broken nor were the soils as thin and infertile a
those in the Smoky Hill Buttes. In short, the agricultural potential of th
French-Canadian townships was somewhat better than in northern Union
Township but not quite as good as in the Swedish lands in Rockville or th
Mennonite lands in Menno and Meridian townships.

French Canadians had virtually no contact with the cattle frontier, sinc
the Republican River valley was far removed from the Texas cattle trails
But French Canadians arriving in this northern part of Kansas were expose
to recurrent Indian attack scares. Between 1866 and 1869 several settlers
none of them French Canadian, lost their lives in annual attacks. Sporadi
army patrols proved ineffective in preventing these lightning raids. Th
last attack occurred in June 1869, when a twelve-year-old boy was kille
six miles above Concordia. The Indian threat, however, had begun to re
cede, and it did not frighten off the French Canadians, who had begun t
arrive in 1868 from Kankakee, Illinois, or interfere with homesteading i
the eastern part of Cloud County.[40]

French-Canadian pioneers were also not deterred by the harsh environ
mental conditions prevailing in Kansas when they arrived. The summer o
1868 was hot and dry. One newspaper editor remembered that

hot winds set in the 15th June, and so fierce were they that it was difficult to breathe and face them. . . . The last rain for nearly five weeks fell [on] June 28th. The eleventh of July corn was all tasseled and a better prospect for a first class crop at this time of the year never occurred and yet not one field of ten or fifty acres yielded one bushel of corn! Here and there on the lowest bottom lands was a little corn, but none whatever on the second bottom and higher land.[41]

On August 14 grasshoppers arrived and devoured whatever the drought ad spared. The worst drought years during the pioneer period were 1868, 870, and 1874, when the corn suffered far more acutely than the wheat rop.

A combination of drought and grasshopper invasions afflicted both corn nd wheat crops. The marauding insects appeared in 1866 and 1868, but n neither year was the devastation equal to that of 1874. The heat and rought had reduced much of the corn crop to withered chaff by the time he grasshoppers arrived on July 20, 1874. Although there was not much eft to destroy, the pests prevented growth of the winter wheat, attacking he kernels in the ground and devouring the blades of young wheat where t sprouted aboveground.[42]

Another test of endurance on the frontier came from prairie fires. In August 1871, barely twelve months after the first French Canadians arrived n Aurora Township, a prairie fire ruined nearly all the hay, destroying one f the great natural resources of the pioneer farmers. Subsequent prairie res in western Cloud County during 1876 and 1879 reminded farmers f the continuing danger.[43] Despite economic failure caused by drought, rasshopper invasions, and prairie fires, the settlers persevered. The local Catholic bishop appealed in Europe for financial help to relieve the distress f his flock in central Kansas, where many were impoverished and on the erge of starvation, but the French Canadians survived the tough pioneer ears without it.

Although their Roman Catholic faith was of great importance, the clergy layed a relatively minor role in the location of the French-Canadian settle-nents. Priests did not organize the migration from Kankakee or Quebec, nd the bishop did not negotiate with railroad companies for blocks of land s the Lutheran pastors and Mennonite elders had done for their commu-ities. The Catholic church suffered from a manpower shortage. Bishop ink of Leavenworth dispatched his priests as circuit riders over central and western Kansas, each with a mission territory, to serve the spiritual needs of is widely scattered flock. The bishop explained, "In order to ward off the angers that threaten the Catholic faith and life of the immigrants we have sought to concentrate them in colonies where in the course of time they can have a church and as soon as possible a school." [44] National colonies gave cohesion to a community and made the knowledge of several languages unnecessary for effective pastors. The bishop's hopes were partly realized by the French Canadians, who segregated voluntarily when creating their communities in the Republican valley.

Fortunately the French-Canadian communities lay within the mission territory of a French-speaking priest, who proved sensitive to the cultural as well as the spiritual needs of his flock. Fr. Louis Mollier was born in France, ordained in Topeka in 1873, and immediately assigned a large mission territory in northwestern Kansas. Although the priest traveled on horseback to various communities scattered throughout the northwestern part of the state, he made his headquarters in Shirley Township and ministered to the French-Canadian settlements in Clyde, Concordia, Clay Center, and Elm Creek, later known as Aurora. Fr. Mollier built a church in St. Joseph in 1874 and one at Elm Creek in 1875.[45] His burden was considerably lightened when in 1880 another French-born priest, Fr. Perrier, arrived as pastor of Concordia and Aurora. Fr. Mollier continued to care for St. Joseph and Clyde.

The danger of immigrants losing their faith on the western frontier was very real. The Chiniquy apostasy in Kankakee during the late 1850s shook the Illinois communities to their foundations. Only a few of Chiniquy's congregation, however, joined the migration to Kansas, and they did not create any serious divisions among French Canadians similar to the dissensions among the Swedes or Mennonites. Isolation from a church or one's fellow countrymen could result in a weakening of the faith. One missionary priest lamented: "An unfortunate French-Canadian (Mr. Robert) who after having been raised a Catholic, now turned out to be a follower of Darwin. Seldom did I find a more foolish man who had neither difficulty nor shame deriving his pedigree from a monkey." [46] This lapsed Catholic denied God's existence, spoke against marriage, and opposed the rights of property ownership. If these were the alternatives to the faith on the prairie frontier, Mr. Robert's case was surely exceptional: few French-Canadian farmers strayed from the Catholic fold.

The great majority of farmers from Kankakee and Quebec were anxious to establish their private property and acknowledge God's bounty. They took up farmland on the second bottom in Shirley Township in 1868 and settlement subsequently spread southward onto the prairie upland. In Aurora Township the first homesteaders appeared in the northeastern cor ner and settlement fanned out southward and westward; the last areas to be settled were in the southwest, where the land was somewhat broken and hilly (fig. 16). A review of entries in government land records suggests that the major wave of settlement swept through in 1870 and 1871 (fig. 17). However, many French Canadians in Shirley actually began farming in 1868 and 1869; there was a time lag between their arrival and the filing of a government land claim similar to the lag among Swedish homesteaders in Union Township. The first French Canadians in Aurora Township were more prompt; th⸍ Letourneau brothers and Henry Demars, who left their families in Waterville during the fall of 1870 while they went west to locate their homesteads, wasted no time. They filed their claims in November 1870 and January 1871.

French Canadians incurred just minor expenses in obtaining farmland because most acquired their farms directly from the government (fig. 18); only a few purchased their land from restless American farmers. Unlike in the Swedish and Mennonite townships, the railroad companies owned none of the land in the French-Canadian townships. Consequently for French-Canadian pioneers the cost of obtaining a farm was little more than the ten-dollar filing fee required under the government's homestead, preemption, and timber-culture regulations.

French Canadians conformed to the conventions of government regulations and the rectangular survey system. Most farms were 160 acres, in conventional single square blocks, unlike those of some American farmers, especially in northern Shirley Township, who obtained land in combinations of forty- and eighty-acre units arranged in various shapes. Little evidence suggests that this subdivision of land into small lots was an attempt by French Canadians to adjust to or take advantage of local features in the physical environment. In the southwestern area of Aurora Township there was considerable divergence from the common 160-acre square lot: the frequency of L-shaped lots suggests that American farmers tried to adjust their farm holdings to the hilly, broken land dissected by small streams. But French Canadians generally avoided these lands, where the high frequency of homestead abandonment underscored the difficulties for farming.

Little distinguished the outward appearance of the French-Canadian settlement from American settlements during the pioneer period. The small village of St. Joseph conformed to the rectangular survey system and bore no resemblance to the straggling *côtes* or linear villages of Quebec. Most French Canadians in Kansas preferred to live on their scattered home-

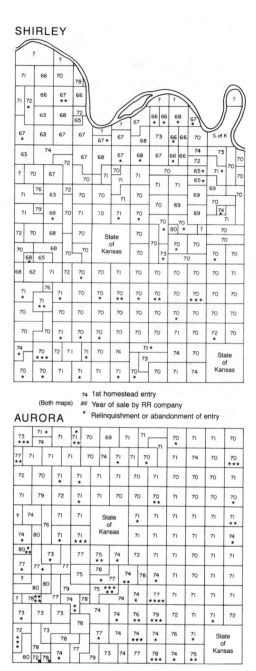

FIG. 16. Year of initial land entry and purchase in Shirley and Aurora townships

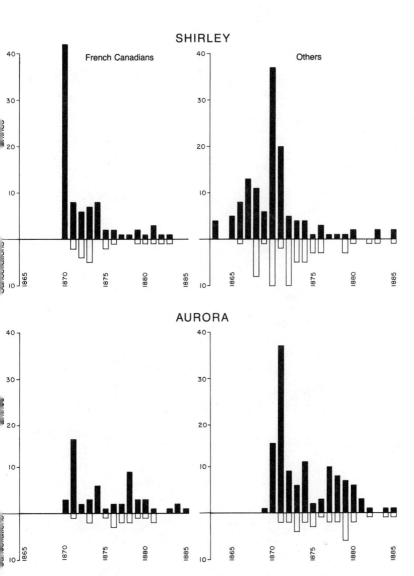

FIG. 17. Homestead entries and cancellations in Shirley and Aurora Townships

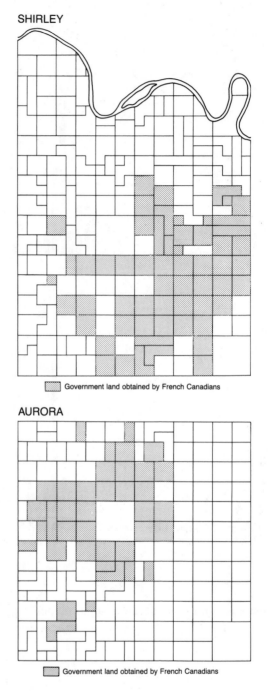

FIG. 18. Lands obtained by French Canadians in Shirley and Aurora townships

steads. The architectural style of the farmhouses and the farm equipment did not differ from those of their American neighbors. French-Canadian pioneers did not produce distinctive crops such as broomcorn or sugar sorghums, which marked the Swedish and Mennonite settlements from their neighbors. During their sojourn in Illinois French Canadians had picked up many American habits and prejudices, particularly in the growing of wheat and corn, that rendered them akin to the American farmers who also came to Kansas from Illinois.

Like all pioneer communities, the French Canadians faced problems of marketing and processing their farm produce. Slowly, small service centers developed marketing facilities. The little village of St. Joseph had no facilities beyond two general stores, a post office, and the church, but at Clyde on the northern edge of Shirley Township a mill was built next to the river. The Republican River also provided power for two mills, a grist mill and a sawmill, built in 1870 ten miles west at Concordia. During the 1870s both Clyde and Concordia saw rapid growth, but Concordia established a clear lead. The location of the land office and county courthouse in Concordia boosted the town's fortunes, and several newspapers that had been established in Clyde during 1870 and 1873 moved to Concordia when the latter's ascendancy became apparent.[47] The growth of the two towns not only eased the difficulties of marketing for pioneer farmers but also provided employment. Hard-pressed French-Canadian farmers earned badly needed cash by hauling goods from the railhead at Waterville to merchants in Clyde and Concordia.

The extension of the railroad westward through the Republican valley widened the pioneer farmers' marketing range and greatly reduced their dependence on local markets. Until 1877, Shirley and Aurora townships were forty miles from the railhead to the east and fifty miles from Salina, on the Kansas Pacific to the south. The need for improved rail connections was apparent, and French Canadians eagerly participated in its planning. The French Canadians Frederick La Rocque of Concordia and Cyrille Lafond of Shirley were among thirteen directors appointed to the Republican Valley Railroad Company, following a railroad convention in Clyde during August 1876.[48] In a special election held soon after a bond issue was approved, and in January 1878 the first trains arrived in Clyde and Concordia. Elevators quickly appeared along the line, bringing farmers in Shirley into direct contact with national market centers. Even Aurora grain farmers had rail outlets in 1878 as close as those of the Swedish and Mennonite farmers in Rockville and Meridian townships.

The farmers in Shirley Township had access to elevators in a new service center, Ames, created on the railroad line along the northern margin of the township itself. The village never fully realized the hopes of the town-site developer, an eastern industrialist, but it did shorten the grain hauling distance for Shirley farmers. A large grain elevator, said to be the largest west of the Missouri River, was built alongside the railroad depot.[49] By 1885 Ames had a population of 150, several stores, a post office, a hotel, and a livery stable. But it never became much more than a small service center for farmers, including French Canadians, in the bottomlands of the Republican valley.

By 1885, toward the end of the pioneer period, the urban ranking was clearly established. Ames and St. Joseph were primary, lowest-order ser-vice centers, the former the more important of the two because of the railroad depot, elevator, and bank. Clyde, on the northern side of the river, was somewhat larger than Ames and boasted two hotels, two newspapers, and three banks, with capital assets totaling $120,000. In 1881 the Clyde Milling Company began to grind corn and later, with the addition of new equipment, wheat. The opening in 1883 of a creamery in Clyde created a new outlet for dairy farmers in the region. Concordia, however, was the largest center in the county. Local boosters enumerated a creamery, two implement factories, the second-largest hotel in the state, four newspapers, and four banks. In addition to twenty general stores, two large elevators, and several small ones, the town had an opera house and several meet-ing halls.[50] The Republican Valley Agricultural and Stock Fair Association elected to hold their annual meetings in the county seat. Concordia's rapid expansion mirrored the increasing prosperity of new farmers along the Republican River lowlands.

French Canadians were prominent in the economic and social develop-ment of Concordia. Eli Lanoue boosted the local economy when in 1870 he built the town's second sawmill and in 1871 a new flour mill. In 1875 he improved the dam on the river, which was used to power the mills, and in 1878 combined with several new investors, George Letourneau, A. Berard, and A. Gosselin of Kankakee, to improve the mill's facilities. Dr. F. L. Marcotte, a graduate of St. Viateur's College in Kankakee and Northwest-ern medical school in Chicago, opened a medical practice in town in 1879. C. A. Betournay became one of the directors of the First National Bank of Concordia when it was established in 1883. One of the activists at the 1876 railroad convention, Frederick La Rocque, operated several businesses in town, including a large meeting hall, which he loaned during the 1870s to Fr. Mollier for religious services, before a parish church was built in 1879. Three years later the first parish priest, Fr. Perrier, built a parochial school and in 1884 assisted the Sisters of St. Joseph in opening Nazareth Academy, a boarding school for girls. J. S. Paradis owned and edited the *Expositor,* one of Concordia's four newspapers.[51]

Despite their high visibility, the French Canadians in Concordia did not create a distinctive cultural and religious focus for rural settlements the way the Swedes in Lindsborg and the Mennonites in Halstead and Newton had. The cultural focal point for rural French Canadians in the Republican valley was the small village of St. Joseph. Here expressions of French-Canadian identity were low key—a few concerts in the winter performed by the students in the boarding school, in summertime the St. Jean Baptiste Day picnic. French-Canadian community leaders in Concordia joined the mainstream booster spirit promoting the town's growth and economic development.

The rural community was outwardly very similar to an American settlement: French Canadians grew the same crops, operated the same equipment, and built similar houses to those of their American neighbors. They were a close-knit community who faced the hazards of nature together, helping each other out after fires, plagues, storms, and droughts. They enjoyed close family ties that had been forged in Kankakee, Illinois, before the migration to Kansas. The community was free from religious dissent even though a few Chiniquy followers lived among their Roman Catholic relatives.[52] The struggle with nature overshadowed other troubles and enhanced neighborly cooperation among French-Canadian farmers.

## Summary

Although the Swedes and French Canadians had a few years head start over the Mennonites in Kansas, the advantage was small and offset by the fact that the Mennonites were closest to the railroad line during the early years of breaking in new farms. During those early years the French Canadians were farthest from the railroad, but by 1878 and 1879, when branch lines were built, all three groups had ready access to external markets.

Several other differences among the three communities had long-term implications for farming. The Mennonites obtained the best farmland. The Swedes obtained some of the best and some of the worst—the land in Rockville Township was as good as the land in either of the Mennonite townships, but the Smoky Hill Buttes in northern Union Township was the least desirable for farming. In general Swedish-owned land was better than French-Canadian land. A simple ranking of farm quality shows that Mennonites obtained the best farmland and French Canadians the poorest of the three immigrant groups.

If the Mennonites obtained the best agricultural land, the advantage was offset by the high capital outlay needed to buy it. The Mennonites did not receive free government land under the Homestead Act or the Timber Culture Act, as the Swedes and French Canadians did. Most Swedes obtained only eighty-acre homesteads, which they combined with eighty-acre lots purchased from the railroad the French Canadians received 160-acre homesteads. Thus, in terms of initial capital outlay, Mennonites incurred the largest and French Canadians the smallest.

Swedes and French Canadians differed in several other homesteading achievements. The Swedes had a much better record of completing their homestead requirements and obtaining title to the land than French Canadians; in Swedish settlements many fewer homestead claims were abandoned (table 1). Further, the immigrants had a better record than their neighbors (mostly American farmers) of completing their homestead requirements. (It may be noted in passing that the preemption law was not widely used by any of the groups and that the Timber Culture Act was largely a failure as a means of obtaining land).

Little evidence suggests immigrant farmers adjusted the shape of their land claims to take advantage of or to counteract local environmental conditions.[53] Instances of immigrants rearranging the shape of their farms for cultural reasons; for example, an attempt to re-create the landscapes of their homeland, were rare. Even if they had had the inclination, French Canadians could not create the long-lot farms fronting on the river that were so typical of the lower St. Lawrence lowlands. When the first French Canadians and Swedes arrived in Kansas, they found that the most attractive wooded land along the river bottoms was already taken. Settlement spread out from these bottomlands to the broken, hilly areas. Most of the land claims were 80- or 160-acre units, not broken up into forties, and they seldom crossed section lines. For immigrants, the rectangular grid represented an absolute framework of land survey and land tenure to which they conformed at once. A few Mennonites, however, developed unusual-shaped farms. In Menno Township, especially in sections 1, 3, and 5, they created a number of elongated forty- and eighty-acre farms, but again the section lines were not violated. In this case, the influence in the develop-

TABLE I    Government Land Claims by Swedes, French Canadians, and Control-Group Farmers

| Township | Group | Homesteads | | | Timber claims | | |
|---|---|---|---|---|---|---|---|
| | | Completed | Cancelled | Commuted | Completed | Cancelled | Preemptions |
| Union | Swedes | 79 | 13 | 1 | 7 | 11 | 2 |
| | Others | 11 | 12 | 4 | 0 | 5 | 5 |
| Rockville | Swedes | 7 | 4 | 0 | 0 | 0 | 2 |
| | Others | 46 | 14 | 3 | 6 | 15 | 14 |
| Meridian | Others | 56 | 32 | 5 | 2 | 8 | 3 |
| Shirley | French Canadians | 56 | 19 | 3 | 0 | 1 | 6 |
| | Others | 55 | 32 | 7 | 0 | 2 | 6 |
| Aurora | French Canadians | 35 | 13 | 2 | 0 | 5 | 3 |
| | Others | 80 | 40 | 13 | 8 | 28 | 9 |

SOURCE: Kansas Tract Books, Bureau of Land Management Records, Washington National Records Center, Washington, D.C.

ment of the strip farms was cultural rather than environmental: it was an attempt to reestablish the village pattern of farming the Mennonites had known in Russia.

By the end of the pioneer period the three immigrant settlements had begun to develop in varying degrees a distinctive self-identity. Religious dissensions, which surfaced in many frontier settlements, may be seen as cathartic events resulting in a reassessment and redefinition of identity. Immigrants sorted themselves out as subgroups within the new community, and so the realignment of loyalties may be considered a first step in the transition from immigrant to ethnic. The tendency toward religious dissension was much stronger in the Swedish than in the Mennonite settlements; among the French Canadians it was very weak.

Several factors affected the ability of immigrant groups to establish a closed community within which an ethnic identity could be developed. Because the pioneer settlement period was much shorter on the western margins than it had been on the northern or eastern sections of the midwestern frontier, three factors were of supreme importance: the rapidity of immigration, the size of the migrant pool, and the determination of the settlers to create a totally closed society. The Mennonites led the field: their immigration was rapidly accomplished within a five-year period, a very large number of Mennonites arrived simultaneously in central Kansas, and they purchased land from speculators rather than sought out homesteads to create their settlements in their determination to create homogeneous communities. Even among Mennonites the Alexanderwohlers were exceptional, in that virtually the entire village was transplanted en masse from Russia. Swedes came second: their immigration extended beyond a decade, it was smaller than that of the Mennonites, and their pastors and colonization companies clearly enunciated their determination to create solid Swedish settlements. French Canadians were last: their immigration took as long as that of the Swedes, but they had a much smaller migrant pool to draw from in filling up the settlement, and they had no migration leaders or colonization company to focus and direct the settlement process. Nonetheless, French Canadians did manage to create a fairly homogeneous settlement by virtue of strong kinship ties to and chain migration from the Illinois settlements. Community spirit was strong in the French-Canadian community, but a robust self-consciousness and distinctive identity were never institutionalized to the same degree as in the Swedish and especially the Mennonite communities.

# GROWTH OF THE
# ETHNIC COMMUNITIES

4

By 1885 farming communities in central Kansas passed beyond the pioneer phase of settlement. The immigrant colonies had put down tentative roots, which had begun to take hold, but their maturing and flourishing depended partly on their ability to survive the roller-coaster rides of economic booms and depressions, and partly on their ability to create a strong sense of community. Ethnogenesis, the creation of a distinctive ethnic identity, was part of this maturing transition from immigrant settlement to ethnic community. Families no longer saw themselves as immigrants in the bewildering mass of a polyglot American society but as members of a cohesive group with a distinctive culture that shared a common language, religion, and national origin.

Ethnogenesis and Americanization were like two opposing magnetic poles. If the ethnic identity was strong, then Americanization of the immigrants was retarded; where ethnic identity was weak, immigrants slipped into the mainstream and Americanization occurred early and easily. The outcome of this tug of war was determined by the ability of the ethnic group to resist the acculturation or Americanization of its members, and to increase its numbers and preserve the territorial foothold it had established on the Kansas prairies.

## Ethnogenesis and Americanization

An ethnic community expressed its solidarity and maintained its distinctive identity in a variety of ways. For example, voting patterns suggest the degree to which group conformity operated to create power blocs in the political arena. The rapidity with which English was adopted in everyday use indicates the willingness of ethnics to interact with their American neighbors and accommodate themselves to American society. Exogamy, or intermarriage with outsiders, suggests something deeper of a community's relaxation of its barriers to the outside world. The immigrants' church played a key role in keeping a distinctive identity alive. Small communities were generally more vulnerable to the pressures of Americanization than large ones, and small towns, the service centers that linked rural areas to the wider world of commerce, were usually ahead of rural communities in accepting American influences. In rural communities voting patterns, the old-country language, and the role of the church in guiding the affairs of the community were slow to change. Let us look at these changes in the Swedish, Mennonite, and French-Canadian communities over the forty years after the pioneer phase had passed in 1885.

### The Swedish Ethnic Community

The Republican party represented the establishment in Kansas when the Swedes first arrived, and they flocked to its banner to show they embraced American ideals. Swedes remained identified overwhelmingly with the Republican party for decades, in part because the leaders and residents in Lindsborg were rock-bed Republicans.[1] But that was not always the case in the rural townships of McPherson County, where farmers did not readily succumb to the conformist pressures of a small-town bourgeois elite. During the 1870s and early 1880s most of the farmers were indeed Republicans, and local leaders in Union Township tried to keep their flock within the Republican fold. But in the 1880s, when Swedish farmers bucked the Republican lockhold and switched to the Grange movement, there was considerable discussion in the Freemount community about whether members who joined the Grange could remain within the church. The Augustana Synod had forbidden Grange membership because it was seen as a ritualistic and secret society. Walter Nugent has commented: "In the politically and economically fractious decade of the nineties, the voting pattern of Swedish precincts was much more disturbed and heterogeneous than in more peaceful times, which may indicate that they and other groups showing similar disturbances put ethnic cohesiveness on the shelf and concentrated on politics and economics when the times demanded."[2]

During the 1890s the differences between Lindsborg and rural areas became even more pronounced. Pastor Swensson, president of Bethany College and senior Lutheran minister in Lindsborg, spoke vehemently against the Farmers' Alliance and the Populists. The result was that in Lindsborg the Republican candidate for governor in 1892 won by 317 to 112 votes, but in the surrounding rural areas the successful Populist candidate won by a margin of three to one.[3] The drift away from the Republican party in rural areas continued in the elections of 1896 and 1900, when more and more Swedes who had not voted Populist earlier in the decade embraced the Democratic ticket. Clearly by the late 1800s the solid voting pattern of the Swedes was beginning to crack, and the Swedish farmers in particular ignored the advice of the Lindsborg leadership and voted their own economic self-interest and protest of the status quo. Thus in the 1890s the ethnic solidarity of the Swedish community in politics showed the first signs of fragmentation and diversification, a sign of their Americanization. The political acculturation of the Swedes was not completed, however, until after World War I.

Another method of measuring Swedish adjustment to American life is their abandonment of the Swedish language in favor of English. During the first years of settlement the clergy urged their parishioners to learn English, although several decades later, as Swedish began to disappear, they became active proponents for preserving the mother tongue. Rev. Olof Olsson organized informal English classes for adults in the early 1870s, soon after he arrived in Kansas. His successor in Lindsborg, Rev. Dr. Carl Swensson, emphasized to the students at Bethany College in 1882 that English be given the same importance as Swedish. During these pioneer years the ideal in Swensson's mind was clear: he encouraged immigrants to become Swedish-American but was not anxious to create yet another "Little Sweden" in America.[4] For the moment he encouraged Swedes to celebrate the Fourth of July and to embrace their responsibilities as American citizens.

In the decades that followed, Swedish continued to be used very widely, especially in the rural areas. Children spoke Swedish at home; they became bilingual only after they went to school. Men learned English earlier than women through business contacts; the women, working mainly in the home, had fewer external contacts and fewer opportunities to use English.[5] But even in Lindsborg, the business center linking rural communities with the wider American world of commerce, the use of Swedish persisted well into the twentieth century.

The use of English in business affairs was one thing, its adoption in church services quite another. During the early phase, when pastors seemed anxious to show that Swedes could be good Americans, English was the language chosen for the first performance of Handel's *Messiah* in 1882 at

Bethany College, although the choir was instructed in Swedish. Some English was also used in church services during the 1880s; the principal reason given was to accommodate Americans in the congregation, a response that demonstrates a willingness to admit Americans to the community. Except for this brief period, Swedish was used exclusively in confirmation and most services. By 1908, however, several confirmations had been performed in English, marking the beginning of the end for the exclusive use of Swedish in church. The older, first-generation Swedes wished to retain Swedish; the younger generation was anxious to use more and more English, and so the trend toward English was accelerated during World War I. Consequently, although in 1909 Swedish was used exclusively in church services, ten years later English predominated. The exception was the Bethany Lutheran Church in Lindsborg, which continued to use Swedish exclusively until 1928.[6]

One medium that kept alive the use of Swedish over the years was the newspaper. By 1880 central Kansas had two local Swedish newspapers, the *Svenska Heralden,* published in Salina, and the *Kansas Staats Tidning,* published in Lindsborg. The latter did not last long, as the two young proprietors offended the town elite with their rowdy and sometimes drunken behavior—their advertising was cut off and they were forced to close down and move out of town. They sold out to the *Svenska Amerikaneren,* published in Chicago with a well-established readership that extended to the rural townships of central Kansas. But there was already competition from another local newspaper, the *Lindsborg Localist,* which published in English and carried news of the Swedish communities. Not until 1889 did a second Swedish newspaper appear, the *Lindsborg Posten,* which was supported by local Swedes in a brave effort to keep the Swedish language alive. The paper continued to appear weekly until it closed in 1930.[7]

The opening of the Swedish community into the American mainstream during the first three decades of settlement can also be seen in the patterns of intermarriage. E. K. Lindquist writes that there were no mixed marriages during Pastor Olsson's ministry from 1869 to 1877:

> In the period November, 1870, to January, 1880, there were seventy-six marriage licenses issued in McPherson County in which both parties were Swedish and only eight in which one party was of that nationality, for a ratio of slightly higher than nine to one. [Most if not all of these mixed marriages took place after 1876.] From March, 1880, to March, 1887, 181 licenses were purchased by Swedish couples to thirty-eight, when only one was Swedish, for a ratio of slightly less than five to one.[8]

The rate of intermarriage continued to increase thereafter, even though American brides were not highly regarded by the older immigrants: they were thought to be poor workers and extravagant in their tastes. The fact that many were not Lutherans also stood against them. But by the 1920s intermarriage was widespread among third-generation Swedes, many of whom had little knowledge of Swedish customs.[9] The effect of this increase in intermarriage after 1890 was to weaken the homogeneity of the community and the strong sense of a distinct Swedish identity.

Bethany College was the center of higher education for the entire area of Swedish settlement in central Kansas, and, as noted above, in the early 1880s English and Swedish were given equal weight. Over the next two decades, however, the college became more important as a means of preserving Swedish than as an instrument of spreading the English language, which many young Swedes seemed anxious to learn anyhow. The college became a focal point in teaching and reminding students of their Swedish culture. According to Lindquist, "Appeals for funds to finance the institution were based upon this identification with Swedish culture. . . . The rapid Americanization of the second generation and the impact of World War I definitely curtailed the Swedish character and interests of the college." [10]

The church always played a very important role in the Swedish communities. The clergy in Lindsborg provided outstanding leadership that included pastor, politician, teacher, and newspaper editor. Rev. Olsson shaped the educational system in McPherson County and in the 1870s became the leading Swedish politician in the Kansas legislature before going on to a professorship and the presidency of Augustana College in Illinois. His successor in Lindsborg, Rev. Dr. Swensson, was president of Bethany College and later became editor of the local Swedish newspaper. But in forging a Swedish ethnic identity the small-town clergy in Lindsborg were atypical, and rural pastors did not always follow their lead. This was due to the fact that Rev. Olsson arrived in Kansas full of the Pietist spirit, whereas the rural pastors, such as the Rev. Dahlsten in Freemount, had ministered in Illinois and were generally more open in their doctrinal views. Olsson was not in the least anxious to develop a "folk church" but was vehemently determined to build up a "pure community" into which only those who submitted themselves to spiritual examination were admitted. He was something of a zealot, even in dealing with the comrades who had invited him to come and minister in Kansas in the first place. In contrast the rural ministers were somewhat more relaxed and accommodating, while still maintaining Swedish customs and the Swedish language. Christmas was the big festival for all the Swedish churches in central Kansas. One historian observed: "It is interesting to note that the Christmas complex survives more completely among the descendants of the Swedish pioneers than does the language, historical tradition, and other aspects of Swedish culture." [11] Cultural traditions and language could survive in the rural townships as well if not better than in Lindsborg, where commerce and social conformity were pervasive.

### The Mennonite Ethnic Community

The Mennonites were far more exclusivist in their communities than the Swedes, and so American influences penetrated them considerably later. The majority of Mennonite settlers in central Kansas, wary of the American democratic system because of its violence, refrained from political activity. As Nugent has said, "A religious sect in the strict sense of the word, the Mennonites believed that the church congregation provided all the social organization that they needed and found such political institutions as voting an unnecessary intrusion." [12] Only a few voted in the 1876 elections, and they voted Republican. In 1881 a few became township officers; others stood for county office in 1885. [13] Slowly more and more Mennonites became involved in politics, almost always as Republicans.

During the 1890s, as younger Mennonites came of age, political participation increased, and many were wooed away from the Republican party. [14] The Mennonite vote for Populist candidates increased from 15 percentage points below the state average in 1890 to 20 percentage points above the average in 1894. Juhnke writes, "Pockets of solid Mennonite Republicanism did emerge, however, and none was more united than the Alexanderwohl congregation spread through Menno and West Branch townships in Marion County." [15] Most of them did not understand the free silver issue in the elections, but they were persuaded to vote for cheap money and that the Democrats were responsible for the "hard times." Even some of the most conservative laid aside their scruples and voted for the first time. [16] Although Mennonite loyalty to the Republican party survived in central Kansas, elsewhere in central Kansas the first cracks in Mennonite political solidarity began to appear under the pressure of the 1890s depression.

A new assault on that solid facade developed in 1898 with the Spanish-American War. Pacifism and the refusal to perform military service, key elements in the decision to leave Russia, were still important moral issues for Mennonites. Consequently, when war broke out many renewed their lapsed military exemption licenses. Although a few young men enrolled in the army, the majority did not. Despite the fact that the Democratic presidential candidate opposed American imperialism overseas, Mennonites gave the Republican candidate 57 percent of their votes in the 1900 presidential election. Juhnke points out that "the lack of a strong Mennonite peace vote in 1900 suggested that Mennonites were not anxious to let their religious doctrines get in the way of their growing confidence in and commitment to America." [17]

Mennonites were much slower than Swedes in adopting the English language, and German remained a powerful barrier to acculturation until World War I. During the initial period of settlement, as American farmers moved elsewhere, local stores were manned by German-speaking clerks and the German language predominated. Local night schools for adult English instruction, organized during the first decade of settlement, disappeared. German continued to be used widely in the highly segregated rural communities, not only at home but also in business affairs and schools. From 1882 onward public schools were organized by the Mennonites themselves and were heavily attended by young people up to twenty-one years of age. The school term ran for three months, and all subjects were taught in German. Extensions to the school year, first to five months in 1903 and then to seven months in 1907, resulted in a reduction of German instruction to two months in the springtime. Individual communities worked out compromises with the county superintendant whereby some German was taught each year in public schools. But anti-German sentiment whipped up in 1917 and 1918 forced abandonment of German instruction. In March 1919 the Kansas legislature passed a law requiring English as the exclusive language of instruction in all elementary schools. Although the law was nullified by the Supreme Court in 1923, teachers and parents were reluctant to continue with the German schools after World War I. [18]

Pressure to abandon the German language came in part from outside the Mennonite communities and in part from within. Young Mennonites were anxious to learn and use English even though their parents continued to insist that speaking German was essential to being a good Mennonite. Gradually that argument lost credence as the second generation came into its own. Ability to speak German, however, remained an important criterion in the selection of pastors for local churches, although Bethel College in Newton emphasized the importance of both German and English in training teachers for Mennonite schools. Townspeople, in any case, were more inclined to favor English over German than their country neighbors.[19]

Use of German was also maintained through newspapers that circulated in the communities. Some newspapers came from Indiana, but most were published locally in central Kansas. Hillsboro became the publishing center of two weekly newspapers in the 1880s, the *Anzeiger* and the *Zions Bote*. Both were thoroughly German, questioning if not openly critical of American ways, and somewhat narrow in their viewpoint. But these were not the only options available to newspaper-reading Mennonites. The 1880s saw a spate of short-lived German-language papers, including the *Phonograph* and the *Intelligencer*. The *Hillsboro Herald*, which appeared in the late 1880s, published one page in English and three in German. But in the 1890s, as the English-speaking population declined, the *Die Kansas Currier*, started in 1893, and the *Hillsboro Journal*, started in 1908, published exclusively in German. Halstead also published German papers but with church affiliations: in 1875 the weekly religious paper *Zur Heimath* appeared but in 1881 was merged with an eastern newspaper to become *Bundesbote*. After 1883 the Halstead newspapers became the organs for various Mennonite groups. Newton, on the other hand, was the center for two secular papers, the *Herold*, which was in German, and the *Mennonite Weekly Review*, in English. The Hillsboro *Vorwaerts*, under the editorship of Abraham Schellenberg, enjoyed a wide readership in the years before World War I and between 1914 and 1917 took a very strong pro-Kaiser position. Carman tells us that there were numerous German language newspapers until World War I, when there was considerable agitation, led by Governor Capper, to suppress them.[20] What distinguishes Mennonite from Swedish communities is the large number of German newspapers they had and the fact that a flourishing press survived up to the end of World War I even though younger readers knew little of the language.

Religion was a far more powerful molding force than language or national origin for Mennonite ethnicity. The inherent individualism of the Anabaptist faiths, which in the past had led to schism and sectarianism, generally succumbed to the tremendous forces for conformity within each Mennonite sect.[21] The most conservative sects, such as the Krimmer Mennonite Brethren or the Kleine Gemeinde, were usually the strictest in terms of discipline. The farmers in Menno and Meridian townships were not members of these sects but belonged to the mainstream General Mennonite Conference. Even within the General Conference the pressures to conform were quite powerful. Public discussion of offenders' misconduct invoked shame and disgrace and acted as a major deterrent to aberrant behavior.

The austerity of Mennonite religious worship and services was somewhat modified over the years, and the churches became more and more accommodating to American life. Increasingly, music became part of the Sunday service. By 1902 a friendly choir competition among the churches —a Saengerfest—was organized; it became an annual event each May. Religion was no longer as heavy and serious as it had once been, and humor began creeping into the sermons. As the strict codes were relaxed, so was segregation within the church by gender, and married men sat in church with their wives. In the nineteenth century the dead were buried in chronological order of death with only a small wooden or stone tablet to mark the grave. By 1920 the American way had been adopted, and burial by family group was permitted.[22]

The main resistance to assimilation was the religious coercion of the church, but over the years the churches also adapted to life in North America. During the 1880s and 1890s, for example, there was little exchange of preachers from one community to another, but by 1914 quite a lot of contact took place. As Mennonites lowered their religious barriers preachers from not only other Mennonite sects but also Baptist and Methodist churches were invited to share their pulpit so long as they could speak German. In a few instances the coercive power survived, especially when it came to entertainment. Theaters, dance houses, and operas were still banned in 1914, and even the movie house in Hillsboro was out of bounds to Mennonites.[23]

American influences penetrated the Mennonite communities through the second generation, with the greatest changes occurring in the social relations between the sexes among young people. After 1900 a Sunday evening gathering of young folk, referred to as "the crowd," became popular in the General Conference communities. The first part of the evening was given over to group games, and then, according to Janzen, "the young people [would] pair off and spend the rest of the evening in spooning." Courtship, which had once been brief, now took much longer. Diamond rings became commonplace, and parents no longer arranged marriages. The simple Sunday afternoon wedding ceremony gave way to elaborate community celebrations. But by the time of World War I quiet family celebrations were again preferred. Janzen observed, "The chief cause of this is undoubtedly the example of neighboring Americans, whom the younger Mennonites are copying increasingly."[24]

Although the majority of Mennonites voted against women's suffrage, the position of women in Mennonite communities was also becoming more and more American. Families tended to be much smaller, and women waited longer before having their first child. Younger Mennonite men ignored the older folks and demonstrated a higher regard for the health of their wives; older men and women objected strongly to the trend but were powerless to stop it. Women no longer worked in the fields but confined their activity to the farmyard and house. But as the suffrage issue demonstrated, there were limits to a woman's independence, and divorce remained rare among Mennonites. Only twenty-two divorce cases involving Mennonites were recorded in Marion County between 1874 and 1924.[25]

Over the years the material well-being of the Mennonites improved and elements of economic individualism appeared. In the early years, when little currency was in circulation, labor was exchanged, farmers pooled their capital to purchase equipment, and cooperation was common at harvest and hog-butchering times, but as the flow of cash increased and people prospered, cooperation declined and each family became increasingly independent. The self-reliance of the Mennonites diminished as they came to rely more and more on American-made goods, and so household industries such as spinning, knitting, and clothes making dwindled. Similarly, thatched roofs had disappeared by 1893 and the old sod houses were used as barns. Houses were large, well equipped, and furnished with rugs and fancy furniture, including such frills as pianos and organs. The telephone first appeared in 1905, and by 1909 there was scarcely a Mennonite home without one. By the 1920s the bicycle was being replaced by the motorcycle and the carriage by the automobile. The world of American commerce and consumerism made deep inroads into the traditional patterns and folk ways of the Mennonites. Cooperation among Mennonite farmers became a thing of the past (except in real emergencies, such as the drought and economic depression in the 1890s), as most farmers preferred to pay cash for labor.[26]

Janzen was concerned that the weakening of the Mennonite faith that accompanied the advance of materialism and economic individualism was not for the best. "The truth is that materialism has made great inroads and religion, tho still strong, is not nearly so dominant as formerly."[27] Clearly the decline in the power of the church and the pervasive influence of religious beliefs in the daily life of Mennonites is evidence of the first steps in their Americanization.

*The French-Canadian Ethnic Community*

The French-Canadian community in central Kansas was much less distinctive than that of the Swedes or Mennonites. Partly this was because of its smaller size and partly because the community, a daughter colony of the Kankakee settlement in Illinois, was twice removed from Quebec. Kankakee did not provide the support needed to develop a strong ethnic identity. Unlike the Illinois settlements, the Kansas community was not served by priests from Quebec; priests who served the Kansas settlements were appointed by the local Catholic bishop, who was often hard pressed to find the necessary personnel to staff his churches. These French-speaking priests at first were circuit riders with a large territory to serve in western Kansas, but by the early 1880s they were appointed as resident pastors in the rapidly growing French-Canadian settlements.

From a commercial viewpoint, Shirley and Aurora townships each had their own small service centers. The village of Aurora served the township of that name, Union Township had the village of Clyde on the northern side of the Republican River, and the village of St. Joseph was in the heart of the French-Canadian settlement in Shirley Township. Clyde became the more important commercial center of the two in Shirley Township and remained ahead of the third village, Ames, which developed in the 1880s on the rail line. All these centers were overshadowed by Concordia to the west, which was the county seat and land office. French-Canadian businessmen and professionals were leading citizens in Concordia as well as in the smaller service centers. Although the Catholic bishop was in Concordia and established the first hospital and higher schools with the help of French-Canadian nuns, the religious center of the French-Canadian community in the Republican valley continued to be St. Joseph.[28] (Rev. R. Scannell was elected bishop in 1887 but was transferred to Omaha in 1891. During the 1890s the diocese was administered from Wichita; a new leader, Bishop Cunningham, was eventually appointed in 1898.) Fr. Perrier, who had come in 1880, helped to found Nazareth Academy in 1884. As important as the academy became, it never attained the position Bethany College held for the Swedes.

French Canadians did not remain isolated on farms but were active in the commercial life of Aurora. The village was founded around St. Peter's Church, built in 1875 on a site close to where the railroad was expected to run. But in 1887, when the railroad was eventually constructed, Aurora came into being and many businesses (and the church) relocated to a new site close to the railroad tracks. I. Gennette moved his hardware store, and Z. Cyrier moved his dry goods, grocery store, and post office to the new site. Turnover within the village was high. Eli Grandpre built the first blacksmith shop but did not stay long. Mrs. Gravelin and Mrs. Letourneau both opened hotels; the former did not stay long either, but the latter remained for years. In 1888 two banks opened, but their tenure was brief; one lasted a short time and the other a few years.[29] By 1901 the town had flour and feed stores, livery stables, a creamery, and a lumberyard. Like many other businesses in town, the three grain elevators were also owned by French Canadians.

The political affiliation of the French Canadians in Kansas was overwhelmingly Republican. Their choice of the GOP ran contrary to the usual alignment with the Democratic party of Catholic immigrants. But in county atlases and histories, the leading French-Canadian businessmen in Concordia and the villages and town areas of central Kansas all listed membership in the Republican party. They had joined the party of the majority. In addition, as their brief biographies indicate, they joined other fraternal organizations and societies such as the Knights of Pythias, the Order of Maccabees, and the Oddfellows. In other words, they showed by the turn of the century an advanced movement into the American political and social mainstream. But the distress caused by the depression of the 1890s resulted in defections from the Republican party, especially in rural areas, and as Nugent noted, southern Shirley Township, heavily French Canadian, voted overwhelmingly Populist in elections at the time.[30] In contrast, townsfolk tended to stick with the Republicans, and so Concordia, Clyde, and Aurora remained Republican. French Canadians behaved much like their American neighbors in terms of party affiliation and voting preferences from the earliest years in Kansas.

Priests from France provided leadership within the French-Canadian communities. Fr. Mollier ministered to St. Joseph and Clyde; Fr. Perrier to Concordia and Aurora. But in 1883 Fr. Pierre Fortier, a young French-Canadian priest, was persuaded to take Aurora as a permanent parish. He had come from Ste. Helene D'Arthabaska to visit a cousin in Aurora Township and remained in the parish as pastor until his death in 1912. These priests were more anxious to preserve the faith of their congregation than to develop a distinctive French-Canadian heritage, although Fr. Mollier introduced the Society of St. Anne, a religious sodality for the womenfolk of the parish that had strong associations with Quebec.

The men of the parish established a branch of the St. Jean Baptiste Society, which was very active in the 1880s in the Kansas communities. This organization for expatriate French Canadians, based in New England, encouraged among its members the maintenance of ties with the homeland but simultaneously promoted American citizenship. When Bishop Fink visited St. Joseph in 1884, the newly established society gave him a warm welcome:

> After Mass the St. John's French National Society, headed by a band, marched to the pastoral residence, and Mr. J. Fortier read an address of welcome to the Bishop, the main purport of which was to ask him to bless the association. His lordship answered the compliment by warmly sanctioning the organization and expressed the hope that the membership might increase, thus serving to foster the spirit of patriotism and unity amongst the congregation.[31]

Three years later, when Quebec's national holiday, the feast of St. John the Baptist on June 24, was celebrated with an annual picnic, the local Catholic newspaper reported on how important St. Joseph was as the center of French-Canadian settlement:

> The young as well as the old people had a grand time. The tables were loaded down with all kinds of refreshments, but as it was on a Friday no flesh meat was to be seen about the place, no whiskey, no disorderly conduct of any kind. People from the adjoining towns were very numerous. From Clyde, Clifton, Ames, Corcordia, Miltonvale—the Ames and Miltonvale bands played remarkably well. Speeches were made in French and English. 700 people took part in the celebration of the grand Holy day. Since the organization of the St. John the Baptist society of this place, three years ago, the society has paid $1,300 toward the erection of the convent school, and this year the amount will foot up to $400, which will go into the treasury for further use.[32]

The society continued to host the annual June 24 celebrations through the 1880s and 1890s; morning mass was followed by a picnic with racing and contests of different kinds, riding the merry-go-round, raffling, and in the evening a sumptuous dinner and play by local schoolchildren. The St. Jean Baptiste Society was an important social organization in the local French-Canadian community.

Perhaps more important in preserving a distinctive French-Canadian identity than these parish organizations was the opening of a school by the Sisters of St. Joseph. The nuns were invited from Newton by Bishop Fink to establish a mother house and open schools in Concordia and St. Joseph.

In the fall of 1885 they began teaching in St. Joseph. They took between forty and fifty boarders from the surrounding settlements and taught subjects up to the third year of high school, including English and French, in addition to the usual school subjects, and dramatics, music, and religion —religion was taught after regular school hours because the school was tax supported. Classical French dramas were not only taught but performed for local audiences in St. Joseph and Clyde. Three of the four nuns who established the school were of French-Canadian extraction.[33]

This order of nuns subsequently opened new schools in other French-Canadian communities, not only in central Kansas but even in Illinois, northern Wisconsin, and Michigan. They recruited postulants in Quebec, Kankakee, and, by 1886, from the local settlements in Cloud County. As a result schools were opened in neighboring Clyde and Clay Center, and eventually in 1905 in Aurora. Enrollment in St. Joseph continued to expand; a peak was reached in 1899 and 1900 with 185 students. Enrollment declined to 100 in 1908, rose suddenly to 180 in 1912, and declined again to between 60 and 70 in the mid-1920s. Presumably part of the decline was attributable to the opening of a school in 1905 in Aurora; by 1914 it had 100 students.[34] The Sisters of St. Joseph were not a French-Canadian order of nuns and catered to other immigrant communities—German and Irish—in central Kansas. But they did establish a network of ties with French-Canadian communities throughout the upper Midwest.

French Canadians, like the Swedes and Mennonites, seem to have made an extra effort to inculcate their religious values, and for a while their distinctive national culture, into their children who attended publicly supported schools. But there was no equivalent in Cloud County of Bethany College, Lindsborg, or Bethel College, Newton, where higher education in the distinctive cultural milieu was available. For the children of French-Canadian parents who could afford it, there was only St. Viateur's College in far-off Kankakee.

French Canadians did not have newspapers through which they could keep in touch with other settlements in the Midwest and sustain the French language. The pressure to speak English was unrelenting. The priests, of course, used Latin for mass, but they preached their sermons in French. When Bishop Fink came to administer confirmation on September 9, 1884, Fr. Mollier preached in French and the bishop gave his address in English. Several years later, when his successor, Bishop Scannell, was appointed, it was noted that he was fluent in French.[35] However, by 1890 Bishop

Scannell was transferred to Omaha, and the next bishop did not speak French.

Use of French was the most distinguishing trait of these Cloud County communities. The journalist Noble Prentis noted in 1881, "So prominent is the French element that notices in the French language are displayed in the stores in Clyde." He did not expect this situation to last long. "All tongues and people coming here are blended into one common current. It is doubtful if the grandchildren of these emigrants will speak French, and in time even family names will become so corrupted and changed as to be unrecognizable. I have known D'Aubigne altered to Dabney, and Ronces-valles to Rounsifer." [36] Children spoke both English and French in school and were sometimes laughed at by other children because of the quaint French phrases they used. But at home it was a different matter, as one vet-eran remembered: "We all spoke French and if we spoke too frequently in English my mother wouldn't answer us. She continued to speak her native tongue, even after we children had arrived and other folks of the [Aurora] community spoke English." [37] The town of Aurora may have succumbed to Americanizing influences relatively early, as one report noted in 1911:

> They are thoroughly Yankee in every respect except that they cling lov-ingly to the French language. The older people, now rapidly passing away, cannot speak English at all. But they foresee the time when the language will drop out of the contest and English will win the day. The young people all speak it with scarcely a trace of a foreign accent. [38]

In rural areas French continued to be used. Carman estimated that the critical date when French gave way to English occurred in the mid-1920s.[39] One of the key indicators he suggested in determining the critical date was the use of English on grave markers for non-Catholic French Canadians.

Carman suggested that the church was the most important social insti-tution for the French Canadians and that none of the Kankakee schism reached the Kansas community.[40] He was correct about the church but not the schism. Prentis observed in 1881 that "the larger number of the French-Canadians of Cloud County are Catholics, but there is a consider-able body of Protestants, the former adherents, I believe, of the famous Father Chiniquy and their descendents." [41] In fact, their numbers warranted the formation of a Presbyterian church, known as the Mulberry Creek con-gregation, on the southern margin of Shirley Township. The minutes of the Kansas Presbyterian Synod noted that the congregation was served by

Eucher Paradis from the 1870s through 1893. Paradis, born in Canada, had come to Kansas from Illinois but was not an ordained minister and so did not have permanent charge of the congregation. It appears that in 1894 the congregation was reorganized in the town of Aurora under Clement Ledoux, but it was dissolved in 1903.[42]

There is no evidence that the Presbyterians encountered or engendered friction with their Catholic French-Canadian compatriots. The infamous Father Chiniquy visited Concordia in early February 1884 and gave lectures in the Presbyterian and Baptist churches denouncing the Catholic church, but none of his antagonism seems to have spread to the rural areas and no record exists of his having preached to the Mulberry Creek congregation.[43] Sermons were preached in that Presbyterian church in French through to the 1890s, although English clearly was used on tombstones erected in the Protestant graveyard in the 1870s. As French Canadians became Americanized, apparently none of the Catholics joined the Presbyterian congregation; rather, there is some evidence that a few Presbyterians returned to the Catholic fold.[44]

## The Changing Number of Farmers

Ethnogenesis and the development of a strong ethnic identity in a rural community depended on population growth and stability. But factors often worked against community stability. In a thorough study of the shifting population in rural Kansas, James Malin suggested that farm population density varied according to periods of economic depression, conditions of drought, and the age of a community. During the earliest years of settlement farms tended to increase in number to a point in excess of what the land would support. A period of adjustment followed, when pioneer farmers emigrated and their farmland was absorbed by those who remained. As a result, following the initial wave of settlement the total number of farms declined and the average farm size increased.[45] After the period of adjustment the density of rural population ebbed and flowed according to periods of rural hardship. For example, between 1885 and 1895 the depression and drought years coincided with a decline along the western edge of the Kansas frontier and an increase in population density back in the older-settled eastern areas of the state.

Changes in the number of farm operators in the six sample townships generally followed the patterns described by Malin (table 2). For most of

TABLE 2    Changes in the Number of Farm Operators, 1875–1925

| Township | 1875 | 1885 | 1895 | 1905 | 1915 | 1925 |
|---|---|---|---|---|---|---|
| Union | 120 (−11) | 107 (−3) | 105 (−10) | 95 (−1) | 94 (−3) | 91 |
| Rockville | 165* | 101 (−24) | 77 (−5) | 73 (+4) | 76 (−1) | 75 |
| Menno | 80* | 151* | 131 (+10) | 144 (−8) | 132 (−8) | 122 |
| Meridian | 71 (+68) | 119 (0) | 120 (−10) | 109 (−7) | 101 (−1) | 100 |
| Shirley | 124 (+22) | 151 (−3) | 146 (+8) | 158 (−10) | 142 (0) | 143 |
| Aurora | 75 (+61) | 121 (−7) | 112 (+4) | 116 (+3) | 120 (−11) | 107 |

*In 1875 Rockville and Menno were part of larger, seventy-two-section townships. Menno did not become a regular thirty-six-section township until 1895. (See appendix A.)

these townships the decade of the 1870s was the initial settlement period when the number of farms increased dramatically. The decade from 1885 to 1895 was the adjustment period; the number of farm operators declined. The years following 1895 represented the ebb and flow in response to the changing conditions of economy and environment. Only two of the townships sampled for this study were somewhat atypical: Union Township was a step ahead of the others because initial settlement occurred in the 1860s rather than the 1870s; Meridian Township lagged behind the others because farmers arrived in the late 1870s. The number of farms in Union Township peaked in 1875, so that the following decade was one of downward adjustment; in Meridian Township the peak number of farms was most likely reached after the census of 1885 was taken. For the majority of townships the decade 1885–95 was one of decline in the number of farms due to the depression and drought that began in 1893. From 1895 to 1915 the economy recovered, albeit slowly at first, and the number of farms declined slightly. (Exceptions to the general trend between 1895 and 1905 in Menno and Shirley townships were eliminated in the decade 1905 to 1915.) After 1915 the decline in the number of farm operators was very small, indicating a degree of stability in farm numbers.

An important consideration in the development of ethnic communities is the origin of the farm families—where they were born and where they had lived before coming to Kansas. American influences would penetrate the community more readily as more and more of the ethnic farmers were second-generation, American born. Conversely, distinctive ethnic traits would persist if the foreign born predominated in the ethnic communities. Comparisons of the three groups show strong similarities between the Swedes and Mennonites. About the same number of farmers in each community, up to 1895, were born in Sweden and Russia respectively. In sharp contrast there were far fewer Quebec born in the French-Canadian communities in 1895, and their numbers dropped rapidly after that. In fact, from 1885 onward the Kansas-born and Illinois-born French Canadians took over more and more of the farms until by 1905 they were in a clear majority. Although there were some midwestern-born farmers, both Illinois and Kansas born, in the Swedish communities, they did not represent more than 50 percent until 1925. The Mennonites, however, were almost entirely Russian born before 1900, except for a few Indiana-born Mennonites in Meridian Township. These data on the origins of the ethnic communities suggest that American influences would have been felt much earlier in the French-Canadian community and that the Swedish community would have Americanized ahead of the Mennonite groups. Because a larger proportion of the Mennonite communities were made up of foreign-born farmers, the old-county ways and ethnic identity would survive longer.

The arrival and departure of farmers over the decades also brought about marked changes within each township. Immigrants sometimes bought up the land of departing American-born farmers, especially in the homogeneous townships. The Mennonites were particularly active in buying up more and more of the land in their township; the Swedes and French Canadians were much less aggressive. In the heterogeneous townships the achievement of ethnic dominance was not as marked as in the homogeneous townships, although again the Mennonites, in Meridian Township, were the most aggressive. The ethnics were able to attain varying degrees of dominance in land ownership over their American-born neighbors not because they were less mobile or less inclined to move on in search of a new farm as the frontier pushed farther and farther west, since an analysis of population turnover in the six townships reveals that the immigrants too were surprisingly mobile.

## Population Turnover

There are several reasons for investigating mobility among the immigrant groups. A stable immigrant community had a much better chance of developing a strong ethnic identity than a community in which the rate of turnover was very high. Furthermore, over time a stable community would accumulate a large core of experienced farmers capable of developing farming strategies to deal with drought and other environmental fluctuations

In addition to achieving a higher level of environmental adaptation, stable farm communities would achieve higher levels of financial success than a group of mobile farmers.[46] Finally, an examination of farm population turnover allows one to address the issue of whether increased mobility within an immigrant community may be equated with Americanization.

Conventional wisdom held that American farmers were much more mobile than immigrant farmers. Malin wrote that "whenever the unstable native American came into competition with the immigrant stock of Germans, Swedes, and Bohemians, the American lost out. . . . The American did not possess love of the soil for its own sake that was so conspicuous among these European stocks." M. Curti doubted this viewpoint, believing that poverty was a major factor in determining mobility. In his study of a Wisconsin county he found that immigrants were often poorer, and therefore more mobile, than Americans. Curti acknowledged that his conclusion was "not in agreement with the traditional conception of the stubborn European peasant, devoted to the land. But perhaps this devotion to the soil is not quite as stubborn as has been thought."[47]

Figures 19, 20, and 21 indicate that the three immigrant groups were indeed more persistent on their farms than their American neighbors. (The only exceptions were the cohorts of French-Canadian farmers in 1895 and Swedes in 1905.) Although conventional wisdom is confirmed at first glance, further reflection produces the following conclusions: the mobility rate for both immigrants and Americans was very high; among the immigrants it was only a little lower than among the Americans, and the differences between each immigrant group and the local American control group were always quite small.[48] Curti may have had a better explanation when he suggested that poverty rather than devotion to the soil was the important factor affecting mobility.

Among immigrant groups the differences were also quite small. A comparison of the three reveals that Swedes had a slightly higher record while French Canadians had the lowest record of persistence. (The persistence curves are analyzed in detail in appendix B.) The surprise is that the Mennonites were much more mobile than expected, although in the later years of settlement the Mennonite communities did appear to be stabilizing. The high rate of mobility among French Canadians may have been due to the fact that increasingly many of them were second generation, born in either Illinois or Kansas. It would be tempting to argue that the young French Canadians were becoming Americanized, as evidenced by their increased mobility. But that suggestion would be difficult to sustain given that the

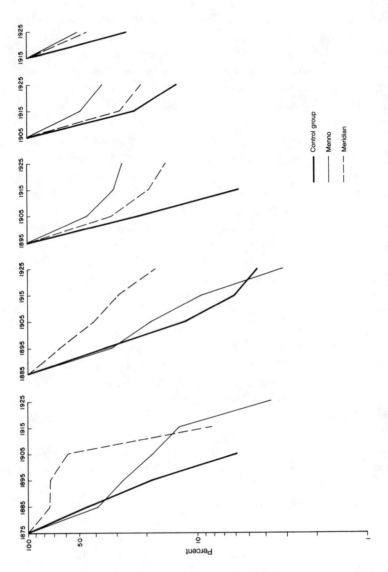

FIG. 19. Comparison of persistence rates among Mennonite samples and control group by decadal cohorts

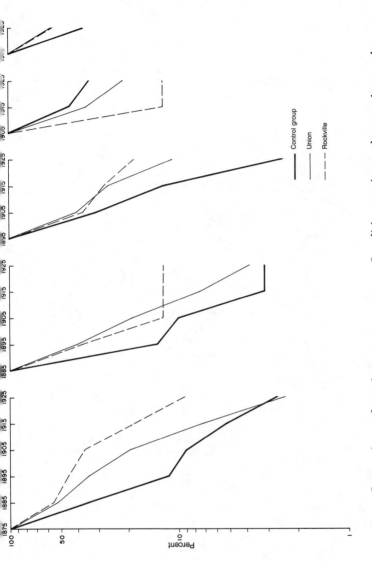

FIG. 20. Comparison of persistence rates among Swedish samples and control group by decadal cohorts

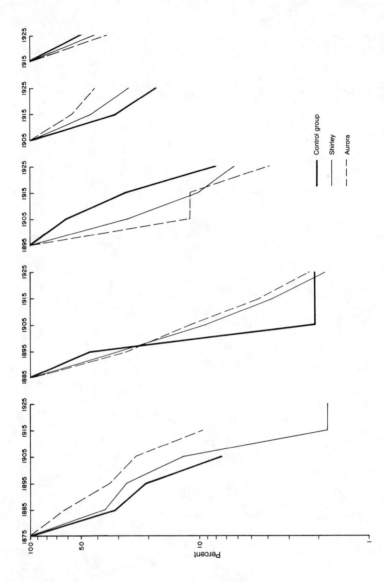

FIG. 21. Comparison of persistence rates among French-Canadian samples and control group by decadal cohorts

differences between immigrants and the American born were always very slight, and the mobility of those who arrived in later years was not much different from that of earlier settlers in the townships.

If one looks for a moment at the immigrant groups individually, one finds noticeable differences in mobility within each group. The Swedes, Mennonites, and French Canadians who lived in the mixed-population townships (Rockville, Meridian, and Aurora), where they had frequent contact with American farmers, were inclined to be more persistent and less mobile than their counterparts in the homogeneous townships, who lived in the heart of the ethnic settlements. In other words, increased contact with American farmers did not result in increased immigrant mobility; on the contrary, it resulted in increased stability.

The evidence seems fairly strong that increased mobility cannot be equated with increased Americanization of the immigrants. In good part, the characterization of mobility as an American trait derives from comparisons of American and European rural societies. The stereotype of European rural society is often of the stubborn peasant tied to his local area, whereas the most extreme stereotype of American rural society is that of the Yankee farmer who mines the soil and rapidly moves on in search of quick profits. The immigrants who came to North America were not stubborn peasants tied to the soil—their most distinguishing characteristic was that they were prepared to pull up roots and migrate. Having broken the bonds of localism in Europe, it was in their nature to be mobile. That distinguishing characteristic was handed on to their successors by each wave of immigrants. Thus one can argue that mobility was not an inherently American characteristic but an immigrant trait perpetuated by their children in the New World.

A detailed statistical analysis of the mobility patterns of each group of farmers, both immigrant and American born, yielded the following conclusions:

1. The control groups (i.e., the mostly American born) were not significantly more persistent than their immigrant neighbors except for one series—the 1875 cohorts. The differences between the Swedes and their neighbors and between the Mennonites and their control group were significant for that year.

2. The three control groups of American-born farmers were equally mobile over the fifty-year period under study. No significant differences existed among these groups.

3. Although the mobility rates among the three immigrant groups were

significant, much of that significance was due to the very high mobility of French Canadians in Aurora Township and the contrasting high persistence rate among Mennonites in Meridian Township.

4. On a few occasions significant differences were found within each immigrant group among those who lived in the heart of the community and those who lived along the fringes. In general, however, segregation did not have a significant impact on mobility or persistence.

5. There were no significant differences within each group among the later arrivals and those who began farming in the 1870s and 1880s.

6. None of the immigrant groups was building up a core of experienced farmers larger than that of the others. For example, among the Mennonite farmers in 1915 there were not significantly more individuals who had begun farming in 1875 or 1885 than among the Swedish or French-Canadian groups.

It is necessary to keep these conclusions in mind for later sections of the study, because they indicate that differences in the agricultural success of each ethnic group and in their ability to establish a territorial base for their communities (French Canadians excepted) cannot be attributed to the fact that one group was significantly more restless than another.

## Territorial Base of the Communities

One of the principal themes in this study is whether the segregation of immigrants retarded their Americanization or reinforced their ethnic identity. I have already noted that the Swedes and Mennonites explicitly stated their desire to create homogeneous communities, and that the French Canadians, without such an overt expression, certainly gave it a try. It is appropriate at this stage to examine the record of each immigrant group in establishing a territorial base.[49]

There are many reasons immigrants would wish to establish a homogeneous territorial base. Ethnic enclaves, whether in cities or rural areas, eased the transition from the tightly knit, stable communities of Europe to the turbulent, mobile, atomistic society of North America. In an ethnic settlement the new immigrants found neighbors who spoke their language, helped them find work and shelter, and shared their religious beliefs. Although rural enclaves have not been studied to the same degree as urban ghettos, many similarities existed. There was comfort and security in ethnic communities, where children could be raised and schooled in the values and religious beliefs of their parents. The enclave imparted a feeling of membership within a community, mitigated the loneliness of pioneer life, facilitated mutual cooperation, and reinforced obligations and responsibilities. Homogeneous ethnic communities, as Suttles noted, "made short-run opportunism a dangerous proposition since the opportunist must continue to live with his victims. . . . Territoriality, then, builds accountability into a society without anyone's having to work at it."[50]

The maintenance of a territorial base may serve as a barometer of ethnic loyalty. If the base continues to expand after a generation of settlement, then group loyalty appears to be strong. But if that base disintegrates, group loyalty and community cohesion obviously are weak. The reasons for disintegration may vary widely. As the nuclear family becomes more and more the norm, ties to the extended family weaken and family pressure to conform weakens correspondingly. As young people increased their contact with American life, they may have looked for marriage partners and other opportunities outside their own ethnic community. Exogamy works strongly against the maintenance of a distinctive ethnic identity. All of these factors are intricately interwoven in the maintenance of an ethnic group's cohesiveness, but they also find expression in the changing patterns of land ownership, the territorial base of the community. Land ownership patterns (figs. 22–27) indicate that the Mennonites were strongest in preserving their territorial base. In Menno Township they quickly bought up all the land until only one section remained beyond their control. (Section 10 belonged to the huge holdings of the Scully family, which stretched throughout the rural Midwest.) In Meridian Township, on the western margin of the Mennonite settlement, these Russian immigrants again revealed how aggressive they could be in expanding the territorial base of their community; they seldom lost land they had come to own, and by 1925 they owned more than half the farmland in Meridian Township.

The Swedes were second to the Mennonites in retaining their land base. The initial Swedish desire for homogeneous settlement resulted in their acquiring over 90 percent of the land in Union Township in 1885, but in the years that followed they lost land to non-Swedish farmers, especially in the drought and depression years between 1885 and 1895. Although much land changed hands, at the end of fifty years of farming there was a very small net gain by the Swedes in Rockville Township. In short, they were considerably less successful than the Mennonites in retaining and expanding the territorial base of their communities.

It should be remembered that the French Canadians never explicitly

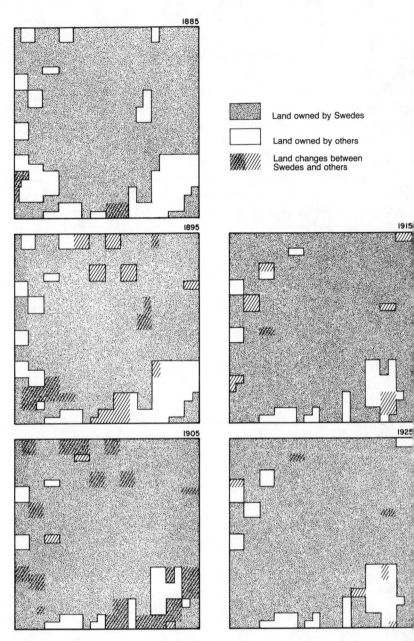

FIG. 22. Changes in land ownership, Union Township, 1885–1925

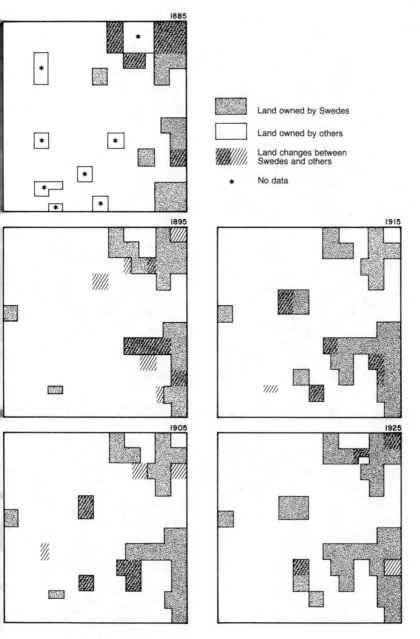

Land owned by Swedes

Land owned by others

Land changes between
Swedes and others

* No data

1895

1915

1905

1925

FIG. 23. Changes in land ownership, Rockville Township, 1885–1925

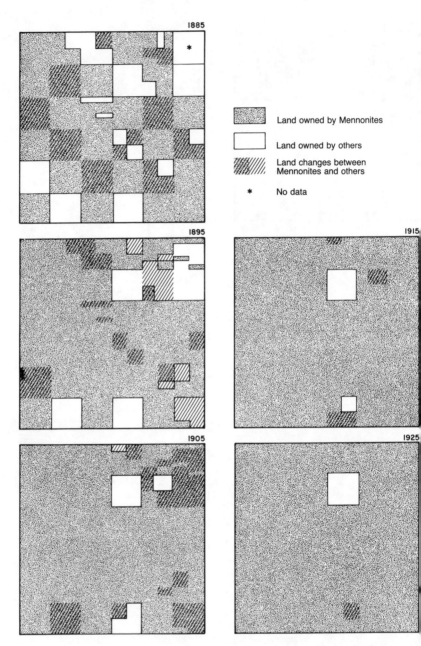

**1885**

Land owned by Mennonites

Land owned by others

Land changes between
Mennonites and others

\*    No data

**1895**

**1915**

**1905**

**1925**

FIG. 24.    Changes in land ownership, Menno Township, 1885–1925

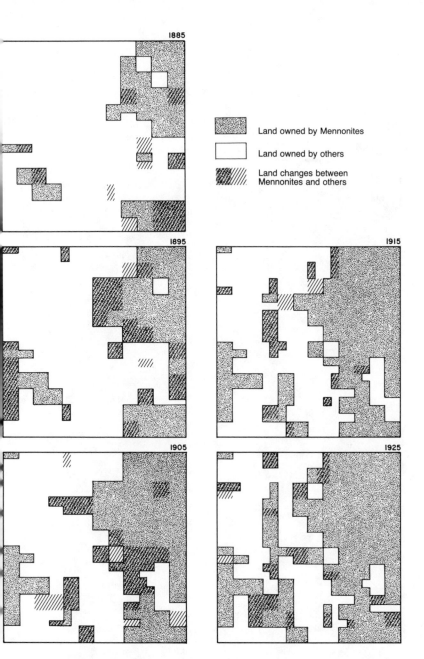

FIG. 25.    Changes in land ownership, Meridian Township, 1885–1925

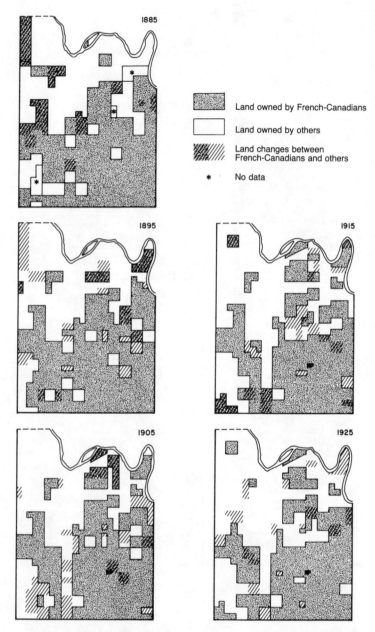

1885

1895       1915

1905       1925

Land owned by French-Canadians

Land owned by others

Land changes between
French-Canadians and others

*    No data

FIG. 26.    Changes in land ownership, Shirley Township, 1885–1925

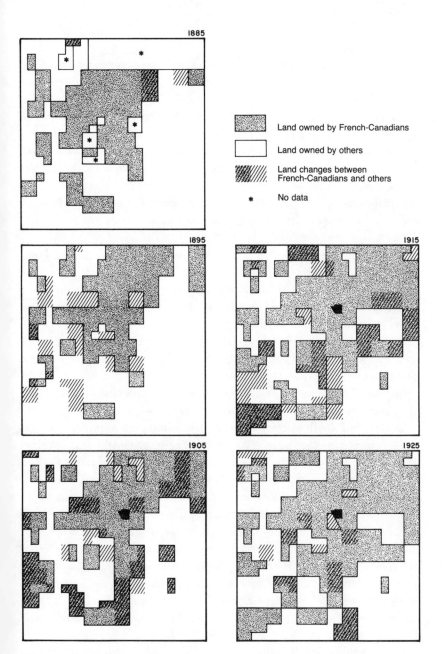

FIG. 27. Changes in land ownership, Aurora Township, 1885–1925

stated their desire to create solid homogeneous communities, and the local priests did not provide leadership in attaining that goal despite the great practical advantages in terms of building a church and providing religious services and education. Nevertheless, new French-Canadian farmers did take up the abandoned homesteads of departing Americans and formed a moderately homogeneous settlement. By 1885 these settlers owned half the farmland in Shirley Township, but after 1895 they steadily lost out to their American neighbors. The pattern was slightly different in Aurora Township, along the fringe of the French-Canadian settlement. Although losses outweighed gains from 1885 to 1895, much of the loss was recovered by 1905 and the Aurora French Canadians continued to expand until 1915. But their record in general was weak compared to that of the Swedes and Mennonites. French-Canadian patterns of land ownership were the most fragmented of the three groups, and their community evidenced the strongest signs of dissolving into the sea of American settlement after fifty years of farming in central Kansas.

Before one can attribute these changes in land ownership to fluctuations in group loyalty or variations in ethnic identity, it is necessary to examine other factors, including the ability of immigrants to weather periods of drought and economic depression and any demographic characteristics that may have been unique to the selected samples.

A recurring myth of the frontier is that immigrants survived the economic buffetings of recession and depression better than American farmers. In a study of land ownership changes in Nebraska, Hollingshead suggested that American farmers, whom he considered financially weaker than their foreign-born neighbors, sold their farms and moved elsewhere during economic recessions.[51] He also suggested that the American farmer was more mobile than the immigrant—a notion that has not been confirmed in this study. In any event, he believed that the foreign born in Nebraska found it easier to expand their territorial base during periods of economic depression. This was not the case in Kansas; immigrants did not benefit at the expense of American farmers during the depression of the 1890s. In fact, during the decade from 1885 to 1895 immigrants suffered their heaviest losses, or at best achieved their smallest gains, of the fifty years covered in this study. There is no evidence to confirm that the depression years accorded the immigrants an opportunity of expanding their territorial bases.

The most direct threat to the territorial homogeneity of a community emerged when farms changed hands, as farmers died, retired, or moved on to some other community. An ethnic replacement was necessary if the farmland was not to pass into the hands of an outsider. The replacement could come from a number of sources: young farmers in the local Kansas community, other communities in the Midwest, or parent communities in Illinois, Quebec, and Europe. Elsewhere I have suggested a "transfusion model" to demonstrate the importance of demographic factors in the survival of ethnic territoriality.[52] The model's three components are hemorrhaging due to population turnover, replacement through high birthrates within the community, and infusion of new blood as a result of immigration from outside the local community.

We have already seen that the immigrants were only slightly less mobile than their American neighbors, and that the differences in population turnover were small. The Swedes did have a slightly more stable population in the early years and the Mennonites a slightly more stable population in the later years of settlement. The French Canadians, however, were about as mobile as the neighboring Americans. The greatest difference in mobility was for the farmers who arrived in 1905, when many French Canadians were on the move, and the net losses in French-Canadian land ownership were greatest in Shirley Township. Mobility appears to have been a factor in French-Canadian territorial losses.

Internal regenerative power is essential for the survival of any community. If a population is not reproducing fast enough to replace those leaving or dying, then the community's survival is in doubt. If, on the other hand, the reproductive energy in a community is high, then the pressure to expand its territorial base is great. Various estimates of fertility and family size suggest that in terms of regenerative power the French Canadians were the most robust and Swedes were the weakest of the three ethnic groups.[53] French Canadians not only had the largest average family size and the lowest percentage of childless families but also the highest fertility rates. Swedes were at the other end of the scale on all three counts, and Mennonites held an intermediate position.

The third element in the demographic transfusion model is the infusion of newcomers to the community. Replacements did not come from the homeland (Sweden, Russia, or Quebec) but from other immigrant colonies scattered throughout the Midwest. The number of Swedish replacements was small, and although many of them had been born in Sweden, they came from the Illinois settlements and from adjacent townships in Kansas. There were more Mennonite replacements than Swedish ones, and they too came largely from adjacent townships in Kansas, since there was no significant overseas Mennonite immigration after 1885. The number of French-Canadian replacements was also small; it declined sharply in 1905 but increased again in 1915 and 1925. Almost all the French-Canadian newcomers came from the Illinois and local Kansas settlements.

When the components of the transfusion model are considered together, they provide new insight into the territorial gains and losses of the three ethnic groups. The strength of the Mennonites in expanding their territorial base cannot be easily ascribed to demographic traits. Although the Mennonites were not as mobile as the French Canadians, their regenerative power was not as great. It seems clear that ethnic loyalty and the desire for territorial homogeneity were much stronger among Mennonites than among French Canadians. Conversely, the Swedish territorial weakness cannot be explained entirely by a weakening of ethnic loyalty and identity; the weakness may have been due to increasing mobility in later years, falling regenerative power within the communities in Kansas, and inability to attract new farmers from the parent communities in Illinois.

The influence of segregation on the development of a distinctive community identity is an important analytical theme in this study. The results outlined above suggest that French Canadians were most susceptible to American influence, as they did not develop and preserve a strong territorial base. Consequently, they had a lot of contact with their American neighbors. In sharp contrast, the Mennonites, as might have been expected, demonstrated a desire to develop a strong territorial base and to remain apart and minimize secular influences in their communities.

## Summary

Differences in the growth and development of the Swedish, Mennonite, and French-Canadian communities in central Kansas were striking in some respects. Chapter 3 showed that the Mennonites were the most successful in laying down the foundation for a closed community, within which a community with a distinctive ethnic identity would be developed, and that the French Canadians were the least successful. Over the succeeding four decades this general pattern was maintained.

Mennonites were slow to enter the American mainstream. They did not become involved in politics in large numbers, and those who did, in particular the Alexanderwohlers, remained loyal to the Republican party even through the depression of the 1890s and the elections preceding

American entry into World War I. Mennonites retained German in their churches, schools, and to a degree in everyday speech until the shattering impact of World War I. They admitted American customs slowly, if not grudgingly, into church practices and everyday life, and they sustained a strong ethnic identity through newspapers and a network of contact with other Mennonite communities in North America. These networks could be very important in reinforcing a sense of Mennonite separateness and distinctiveness within the republic.

Swedes were at once anxious to participate in American political and economic life but wary of American social values and morals. Rev. Olsson quickly became a citizen and a stalwart supporter of the Republican party in the state legislature. But he and his successor, Dr. Swensson, emphasized the importance of Christian morals, a deep Pietist faith, and observance of strict standards in social behavior. Their efforts to enforce conformity with their views were not successful in rural settlements. During the 1890s depression many Swedish farmers defected to the Populists, and struggling farmers retained their Pietist faith without becoming involved in theological dissension or the power struggles among small-town elites. The Swedish language survived into the first decade of the twentieth century, and churches gradually adapted to American customs and educational practices. The major cultural event of the year, the Easter presentation of the *Messiah,* was not an especially Swedish event, though it did provide a focus for Swedish pride in their community. Ties with a network of Swedish communities throughout the Midwest were maintained largely through Augustana College in Illinois and the Lutheran Synod.

The French Canadians were perhaps most representative of small ethnic enclaves throughout the Midwest. They were relatively small in numbers and established a church-centered community. The priests and nuns who served them were committed to preserving the faith rather than a cultural heritage or linguistic distinctiveness, although French seemed to survive longer than Swedish in rural communities. French Canadians generally voted Republican, although some farmers joined the Populists during the 1890s, as many American farmers did. French Canadians moved readily into business opportunities in town and seem to have been more akin to their American neighbors than either of the other two groups.

The patterns of acculturation outlined above were reflected in territorial trends within the ethnic communities. Mennonites, the most resilient in resisting American influence, were the most aggressive in gaining control of the land in their community. The development of a strong ethnic identity and a solid territorial base seem closely correlated in the Mennonite community; in the French-Canadian community ethnic identity weakened and the territorial base dissolved, especially as the second generation came of age in the 1890s. Swedes held an intermediate position. The next chapter will discuss whether or not variation in the rate of Americanization affected the ability of each group to become successful farming communities.

# 5

# THE IMPROVEMENT OF FORTUNES

A popular impression of the transatlantic migrations to North America is that immigrants belonged to one of two groups: refugees from religious and political persecution seeking the freedom of the New World, where they could profess their beliefs unmolested by government authorities, and the starved and impoverished, who fled the famines and overpopulated rural areas of Europe for the new land of plenty, where fear and threat of famine were unknown. Persecution and hunger were supposedly the major determinants that produced the great transatlantic migration. In fact, these were merely extreme factors that produced some of the more spectacular migrations in the nineteenth century.

The decisions of most emigrant groups to emigrate, including those of the Swedes, Mennonites, and French Canadians, do reflect some of the extreme conditions cited above. For example, the conflict between the state Lutheran church and the evangelical Pietists was responsible for the early Swedish migration to Illinois during the 1840s. The demands of the Russian imperial authorities that the Mennonites give up their German language, separate schools, and pacifist beliefs and enlist in the imperial army contributed powerfully to the Mennonite emigration. For the French Canadians, it was a matter of hunger rather than conscience, of increasing population pressure rather than religious or political persecution, that produced emigration from Quebec in the midnineteenth century. To suggest that either hunger or persecution was the sole determinant of emigration, especially of Swedes and French Canadians, would be a gross oversimplification and would poorly characterize the motivation of the great majority of emigrants.[1]

In the late nineteenth century, that majority were neither idealist refugees nor wretched to the point of starvation. Rather they were ambitious folk, anxious to avail themselves of the opportunities in North America to increase their fortune, improve their status in society, and become, as far as possible, financially independent. This was certainly true for the Swedish and French-Canadian farmers who left Illinois to seek new farms and a new opportunity for their families in Kansas. Even the Mennonites who finally decided to leave Russia appreciated the opportunities offered in the New World. The imperial authorities, alarmed by the unrest in the Mennonite communities, had moderated their demands, suggesting that the Mennonites retain their pacifist beliefs and perform forestry service in lieu of military duty. By that stage, however, the leaders were aware that in North America they not only could retain their language and religious beliefs but also could improve the opportunities for young farmers. After the difficult years during the 1860s of the Anwohners' dispute, the opportunity of farmland in abundance for everyone appealed to Mennonite leaders. Free land, access to markets, and the chance for financial success were the major advertisements that induced American, Canadian, and European farmers alike to move westward to the agricultural frontier.

The improvement of fortunes and achievement of financial independence were parts of the process whereby immigrants adapted to the economic milieu and were Americanized. The increasing emphasis on materialism and economic individualism was not peculiarly American. By the midnineteenth century, these and parallel trends (from Gemeinschaft to Gesellschaft, from subsistent peasant to commercial farmer) were already under way in the cultural hearths of the three groups in Sweden, southern Russia, and Quebec. What was distinctively American was the abundance of cheap land, which accelerated the process. As opportunities for material success increased, so did temptations to adopt the ethos of economic individualism and abandon the old values deeply embedded in religion.

Frederick Jackson Turner suggested that the opportunities for upward mobility were greatest in new areas of agricultural settlement. The western frontier was the land of opportunity, where the basic institutions of American democracy and the abundance of natural resources guaranteed equality and success for the immigrant. The Turner thesis states basically that although differences in individual wealth might exist among recently arrived immigrants, with the equality of opportunity in obtaining land, particularly after passage of the Homestead Act in 1861, these differences would quickly diminish and disappear. Turner did not investigate the possibility that immigrants might form communities, pool their resources, and achieve higher levels of financial success (though not of financial independence) than was possible with simple economic individualism. But this is a separate issue that will be dealt with later.

Curti described the essential elements of the Turner thesis and its antithesis fairly succinctly:

> Certainly many immigrants came from areas where bitter poverty prevailed. It might be thought that the "artificial equality" in the amount of land acquired by different groups would be merely temporary—that after a few years certain peasant stocks would lapse into their Old World acceptance of poverty and social inferiority as a natural lot. In that case, differences between groups in acreage, property, and produce would become greater with the years, not less: the rich might become richer, the poor poorer. Turner of course expected the opposite. Farmers, then, who had smaller amounts of cash and equipment should gain more rapidly in the economic values represented in the census figures than those of high economic status. All groups should gain, but if the theory is sound, the rate of gain should be differential, so that gradually over the years the disparity between high and low would be less. Frontier conditions would encourage the less privileged and favor their economic advance.[2]

The two models outlined above are somewhat extreme. The first postulates an increasing gap between rich and poor (somewhat similar to a Latin American model of development), an increasingly bimodal distribution of the various indices of wealth and success as time went on. The second suggests the evolution of an egalitarian society, where there was not only equality of opportunity but also a trend toward equal achievement. A more realistic model of development might postulate: (1) the gradual development of a statistically normal curve for the various measures of success in each immigrant group, and (2) with the passage of time the disappearance of differences in the levels of success for each immigrant group. The equalizing effect of the frontier should not exclude the possibility that individual farmers within a group might accumulate greater amounts of wealth than their neighbors. Thus the enterprising Swede, Mennonite, or French Canadian would be as likely to achieve the same success as the most enterprising Yankee or southern farmer, while there would still be poor Swedes, Mennonites, French Canadians, Yankees, and southerners.

The purpose of this chapter is to investigate the levels of financial success and achievement for each of the three ethnic groups and how the indices of success changed over time.[3] The Swedes, Mennonites, and French Canadians can be ranked at different points along a work-ethic continuum based on their performance in agriculture before migrating to the American Midwest. The Mennonites were the acme of the Protestant work ethic. They worked hard, were frugal in their consumption habits, and reinvested their capital earnings in farming. In addition, the Mennonite value system emphasized community cooperation and mutual assistance in the attainment of common goals. French Canadians occupied a position at the opposite end of the spectrum. They have been described as slovenly, lazy, and spendthrift. They were not ambitious farmers, and their value system reputedly emphasized obligations to the extended family—obligations that often retarded individual financial achievement. Swedes occupied an intermediate position between Mennonites and French Canadians. Although they held a reputation for being good workers, there was not the singular emphasis on self-sacrifice and mutual assistance found in the Mennonite system of values. Given the priorities of each group, the hypotheses to be tested in the following sections are: that the Mennonites achieved the highest and the French Canadians the lowest level of success for the three ethnic groups, that the differences between the three groups diminished over time, that the difference between each group and its control group of mostly American farmers increased over time, and that the impact of segregation was to retard the adoption of American culture and achievement of financial success. The indices of success are discussed under three broad categories: farm size, investment in farming, and the nature of farm tenure. In each case a standard format will be used: first, the pattern will be reviewed in general before a comparison of the three ethnic groups is made; second, the ethnics will be compared with their local control groups to determine which were becoming more like their American neighbors; and third, the impact of segregation will be measured by comparing the achievements of farmers in the core township with the fringe township for each ethnic group.

## Farm Size

Farm size by itself is not a complete measure of financial success; income depends not only on acreage but also on the quality of land and the intensity of its use.[4] Nevertheless, size is a useful starting point in the analysis of farming success because fluctuations in average farm size reflected government land-granting policies and changes in the settlement history of a farming community and in the financial pressures farmers had to bear in building up a profitable farm. Changes in settlement history involved improved accessibility to markets, increased population pressure, and, with the increased competition for farmland in a maturing community, land speculation. Changes in technology also affected the size of farm that a family could operate, although the effectiveness of technological breakthroughs depended directly on the supply of capital in the mortgage market.

During the 1870s, when Kansas was opened up to settlement, the Homestead Act had been law for over a decade. Despite the boosterism of the local western press, the question was already being raised of whether or not 160 acres were enough to ensure a farmer's success on the dry western margins of the prairies. The federal government responded with new legislation: the Timber Culture Act of 1873 was but one of several legislated attempts to make it possible for the western farmer to obtain a farm large enough to ensure his survival. Farmers on the agricultural frontier disagreed among themselves on the need for this new legislation. One of the leaders in the farming community in Dickinson County, T. C. Henry, held the view that the quarter section was indeed too small, arguing that larger farms capable of incorporating more livestock farming were needed in the western regions of decreasing rainfall. Others opposed this viewpoint. T. Dunlap argued in 1879: "I have become satisfied that we as farmers in Dickinson County are trying to farm too much land. We must sell off part of our land, go on a smaller scale, and farm a good deal better."[5] Another farmer, J. W. Robson, believed that 160 acres were more than adequate for a farmer if he used eighty acres for cropland and the other eighty for pasture.

Whatever the merits of each side of the argument, it is doubtful that the government's land-granting policy seriously impeded the farmer's struggle for success. J. C. Malin pointed out that in the pioneer days, there was often plenty of unclaimed government and railroad land that the new farmers used as commons to graze their livestock, so that more land was available than most farmers could use:

> Even if the pioneer had received larger acreages, under the terms of the governmental land policy, he seldom had the capital to finance even the traditional quarter-section farm—the buildings, fences, machinery, horse-power, and man-power. Whether he could have marketed, profitably, large production is open to question. The early years were usually marked by the severest struggle to cultivate even small acreages.[6]

The major characteristics of the first phase of settlement were an abundance of land and a marked shortage of labor.

The abundant supply of unclaimed government and railroad lands that could be used as grazing commons for livestock did not last very long. With the construction of a network of branch lines feeding into the major transcontinental railroad lines, the demand for farmland increased sharply. The formerly pioneer areas became readily accessible to markets, and a second wave of migration, larger than the first, invaded the agricultural frontier. The second phase of settlement was marked by a rapid increase in population and the creation of a large number of new farms. Some were established on areas that later were considered marginal for agriculture. In central Kansas the second phase of settlement began in the late 1870s with the construction of branch railroad lines, and by 1885 the process was almost completed.

There is ample evidence that many pioneer farmers throughout the Midwest engaged in some form of land speculation. They acquired more land than they could manage or cultivate, retaining a "surplus" that they would sell at a later date when land values rose. Malin reported that pioneer farmers in Kansas also engaged in land speculation.[7] Ideally these small-scale speculators should have unloaded their surplus holdings when demand was at a peak—when the second wave of farmers swept through. Inevitably this would have resulted in a reduction of the average size of farms. However, there were always a few farmers who waited for land prices to climb higher than before, even after the market had peaked. These "late speculators" sometimes clouded the issue of farm-size adjustment during the second phase of settlement.

The third phase of settlement marked the maturing of an agricultural community after the boom conditions had passed. If the farming community had overextended itself during the second phase of settlement, either in creating farms that were too small or in creating farms on marginal agricultural land, then there was a contraction during the third phase of settlement.[8] The third phase allowed little leeway for marginal farmers and was characterized by conditions of financial stringency and increased competition for access to farmland. Usually the smallest farms and the marginal farmlands were amalgamated into the larger farm units, and the general trend was toward an increase in the average size of farms. In central Kansas boom conditions had passed and adjustments in farm sizes had begun by the late 1880s.

Changes in farm technology also had an impact on average farm sizes.

Finley demonstrated that there were technological limits to how much land the farmer could cultivate if he relied on labor from within his own family. He concluded, "A larger homestead would not necessarily have solved the settlers' basic problem; had the larger tract of land been granted, it is not unreasonable to conjecture that abandonment and commutation might not have lessened, and adjustments still would have waited until technology, experience and the appropriate type of farming caught up."[9] Between 1870 and 1890 there were several major technological innovations in prairie agriculture. New horse-drawn machinery—plows, harrows, seeding drills, mowers, and harvesters—permitted the prairie farmer to cultivate and harvest larger and larger acreages, as did new laborsaving machinery. To obtain the new machinery he needed capital, and access to capital was critical to the farmer's success.

The farmer's ability to raise capital was related directly to the condition of the economy. Most farmers obtained additional capital by taking out mortgages on their farms; their ability to bear a mortgage depended on their income.[10] Income, in turn, depended on the weather and the market. A severe winter with extensive winterkill, late spring and early fall frosts, moisture shortages during the growing season, and the severity of the hot, desiccating winds of July and August all contributed to a reduction of the farmers' income. For the farmers of central Kansas the most serious of these problems was drought, which might last for several months or even extend over several years. But farm income also varied with fluctuations in the market price for produce, and so the condition of the economy was also a major factor that influenced farm size.

The nature of the relation between farm size adjustments and fluctuations in the economy was outlined by Malin in a study of Kanwaka Township in eastern Kansas: "During the periods of rural depression the size decreased, or in other words, the number of farms of 160 acres or less increased. In prosperous times the smaller farms were consolidated in part into units of 160 acres or larger." In 1860, before the Civil War, 90 percent of all the farms in Kanwaka Township were quarter-section farms. After the depression of 1872 there was tremendous land subdivision in eastern Kansas, where some 50 percent of the farms were either forty- or eighty-acre lots. Then in the boom years of the 1880s size increased remarkably: 37 percent were approximately a half section or larger, and the forty-acre farms practically disappeared. According to Malin, "the depression of the '90s broke up the big farms, restoring a moderate number of 80-acre and 40-acre operators, and it was not until 1920, as a result of the World War boom, that the large farms again came back in approximately the same proportion as in 1885." [11]

Government land-granting policies, the stage of settlement, climate, and the condition of the economy were major factors that could explain fluctuations in average farm size. I shall now examine the extent to which these factors affected average farm size among Swedes, Mennonites, and French Canadians in central Kansas.

Government land-granting policies do not seem to have had any impact on the average size of farms reported by Swedes, Mennonites, and French Canadians in the 1875 census. French Canadians had been able to obtain 160-acre homesteads in every section, odd numbered and even numbered, in Shirley and Aurora townships. Their capital outlay in obtaining farms was the smallest of the three groups. The Swedes were able to obtain only eighty-acre homesteads in Union Township; additional land had to be bought from the railroad companies. The Mennonites bore the heaviest capital costs of the three groups. No government land was available for homesteading in Menno Township, so that farmland had to be bought either from the railroad company or land speculators. Despite these major differences, the average size of Swedish, Mennonite, and French-Canadian farms in 1875 was very similar. Almost all the farms reported by each group in the census were of quarter-section size (fig. 28), and so government policy had little or no effect on the average size of immigrants' farms.

Furthermore, the initial capital advantage enjoyed by the French Canadians and Swedes over the Mennonites was probably short-lived. A. G. Bogue pointed out that many midwestern farmers bought their farms second-, third-, or fourth-hand because of the high rate of population turnover in pioneer farming areas. [12] This certainly applied to the Swedes, Mennonites, and French Canadians. In all of the sampled communities fewer than 30 percent of those recorded in the 1875 census were still farming in the same township in 1895.

Some evidence shows that the average size of immigrants' farms adjusted to the phases of settlement. Although the census does not record any information on land speculation, the increase in the number of farms indicates that in Mennonite townships (Menno and Meridian) and French-Canadian townships (Shirley and Aurora) the second phase of settlement was reached in 1885. (Population in Union Township may have peaked somewhat earlier and in Rockville Township somewhat later than in the other townships.) In the French-Canadian and Mennonite settlements the average size of farms declined from 1875 to 1885; only in the Swedish

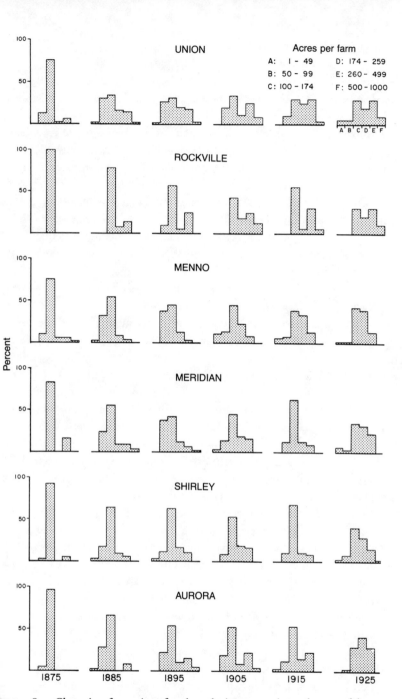

FIG. 28. Changing farm sizes for the ethnic groups in each township

SOURCE: Manuscript of Kansas State Censuses, 1875–1925

settlements did the average size increase during this decade. By 1895 the third stage of settlement was well under way, and the average size of farms for all groups increased.

Changes in the condition of the economy cannot be readily related to adjustments in farm size. The early 1880s were boom years in central Kansas, and the early 1890s were years of acute economic depression. According to Malin's hypothesis the average size of farms should have increased in 1885 and decreased in 1895; in fact, the opposite occurred. The only exception was among Mennonites in Meridian Township, where the number of small farms actually increased between 1885 and 1895. In the subsequent decade, a period of economic recovery, the modest trend toward larger farms continued without any dramatic changes.

The dominant feature of the decade from 1905 to 1915 was the dramatic increase in farm produce prices following the 1914 outbreak of war in Europe. The census year 1915 is a difficult sampling point because it came quickly on the heels of the dramatic market surge, although probably too soon for the new market conditions to have affected farm sizes. Among the Swedish farmers in Union and Rockville townships and the Mennonites and French Canadians in Meridian and Shirley townships respectively, the average size of farms declined from 1905 to 1915. But among the Mennonites of Menno and the French Canadians of Aurora, the average size of farms increased. When the war ended, the market for farm produce declined, and the early 1920s witnessed a minor recession. Nevertheless, in all of the sampled townships the average size of farms increased as new, large farms were created between 1915 and 1925.

In summary, the adjustments in farm size over the period from 1875 to 1925 do not seem to bear out Malin's hypothesis that average farm size decreased during periods of depression and increased during periods of economic recovery and expansion. The general trend for the fifty-year period was upward, toward farms larger than the quarter section. There was no sharp break in that trend to correspond either with the boom years of the early 1880s or the depression of the 1890s. Although some evidence suggests that farm sizes responded to improved market conditions between 1905 and 1915, no evidence shows a response to the poor market years of the early 1920s.

There are several possible explanations for the failure of Malin's hypothesis. One is that the foreign born were less sensitive to and less deeply affected by fluctuations in rural prosperity than the native-born American Malin studied in Kanwaka Township. However, an analysis of farm-size ad-

TABLE 3    Changes in Percent Distribution and Frequency of Farm
Sizes for Control-Group Farmers, 1875–1925

| Acres | 1875 % | (no.) | 1885 % | (no.) | 1895 % | (no.) | 1905 % | (no.) | 1915 % | (no.) | 1925 % | (no.) |
|---|---|---|---|---|---|---|---|---|---|---|---|---|
| | | | | | Rockville | | | | | | | |
| 1–49 | 0 | (0) | 0 | | 0 | (0) | 0 | (0) | 1.5 | (1) | 0 | (0) |
| 50–99 | 18.2 | (14) | 10.7 | (9) | 12.1 | (7) | 7.4 | (4) | 1.7 | (1) | 5.6 | (3) |
| 100–174 | 58.4 | (45) | 63.1 | (53) | 58.6 | (34) | 70.4 | (38) | 67.8 | (40) | 43.4 | (23) |
| 175–259 | 3.9 | (3) | 9.5 | (8) | 5.1 | (3) | 5.5 | (3) | 0 | (0) | 9.4 | (5) |
| 260–499 | 16.9 | (13) | 10.7 | (9) | 12.1 | (7) | 11.1 | (6) | 27.1 | (16) | 39.6 | (21) |
| 500–999 | 2.6 | (2) | 5.9 | (5) | 12.1 | (7) | 5.5 | (3) | 3.4 | (2) | 0 | (0) |
| | | | | | Meridian | | | | | | | |
| 1–49 | 0 | (0) | 1.1 | (1) | 1.4 | (1) | 2.2 | (1) | 5.1 | (2) | 3.1 | (1) |
| 50–99 | 3.4 | (2) | 23.3 | (21) | 15.7 | (11) | 11.1 | (5) | 15.4 | (6) | 3.1 | (1) |
| 100–174 | 79.6 | (47) | 63.3 | (57) | 51.4 | (36) | 55.6 | (25) | 38.5 | (15) | 31.2 | (10) |
| 175–259 | 3.4 | (2) | 3.3 | (3) | 10.0 | (7) | 11.1 | (5) | 20.5 | (8) | 34.4 | (11) |
| 260–499 | 8.5 | (5) | 5.6 | (5) | 17.1 | (12) | 15.6 | (7) | 20.5 | (8) | 25.0 | (8) |
| 500–999 | 5.1 | (3) | 3.3 | (3) | 4.3 | (3) | 4.4 | (2) | 0 | (0) | 3.1 | (1) |
| | | | | | Aurora | | | | | | | |
| 1–49 | 0 | (0) | 0 | (0) | 6.4 | (4) | 1.4 | (1) | 3.6 | (2) | 5.7 | (3) |
| 50–99 | 0 | (0) | 14.3 | (9) | 17.4 | (11) | 15.3 | (11) | 10.9 | (6) | 5.7 | (3) |
| 100–174 | 95.8 | (46) | 69.8 | (44) | 41.3 | (26) | 52.7 | (38) | 58.2 | (32) | 49.1 | (26) |
| 175–259 | 0 | (0) | 4.7 | (3) | 11.1 | (7) | 16.6 | (12) | 20.0 | (11) | 20.7 | (11) |
| 260–499 | 4.2 | (2) | 11.1 | (7) | 23.8 | (15) | 12.5 | (9) | 5.4 | (3) | 18.8 | (10) |
| 500–999 | 0 | (0) | 0 | (0) | 0 | (0) | 1.4 | (1) | 1.8 | (1) | 0 | (0) |

justments by control groups of farmers in Rockville, Meridian, and Aurora
townships, most of whom were American, shows conformity to the pattern outlined for the ethnic groups rather than the pattern described by
Malin. The general trend for the control groups was also toward larger and
larger farms (table 3). The depression did not cause an abrupt increase in
the number of small holdings in 1895, nor did the market boom cause an
increase in large farms by 1915. The changes in farm-size distributions for
the three ethnic groups closely parallel the changes for the control group
of farmers in Rockville, Meridian, and Aurora townships.

Another possible explanation for the failure of Malin's hypothesis may
be the differences between central and eastern Kansas in types of farm-

ing. The general patterns of data Malin presented for several townships in central Kansas also fail to confirm the trends he outlined for Kanwaka in eastern Kansas. Although he did not elaborate on the little impact the depression of the 1890s had on the trend toward large farms in the central Kansas townships, the differences are explained by variations in the type of farming. Eastern Kansas was an area of mixed farming, so one would expect farm-size adjustments in response to changing economic conditions to be quite different from those in the west-central townships, where there was considerable farm specialization, either in livestock or in winter wheat.

Perhaps the most important factor of all in determining farm size, one Malin did not mention (although he alluded to it in his early study of farm population turnover), is how economic fluctuations affected the ebb and flow of migrants along the outer edge of frontier settlement. An economic recession often slowed down the supply of pioneer farmers to the outer edge, resulting in a buildup of farmers in the mature settlements well to the east of the frontier line. The mature settlements provided financial security and access to markets and had reached stage three of the settlement process some years previously. A recession, then, temporarily halted the normal adjustments in farm size only in those areas that had reached stage one or stage two in the settlement process.

The general trends in farm-size adjustments described by M. B. Bogue in her study of prairie farming in Illinois confirm this hypothesis. The initial wave of settlement moved across central Illinois in the 1850s. The first few years of high prices and excellent crops were followed in 1857 by a huge drop in prices for farm produce, accompanied by poor harvests resulting from insect attacks. Although agricultural prices recovered during the 1860s and were high throughout the Civil War years, the decade was one of excessive farm subdivision. Bogue noted, "In 1870 operating units of less than one hundred acres dominated the land use and ownership pattern of Champaign, Ford, Iroquois, Kankakee, Livingston, McLean, Piatt, and Vermillion counties more completely than ever before or since. Sixty-four percent of all farms fell in that category." Many of the small farms in east-central Illinois in 1870 were tenant operated. The economic depression of 1872 reversed the trend toward small farms and eliminated many of the small farmers. There was a general tightening up of the agricultural economy as increasingly efficient farming practices were introduced. Hired help was eliminated in favor of family labor and unimproved land brought into production. The corn-oats-hogs pattern of farming began to predominate in this part of Illinois. Bogue noted, "Hogs dominated the livestock industry, with feeder beef and dairy cattle in a position of secondary importance."[13] Along with the extension of this type of farming went a decline in the number of small farms. The need for additional machinery and livestock on the farm could be resolved only with more capital, and many of the small farmers were unable to borrow more money to expand.

Once the trend in Illinois toward large farms was begun in the 1870s, it continued through the 1880s and 1890s, although for different reasons than for the earlier period, according to Bogue:

> The physical growth of larger farm units in the 1880s and 1890s differed substantially from that of the 1870s. No longer were [farm] boundaries extended by bringing hitherto untilled land into cultivation. The region's many new units of 100 to 160 acres originated in the consolidation of smaller farms and in the subdivision of farms of 500 to 1,000 or more acres.[14]

Some of the large landowners who held land for speculative purposes began to sell part of their property to farmers who would operate their own farms. The overall trend for the last three decades of the century in east-central Illinois was toward large farms, with little regard for changing conditions in the rural economy.

Among the Swedes, Mennonites, French Canadians, and control-group farmers in central Kansas the pattern was similar to the one for Illinois. A high degree of uniformity in farm size existed at the time of initial settlement in 1875, with quarter-section farms predominating. Within the first decade short-term adjustments took place: a decline in the number of medium-size, quarter-section farms and an increase in the number of small farms. A few large farms also were reported in the censuses, and the distribution of farm sizes in the second decade of settlement began to approach the normal curve. Thereafter long-term adjustments toward large farms began. At this mature stage of settlement it is reasonable to ask: Were the farmers of one ethnic group more successful than those of another group in developing large farms? Were the ethnic groups more successful than control groups in obtaining farmland? Did segregation have an observable impact on the size of farms acquired by farmers within each ethnic group?

An analysis of variance test indicates that differences among the three ethnic groups were indeed significant from 1885 onward (table 4). Throughout the period, Swedish farms on average were the largest and Mennonite farms the smallest. The difference between the two groups continued to increase until 1905, then narrowed. In contrast, the difference between Mennonites and French Canadians narrowed from 1885 to 1905

TABLE 4    Average Size of Farms in Acres of Swedes, Mennonites, and French Canadians, 1875–1925

|  | 1875 | 1885 | 1895 | 1905 | 1915 | 1925 |
|---|---|---|---|---|---|---|
| Swedes | 159.8 | 184.3 | 192.9 | 251.2 | 239.5 | 276.1 |
| Mennonites | 185.0 | 141.6 | 140.9 | 160.9 | 172.2 | 195.9 |
| French Canadians | 163.7 | 152.8 | 175.1 | 184.3 | 176.7 | 213.6 |
| F ratio | 2.54* | 9.08* | 12.25* | 19.84* | 18.43* | 11.45* |
| Degrees of freedom | 2/233 | 2/414 | 2/414 | 2/418 | 2/422 | 2/391 |

*Significant at the .05 confidence level.

and then began to increase again. The French Canadians occupied an inter mediate position between Swedes and Mennonites in terms of increasing farm size. Difference of means tests for each pair of ethnic groups indicate that the differences are all significant, except for that between French Cana dians and Swedes in 1895 and between French Canadians and Mennonites in 1905. In 1895 the first Kansas-born French Canadians appeared in the census manuscripts, and the new, second-generation French-Canadian farmers may have had an important influence on the general increase in farm size within their communities. From 1905 onward the difference be tween French-Canadian farmers and Swedish farmers diminished, while the difference between them and Mennonite farmers increased.

The Swedish and French-Canadian farmers compared favorably with their American neighbors in developing large farms. Although Swedish farms were smaller than neighboring American farms in 1885, 1895, and 1915, the difference of means tests indicate that the differences were signifi cant in only one census year, 1895.[15] In general, Swedes were progressing at the same rate as their American neighbors. French-Canadian farms were significantly smaller than those of their neighbors only in 1885. There after, French-Canadian farms increased in size until 1915, when they were slightly larger than those of their control group. French Canadians eventu ally caught up with and surpassed their American neighbors in acquiring large farms. The Mennonites, on the other hand, had consistently smaller farms than their control group. Although the differences in farm size did not fluctuate widely, the differences between Mennonites and their Ameri can neighbors were significant for every census year except 1915.

Finally, there is the question of how important segregation was in the acquisition of large farms—whether ethnic farmers living on the fringe of a large settlement were able to acquire larger farms than their counterparts living in the core of the community. Generally, ethnic farmers who lived in the nonsegregated townships did have larger farms in all of the census years. However, the differences between the segregated and nonsegregated samples were significant in only a few instances—for the Mennonites in 1885 and 1905 and the French Canadians in 1915 and 1925. The difference of means tests reveals that at no time were the differences between the two Swedish samples significant.[16] Consequently, although farm size was consistently lower in the segregated communities, segregation does not seem to have had a significant impact on the acquisition of large farms by members of the three ethnic groups.

The foregoing comments might suggest at first glance that between 1875 and 1925, the Swedes were the most successful and Mennonites the least successful farmers. It is important to emphasize again, however, that farm size by itself is not a complete guide to success. One must consider the quality and intensity of land use in conjunction with farm size when estimating the success of any farming group. For example, it might be argued that the large size of Swedish farms was due more to the poor quality of land in Union Township than to Swedish enterprise. The northern parts of Union are characterized by thin soils and moderate slopes, an environment that requires extensive rather than intensive land-use practices. I have shown elsewhere that variations in land quality had only a small impact on farm sizes.[17] Furthermore, the Swedish farms in Rockville Township, a fertile, level agricultural area, were even larger than the farms of Union Township. Although land quality seems to have had a varying impact on farm size, to determine fully what influenced it one must examine the intensity of land use and the investment in farming by each group.

## Investment in Farming

Intensity of land use cannot be measured directly from any surviving records, but it can be inferred from the capital investment in farming where such records exist. Unfortunately the record is not complete. Information on farm values and farm equipment was not collected after 1905, and even in the early censuses the enumerators recorded this information somewhat sporadically. Farmers have always been sensitive about reporting the value of their possessions to any government agency, despite guarantees of confidentiality, and so the value of farms was often omitted in the early census returns. In 1875 only five farmers in Rockville and seven farmers in Aurora Township reported the value of their farms to the census enumerators. (None of the five in Rockville were Swedish, and all seven of those who reported in Aurora were French Canadian.) If information was not volunteered by the farmer, the census enumerator was required to make an estimate of the value. However, in 1875 and 1885 many enumerators simply did not bother, so the census records for farm and equipment values must be treated with care, especially for the first years of settlement.

A second problem in dealing with values for the early census years concerns the statistical distribution of the data. Many tests comparing, for example, the average value of farms from one group to another (difference of means tests and analysis of variance tests) require that the data be distributed along a statistically normal curve. The data on farm values and equipment values for 1875 and 1885 are not normally distributed but highly skewed. With these data, the reliability of the test results is questionable. Accordingly, I decided to calculate the coefficient of variability as a measure of how the data are distributed about the mean.[18]

$$V = s / \overline{X}$$

where $V$ equals the coefficient of variation, $s$ equals the standard deviation, and $\overline{X}$ equals the mean. The coefficient of variability also gives some insight into the distribution of values within each group. If the value of the coefficient is small, then within the group there are some highly successful farmers, many moderately successful, and some unsuccessful farmers. If the value of the coefficient is high, then there are either a large number of unsuccessful farmers and a few highly successful ones or a large number of successful farmers and a few very unsuccessful ones, depending on the direction of skewness.

Table 5 illustrates that farm values generally increased in the years from 1875 to 1905. The census of 1895 was an exception. The average value of farms in all townships except Aurora and Rockville declined in 1895, reflecting the effect of the general economic depression. The average value of all Swedish farms (both townships combined) was highest for the three groups: $3,625 in 1895 and $6,941 in 1905.[19] The French Canadians occupied second position, with combined averages per farm of $2,582 in 1895 and $5,446 in 1905. The Mennonites occupied the least valuable farms in 1895 ($2,541) and 1905 ($4,611). The values unfortunately are highly skewed, particularly in the Swedish samples, and it is not possible to determine if the differences are statistically significant. It should

TABLE 5    Mean Values in Dollars and Coefficients of Variability for
Farm Values in the Six Townships

| Township | Group | | 1875 | 1885 | 1895 | 1905 |
|----------|-------|---|------|------|------|------|
| Union | Swedes | M | 545.30 | 3,882 | 3,704 | 6,957 |
| | | V | 0.758 | 0.719 | 0.659 | 0.653 |
| Rockville | Swedes | M | — | 1,733 | 3,346 | 5,692 |
| | | V | — | 0.472 | 0.576 | 0.719 |
| Rockville | Others | M | 968.50 | 1,844 | 3,238 | 5,335 |
| | | V | 0.570 | 0.654 | 0.732 | 0.817 |
| Menno | Mennonites | M | 671.20 | 3,019 | 2,381 | 3,686 |
| | | V | 0.526 | 0.450 | 0.395 | 0.462 |
| Meridian | Mennonites | M | 1,420.00 | 4,564 | 2,961 | 6,822 |
| | | V | 0.706 | 0.666 | 0.508 | 0.458 |
| Meridian | Others | M | 1,401.90 | 4,902 | 3,090 | 7,767 |
| | | V | 0.667 | 0.963 | 0.565 | 0.638 |
| Shirley | F. Canadians | M | 791.10 | 3,447 | 2,356 | 5,920 |
| | | V | 0.465 | 0.520 | 0.346 | 0.561 |
| Aurora | F. Canadians | M | 1,671.40 | 2,513 | 3,038 | 4,284 |
| | | V | 0.565 | 0.661 | 0.757 | 0.446 |
| Aurora | Others | M | — | 2,843 | 3,144 | 3,970 |
| | | V | — | 0.456 | 0.640 | 0.563 |

$M$ = mean value
$V$ = coefficient of variability

be noted, however, that the distribution of the indices of wealth is more
uniform among Mennonites than Swedes. In the Swedish settlements there
were a few highly successful farmers and a large number of less well-to-do
farmers.

It is a great pity that the censuses after 1905 did not continue to record
farm values. If such information was available it might be possible to make
reliable comparisons among the groups and to establish a definite trend in
farm-making success. An alternative source of information to the census,
however, is in the county tax rolls, and an attempt was made to obtain real
estate tax data for the farmers listed in the censuses. Not all farmers owned
their farms and so did not appear on the tax rolls. In addition, the tax rolls
tend to be a little out of date, continuing to record a previous owner's name
long after he had sold the property or died. A further difficulty in using
tax records is that differences among groups in the value of their real estate
may be a result of variations in evaluation methods used by tax assessors.

TABLE 6    Mean Values in Current Dollars and Coefficients of
Variability for Real Estate in the Six Townships

| Township | Group | | 1875 | 1885 | 1895 | 1905 | 1915 | 1925 |
|---|---|---|---|---|---|---|---|---|
| Union | Swedes | M | 440 | 780 | 848 | 643 | 5,702 | 8,024 |
| | | V | 0.731 | 0.680 | 1.016 | 0.863 | 0.596 | 0.715 |
| Rockville | Swedes | M | — | 390 | 501 | 708 | 8,194 | 10,036 |
| | | V | — | 0.163 | 0.021 | 0.381 | 0.145 | 0.238 |
| Rockville | Others | M | 545 | 530 | 756 | 989 | 11,824 | 8,178 |
| | | V | 0.361 | 0.567 | 0.557 | 0.945 | 0.994 | 0.602 |
| Menno | Mennonites | M | — | 558 | 704 | 891 | 7820 | 8,951 |
| | | V | — | 0.601 | 0.799 | 0.791 | 0.576 | 0.583 |
| Meridian | Mennonites | M | 742 | 1,005 | 1,021 | 1,056 | 10,699 | 15,994 |
| | | V | 0.393 | 0.692 | 0.724 | 0.642 | 0.593 | 0.803 |
| Meridian | Others | M | 975 | 896 | 974 | 1,237 | 9,627 | 10,472 |
| | | V | 0.696 | 0.756 | 0.886 | 0.726 | 0.627 | 0.736 |
| Shirley | F. Canadians | M | 423 | 628 | 838 | 919 | 7,125 | 8,419 |
| | | V | 0.439 | 0.555 | 0.658 | 0.606 | 0.491 | 0.455 |
| Aurora | F. Canadians | M | 467 | 430 | 766 | 953 | 8,880 | 11,614 |
| | | V | 0.523 | 0.569 | 0.635 | 0.887 | 0.608 | 0.590 |
| Aurora | Others | M | 419 | 404 | 681 | 714 | 5,845 | 7,041 |
| | | V | 0.408 | 0.597 | 0.590 | 0.563 | 0.554 | 0.667 |

M = mean value
V = coefficient of variability

This particular problem is less serious for the later years of settlement than
for the early years.[20] The distinct advantage in using tax records is that they
are available for the full fifty-year period covered in this study—a period
long enough to establish reliable trends.

The information obtained from the tax rolls and shown in table 6 indicates that farms, for taxation purposes, were not assessed at their full value.
Nevertheless, the rank order of real estate values for the various samples
seems to confirm the patterns for farm values derived from census data.
There is, however, some indication by 1905 that the Swedes were not as
far ahead of the other groups as the census data showed. The average value
of Swedish real estate (in Union and Rockville townships combined) in
1905 was $656, compared with $948 for Mennonites and $933 for French
Canadians. By 1915 the averages of the combined samples were $8,663
for Mennonites, $7,863 for French Canadians, and $6,073 for Swedes.
In 1925 the Mennonites had pulled even farther ahead, with an average

TABLE 7    Results of Analysis of Variance Test for Per-Acre Value
of Real Estate in Current Dollars among Swedes, Mennonites, and
French Canadians, 1895–1925

|  | 1895 | 1905 | 1915 | 1925 |
|---|---|---|---|---|
| Swedes | 4.70 | 3.45 | 37.41 | 50.26 |
| Mennonites | 4.42 | 5.19 | 46.88 | 61.01 |
| French Canadians | 5.13 | 5.62 | 47.01 | 56.85 |
| F ratio | 10.73* | 30.13* | 16.88* | 10.66* |
| Degrees of freedom | 2/65 | 2/273 | 2/241 | 2/221 |

*Significant at the .05 confidence level

real estate value of $11,237 compared with $9,563 for French Canadians
and $8,455 for Swedes. What the real estate data show is that the value of
Mennonites' real estate always ranked highest, except in 1885 and 1895;
that the value of the Swedes' real estate always ranked lowest, with the exception of 1885 and 1895; and that the French Canadians invariably ranked
second throughout.

A major limitation to the statistics cited above is that they indicate the
value of taxable real estate belonging to individuals who could be identified
both in census manuscripts and in the tax rolls. These individuals most
often were farm operators who owned rather than rented their farms; they
are not necessarily representative of all farmers in their group. Furthermore, the statistics tell us nothing about the quality of farmland owned
by these farmers or whether differences in the value of real estate might be
attributable to differences in land quality. Accordingly, the per-acre value
of real estate has been calculated for each farm and the results compared
among the three groups. The results of the analysis of variance test (table 7)
indicate that from 1895 to 1915 French Canadians held the most valuable
farmland of the three groups. In 1925 the Mennonites moved into first
place. Throughout the period, Swedes ranked lowest in per-acre value of
real estate, probably reflecting the poor quality of farmland in northern
areas of Union Township. The per-acre value of real estate also reflects the
intensity of land use. A higher value of taxable real estate not only indicates that farmland which is naturally the most fertile but also the land on
which the most valuable improvements have been made. The fact that the
Mennonites had moved into first place in terms of per-acre value of real
estate suggests that they were investing more capital than the other groups

in improving the value and productivity of their farms. The data also suggest that the Swedes were less involved than the other groups in improving the productivity of their farms. These measures of farming intensity are only indirect measures at best. A direct measure of farming intensity is the investment in farm implements and machinery by each farmer.

### Farm Implements and Machinery

One of the first objectives of the new farmer in central Kansas was to obtain equipment and machinery that enabled him to bring his farm into full production. We have seen that with the use of simple tools and reliance on his own labor and that of his family, there were severe limitations on how much land the farmer could bring into and maintain in production.[21] The investment in farm equipment was a critical factor in the breakthrough from small-scale farming to commercial agriculture. In each of the censuses from 1875 to 1905, the enumerator recorded, or should have recorded, the value of equipment on each farm. Unfortunately, as with the value of each farm, the data are often incomplete and cover only the first thirty years of farming in central Kansas. Nevertheless, they serve to confirm some of the patterns outlined tentatively above.

Table 8 shows the mean values of farm implements and machinery for each ethnic group and its control group, along with the coefficient of variability for the years from 1875 to 1905. The single exception is Shirley Township in 1875, where the census enumerator failed to record these values. It is apparent from the coefficients of variability that with only two or three exceptions, the data are not normally distributed during the 1875 or 1885 census years. Generally speaking, however, the size of the coefficient declines over the years as the distribution of values of farm equipment more closely approximates a normal curve. Since many of the distributions are skewed to the right, the mean value often tends to underestimate the value of investments in farm implements and machinery; the greater the degree of skewness, the more unreliable the estimation of the mean.

In comparing the three ethnic groups in 1875 and 1885, the variability in degree of skewness and mean values is so great that establishing a rank order is very difficult. At a crude level, one can state that the value of farm implements and machinery was increasing from 1875 to 1885, and that French Canadians seemed to have had a slightly higher level of investment than the Mennonites or Swedes. Perhaps the French Canadians, with their years of farming experience in Illinois before coming to Kansas, were more

TABLE 8   Mean Values in Dollars and Coefficients of Variability for
Farm Implements and Machinery in the Six Townships

| Township | Group | | 1875 | 1885 | 1895 | 1905 |
|----------|-------|---|------|------|------|------|
| Union | Swedes | M | 61.51 | 105.88 | 59.83 | 78.49 |
| | | V | 1.433 | 0.854 | 0.607 | 0.338 |
| Rockville | Swedes | M | 19.87 | 100.00 | 99.23 | 131.82 |
| | | V | 0.590 | 0.471 | 0.527 | 0.752 |
| Rockville | Others | M | 49.37 | 99.34 | 108.49 | 142.30 |
| | | V | 1.069 | 0.674 | 0.714 | 0.626 |
| Menno | Mennonites | M | 24.00 | 116.86 | 47.96 | 51.59 |
| | | V | 1.119 | 0.473 | 0.556 | 0.351 |
| Meridian | Mennonites | M | 96.40 | 55.70 | 41.70 | 199.05 |
| | | V | 1.574 | 0.744 | 0.434 | 0.438 |
| Meridian | Others | M | 64.43 | 41.70 | 40.24 | 199.40 |
| | | V | 1.492 | 1.104 | 0.977 | 0.472 |
| Shirley | F. Canadians | M | — | 191.30 | 56.46 | 150.33 |
| | | V | — | 2.062 | 0.443 | 0.636 |
| Aurora | F. Canadians | M | 29.46 | 56.36 | 40.95 | 173.50 |
| | | V | 1.058 | 0.974 | 0.705 | 1.012 |
| Aurora | Others | M | 24.71 | 76.15 | 46.58 | 169.00 |
| | | V | 1.164 | 0.789 | 0.544 | 0.786 |

M = mean value
V = coefficient of variability

willing than the other groups to mortgage some of their property in order
to buy equipment for their farms during the 1870s.

By 1895, the investment in farm equipment seems to have been more
normally distributed among the three groups than in previous decades. The
Swedish farmers had the largest average value at $64.90 per farm, whereas
the French Canadians and Mennonites attained an average of $51.24 and
$46.18 per farm respectively. An analysis of variance test indicates that
these differences are significant within the .05 confidence limit. The value
of the $F$ ratio is 30.81, with 2 and 382 degrees of freedom. In 1905 the rank
order of investment in machinery had changed. Now the French Canadians were first, with a mean value of $158.39, followed by the Mennonites
with $99.37 and the Swedes with $89.67 worth of implements. Again the
analysis of variance test indicates that these differences are significant at the
.05 confidence level; with 2 and 396 degrees of freedom the value of the
$F$ ratio is 12.25.

TABLE 9 Results of Analysis of Variance Test for Per-Acre Investment in Farm Equipment among Swedes, Mennonites, and French Canadians, 1875–1905

|  | 1875 | 1885 | 1895 | 1905 |
|---|---|---|---|---|
| Swedes | 0.38 | 0.66 | 0.42 | 0.43 |
| Mennonites | 0.22 | 0.86 | 0.35 | 0.66 |
| French Canadians | 0.24 | 0.91 | 0.33 | 1.02 |
| $F$ ratio | 3.03 | 0.93 | 5.23* | 19.04* |
| Degrees of freedom | 2/140 | 2/391 | 2/391 | 2/391 |

*Significant at the .05 confidence level.

When the per-acre value of investment in farm equipment is calculated for each farm and compared among the three groups, the pattern of changes in farming intensity are confirmed (table 9). In 1885 French Canadians ranked first and Swedes third in equipment value per acre, although the differences were not significant. In 1895, at the end of the 1890s depression, Swedes apparently held a slight edge over the other two groups. But by 1905 the differences were much sharper: French Canadians again ranked first and Swedes third among the three immigrant groups.

The pattern, albeit a rather weak one, that emerges from these data is that the French Canadians were doing rather well in farming. Thus, unlike French-Canadian farmers in Quebec in the early nineteenth century, those who had emigrated to the American Midwest seemed to be ahead of other groups in their investment in equipment and in the intensity of land use. French-Canadian hegemony cannot be attributed to differences in age structure between their communities and the Mennonite and Swedish communities. Although there were more Kansas-born French Canadians in 1905 than Kansas-born Mennonites or Swedes, the younger generation of farmers owned less-valuable property and less-valuable equipment than their elders in all three groups.

Furthermore, when the ethnic groups are compared with their control groups, French Canadians again appear to have done well. They registered a consistently higher value for real estate then their neighbors in each decade from 1875 through to 1925. Mennonites, however, generally had a lower value of real estate than their neighbors, at least in each census year before 1925, but by 1925 the Mennonites' real estate value was higher than that of their neighbors for the first time. Swedes generally had a lower value of real estate than their American neighbors, although the two groups alternated and no strong pattern emerges. The data on farm implements and machinery indicate that French Canadians were closest to their control group. What is perhaps striking is that in 1885 the value of farm implements for each ethnic group is higher than for the control groups. In 1895 the difference between each pair diminishes, and in 1905 the control groups have a generally higher value for farm equipment. In general, however, French Canadians were the most similar to their American neighbors.

Segregation may have had an impact on the success of the immigrants, because those who lived in mixed or heterogeneous communities registered higher levels of investment in farming than their counterparts in the solidly homogeneous settlements. In the early years of farming the homogeneous settlements of Swedes and French Canadians recorded higher values of real estate than those living in the mixed communities. But after 1895, the average value of real estate was higher in the mixed townships, and the gap between the segregated and nonsegregated samples increased over time.[22] There were also quite substantial differences in the value of farm equipment between the segregated and nonsegregated samples for each group. In 1885, those living in the segregated townships had a higher value for farm equipment than those in the mixed-population townships. In the next two decades the positions were reversed. By 1905, the differences resulting from segregation were greatest for the Mennonites and least for the French Canadians. One should not immediately claim a higher level of success for those in the mixed townships. It may have been that as communities matured, those living in the homogeneous communities found ways of cooperating during peak labor periods of spring and fall, making it unnecessary for everyone to buy the new and expensive seeding drills and harvesters. In mixed-population townships, opportunities for mutual help would have been less common and the need to buy one's own equipment greater.

This review of farm investment indicates that although Mennonites occupied the smallest farms, by 1925 the per-acre value of their real estate was the highest of the three groups. Furthermore, although data on investment in farm equipment are not available beyond 1905, the pattern in that year was very similar to that of the real estate values. The French Canadians, contrary to what might have been expected of them because of their poor reputation in Quebec, were able to increase the intensity of their farming operations, more so than Swedish farmers. In addition, French Canadians were more like their American neighbors in this regard than either Swedes or Mennonites. An important factor related to the issue of investment in farming, however, is the nature of farm tenure—the extent to which farmers decided to invest their capital in land (thereby obtaining ownership of their farms), used their farms to raise additional capital (by mortgaging their farms), or simply rented their farms (saving their limited capital resources for other farm needs).

## Farm Tenure

A measure of success for many farmers who migrated to the agricultural frontier was their ability to obtain ownership of their farms and homes. The "agricultural ladder" theory provides recognizable steps that indicate a farmer's progress to success. According to the theory, a young man first gained farming experience as a hired hand before renting a farm to operate by himself. After several years he accumulated enough capital to make a deposit on a mortgaged farm. Eventually, after years of hard work and careful management, he paid off the mortgage and owned his farm free from debt.[23] Farm ownership was a goal that was deeply embedded in the value system of rural communities.

Preference for land ownership was also strong among immigrants.[24] The Swedes, Mennonites, and French Canadians had come from homelands where land hunger was a serious problem. In those homelands tenancy was associated with domineering landlords, social inferiority, and economic subservience, and these associations were difficult to shake off. Even the Swedes and French Canadians who had lived for some time in Illinois were aware that problems of land hunger could reappear in the Midwest. What drew all of them to Kansas was the availability of undeveloped land where they could obtain their own farms free from debt or encumbrance.

### Farm Renting

Despite the high hopes of immigrants to central Kansas, the incidence of farm renting increased as settlements matured. The phenomenon is observable throughout the Midwest. In Illinois and Iowa the average rate of renting was between 7 and 11 percent in 1850; by 1900 it was almost 50 percent.[25] The trend is found between 1900 and 1925 in the statistics published by the Federal Censuses for the four counties of central Kansas in which the sample townships are located (table 10).

TABLE 10    Rented Farms as a Percentage of All Farms in Four
Kansas Counties, 1900–25

| County | 1900 | 1910 | 1920 | 1925* |
|--------|------|------|------|-------|
| Cloud | 37.6 | 41.7 | 47.4 | 47.9 |
| McPherson | 34.4 | 42.3 | 47.0 | 44.9 |
| Marion | 36.8 | 39.5 | 43.4 | 48.5 |
| Rice | 37.8 | 44.7 | 46.9 | 47.0 |

*Data derived from Kansas State census

The increase in farm tenancy was viewed with alarm by agricultural administrators in the federal government during the 1920s. It was feared that American farmers were increasingly becoming a class of economically distressed workers. Farm renting had long been associated with rural instability, the rape of the land, single crop emphasis, and soil destruction. The causes for an increase in farm renting were variously attributed to the failure of government land policies, speculation, and the rising capital costs of farming, which delayed a young farmer's progress up the agricultural ladder. Two major studies carried out during the 1920s concluded that the increase in farm tenancy was part of the maturing process in an agricultural community.[26] As the initial settlers and homesteaders grew older and were no longer able to work their land, they leased their farms to sons, sons-in-law, or other young farmers. The rent derived from leasing supported the older farmers in their retirement. Young farmers operated almost all of the rented farms in a mature agricultural community.

French-Canadian farmers, somewhat older than their Swedish and Mennonite counterparts, were soon replaced by young, Kansas-born French Canadians. It is not surprising, therefore, that the rate of farm renting was highest in the French-Canadian group in 1885 and 1905. By 1915 and 1925 Swedes had caught up with French Canadians and their rates of farm renting were approximately equal. Throughout the entire period, however, the Mennonites rented considerably fewer farms than the others, even in 1925, when all the agricultural communities had matured. The distinctiveness of the Mennonites in resisting farm tenancy is apparent in the statistics for Menno Township, where in 1925 only 36 percent of the farms were rented. The differences in the number of rented farms among the three groups remained fairly consistent from 1885 to 1925.

Historians have been intrigued as to whether farm renting was more prevalent among immigrants than native-born farmers. On the one hand, immigrants were known to have very small cash reserves—seldom enough to purchase a farm. By renting a farm on the frontier they had an opportunity to begin accumulating enough cash for a down payment and time to select their farms. On the other hand, immigrants were more aware of the evils of tenancy and landlordism than were the American born. Their resistance to land renting, therefore, was believed to be greater than that of the American-born farmer. Historians' investigations of census manuscripts tend to confirm the latter viewpoint. Curti found in Trempealeau County, Wisconsin, that the proportion of tenants among native-born Americans was higher than among the foreign born. S. Cogswell found that tenants were more frequent among the American farmers of eastern Iowa in 1850 than among the foreign born, but by 1880 the positions were reversed. E. A. Goldenweiser and Leon Truesdell found that among white farmers in the United States in 1920, the percentage of rented farms was over 33 percent for American-born and only 18 percent for foreign-born farmers. They wrote, "This difference is due partly to the fact that the foreign-born white farmers as a group are considerably older than the native white farmers, and partly to the fact that the immigrants of a generation ago had a very strong desire to acquire the ownership of land and found it relatively easy to do so." [27]

A comparison of the rate of renting among the ethnic group farmers to that of the control group of farmers makes several points clear (table 11). First, the rate of tenancy for the control groups was always higher than for either Swedes or Mennonites. Only French Canadians had higher rates of tenancy than others. Second, until 1915 differences between the control groups and Swedes and Mennonites were increasing; for French Canadians the differences were diminishing. By 1925 the increase in rented farms had begun to slacken off for the control groups, although that of each of the three ethnic groups increased slightly. What emerges from the comparisons is that immigrants rented farms much less frequently than the native born. The French Canadians resembled their American neighbors more than anyone else, whereas the Mennonites were most distinctive in having low rates of farm renting.

What was the impact of segregation on tenancy? A. G. Bogue suggested that the foreign born were most likely to become tenant farmers in those areas where they were already concentrated: "A township by township study of the tenants in Johnson County, Iowa, in 1880 seemed to show mainly that foreign-born tenants were most common in areas where foreign-born owner-operators were most common, and that native-born

TABLE 11    Percentage Rates of Farm Tenancy in the Six
Townships, 1885–1925

| Township | Group | 1885 | 1905 | 1915 | 1925 |
|----------|-------|------|------|------|------|
| Union | Swedes | 10.3 | 36.6 | 49.4 | 48.7 |
| Rockville | Swedes | 7.2 | 23.5 | 38.5 | 50.0 |
| Rockville | Others | 10.3 | 43.6 | 60.8 | 64.8 |
| Menno | Mennonites | 15.3 | 29.6 | 27.1 | 36.4 |
| Meridian | Mennonites | 3.8 | 21.7 | 39.3 | 44.8 |
| Meridian | Others | 24.5 | 42.8 | 67.5 | 56.2 |
| Shirley | French Canadians | 18.9 | 48.8 | 50.0 | 52.5 |
| Aurora | French Canadians | 10.5 | 36.4 | 42.2 | 43.4 |
| Aurora | Others | 15.6 | 31.9 | 32.1 | 52.8 |

NOTE: Information on tenancy was not recorded in the state censuses of 1875 and 1895.

tenants were most often found closely adjacent to native-born owners." [28]
A comparison of segregated and nonsegregated townships for each ethnic
group confirms this observation—in almost every case the proportion of
renters was higher in homogeneous townships than in the mixed communities. The main exception was Meridian Township in 1915 and 1925, where
the Mennonites in any case were taking over more and more of the land
after 1915. There were several reasons for the immigrants' tendency to become tenant farmers in the homogeneous townships. Many young farmers
were renting their parents' farm, not yet having obtained ownership of
the property, while others found it easy to rent land from landowners who
belonged to the same ethnic group. Farmers living in a township where
their ethnic group was in the minority were disinclined to become tenant
farmers.

Farm renting was not the most desirable form of land tenure on the
American prairies. Tenant farmers were sometimes obliged to follow cropping practices and to make improvements specified in their leases. [29] Furthermore, the rapid rise in land values favored the farm owner, not the
tenant. It was to the immigrant's advantage to acquire ownership of a farm
even if it required heavy mortgaging.

*Farm Mortgaging*

The issue of farm mortgaging is one of the most clouded in western historiography. Rooted in the Populist tradition and expressed in radical rhetoric
was the idea that eastern moneyed interests were gouging the struggling

farmer on the frontier by charging high interest rates, thereby making success increasingly difficult. Recent studies have shown that mortgage companies were often caught from both sides during periods of rural depression, and that the majority had no interest in acquiring farm property by foreclosure. When farmers were not able to meet their payments and foreclosure ensued, many mortgage companies became overburdened with real estate and suffocated from the lack of cash that was required to keep their system alive. The payment of rates and taxes, not to mention litigation over disputed payments, was a further drain on the mortgage companies' cash reserves. While a few companies survived the crises of rural depression, many collapsed under the strain. In good times, however, they served a vital function in helping farmers establish and develop viable farms. In doing so they probably retarded the increase in farm renting.[30]

In Kinsley Township, Edwards County, Kansas, immediately west of the study area, Bogue discerned three peak periods of mortgaging—1879, 1886, and 1905. The first peak occurred as the newly arrived farmers obtained title to their land and applied for mortgages to buy implements and machinery: "During the real estate boom of the 1880s land sales and refinancing accounted for a much larger proportion of the first mortgages than during the 1870s. Of the 90 first mortgages recorded during 1885, 1886, and 1887, there were 58 or 64 percent which were obviously for refinancing or related to real estate transactions. By the years 1903, 1904, and 1905 this percentage had risen to 71 percent." A further investigation of mortgaging in nearby Pawnee County indicated that less than 10 percent of the mortgages in 1890 were negotiated to relieve acute financial distress, even though hardships caused by droughts and poor harvests were being felt. According to Bogue, "More than 90 percent of the first mortgages had been negotiated for purposes which were ostensibly productive. Presumably much the same condition held true in other counties of the middle border country."[31]

The enumerators of the Kansas state censuses did not record information on farm mortgaging until the census of 1905, so that information on mortgaging patterns must be inferred from other sources for the early decades. The 1885 census manuscripts reveal a sharp increase from the 1875 census not only in the value of farm implements and machinery but also in the numbers of livestock on farms, in all the sample townships except Meridian. It seems highly probable that the capital needed to pay for the new farm equipment and livestock was obtained from loan or mortgage companies, since no increase is found in the value of assessed personal property on the tax rolls to account for the increased capital outlays.

The deed records in the various county courthouses provide detailed and voluminous information on farm mortgaging. Seven sections were sampled in Union, Menno, and Shirley townships to provide accurate information on the frequency of mortgaging for the years before 1905. The farm mortgage data indicate that of the three immigrant groups the Swedes used farm mortgages most frequently and most heavily and Mennonites used mortgages least frequently and least heavily during the early period (fig. 29). The data shown in figure 30 represent the total number of foreclosures among the immigrants in Union, Menno, and Shirley townships in the years from 1885 to 1925. Almost all the mortgage foreclosures for the fifty-year period took place in the years between 1886 and 1901, with the worst experiences in 1897, and especially high rates in 1890 and 1893. Mennonites were much more successful than either French Canadians or Swedes in avoiding foreclosure, especially during the worst years of the 1890s. It may be argued, on the one hand, that the rate of Mennonite foreclosure was low because they did not mortgage as frequently or as heavily as the others did. On the other hand, it should be noted that the number of Mennonite farmers was much higher than the number of French-Canadian or Swedish farmers in their respective townships. Consequently, the incidence of mortgaging and of foreclosure among Mennonites was much lower proportional to the number of farmers than figures 29 and 30 suggest. No matter how one looks at the data, the inevitable conclusion is that the Mennonites avoided the pitfalls and hardships of mortgage foreclosure more successfully than did Swedes or French Canadians.

For the period 1905 onward, with mortgaged farms recorded in the censuses, not only frequency but also the impact of mortgaging on farm size is easier to determine than for the period before 1905. The rate of mortgaging was highest among the Mennonites after 1905 and the incidence of mortgaging fairly constant, ranging from 30 percent to 27 percent (table 12). The rate of mortgaging was also stable among French-Canadian farmers. Only the Swedes increased the number of mortgaged farms between 1905 and 1925. By 1925, however, there was very little difference in the rate of mortgaging among all three immigrant groups. Many farmers seem to have used a mortgage to increase the size of their operations, since the average size of mortgaged farms was often larger than the average size of rented farms and those owned debt-free.

Herein lies the nub of the problem in using farm mortgaging to measure farmers' success. On the one hand, a mortgage represented a major risk. If the farmer was unable to meet his payments, either because of poor harvests resulting from bad weather or because of depressed market prices,

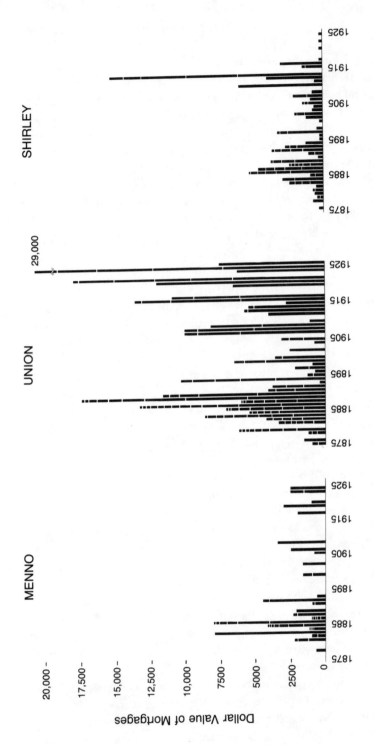

FIG. 29.    Frequency and amount of mortgaging among ethnic farmers in Union, Menno, and Shirley townships

SOURCE: Based on data drawn from seven sections in each township

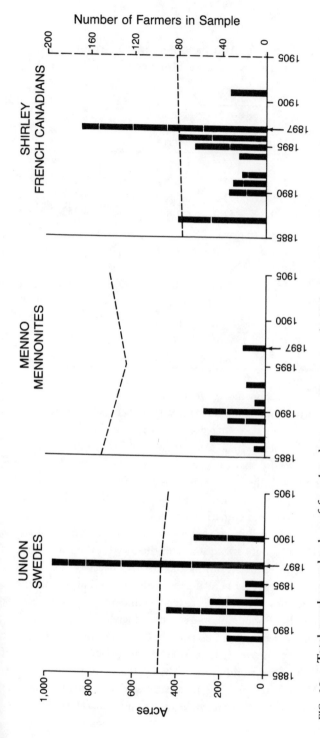

FIG. 30. Total number and value of foreclosed mortgages among ethnic farmers in Union, Menno, and Shirley townships, 1885–1925

TABLE 12   Average Size in Acres and Percent Distribution of Farms Owned Debt-free, Rented, or Mortgaged by the Three Ethnic Groups, 1905–25

| | 1905 | | 1915 | | 1925 | |
|---|---|---|---|---|---|---|
| | Acres | % | Acres | % | Acres | % |
| *Swedes* | | | | | | |
| Owned | 266.2 | (48) | 212.2 | (33) | 190.6 | (26) |
| Rented | 223.8 | (34) | 238.2 | (48) | 316.8 | (49) |
| Mortgaged | 280.2 | (18) | 208.9 | (19) | 251.7 | (25) |
| *Mennonites* | | | | | | |
| Owned | 161.9 | (43) | 156.4 | (39) | 174.8 | (34) |
| Rented | 141.5 | (27) | 139.1 | (31) | 161.9 | (39) |
| Mortgaged | 163.9 | (30) | 188.3 | (29) | 212.2 | (27) |
| *French Canadians* | | | | | | |
| Owned | 156.1 | (33) | 190.9 | (30) | 189.1 | (28) |
| Rented | 171.6 | (44) | 170.1 | (47) | 197.5 | (49) |
| Mortgaged | 212.5 | (23) | 172.2 | (23) | 234.7 | (22) |

he ran the risk of having his mortgage foreclosed and losing everything he owned. On the other hand, the mortgage was a means whereby the farmer obtained additional capital to increase his acreage and to buy his equipment and livestock, thereby increasing the size of his farm operation and becoming more successful than he would have been otherwise. In the years before 1900, and especially during the crisis years of the 1890s, mortgaging was risky. But after 1895 the farmers of central Kansas had a better measure of market risks and climatic hazards.

Of the three immigrant groups, before the turn of the century it seems the Mennonites were the most cautious and the Swedes the least cautious about mortgaging. In addition, during the first two decades of settlement many Mennonite mortgages were underwritten by fellow Mennonites. From 1905 onward, however, they were more confident than the Swedes or French Canadians about obtaining mortgages to increase farm production. The Swedes seem to have been hesitant about reentering the mortgage market; furthermore, the mortgaged Swedish farms were not the largest farms within the Swedish community.[32] The evidence presented here suggests that the Mennonites were the most successful and Swedes the least successful in using mortgages to improve their condition as farmers.

TABLE 13  Percentage Rates of Mortgaging in the Six Townships, 1905–25

| Township | Group | 1905 | 1915 | 1925 |
|----------|-------|------|------|------|
| Union | Swedes | 19.5 | 22.4 | 22.4 |
| Rockville | Swedes | 5.9 | 0.0 | 33.3 |
| Rockville | Others | 3.6 | 8.7 | 18.5 |
| Menno | Mennonites | 30.9 | 31.0 | 29.8 |
| Meridian | Mennonites | 28.3 | 26.2 | 22.4 |
| Meridian | Others | 12.2 | 10.0 | 18.8 |
| Shirley | French Canadians | 18.3 | 23.9 | 18.7 |
| Aurora | French Canadians | 29.5 | 23.4 | 28.3 |
| Aurora | Others | 29.2 | 35.7 | 32.1 |

Willingness to borrow money to increase farm acreage or to add new equipment and livestock involved taking a degree of risk and a dependence on unknown financiers that has been attributed to native-born Americans but not the foreign born. E. Brunner reported that "the foreign-born were more conservative in the financial management of their farms. They were less likely than the native farmers to borrow for improvements, for machinery. . . . This aversion to incurring debt was reported from many sections of the country."[33] This aversion is not apparent when the three immigrant groups are compared with the control groups of neighboring American farmers (table 13). The Swedes and Mennonites had consistently higher rates of mortgaging than their American neighbors. Only the French Canadians had a smaller percentage of mortgaged farms than their neighbors. In general, after 1905 the immigrants to central Kansas were as inclined as their American neighbors to take mortgaging risks in order to improve the size of their farms and their farming investment.

It is therefore not surprising that contact with American farmers did not have an appreciable effect on the rate of mortgaging within each of the ethnic groups. In fact, mortgages were less frequent among Swedes and Mennonites who lived in the mixed-population townships (Rockville and Meridian) than for the Swedes and Mennonites who lived in the homogeneous townships. (Too much emphasis must not be placed on the data for Swedes in Rockville Township, since the number of Swedish farms was less than twenty and an increase of three or four mortgaged farms produced a significant change in the percentage figures.) Among French Canadians

TABLE 14   Debt-free, Owner-Operated Farms as a Percentage of
All Farms, 1885–1925

| Township | Group | 1885* | 1905 | 1915 | 1925 |
|----------|-------|-------|------|------|------|
| Union | Swedes | 89.7 | 43.9 | 28.2 | 28.9 |
| Rockville | Swedes | 92.8 | 70.6 | 61.5 | 16.7 |
| Rockville | Others | 89.6 | 52.7 | 30.4 | 16.7 |
| Menno | Mennonites | 84.7 | 39.4 | 41.8 | 33.8 |
| Meridian | Mennonites | 96.2 | 50.0 | 34.4 | 32.8 |
| Meridian | Others | 75.5 | 44.9 | 22.5 | 25.0 |
| Shirley | French Canadians | 81.1 | 32.9 | 26.1 | 28.8 |
| Aurora | French Canadians | 89.5 | 34.1 | 34.4 | 28.3 |
| Aurora | Others | 84.4 | 38.9 | 32.1 | 15.1 |

*Data for 1885 did not distinguish between mortgaged farms and those owned debt-free.
Hence the column for 1885 most likely includes mortgaged farms.

mortgaging was more frequent in the mixed-population township (Aurora)
than in the homogeneous township (Shirley). Segregation does not seem to
have had a uniform effect on the incidence of mortgaging: if an immigrant
farmer decided to obtain a mortgage, it did not make much difference
whether he lived in a highly concentrated ethnic community or in an area
dominated by American farmers.

*Debt-Free Ownership*

Many recent studies of farm tenure on the agricultural frontier have re-
dressed the imbalance and bias against tenancy and mortgaging. When an
agricultural community had stabilized, tenant farmers were as careful and
efficient in their farming operations as any others, and a mortgage, rather
than being an article for the enslavement of the western farmer, provided
the cash necessary to convert a quarter section of prairie into a viable family
farm. Both factors played a vital economic function in the development
of agriculture, and after fifty years of farming the stigma that may have
been attached to them in the early years was gone. Nevertheless, the historians who reappraised the roles of renting and mortgaging asserted that
debt-free ownership of the family farm was still the most desirable goal
for farmers.[34] And yet attainment of that goal seemed increasingly difficult
with each passing decade (table 14).

The general trend in the percentage of farms owned debt-free was downward. Although the census of 1885 did not distinguish between farms that were mortgaged and those that were not, the rate of owner-operated farms would still have been quite high even if mortgaged farms had accounted for 30 percent of all farms. Swedes had the highest ratio of owner-operated farms in 1905 (48 percent) and French Canadians the lowest (33 percent). Over the next two decades the proportion of debt-free farms in the Swedish samples dropped sharply to 26 percent, whereas the French-Canadian decline reached 28 percent. Over the same period the decline among Mennonites was from 43 percent to 34 percent. The decades from 1905 to 1925 were when younger, second-generation farmers were taking over from their immigrant parents; it is clear that the Old World desire for a debt-free farm survived most strongly among the Mennonites and least among the Swedes, where tenancy and mortgaging were still on the increase.

Brunner, comparing the patterns of farm ownership of immigrants with those of the native born in the 1920s, concluded that if "ownership of the land one tills be taken as an index of success in agriculture, the foreign-born farmer ranks high. The proportion of farm owners among immigrants exceeds the proportion of native-born white farm-operators."[35] In general that observation is confirmed by a comparison of the ethnic groups with the control groups. Only in 1905 did the control-group farmers have a slight edge in the percentage of debt-free, owner-operated farms. The Mennonites were consistently ahead of their control group in this measure of farming success, although the difference was diminishing over the years.

The percentage of debt-free farms was usually higher in the nonsegregated townships than in the homogeneous ones. The impact of segregation on debt-free ownership was greater among the Swedes and Mennonites than among the French Canadians. By 1925, however, differences between the pairs of samples were negligible, and segregation seemed to have little or no effect on whether or not outright ownership of the family farm could be achieved.

Caution must be exercised against overstating the importance of levels of farm tenure as an index of success in rural communities. The census enumerator distinguished only among those farms that were predominantly rented, mortgaged, or owned free of debt; he did not distinguish land that was partly rented, mortgaged, or owned. This information was obtained in the 1920 state census, based on which Malin argued that partly rented land played an important role in the success of family farms. Farmers who combined rented land with their own farms had a higher rate of persistence than farmers who did not. The rented land provided a margin of elasticity whereby the farmer could increase the scale of his operation without undertaking massive outlays of capital during years when market conditions were booming. During periods of low market prices some of the rented land need not be taken up. In this way the risk of poor markets was not borne by the farmer alone but also by landowners who elected to rent their land rather than farm it themselves.[36]

## Summary

This survey of farming success from 1875 to 1925 confirms some elements of the Turnerian thesis. The immigrant peasant stock certainly did not lapse into an Old World acceptance of poverty and social inferiority. Swedes, Mennonites, and French Canadians achieved a considerable measure of success in central Kansas, although the differences in levels of success among the three groups did not always narrow. Although there is no evidence to suggest that the rich were getting richer or the poor were getting poorer, neither does the evidence suggest that all three immigrant groups were coming closer together in terms of levels of achievement and success. In some instances this was true, as in the case of Swedish and French-Canadian immigrants, but rarely for Mennonites.

In the early years the Swedes appear to have been the most successful farmers: they had the most valuable and also the largest farms, according to information obtained from state censuses. After 1905 the average size of farms continued to increase, faster among Swedes and French Canadians than Mennonites. In fact, the difference in size between Swedish and French-Canadian farms was diminishing. When measures of success other than farm size are examined, a very different picture emerges. The value of Mennonite real estate, according to the tax rolls, began to exceed that of Swedes and French Canadians after 1905, and by 1925 the difference between the Mennonites and the others was still growing. This suggests that the Mennonites were investing their capital to intensify production on existing farms while Swedes and French Canadians were using their capital to increase their farm acreage.

None of the indices of progress in farming suggest that the immigrant groups failed to keep up with their American neighbors or that the immigrants were sliding into poverty. Investment in farm implements and machinery is the only anomalous index. In the first two decades of farming, ethnic groups had a higher average investment in equipment than the control groups, but in 1905 the control groups' investment was greater. Unfortunately, information on the value of farm equipment is not available in the censuses taken after 1905; however, in terms of real estate value, farm size, and proportion of debt-free farms, the immigrants were ahead of the control groups. Of the three immigrant groups French Canadians were the most similar to their American neighbors and Mennonites least similar.

The effect of segregation on achievement within the three ethnic groups was quite small; proximity to American farmers does not seem to have had a marked influence on immigrants' success. Those who lived in the core of the ethnic community tended to have a higher value of real estate, slightly smaller farms, and somewhat more tenant farms than their compatriots who lived along the margins of the ethnic community. Nevertheless, few of the tests of differences between the pairs of townships produce significant results. In other indices of progress (value of farm equipment, farm value, and degree of mortgaging) the patterns show no consistency: the impact of segregation on the rate of success for each of the three ethnic groups appears to have been negligible.

The analysis above does not take into consideration how cooperation within an ethnic community may have contributed to levels of success, because such information is difficult to obtain and measure at this remove in time. But there are some indications that community cooperation existed in the Mennonite settlements during the first decade or two of settlement. The organization of the first villages and the distribution of strips of land in Menno Township during the early settlement phase (albeit short-lived) suggest a considerable degree of cooperation. In addition, many of the early Mennonite farmers who took out mortgages did so from fellow Mennonites, which also suggests a degree of cooperation. There is no evidence of cooperation beyond about 1890, and one may assume that economic individualism and financial independence were widespread by then among Mennonites, Swedes, and French Canadians.

Over the fifty-year period from 1875 to 1925 the stereotypes of ambitious and hardworking Swedes, efficient and frugal Mennonites, and inattentive and spendthrift French Canadians are not all confirmed. Mennonites indeed exhibited work-ethic traits most strongly and appear to have been the most successful farmers. Their farms may have been the smallest but were the most valuable and most intensively used of the three groups. French Canadians, on the other hand, attained a higher level of financial success than Swedes, shattering their stereotype. In addition, French Canadians appear to have Americanized most rapidly, for of the three groups they most resembled their American neighbors. What emerges from these results is that material or financial success cannot be equated directly with Americanization. It was possible for an immigrant group to surpass the financial success of their American neighbors and still retain an ethnic identity. As the Mennonites demonstrated, financial success and material improvement did not result in a rapid corrosion of their ethnic identity.

The foregoing discussion is concerned with measuring the success of farmers who came to central Kansas and stayed. But what of those who came and left? There is no way at present of determining how many of those who left did so because of failure, but the numbers must have been high. Central Kansas was probably much less tolerant of those who were barely surviving on their farms than many other areas in the central and eastern Midwest. In the transition zone between the western edge of the prairies and the high plains, the impact of drought, sometimes subtle, sometimes overwhelming, but always unpredictable, was such that weak farmers were rapidly weeded out. Those who survived and were successful did so because they developed farming strategies that minimized some of the major risks to farming in central Kansas. Material well-being is only one measure of success; adaptation to the environment is yet another.

# Farming Decisions over Fifty Years

6

The development of an agricultural system that was specifically suited to the special moisture conditions in central Kansas was not immediately achieved, although many self-appointed experts in those early years, particularly local newspaper editors, believed they had the solution. The majority of American farmers coming into central Kansas during the early 1870s were from the Corn Belt states, and their first attempts in farming duplicated the systems they had known in Iowa, Illinois, Wisconsin, Missouri, and Indiana. Consequently, corn was the preeminent crop in the early 1870s, but with crop failures and depressed prices following 1873, corn began to give way as the major crop to soft winter wheat.

As the soft winter wheat boom gathered momentum during the second half of the 1870s, few urged a diversified farming system to counteract the unpredictability of market prices and crop yields. With the onset of poor harvests in 1879, 1880, and 1881, however, the cry for a diversified farming system rose again. Editors urged farmers to raise hogs, sheep, and cattle in addition to growing wheat, and the editor of the Salina *Herald* in January 1880, stoutly maintained: "The raising of stock must soon take the place of grain growing in this part of Kansas, and the sooner the farmers take hold of this great interest the better for them. Sheep and cattle will put more money in your pocket than wheat farming."[1] Even sheep production enjoyed a short-lived boom, and T. C. Henry of Dickinson County, well known for his advocacy of corn production in the early 1870s, was now engaged in sheep raising and urging other farmers to become involved in livestock production.[2]

The fluctuations in crop yields continued through the 1880s, but in the early years of the decade, crop returns in general were good. (The relation between crop yields and climate is presented in appendix C.) From 1885 to 1887 yields dropped again and, combined with the collapse of the real estate boom, brought new cries for more careful farming and less dependence on wheat. The years that followed, 1888 to 1890, produced some of the best wheat harvests to date, and the summer drought of 1890 that greatly reduced corn yields did not affect the wheat crop.

During those first two decades of farming many solutions to the fluctuations in yields and market prices were proffered. When market prices were low or harvests poor, many urged a diversification of farm enterprises. But when crop returns were good and market prices high, those who spoke out against farm specialization won few adherents. For the farmers themselves decisions on which crops to plant and on the degree of farm specialization were made under conditions of uncertainty rather than of risk.[3] It was not until after 1895, after the first major economic depression and major drought had passed, that farmers became fully aware of the magnitude of the risks involved.

An accurate perception of the hazards of market prices and crop yields was only the first step in developing a successful farming system for central Kansas. Another requisite for success was some degree of managerial ability. Malin believed this was a critical factor in the subhumid environment of the western prairies: "The most intangible but certainly not the least important factor in success anywhere commercial agriculture is practiced is that of managerial ability and business judgment. Some have it— a sort of sixth sense—some do not. . . . One is tempted to assume that the management factor is more critical to farming success in a subhumid environment than elsewhere, but possibly that cannot be proved."[4] Malin was not really specific on the nature of "managerial ability," but for our purposes it may be described as the allocation of a farm's resources to achieve specified goals in the light of assumed risks and uncertainties.

## Risk and the Variability of Farm Income

Throughout the Midwest, farm income was notoriously unstable during the latter decades of the nineteenth century. Fluctuation in market prices of the major agricultural products contributed significantly to the variability of farm income (fig. 31). In central and western Kansas the problem of fluctuating crop yields as a result of moisture shortages was another major source of variability in farm income (appendix C). Malin believed that in "overall effect, the hazards of weather on crops and prosperity were greater

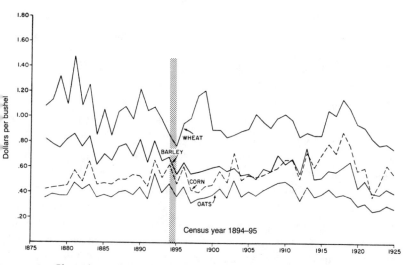

FIG. 31. Changing prices of farm commodities in Kansas based on a three-year moving average, 1875–1925

than the hazards of price. To ponder agriculture in this perspective brings the historian face to face with the stark realism of rural life." Nevertheless, E. N. Castle suggested that there was a strong tendency for low prices to coincide with poor yields and high prices to coincide with good yields.[5] The combined effect of climatic and market fluctuations was to accentuate the variability of farm income.

The purpose of this chapter, then, is to examine the farming decisions of each ethnic group in each census year in order to determine their adaptation to the environmental milieu and, consequently, variations in their rates of Americanization. Specifically, the analysis focuses on how their farming systems differed in terms of risk and adaptation to the uncertainties of markets and climate. Over a period of fifty years immigrant farmers (and their children who succeeded them on their farms) developed farming strategies that were attuned not only to the problem of markets and moisture supply but also to their goals, to security of income, to family continuity, and to the ownership of their homes and farms. These goals could be achieved either by farming decisions that were either risky or minimized risks. As time passed, farmers realized that there was a trade-off between profit maximization and risk minimization. If a farmer went entirely into wheat production the return could be very high, but so could the risks. If, however, he balanced wheat and several other small grains with a variety of livestock, for which market demand was not strong, he could not only lower the level of risk but also the level of his income.

Herein lay a perceived difference between immigrant and American farms. Immigrants often came from a modified European commercial agricultural economy in which there was still an element of subsistence farming, whereas Yankee farmers in the Midwest were well acquainted with the world of commercial farming. Historians have portrayed the immigrant farmer as taking the long-term view—he put down deep roots and was committed to his community, devoted to the preservation of his family farm, and anxious to establish security for his children. On the other hand, the eastern farmer moving westward along the frontier was characterized as inherently mobile, forever looking for new opportunities to get rich quick —he took the short-term view, frequently mined the soil for a quick return on his investment despite the high risks, and then moved farther west in search of another opportunity. The stereotypes are obviously inaccurate, for as the farmer turnover study in Chapter 5 showed, immigrants were just as mobile as American farmers. But the degree to which immigrants adopted a profit-maximizing strategy has not been fully investigated, and doing so can reveal something of their transition from European to North American.

At this point a word is necessary about several underlying assumptions in the analysis that follows. First, it is assumed that most farmers moved to Kansas to improve their economic status and that of their families. Second, many of the ethnic farmers arrived full of idealism for the creation of a community with a strong religious element. Over time, however, as they adopted American ways, an increasing number at one end of the spectrum embraced a spirit of materialism, consumerism, and economic individualism in varying degrees. Gradually these immigrants were drawn away from the obligations of community into the world of North American commercial agriculture, in which individualized profit predominated. At the other end of the spectrum were immigrants who continued to "spurn the rage of gain," remaining outside the commercial maelstrom and clinging to the principles of a simple way of life. These farmers would grow a variety of crops and raise livestock, diversifying in order to meet family needs rather than specializing in cash grain production. Over the years, these farmers would decline in numbers as the immigrants became Americanized. Within each group it is assumed that there were some farmers who adopted high-risk strategies and some who did not. It is the changing proportion of these two groups that reflects the adaptation to American life.

A critical appraisal of farm management decisions for each ethnic group, then, reveals something of the perception of market and climate hazards and also the degree of risk or uncertainty tolerated in the attainment of its goals. Insight into decision making can reveal a great deal more of the character of an ethnic group and how it is changing, the deeper currents that distinguish one group from another, and the basic differences in value systems, which are probably more important in ethnic differentiation than such often-cited features as architectural preferences, observance of seasonal festivals, or even differences in language. Often the source of conflict between ethnic groups is found in subliminal differences in goals, in what constitutes the good life, and in decisions as to how that concept of the good life is to be attained.

In this appraisal, measurement of farm income variability and the risk involved in different farming strategies is important. A detailed measurement is described in appendix D but summarized briefly here. The acreage in various crops and the numbers of livestock on each farm recorded by census enumerators were converted into labor units; this information represents the decision of each operator in organizing the resources of his farm. The next step was to separate major enterprises on each farm from minor activities not significant in terms of farm income. The major enterprise combinations reveal the truly important activities on each farm. An independent estimate of risk was developed from data gathered by the Kansas State Board of Agriculture, which included annual estimates of crop yield per acre for each county in addition to current market prices for crop and livestock. Thus it was possible to develop an index of variability for each crop and livestock combination based on yield variations resulting from weather and price fluctuations. Corn monoculture was the highest-risk crop, whereas wheat frequently was less risky than other small grains such as oats or barley. For example, corn monoculture in Cloud County and McPherson County produced a coefficient of variation of 56.5 and 46.5 respectively; the coefficients for wheat monoculture in both counties were 41.9 and 37.4. But when hog production or dairying is added to several crops in a farming strategy, the risk level drops dramatically. A wheat-corn-hog combination, for example, produces a coefficient of 12.8

in McPherson County and 13.7 in Cloud County. These independent estimates allow one to determine the level of risk in actual farming strategies for each farm obtained from the census manuscripts.

When one reviews the farm strategies for each group over the fifty-year period, several important points should be borne in mind. The *number* of enterprises in a farm strategy indicates the level of risk: one- and two-enterprise strategies represent a high degree of risk; three- and four-enterprise strategies indicate a much lower level of risk. The nature of the enterprise combination is also important. Corn is a high-risk crop and wheat a moderately risky crop. When livestock appear in a combination or farm strategy, the risk level is fairly low. But with livestock in the farm strategy one should also remember market demand: in general, hog production was a commercial venture, whereas dairying was usually for domestic consumption. Finally, important indicators that appeared in the post-1895 censuses were the new drought-resistant crops such as alfalfa, millets, and sorghums. Although the new crops were never widespread enough to appear in the enterprise combination, the fact that ethnic farmers were growing them indicates an effort to minimize risk while increasing profits; that is, successful adaptation to environment and markets.

## Farming Patterns over Fifty Years

In 1875, farming was still in the pioneer stage in central Kansas, and almost everyone was preoccupied with breaking the prairie sod and extending the cultivated acreage on his farm. The Mennonites were still arriving in large numbers when the census was taken, and no distinctive pattern of farming was yet observable. Within three or four years, however, Mennonite farms attracted attention. Travelers often commented on the unusual crops produced by the Russian immigrants:

> Besides the raising of wheat, corn, rye and barley, the agricultural activities of the Mennonites are somewhat more manifold than those of the American farmers. They raise all the green forage crops such as millet as well as bulbous and tuberous plants. They immediately planted large gardens of vegetables, fruits, and flowers, using besides common varieties those which they had brought from Russia. The orchard contains cherry, apple, and peach trees, as well as plums and a fine blackberry patch.[6]

There was even an attempt to plant silk and mulberry trees, especially in southern Marion County. The crop most often associated with Mennonites, however, is hard winter wheat, particularly Turkey red wheat. Controversy exists over whether the Mennonites were the first to bring the crop to Kansas, but as Malin affirmed, "If the Mennonites were not the first or the only ones to introduce the hard winter wheat, at any rate they grew it extensively."[7]

Swedish farmers in the Smoky Hill valley were urged to plant a variety of crops, including wheat, oats, buckwheat, potatoes, and broomcorn.[8] The census manuscripts reveal that all of these crops were grown on Swedish farms but that corn or wheat predominated as a single-enterprise operation. Swedish pioneer farms took a high degree of risk. Corn and wheat were also widely grown in the French-Canadian settlements. Corn was the most important crop, and in 1875, French Canadians grew much more spring wheat than winter wheat—the only occasion on which spring wheat figured significantly in any of the census returns. Presumably the Swedes and French Canadians brought this corn-wheat strategy with them from their former settlements in Illinois.

When labor units are applied to the crop acreages and livestock numbers, the pattern of farming that emerges is of one- and two-enterprise farm combinations (fig. 32). Dairying was the dominant activity, and its importance in the farm combination is due to the fact that crop acreages were still very small, and the care of livestock, even two or three dairy cows, tended to be labor demanding. If it had been possible to include farm labor spent on fencing, clearing the land, and preparing it for the first crop, the importance of dairying in the total labor inputs of the new farms would be greatly diminished. One must be careful, then, not to read too much into the farming differences in the pioneer years of farming. The largest difference appeared between Swedes and French Canadians: the latter generally had more diverse farm operations and fewer livestock. The control groups of American farmers had more diverse farming activities than the immigrants (fig. 33).

## Farming Patterns in 1885

By 1885 the winter wheat boom was already well under way in central Kansas, and although harvests in the years 1879–81 were disappointing, crop yields in 1882, 1883, and 1884 were good. Nevertheless, there was little evidence that "wheat fever" had taken hold of many of the farmers in the sample townships. Winter wheat was assigned a secondary role in the farm combinations in 1885 for all groups except the Mennonites in

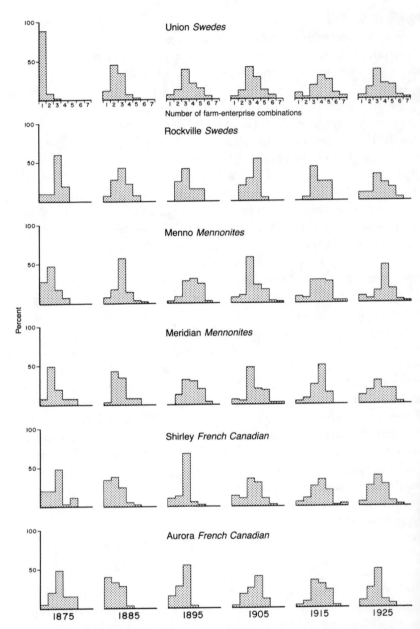

FIG. 32. Percent distribution of farm-enterprise combinations for the ethnic groups, 1875–1925

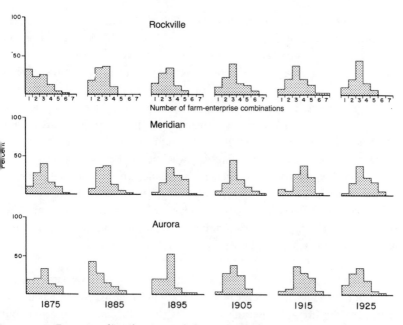

FIG. 33. Percent distribution of farm-enterprise combinations for the control groups, 1875–1925

Menno Township. Farming systems had become increasingly diversified over the preceding decade, but corn was still the preeminent crop in the system of Swedes, French Canadians, and neighboring American farmers. The Swedes had diversified their operations considerably: 45 percent of the Swedish farms in Union Township were two-enterprise and 35 percent three-enterprise combinations. In Rockville Township the range of enterprises had changed very little on Swedish farms, although there was a slight drop in the number of three-enterprise and an increase in the two-enterprise combinations. Among the Mennonites in both Menno and Meridian townships, since 1875 the number of three- and four-enterprise combinations significantly increased, accompanied by a decrease in the single- and two-enterprise combinations. The French Canadians, in contrast to the Mennonites and Swedes, showed evidence of increased specialization rather than diversification: the number of single- and two-enterprise combinations increased between 1875 and 1885 while three-enterprise combinations declined.

Within the Swedish townships were other signs that a more commercial farming system had developed since 1875. The emphasis on dairying and beef cattle was much less apparent than before: corn and wheat production ranked first and second as the most important activities on Swedish farms (table 15). What was really distinctive in Swedish farming patterns, however, was the production of broomcorn in both Union and Rockville townships. On Mennonite farms corn and wheat production were the major activities in both sample townships, although wheat was slightly more important in Menno Township. Dairying was the most popular third-ranked activity on Mennonite farms. French Canadians, who had specialized their production patterns since 1875, were now putting more effort into corn production and dairying activities and somewhat less into wheat growing than before. The typical farm combination in Shirley and Aurora townships was corn-dairy, with oats or wild prairie hay as a third activity on a few farms.

In the years between 1880 and 1885 the market price of wheat fell while prices for corn and livestock rose (fig. 31). The combination of wheat and corn over the fifty-year period shows a high coefficient of variation, but given the moisture fluctuations in the early 1880s, the two crops were a complementary combination. The addition of dairying activities to such a combination was an added factor in reducing the variability of farm income. Mennonites spread their risks to a greater degree than Swedes, who seem to have taken advantage of improved market conditions to increase corn and broomcorn production. The French Canadians, however, were taking even greater advantage of these conditions by increasing their corn and greatly reducing their wheat acreages. With dairying and beef production common on French-Canadian farms, they were creating a farming system with a less risky source of income than the Swedes or even the Mennonites.

The control-group farmers in Aurora Township also specialized their farm production. There were more two-enterprise and fewer three-enterprise combinations, more acres of corn, and fewer acres of wheat than in 1875. Among the control-group farmers in Rockville and Meridian townships the number of two-enterprise combinations increased (fig. 33) but not at the expense of the three-enterprise combinations. In general, the trend was toward an increasingly diversified system, with corn-wheat-dairy combinations, more acres of corn, and fewer acres of wheat than in 1875. Broomcorn was also an occasional third crop in the farm combinations of Rockville Township. Although all three ethnic groups had farming prac-

TABLE 15  Percentage Distribution of Labor on Swedish, Mennonite, and French-Canadian Farms, 1885

| Group | Swedes | | | Mennonites | | | French Canadians | | |
|---|---|---|---|---|---|---|---|---|---|
| Township | Union | Rockville | Others* | Menno | Meridian | Others | Shirley | Aurora | Others* |
| Wheat | 21.6 | 9.1 | 10.2 | 36.5 | 33.4 | 31.1 | 2.6 | 2.3 | 2.7 |
| Corn | 47.1 | 45.1 | 53.3 | 33.1 | 40.3 | 40.0 | 67.7 | 69.5 | 66.9 |
| Oats | 7.4 | 0.0 | 0.5 | 8.8 | 7.3 | 6.1 | 6.0 | 5.9 | 4.9 |
| Potatoes | 1.8 | 0.0 | 0.2 | 3.4 | 1.5 | 1.9 | 1.5 | 1.3 | 2.1 |
| Sorghum | 0.1 | 0.0 | 1.4 | 0.3 | 0.4 | 0.2 | 0.0 | 0.0 | 0.1 |
| Broomcorn | 12.3 | 12.5 | 5.2 | 0.0 | 0.0 | 0.1 | 0.0 | 0.0 | 0.0 |
| Millets | 0.8 | 3.6 | 0.8 | 1.0 | 2.1 | 2.2 | 2.1 | 2.5 | 2.6 |
| Tame grass | 0.1 | 0.0 | 0.0 | 0.0 | 1.4 | 0.6 | 0.1 | 0.1 | 0.5 |
| Prairie grass | 7.5 | 0.4 | 0.9 | 0.2 | 5.8 | 7.5 | 3.4 | 2.9 |  |
| Dairy cows | 0.1 | 13.1 | 14.2 | 12.9 | 6.4 | 6.6 | 12.8 | 12.5 | 11.7 |
| Beef cattle | 0.1 | 1.8 | 1.5 | 0.7 | 0.4 | 1.7 | 0.8 | 0.7 | 1.2 |
| Sheep | 0.0 | 0.0 | 0.1 | 0.0 | 0.0 | 0.0 | 0.0 | 0.0 | 0.0 |
| Hogs | 0.0 | 2.3 | 1.6 | 0.5 | 0.5 | 0.8 | 2.0 | 1.7 | 2.2 |
| Other | 1.1 | 2.1 | 10.8 | 2.5 | 0.5 | 1.2 | 1.0 | 0.6 | 0.8 |

*Others refers to the control-group farmers from the non-segregated township (Rockville, Meridian, and Aurora).

tices very similar to those of their control groups, the French Canadians were again the closest to the neighboring control-group farmers.

*Farming Patterns in 1895*

The census of 1895 was taken during the first very serious setback to farming in central Kansas. Not only had there been a disastrous and prolonged drought beginning more than two years earlier but also a major economic recession that sent the market price for farm produce tumbling. It was a severe setback for everyone, but it was the most serious for farmers who had gone out on a limb and specialized their farm production. The farmers best able to survive the catastrophe had minimized the risk of losses and diversified their farming patterns. For those who had specialized, the only solution was to try to diversify as quickly as possible or else continue to run the risk of being wiped out financially.

The Swedes in both Rockville and Union townships continued to diversify their farm operations, with an increase in the number of three-, four-, and five-enterprise combinations from 1885 to 1895. In Union Township the percentage of four- and five-enterprise combinations increased from 6 percent to 22 percent respectively, and from 1 percent to 16 percent between 1885 and 1895. Mennonites also showed signs of diversifying during this period of stress. In Menno Township the representation of four-enterprise farms increased from 14 percent to 32 percent and of five-enterprise farms from 3 percent to 26 percent. In Meridian Township the increases in five-enterprise combinations were from 8 percent to 20 percent. The French-Canadian farmers, however, did not achieve the same degree of enterprise diversification. Although numbers of one- and two-enterprise combinations on French-Canadian farms declined and three-enterprise combinations significantly increased, there was no trend toward more four- and five-enterprise combinations, as found among the Swedes and to a greater extent among the Mennonites.

The Swedes had trimmed their sails to the sudden change in the economic climate, although the major crop on many of their farms was still corn (table 16). Wheat and broomcorn were alternative cash crops as the second most important enterprises in the combination. Dairy farming had now returned to a prominent position in the Swedish farming system as a third enterprise, and prairie hay was a fourth. The typical combinations on Swedish farms, then, were corn-wheat-dairy–prairie hay or corn-broomcorn-dairy–prairie hay. A similar pattern prevailed among Swedish

TABLE 16 Percentage Distribution of Labor on Swedish, Mennonite, and French-Canadian Farms, 1895

| Group | Swedes | | | Mennonites | | | French Canadians | | |
|---|---|---|---|---|---|---|---|---|---|
| Township | Union | Rockville | Others | Menno | Meridian | Others | Shirley | Aurora | Others |
| Wheat | 18.4 | 11.0 | 11.3 | 29.6 | 23.8 | 16.4 | 0.5 | 2.3 | 0.4 |
| Corn | 36.6 | 43.4 | 49.2 | 24.9 | 33.0 | 43.1 | 56.1 | 63.4 | 58.0 |
| Oats | 3.5 | 4.7 | 2.7 | 9.6 | 7.3 | 7.1 | 20.4 | 14.4 | 12.7 |
| Potatoes | 1.9 | 0.4 | 0.7 | 2.0 | 1.0 | 0.8 | 0.4 | 0.5 | 1.1 |
| Sorghum | 0.9 | 0.7 | 1.7 | 1.9 | 2.7 | 2.2 | 1.2 | 0.9 | 2.0 |
| Broomcorn | 12.6 | 12.9 | 11.9 | 0.0 | 0.0 | 0.0 | 0.0 | 0.0 | 0.0 |
| Millets | 0.5 | 1.1 | 1.0 | 0.4 | 2.1 | 4.0 | 1.9 | 1.0 | 2.5 |
| Tame grass | 1.4 | 0.4 | 0.4 | 0.0 | 0.1 | 0.2 | 0.0 | 0.2 | 0.5 |
| Prairie grass | 10.6 | 7.7 | 6.4 | 9.0 | 7.1 | 7.2 | 7.8 | 7.1 | 7.8 |
| Dairy cows | 10.1 | 14.6 | 10.7 | 17.7 | 17.5 | 4.8 | 10.6 | 10.4 | 13.2 |
| Beef cattle | 1.7 | 1.9 | 2.5 | 0.8 | 1.0 | 1.0 | 0.7 | 0.5 | 0.8 |
| Sheep | 0.0 | 0.0 | 0.1 | 0.0 | 0.0 | 0.0 | 0.0 | 0.0 | 0.0 |
| Hogs | 0.8 | 1.2 | 1.0 | 0.9 | 1.1 | 0.9 | 0.4 | 0.4 | 0.6 |
| Other | 1.0 | 0.0 | 0.4 | 3.2 | 3.3 | 2.3 | 0.0 | 0.4 | 0.4 |

farmers in Rockville Township, except that dairying was frequently ranked second and the wheat/broomcorn alternatives were third. Dairying had also assumed a prominent position in Mennonite farming—it ranked first among the farmers in Menno Township and second in Meridian Township. Wheat, on the other hand, was somewhat less important in the farming system, having slipped to second place in Menno and third in the farm combinations of Meridian Township. The representative farm combination for Menno Township was dairy-wheat-corn-oats, with possibly prairie hay as a fifth enterprise. Corn was overwhelmingly the most important crop on French-Canadian farms—wheat seemed to have been dropped almost completely from the farming system. The most frequent combination on French-Canadian farms in Shirley Township was a corn-oats-dairy one and for Aurora Township corn-dairy-oats.

The evidence is strong that many farmers adjusted their farming system to the prevailing climatic and economic conditions of the early 1890s; increased emphasis on dairying is just one example of this. The Swedes, however, still clung to several of their cash crops—wheat and broomcorn —whereas the Mennonites reduced the relative emphasis on wheat growing. The appearance of prairie hay in the farming combinations during this period also suggests that more attention was being given to livestock. The importance of corn is further evidence of an attempt to shift to livestock, either cattle or hogs. Although the price of beef cattle had fallen sharply since 1890, the price of hogs had actually begun to rise by 1895. On French-Canadian farms, however, considerably more emphasis was given to corn production than on Swedish and Mennonite farms, and the change in emphasis represented a greater risk in terms of farm income.

The French-Canadian farmers, having specialized their farming patterns in the 1880s, seemed unwilling to adjust and diversify their system quickly when the disaster period began in 1892. In contrast, the Mennonites were much better able to adapt their system of farming than were the others during the early 1890s.

The three control groups of farmers also showed signs of adapting to this difficult period in farming. In all three samples—Rockville, Meridian, and Aurora townships—from 1885 to 1895 the number of single- and two-enterprise combinations decreased and the number of three-, four-, and five-enterprise combinations increased. However, the control-group farmers usually placed a heavier emphasis on corn production than their Swedish and Mennonite neighbors; the French Canadians were very similar in this respect to their control group. There is no evidence that the control groups had developed a better system of farming or adjusted more rapidly to the special conditions of 1895 than the ethnic groups.

## Farming Patterns in 1905

The decade between 1895 and 1905 was one of slow recovery from the depressed market conditions and disastrous droughts of the early 1890s. In the years from 1895 to 1900 crop yields generally were good and market prices rose. After the turn of the century there were two short-lived droughts, one in 1901 and another in 1904, which reminded farmers that crop failure could occur again. After 1900 the market for farm produce began to fluctuate once more as the initial recovery came to an end. The economic recovery of the late 1890s did not become an economic boom, and a certain nervousness persisted. Only the most adventurous gamblers would have been tempted to specialize their farming system. For the majority of farmers it was a time for caution and consolidation of the changes made to the farming system in the early 1890s, with, perhaps, the introduction of additional drought-resistant feed crops, which were being recommended to farmers in Kansas.

The trend in the farming system toward diversification with a larger number of enterprises continued on Swedish farms through the decade from 1895 to 1905 as the percentage of three- and four-enterprise farms increased yet again. On Mennonite farms, few farmers were organizing four- and five-enterprise farms, and there was a small shift toward three- and two-enterprise farms. French-Canadian farmers, however, evidenced the greatest change toward diversification, with substantial increases in the number of four- and five-enterprise farms. Despite the fact that many French-Canadian farmers were making adjustments in the diversification of their farms, this group still operated considerably more single- and two-enterprise farms than anyone else. In Shirley and Aurora townships these two categories accounted for 25 percent and 20 percent of all French-Canadian farms, in Menno and Meridian townships 17 percent and 12 percent of Mennonite farms, and in Union and Rockville 14 percent and 12 percent of Swedish farms.

Between 1895 and 1905 some small changes occurred in the cropping and livestock patterns of Swedish farms. Fewer Swedish farmers selected corn as their most important enterprise, and more selected wheat growing and dairying than in 1895 (table 17). The production of broomcorn, however, had declined considerably since 1895. The most popular farm

TABLE 17  Percentage Distribution of Labor on Swedish, Mennonite, and French-Canadian Farms, 1905

| Group | Swedes | | | Mennonites | | | French Canadians | | |
|---|---|---|---|---|---|---|---|---|---|
| Township | Union | Rockville | Others | Menno | Meridian | Others | Shirley | Aurora | Others |
| Wheat | 20.1 | 14.4 | 13.4 | 25.1 | 23.4 | 19.5 | 8.7 | 7.6 | 7.5 |
| Corn | 36.0 | 41.3 | 46.0 | 26.3 | 28.0 | 33.7 | 42.8 | 36.9 | 40.7 |
| Oats | 2.3 | 2.3 | 1.9 | 9.3 | 7.5 | 6.9 | 11.5 | 14.5 | 9.5 |
| Potatoes | 0.1 | 0.8 | 1.1 | 1.4 | 1.5 | 1.7 | 1.1 | 0.0 | 0.6 |
| Sorghum | 0.0 | 0.2 | 0.6 | 2.2 | 1.2 | 1.2 | 0.6 | 0.8 | 1.1 |
| Broomcorn | 6.2 | 2.2 | 1.0 | 0.0 | 0.0 | 0.0 | 0.0 | 0.0 | 0.0 |
| Millets | 2.2 | 1.3 | 1.1 | 1.4 | 1.5 | 1.2 | 1.6 | 2.5 | 1.7 |
| Tame grass | 2.5 | 3.2 | 3.8 | 0.6 | 2.2 | 2.9 | 2.4 | 1.2 | 1.3 |
| Prairie grass | 11.9 | 13.6 | 8.0 | 9.1 | 9.1 | 10.9 | 6.5 | 11.2 | 10.1 |
| Dairy cows | 12.4 | 11.5 | 17.3 | 21.8 | 21.4 | 17.0 | 19.0 | 21.0 | 22.8 |
| Beef cattle | 4.2 | 6.6 | 3.5 | 1.3 | 1.9 | 2.5 | 2.3 | 2.5 | 2.1 |
| Sheep | 0.0 | 0.0 | 0.0 | 0.0 | 0.0 | 0.0 | 0.0 | 0.0 | 0.0 |
| Hogs | 1.1 | 2.4 | 2.2 | 0.6 | 1.2 | 1.5 | 3.5 | 1.7 | 2.5 |
| Other | 1.0 | 0.2 | 0.1 | 0.9 | 1.1 | 1.0 | 0.0 | 0.1 | 0.1 |

combination was a corn-wheat-dairy combination, with prairie hay as a fourth enterprise on some farms. Also on Mennonite farms few changes had taken place in the farming systems from 1895. There was a very slight decline in the emphasis given to corn and a slight increase in wheat production. Consequently dairying, corn growing, and wheat growing were of approximately equal importance. The rank order of the most frequent farm combination, however, was dairy-wheat-corn, with prairie hay and oats as a fourth enterprise in some combinations. The most remarkable changes occurred on French-Canadian farms: corn, although still top crop, was much less important than it had been in 1895, increased attention was given to wheat farming, and livestock (including not only dairying but also beef cattle and hog production) appeared with greater emphasis in the farming combinations. The typical farming pattern was a corn-dairy-oats-wheat combination, with some prairie hay also apparent in the system.

Although dairying along with corn and wheat production appeared in the farming combinations of all three groups, the rank order of various activities and the emphasis given to each within the combination suggest differences in the level of risk taken. Given that corn production was more risky and dairying less so, Mennonites adopted the lowest-risk farming strategy, since they placed a greater emphasis on dairying and a lesser emphasis on corn than anyone else. Although the French Canadians had increased dairying activities to the same level as the Swedes (and perhaps even slightly higher), the emphasis given to corn on French-Canadian farms was still higher than on Swedish ones, and so the level of risk was higher on the French-Canadian farms.

Finally, another method of lowering risk on central Kansas farms was the adoption of new drought-resistant crops, such as the sorghums and alfalfa. Although acreages were still very small, more alfalfa and more kafir corn was grown on Swedish and French-Canadian farms than Mennonite farms. The Mennonites for their part cultivated a few acres of sorghum, while the others did not seem to favor it at all. The acreages devoted to special drought-resistant crops were still very few in 1905, and the acreage differences between the three ethnic groups were so small as to be insignificant.

The changing systems of farming among the control-group farmers followed the same general trend as that of their ethnic neighbors. In Rockville Township the Swedes' neighbors reduced risks with a decline in single- and two-enterprise combinations and an increase in three-, four-, and five-enterprise combinations. The changes among the Mennonites' neighbors followed the shift on Mennonite farms from fewer four- and five-enterprise to more three-enterprise farms than in 1895. In Aurora, however, the control-group farmers did not diversify, not even a little as their French-Canadian neighbors had done; there was an increase in two- and three-enterprise combinations and a drop in five-enterprise farms. The shift in farming patterns was also small among the control groups between 1895 and 1905. Although the farmers in Aurora Township gave more attention to dairying than their French-Canadian neighbors and those in Rockville and Meridian still stressed corn production to a greater degree than their Swedish and Mennonite neighbors, these contrasts in farming emphasis served to make the control groups more similar to their ethnic neighbors, even though their systems were still somewhat riskier than those of the ethnic farmers.

### Farming Patterns in 1915

When the census was taken in the spring of 1915, war had broken out in Europe and market prices, although climbing rapidly, still had not reached wartime peaks. In fact, only the prewar increase in farm prices affected farming decisions for the crop year of 1914, which were reported to the census enumerator. Consequently the conditions on which farming decisions were made in 1914 were of steadily improving farm prices, but not the spectacular increase that began later that year and continued through 1915. The market outlook was good in the spring of 1914—the only negative factor was the short, sudden drought that had severely affected the corn crop in 1913. Wheat yields had also been low in 1913, but to a lesser degree than corn yields. The cause was a slightly wetter-than-average spring in 1913 rather than the midsummer drought, which came after the wheat had been harvested. For the increasing number of young farmers who operated farms in 1914, the market prospect must have looked good. The moisture shortage of 1913 was a warning that the daring might choose to ignore, and the temptation must have been strong to specialize in wheat production.

The Swedish farmers did not succumb to that temptation: their proportion of three- and two-enterprise farms declined and four-, five-, and six-enterprise combinations increased in 1915. The shift toward four- and five-enterprise farms was found among the Mennonites, where there was also a decline in the percentage of three-enterprise combinations. The French Canadians in Shirley Township also shifted to four- and five-enterprise combinations, and although those in Aurora Township increased the percentage of three- and five-enterprise farms, the percentage of four-enterprise farms decreased. The trend toward diversified farming systems that began in 1895 continued through 1915. The Swedes were now the most diversified and the French Canadians the least diversified, although the differences among the three groups were declining.

By 1915 the production of corn had dropped on the Swedish farms in Union Township, but there was almost no change in the status of wheat growing and dairying (table 18). Slightly more attention was given to beef cattle and the production of hay than in 1905. Among the Swedish farmers in Rockville Township changes were even smaller, for although wheat was slightly more important than in 1905, the status of corn production had not changed at all. The representative farm combination for these Swedes was corn–dairy–wheat–prairie grass, with the cultivation of tame grasses or beef cattle production as possible fifth enterprises. Among the Mennonites and especially among the French Canadians there was a very marked shift to wheat farming and a decline in corn production. This obviously put them in an excellent position to capitalize on the rapidly increasing price of wheat in the latter part of 1914 and in 1915. Dairying was still as important in the second-ranked position of the farm combination as it had been in 1905. The usual combination on the Mennonite and French-Canadian farms in Shirley Township was wheat-dairy-corn-oats, with prairie grass as an alternative to oats or as a fifth enterprise. The French-Canadian farmers in Aurora Township frequently chose prairie grass as a third enterprise, with oats and corn as alternative fourth or fifth enterprises.

It is difficult to determine which of these combinations represented a greater degree of risk than the others. The Swedes gave as much emphasis to corn as the Mennonites and French Canadians gave to wheat; they also gave as much emphasis to wheat as the Mennonites and French Canadians gave to corn. The emphasis Swedish farmers placed on corn involved a high degree of risk, because corn yields fluctuated more than wheat yields, and the corn record had not been nearly as successful as that of wheat since the recovery of the late 1890s. Corn was fed to livestock, and so it appears that the Swedes were bent on a strategy of lowering risks by turning to livestock rather than wheat. Indeed, the Swedes placed considerably more emphasis on beef cattle and hog production than the other ethnic farmers. The switch to livestock on Swedish farms may be explained in part by the quality of the land in Union Township: the northern half of the township, the Smoky Hill Buttes, are best suited for cattle grazing. But the poor quality of the land is not a complete explanation for the prudent farm-

TABLE 18 Percentage Distribution of Labor on Swedish, Mennonite, and French-Canadian Farms, 1915

| Group | Swedes | | | Mennonites | | | French Canadians | | |
|---|---|---|---|---|---|---|---|---|---|
| Township | Union | Rockville | Others | Menno | Meridian | Others | Shirley | Aurora | Others |
| Wheat | 18.3 | 17.3 | 17.7 | 29.1 | 39.0 | 34.3 | 31.8 | 31.6 | 26.1 |
| Corn | 29.9 | 41.6 | 43.4 | 18.8 | 19.6 | 20.0 | 18.9 | 8.3 | 29.9 |
| Oats | 1.6 | 3.3 | 2.9 | 9.3 | 10.5 | 8.7 | 9.0 | 9.6 | 6.7 |
| Potatoes | 1.8 | 0.7 | 0.6 | 0.9 | 1.0 | 1.3 | 0.9 | 0.0 | 0.6 |
| Sorghum | 0.0 | 0.8 | 0.2 | 1.8 | 1.0 | 1.4 | 2.4 | 1.7 | 1.1 |
| Broomcorn | 0.0 | 0.0 | 0.0 | 0.0 | 0.0 | 0.0 | 0.0 | 0.0 | 0.0 |
| Millets | 4.8 | 2.3 | 3.4 | 1.1 | 1.0 | 0.8 | 1.7 | 2.2 | 1.5 |
| Tame grass | 8.1 | 5.2 | 5.1 | 1.2 | 2.2 | 3.6 | 2.4 | 2.9 | 4.9 |
| Prairie grass | 9.4 | 7.4 | 9.2 | 10.6 | 7.8 | 8.8 | 8.3 | 15.5 | 12.3 |
| Dairy cows | 15.1 | 14.3 | 10.2 | 25.1 | 12.8 | 14.4 | 21.5 | 25.4 | 20.3 |
| Beef cattle | 6.2 | 4.9 | 4.0 | 1.0 | 3.1 | 4.3 | 2.0 | 2.1 | 1.6 |
| Sheep | 0.0 | 0.0 | 0.0 | 0.0 | 0.0 | 0.0 | 0.0 | 0.0 | 0.0 |
| Hogs | 3.3 | 1.9 | 2.8 | 0.6 | 1.2 | 1.7 | 0.6 | 0.6 | 2.6 |
| Other | 1.5 | 0.3 | 0.5 | 0.5 | 0.8 | 0.7 | 0.5 | 0.1 | 0.4 |

ing strategy, since these uplands were generally unsuited for fodder crops, especially corn. The Swedish system was, however, increasingly diversified, and the income from livestock was spread over categories other than dairying, which served to reduce further Swedish income variability.

Quite apart from the diversification of livestock on Swedish farms, the Swedes' cautious approach is evidenced in the fact that they grew more drought-resistant crops than the Mennonites or French Canadians. The Swedish systems produced considerably more alfalfa and millet, and the percentage of farm labor given to kafir corn and feterita, though small, was still proportionally greater than on Mennonite and French-Canadian farms. Thus Swedish farmers, in making their farming decisions in 1915, showed greater caution than the Mennonites and French Canadians, but in doing so they minimized the windfall profits that could be made in 1915, when market prices for farm produce soared, especially wheat.

The control-group farmers also continued the trend toward more diversified farming systems in 1915. (The percentage of two- and three-enterprise farms declined and the proportion of four- and five-enterprise farms increased from 1905.) The cropping and livestock patterns, however, varied considerably. The control-group farmers in Rockville Township employed a system very similar to that of the Swedes—a corn-wheat-dairy combination with prairie hay as a fourth enterprise, and either beef cattle production or the cultivation of tame grasses such as timothy, clover, and alfalfa as a fifth enterprise. For the other farmers who lived in Meridian and Aurora townships, the usual combination was wheat-dairy-corn and prairie hay or oats alternating as fourth and fifth enterprises. The emphasis given to wheat and dairying in Aurora was about equal for control-group farms, whereas in Meridian corn production and dairying were about equal in importance. In general, dairying was not so strongly emphasized on control-group farms as it was on the local ethnic-group farms, and corn production was slightly more important than dairying. The reduced emphasis on dairying, combined with the fact that other livestock enterprises such as beef cattle and hog production were small-scale activities on the control groups' farms, resulted in a slightly higher level of risk for their farming patterns than those of their ethnic neighbors.

## Farming Patterns in 1925

The decade between 1915 and 1925 brought a sharp rise in the market price for farm produce after the outbreak of war in Europe, but when the war ended, prices fell sharply as the postwar depression set in after 1919 (fig. 31). A few years of good yields alternated with poor yields throughout the ten-year period, and there were no acute moisture shortages such as had adversely affected all crops in preceding decades. Thus nature provided no sharp reminders that farmers should keep their farm operations diversified. With market prices dropping sharply after 1919, many farmers must have felt pressure to specialize their farm production to a greater degree than before in order to maintain their existing level of income.

A return to farming specialization was indeed evident in the changing number of farm enterprises in the sample townships. A general decline took place in the number of four- and five-enterprise combinations and an increase in the number of one-, two-, and three-enterprise farms (fig. 32). On the Swedish farms in Union Township the biggest increase was in the three-enterprise category; in Rockville Township the changes were much smaller than in Union, but single- and two-enterprise farm combinations increased slightly. The biggest changes occurred on French-Canadian farms in both Shirley and Aurora townships, where there was a sharp swing toward two- and three-enterprise combinations and a significant drop in the percentage of four- and five-enterprise combinations below the levels of 1915. The exceptional group was the Mennonites. Although those living in Meridian Township increased the percentage of single-, two-, and three-enterprise farms at the expense of four-enterprise combinations, the majority of Mennonites (in Menno Township) did not return to a specialized farming system. Despite the fact that the percentage of five-enterprise farms declined from 27 percent to 18 percent and the proportion of three-enterprise farms from 28 percent to 16 percent, there was a sharp increase in four-enterprise combinations from 28 percent in 1915 to 47 percent in 1925. With this single exception, however, the general trend in the sample townships was toward specialized farming systems.

From 1915 to 1925, the emphasis given to different crop and livestock activities within the Swedish system did not change much. The relative importance of corn production, dairying, and wheat growing remained almost unchanged, although the importance of corn in the system was slightly reduced (table 19). The only noticeable changes since 1915 were in the acreages devoted to the new feed crops: the sorghums (kafir corn, feterita, and Sudan grass) and alfalfa, which appeared more frequently in the farm combinations of 1925. Dairying on the Mennonite farms seems to have accounted for a larger proportion of farming activity than in 1915, and it even ranked slightly ahead of wheat production in the farm combination.

TABLE 19 Percentage Distribution of Labor on Swedish, Mennonite, and French-Canadian Farms, 1925

| Group | Swedes | | | Mennonites | | | French Canadians | | |
|---|---|---|---|---|---|---|---|---|---|
| Township | Union | Rockville | Others | Menno | Meridian | Others | Shirley | Aurora | Others |
| Wheat | 17.4 | 17.7 | 17.7 | 29.4 | 35.2 | 34.0 | 16.1 | 6.5 | 8.6 |
| Corn | 30.0 | 34.6 | 36.5 | 13.6 | 11.2 | 15.9 | 34.5 | 27.2 | 38.6 |
| Oats | 2.5 | 4.7 | 4.0 | 10.0 | 10.3 | 8.0 | 6.9 | 11.6 | 6.8 |
| Potatoes | 0.5 | 0.4 | 1.9 | 0.9 | 1.2 | 0.8 | 0.7 | 0.3 | 1.5 |
| Sorghum | 1.6 | 0.5 | 1.8 | 2.7 | 1.4 | 0.9 | 1.8 | 2.3 | 1.5 |
| Alfalfa | 5.6 | 5.1 | 3.5 | 2.1 | 3.8 | 6.2 | 3.1 | 3.7 | 3.7 |
| Millets | 3.9 | 0.8 | 2.0 | 1.1 | 0.9 | 2.2 | 2.4 | 1.9 | 2.0 |
| Tame grass | 2.1 | 0.1 | 1.6 | 3.3 | 2.0 | 1.0 | 2.2 | 1.5 | 2.8 |
| Prairie grass | 2.3 | 0.2 | 0.2 | 1.9 | 2.3 | 1.3 | 0.4 | 1.0 | 0.9 |
| Dairy cows | 21.7 | 26.6 | 21.8 | 31.7 | 28.5 | 25.3 | 26.3 | 41.4 | 28.6 |
| Beef cattle | 9.6 | 6.3 | 7.0 | 2.0 | 1.8 | 2.5 | 3.7 | 1.9 | 2.4 |
| Sheep | 0.0 | 0.0 | 0.5 | 0.1 | 0.4 | 0.0 | 0.0 | 0.0 | 0.0 |
| Hogs | 2.1 | 1.9 | 1.3 | 0.8 | 0.6 | 0.8 | 1.9 | 0.5 | 2.2 |
| Other | 0.7 | 1.1 | 0.2 | 0.4 | 0.4 | 1.1 | 0.0 | 0.2 | 0.4 |

The typical combination on Mennonite farms in 1925 was dairy-wheat-corn-oats, with about equal emphasis given to the first two enterprises. As always, the biggest changes seemed to have been registered on French-Canadian farms. Wheat growing, which had been so important in 1915, was now relegated to a much lower position in the cropping pattern and corn was reestablished as the major crop. In Shirley Township the usual farm combination was corn-dairy-wheat, with some oats, beef cattle, or alfalfa growing as a fourth enterprise. In Aurora Township dairying seems to have demanded more labor than corn, and the representative combination was dairy-corn-oats, with a little wheat as a possible fourth enterprise.

So far as risk was concerned, the farming decisions of the Swedes and the Mennonites had changed only slightly since 1915. The small reduction in emphasis given to corn and the small increase in dairy herds only served to reduce the risk factor slightly. Of the two groups the Mennonites placed a greater emphasis on dairying and a lesser emphasis on corn production. The changes in corn and dairying, combined with the increase in multiple-enterprise combinations, suggests that their farming system involved fewer risks than the Swedish system. In farming patterns the French Canadians were more akin to the Swedes than the Mennonites, with their greater emphasis on corn and reduced emphasis on wheat. Although dairy herds were common on French-Canadian farms, the general livestock picture was not as diversified, so that the French-Canadian system probably involved a slightly higher level of risk than the Swedish system.

French Canadians also seem to have been less interested in the new feed and forage crops that were able to withstand the moisture shortages of central Kansas. The acreage given to sorghum crops—kafir corn, and Sudan grass—and alfalfa was generally smaller than on Swedish and Mennonite farms. During this decade the use of prairie hay disappeared from most of the farms in the sample townships, and alfalfa seems to have taken its place as the major forage crop. Although the differences in risk levels between the three groups seem to have diminished during this period, the Swedish system probably involved the lowest level of risk and the French-Canadian system the highest.

The control-group farmers demonstrated the same shift as their ethnic neighbors: away from four- and five-enterprise farms to two- and three-enterprise ones. This represented an adjustment to the market conditions for agricultural produce rather than to any special climatic conditions between 1915 and 1925. In Rockville, Meridian, and Aurora townships the percentage of three-enterprise farms rose to 46, 37, and 35 percent, respectively, whereas four-enterprise farms declined to 16, 22, and 18 percent, respectively (fig. 33). From 1915, the major changes in control-group farming systems were that American farmers in Rockville and Meridian townships reduced their emphasis on corn and increased the attention given to dairying, although not to the extent of their Swedish and Mennonite neighbors. The control-group farmers in Aurora Township dropped wheat growing from their farming system, just as the French Canadians had done. They also increased corn production, and since they had not abandoned corn to the same extent as the French Canadians had in 1915, by 1925 the control-group farmers had a greater corn emphasis than their neighbors. The representative farm combinations for the control-group farmers in 1925 were corn-dairy-wheat in Rockville Township; wheat-dairy-corn, with oats as a fourth enterprise, in Meridian; and a dairy-corn-wheat combination, with oats as an alternative third enterprise to wheat, in Aurora Township. The magnitude of the changes from 1915 to 1925 in the farming systems of the control-group farmers was greater than in the Swedish and Mennonite systems, though approximately equal to or even less than the sharp changes in the French-Canadian farming patterns.

Over the fifty-year period from 1875 to 1925 the farming systems in central Kansas became increasingly diversified, and new patterns of farming emerged that were better suited to the problems of uncertain moisture supply and fluctuating market prices. The Mennonites took the lead in the diversification of farming activities and by 1925 had achieved it to a greater degree than either of the other two ethnic groups. The French Canadians, on the other hand, fluctuated most widely, changing their farming system to a greater degree than anyone else and in such a way as to suggest that their farming decisions were more finely attuned to the condition of the market than to the hazards of climate. This was particularly true in 1895 and 1925, when market prices were falling: farmers tried to survive by specializing their farm production. The Mennonites' farming decisions seem best adapted to the combined effects of weather and the economy, so that their farming pattern gave them advantages in overcoming the disastrous conditions of the early 1890s and in taking advantage of the excellent market conditions for wheat in 1915. In contrast, the Swedes seemed to have adjusted slowly to the changing economic conditions, and after 1895 their concern about the uncertainty of climatic conditions was always evident, especially in 1915, when cautious farming strategies prevented them from maximizing profits on their farms.

TABLE 20   Value of the $D^2$ Statistic for Differences between
Swedish, Mennonite and French-Canadian Farming Systems,
1875–1925

| Groups | 1875 | 1885 | 1895 | 1905 | 1915 | 1925 |
|---|---|---|---|---|---|---|
| Swedes/Mennonites | 16.02 | 20.02 | 25.82 | 53.83 | 53.87 | 21.41 |
| Swedes/French Canadians | 38.55 | 46.11 | 77.54 | 29.70 | 34.68 | 8.02 |
| Mennonites/French Canadians | 9.49 | 53.45 | 80.02 | 27.25 | 5.37 | 24.05 |

## Ecological Adaptation and Americanization over Fifty Years

Although substantial differences still existed among the ethnic groups in 1925, their farming systems did appear to be much more similar to one another than they had been in the 1870s and the 1880s. Each group in its own way adjusted to the special ecological conditions in central Kansas, but the questions of the rate at which the changes were made and whether indeed the adaptation of all three groups was a continuous and unbroken process remain to be answered. There is also the question of which group was becoming the most similar to the local, American-born control group, as evidence of its rapid rate of Americanization. And finally, the importance of segregation in the rate of assimilation and Americanization of the three ethnic groups remains to be determined. Discriminant analyses have been used to investigate these questions, the results of which are presented below.

Discriminant analysis is a multivariate statistical analysis for more than one variable of the relations among several groups. In this case, the groups are the sample populations of Swedes, Mennonites, French Canadians, and control-group farmers in central Kansas; the variables are the percentage labor input values for the different crop and livestock enterprises on each farm. In the discriminant analysis model a critical level of .05 is established for including variables. One of the products of this analysis is the Mahalanobis $D^2$ statistic, which is a numerical value of the similarity between each pair of groups being tested.[9] The larger the size of the $D^2$ statistic, the greater the difference between the groups. The $D^2$ statistic is used in the subsequent discussion as a measure of the similarity among the different sample populations or groups in terms of their farming systems (table 20).

In the years before 1900, the differences between each pair of ethnic groups continued to widen; the really anomalous group was the French

TABLE 21    Values of the $D^2$ Statistic for Differences between
Ethnic and Control-Group Farming Systems, 1875–1925

| Groups | 1875 | 1885 | 1895 | 1905 | 1915 | 1925 |
|---|---|---|---|---|---|---|
| Swedes/others | 14.86 | 17.49 | 7.35 | 6.59 | 4.89 | 3.19 |
| Mennonites/others | 4.95 | 6.30 | 12.00 | 4.98 | 4.33 | 4.77 |
| French Canadians/others | 5.18 | 1.58 | 5.63 | 5.53 | 3.74 | 2.72 |

Canadians, whose pattern of farming was quite different from that of the Swedish and Mennonite groups. The years of drought and economic recession in the 1890s, however, seemed to have had an equalizing effect, drawing the three groups closer together than before—by 1905 the distances between each pair of groups were approximately similar. In 1915 both the Mennonites and the French Canadians had adjusted their farming systems to increase wheat production and the patterns were fairly similar, whereas the Swedish farmers diversified their operations. But once the expansion of farm prices had subsided after World War I, it was the Mennonites who were anomalous, having the most diversified farm operations in 1925. Thus, although the patterns of farming were becoming more similar after 1900, by 1925 the Mennonites were still the anomalous group; the Swedes and French Canadians were more alike in their farming decisions.

The French Canadians were often the most similar to the local control group (of mostly American-born farmers) than the Swedish or Mennonite farmers were to their neighbors, at least before 1900. French Canadians, with long experience in farming in North America and particularly in the American Midwest, had adopted most rapidly the farming patterns of the American born. The Mennonites at first also seemed to follow the lead provided by their American neighbors, except in 1895 when they made their own adaptations to the special circumstances then obtaining. Swedish farmers seem to have been slow to follow the patterns established by their American-born neighbors, although by 1895 their farming systems were more in line than they had been. After 1900 the differences between the ethnic groups and their respective control groups became smaller and smaller. French Canadians were becoming most like their American neighbors, and the Swedes appeared to be taking on characteristics of the Americans more rapidly than the Mennonites, although the differences were quite small by 1925 (table 21).

The growing similarity between the immigrants and their American

TABLE 22    Values of the $D^2$ Statistic for Differences between
First- and Second-Generation Ethnics and Control-Group
Farming Systems, 1905–25

| Group | 1905 | 1915 | 1925 |
|---|---|---|---|
| S1/control group | 5.72 | 2.53 | 2.09 |
| S2/control group | 1.42 | 2.02 | 3.67 |
| M1/control group | 6.00 | 3.69 | 3.16 |
| M2/control group | 1.64 | 2.27 | 3.87 |
| F1/control group | 1.34 | 1.47 | 1.57 |
| F2/control group | 1.83 | 3.85 | 2.56 |

S1: First-generation Swedes                    M1: First-generation Mennonites
S2: Second-generation Swedes                   M2: Second-generation Mennonites
F1: First-generation French Canadians
F2: Second-generation French Canadians

neighbors after 1905 was due in part to the increasing number of second-generation (i.e., American-born) ethnics who were taking over the operation of farms (table 22). In 1905 the second-generation ethnics were more similar to the control group of American farmers, except French Canadians, where the differences were already quite small. By 1925, the differences between the first-generation immigrants and the Americans had diminished considerably. It is of some note that when the Kansas-born ethnics took over the management of farms in large numbers (for French Canadians in 1915, for Swedes and Mennonites in 1925), their farming patterns diverged slightly from those of local American farmers. A reemergence of a distinctively ethnic approach in farming is not unlikely; the divergence is probably explained by the youthfulness of the new generation of ethnic farmers and the difficulties of young farmers in building up their capital investment for farming. By 1925 the difference between the second-generation French Canadians and the control group of local American farmers was again declining.

The differences between farming systems in the segregated and non-segregated Swedish townships were greater than for the Mennonite and French-Canadian townships in the early decades of farming in central Kansas (table 23). The larger difference is perhaps a reflection of the different origins of the two Swedish populations: those living in Rockville Township had come primarily from the Illinois settlements, whereas many of those in Union Township had come directly to Kansas from Sweden. After

TABLE 23   Values of the $D^2$ Statistic for Differences between Segregated and Nonsegregated Samples of Swedish, Mennonite, and French-Canadian Farming Systems, 1875–1925

| Group | 1875 | 1885 | 1895 | 1905 | 1915 | 1925 |
|---|---|---|---|---|---|---|
| Swedes | 22.28 | 34.82 | 3.03 | 2.23 | 4.05 | 2.38 |
| Mennonites | 6.36 | 3.70 | 4.85 | 3.69 | 8.72 | 4.22 |
| French Canadians | 15.06 | 0.57 | 2.15 | 5.95 | 11.63 | 7.77 |

TABLE 24   Values of the $D^2$ Statistic for Differences between Segregated and Nonsegregated Samples and Control-Group Farming Systems, 1875–1925

| Groups | 1875 | 1885 | 1895 | 1905 | 1915 | 1925 |
|---|---|---|---|---|---|---|
| SA/control group | 26.73 | 40.20 | 6.10 | 6.23 | 5.74 | 3.79 |
| SB/control group | 0.82 | 1.64 | 1.45 | 1.47 | 1.41 | 1.44 |
| MA/control group | 7.59 | 8.42 | 15.68 | 6.76 | 7.32 | 6.31 |
| MB/control group | 0.92 | 0.86 | 2.74 | 1.46 | 0.81 | 1.99 |
| FA/control group | 7.42 | 1.64 | 5.08 | 9.54 | 11.70 | 4.75 |
| FB/control group | 2.34 | 1.51 | 2.27 | 1.65 | 1.23 | 3.11 |

SA: Union Swedes     MA: Menno Mennonites     FA: Shirley F. Canadians
SB: Rockville Swedes     MB: Meridian Mennonites     FB: Aurora F. Canadians

1900, however, the differences between the two Swedish samples were smaller than those between either the Mennonite or the French-Canadian samples. There was, however, considerable variability in the farming decisions of the French Canadians as young, Kansas-born French Canadians took over their parents' farms. However, in order to determine whether a segregated pattern of living affected the rate of assimilation of each ethnic group, it is necessary to compare the farming system of the segregated and nonsegregated ethnic samples with the local control group.

The statistics in table 24 make apparent that the nonsegregated samples were always similar to the control groups in their approaches to farming. Nevertheless, in the early years of farming segregation did seem to have an impact on the adaptation of Swedish farmers, and the residual effect of segregation was greatest for the Mennonites in later years of farming in central Kansas.

## Summary

In the early decades of farming in central Kansas the Swedish seemed to be the most uncertain of the three ethnic groups in making their farming decisions. They were slow to acquire the flexibility in decision making of the local American farmers or even of the Mennonites and French Canadians. The drought and depression of the 1890s had a great impact on the Swedes, so much so that the trend toward farm-enterprise diversification begun in 1895 continued through 1905 and 1915. By 1925, however, the Swedes returned to the general trend of reducing the number of enterprises per farm, thereby increasing not only the level of risk in their farming decisions but also their ability to maximize profits.

The Mennonites were also somewhat cautious in the early years of farming, but their farming decisions seem to have become increasingly assured as the decades passed, and they apparently had an uncanny ability to create the right system for the times. In 1895 their diversified system was better suited to the years of drought and low prices than the specialized farming of the French Canadians, and in 1915, a time when prices were rising, they seem to have been able to maximize their profits without greatly affecting the variability of their income. In 1925 they were the only group that increased the number of enterprises per farm, again exercising greater caution after the boom years had passed than either of the other two groups. They created the best balance in farming decisions—reducing the variability of income on the one hand, and maximizing profits on the other.

The French Canadians apparently were the least cautious of the three ethnic groups in the early years. Their changes in farming systems from one decade to the next suggest a high degree of flexibility in decision making, and also that their decisions were influenced by changing market conditions to a greater degree than those of the other two ethnic groups. This was particularly evident not only in the years of declining market prices (1895 and 1925), when they attempted to maintain their farm income by increased emphasis on corn production, but also in the years of rising market prices, such as 1914, when they switched over to wheat production. In this ability to turn from specialization in one crop to another from one decade to the next, they were more akin to the American-born farmers than were either the Swedish or Mennonite farmers.

In the early decades, there was also greater variability within the French-Canadian group in terms of different combinations of crops and livestock, although by 1915 the Swedish farmers were trying a variety of enterprise combinations. The Swedes in particular evidenced an increasingly varied livestock pattern on their farms. More evidence of beef cattle and hog production, alfalfa growing, and the new sorghum crops could be found on the Swedish farms than elsewhere. The increased interest in livestock may be explained in part by the fact that the hilly upland in northern Union Township was better suited to grazing than to crop production. The Mennonites, however, demonstrated great internal uniformity: most of the farmers employed the same crop and livestock enterprises, and there was less variation in the rank order of these enterprises within the combination than for Swedes and French Canadians.

By 1925 it was clear that the French Canadians were more similar to the American born than either the Swedes or Mennonites, although in the final decade of the study, the Swedes had also become like the American born. The Mennonites also *appear* to have taken on some characteristics of American farming, but not to the same degree as the others. The Mennonites, however, had developed a system of farming that seems to have been better suited to conditions in central Kansas than either the Swedes, the French Canadians, or even the American born. Consequently, there is a problem here in equating Americanization with ecological adjustment, because it implies that American farmers would be the first to develop farming systems ideally suited to the special climatic conditions of Kansas. But, it may be argued that American farmers from Iowa, Wisconsin, and Illinois suffered the greatest handicap of all the farmers who came to central Kansas. These midwestern farmers had to learn that the system of farming that had worked so well in the humid, central Mississippi lowlands would not work in Kansas. They would have to put aside the farming strategies and techniques to which they were accustomed and develop new ones. Furthermore, it cannot be assumed that the exchange of information among farmers in central Kansas was in one direction, from Americans to the immigrants. Indeed, the influence of the ethnic groups, particularly the Mennonites, on the evolution of a successful American system of farming may have been greater than has generally been believed, especially in the years after 1900.

# 7

## Summary and Conclusions

The transition zone from the western prairies to the eastern high plains provides an ideal laboratory for observing the Americanization of immigrants and changes in farming patterns made by both ethnic and native-born American farmers as they adapted to unfamiliar moisture supply conditions. The problem of droughts was recognized rather crudely in the early years of settlement: only after several decades were the frequency, variations, and subtleties of the moisture problem fully appreciated. In passing through periods of uncertainty in the beginning and of imputed risk in the later years, farmers made a host of decisions on how large their farms should be, how the farms should be financed, the degree of mechanization that could and should be adopted, and also the combination of crops and livestock that would prove most successful in attaining their goals. In making these decisions the immigrant farmers revealed something of their value system, the degree to which they were prepared to take risks in order to attain those goals, and how they were adapting to American life within the context of North American commercial agriculture.

The assimilability of an immigrant depended on the extent to which he was prepared to break with his past—to loosen the bonds that tied him to family and kin-group—and strike out on his own as an independent individual. He would then be free to join (or to leave) that loose coalition of neighborliness that represented "community" on the agricultural frontier. Signs of latent independent individualism can sometimes be detected in changing attitudes toward the family and the church and its authority in the old country. On these grounds the Swedes would have seemed assimilable. The increasing frequency of the stem family in late nineteenth-century Sweden, on the one hand, and the Pietist revolt against the authority of the old order embodied in the state Lutheran church, on the other, suggest that individualism was slowly spreading in Swedish society. Strains similar to those in the Pietist protest were clearly evident in the Anwohner revolt among the Mennonites in southern Russia. But the old patriarchal family structure remained strong, and when the Czar's Russianization program threatened their distinctive identity and community life, Mennonites closed ranks. The Mennonites enjoyed a strong ethnic identity before they left Russia. Although French Canadians had a reputation for spirited independence since the earliest days of the fur trade, their sense of alienation in the Anglophone world of late eighteenth and nineteenth-century North America reinforced their distinctive identity. *La survivance* had been their watchword, and the bonds of extended family ties were powerful and pervasive along the lower St. Lawrence lowlands in the nineteenth century. Few would challenge the authority of the Roman Catholic church, which had played a critical role in preserving the French-Canadian cultural identity. Thus at the moment of leaving their homelands, the Swedes appeared eminently more assimilable than either the Mennonites or the French Canadians, although by the time of their arrival in Kansas, the French Canadians had faced a major challenge to church authority.

At first glance, religious fragmentation was a puzzling and fairly common phenomenon along the frontier. The three ethnic groups studied here were not exceptions. On one level the Chiniquy schism can be seen as the refusal of a proud French-Canadian priest to bow to the will of his Irish bishop and superior in Chicago. But on another level it can be seen as a culture-shock response to his first encounter with pluralism. Schism entered the Swedish settlements as part of a power struggle within the local community between the newly arrived pastor from Sweden and the founders who had invited him to come to Kansas. The issue over which they split concerned the right of the individual conscience to depart from conventional wisdom on the doctrine of atonement. The issue of individual rights, then, had penetrated the realm of theology and risen up to challenge Lutheran orthodoxy. Even among Mennonites there was some religious fragmentation (although less in central Kansas than in western Canada), with congregations distinguishing themselves from their neighbors on theological issues. Fragmentation may be interpreted as an element in the first stage of ethnogenesis: as each immigrant group adjusted to its new social environment, it began to forge a new identity by redefining its position vis-à-vis ecclesiastical authority. The redefinition of identity lay at the very core of ethnogenesis.

It should come as no surprise that immigrants began to redefine their identity in terms of small, localized communities, for they faced problems of anomie created by a landscape that seemed to overwhelm them. The great dome of prairie sky and the endless stretch of flat grassland reduced their initial pioneering efforts to minuscule proportions. But soon they imposed their own geometry on the landscape, with field boundaries that ran north-south and east-west following survey lines. They built simple shelters against the prairie wind and erected small churches, where they gathered and worshiped. Nearby, they marked off graveyards and buried their dead. In time the community took root, and the slowly domesticated landscape became familiar. The eye, no longer dominated by the horizon, picked out the bottomlands filled with lush corn and the river terraces trimmed in wheat stubble. Livestock browsed in the distance along the flanks of the buttes. This was their new home.

As the community developed, a new folklife emerged. To be sure, some traditions from the old country were retained: on Christmas morning, Swedes continued to rise in the early morning darkness and tramp along frosty roads with lanterns aloft to worship at first light. But new traditions were established too: the performance of Handel's *Messiah* at Easter in Lindsborg soon became a permanent fixture in the Swedish calendar throughout central Kansas. Communities spun a new folklore based on battles with scorching summer heat, invading grasshoppers, terrifying prairie fires, and the dangers of sudden blizzards and tornadoes. The earliest years were tough and trying, so that the accepted wisdom from an earlier home had short life on the Kansas prairies. Only in later decades would the settlers look back with nostalgia and retell tales of heroism and endurance as pioneers transformed an impersonal prairie landscape into the comforting countryside they now called home.

At an early stage in the settlement process, immigrant farmers reached out to make contact with their own kind in adjacent local communities, then with similar settlements scattered across the Midwest and eventually across the continent. The creation of an ethnic network marked a second stage in ethnogenesis: the affirmation of a distinctive identity. The network was established first as a consequence of chain migrations, whereby new arrivals brought news of fellow countrymen elsewhere in central Kansas or the Midwest. The process was developed by contacts among pastors who belonged to the same synod, by local and regional newspapers that circulated throughout the Midwest, or by membership in national organizations such as the St. Jean Baptiste Society, which maintained branches across the

United States. Networks reinforced an ethnic identity and gave it currency that extended far beyond the bounds of a local community.

Intertwined with social adjustment to the New World were economic adjustment and the readiness with which each group seized opportunities in North American commercial agriculture. Swedes, Mennonites, and French Canadians had all faced problems of increasing population pressure on the land, arising from rapid population growth and the dangers inherent in excessive farm subdivision. Russian Mennonites proved most successful in meeting that challenge in Russia in the late 1860s; French Canadians in Quebec seemed to have had the least success of the three groups. Swedes and French Canadians alike attempted to solve the problem of farm subdivision by mortgaging their property to pay off coinheritors and then producing a small cash crop to pay off the mortgage. Although this strategy did not convert them into commercial farmers overnight, neither could it be said that they were self-subsisting peasants, living in isolation within their highly localized communities and oblivious to the world of commercial markets.

Of the three ethnic groups the Mennonites in southern Russia enjoyed the most efficiently organized, commercialized, and innovative system of farming in the old country. In the early years of the nineteenth century they produced textile fibers, first silk and later wool, for the Russian market. Later, as transportation contacts with the outside world improved, they turned to wheat production as their major commercial product. Agricultural reform in Sweden during the nineteenth century also developed an increasingly commercial pattern of farming, although the emphasis was not on wheat production. Climatically, Sweden was on the northern margins of European wheat farming, notwithstanding scientific advances that produced fast-maturing varieties of wheat; by the end of the century wheat was a minor crop in the Swedish farming system. Wheat was also a marginal crop in Quebec, but it was the cash crop on which the *habitant* depended for decades to feed his family and to pay for his loans and mortgages. Of the three immigrant groups the French Canadians in midnineteenth century Quebec had a reputation for isolationism and withdrawal, for a basic conservatism and resistance to innovation in their farming methods, and for having the least efficient of farming systems.

In terms of the social history of the three groups Swedes were potentially the most assimilable and French Canadians the least, but in terms of their economic history the Mennonites had an edge over Swedes as the most assimilable to the world of commercial agriculture in the American Midwest. Swedish farmers had been assuming mortgages and moving with assurance into farm management and production for international markets, but they were not expert wheat farmers. Mennonites had displayed a remarkable ability to produce for markets in Russia and beyond; they were innovators in finding new products for those markets and had been especially successful as wheat farmers. But the Mennonites had the reputation of remaining aloof and of being self-reliant only in terms of capital accumulation for agriculture in southern Russia. French-Canadian farmers had a rather poor record as wheat farmers and competitors for international markets. Agricultural innovation was weak, and throughout the first half of the nineteenth century capital investment in Quebec farming was low. French Canadians would not have been expected to do well in midwestern commercial agriculture.

Closely related to the social and economic adjustment of the ethnic groups was their adaptation to the new physical environment. A common characteristic in the backgrounds of the French Canadians and Swedes is that they experienced more than a decade of farming in Illinois before coming farther west to central Kansas. During those years they had an opportunity, which the Mennonites who came to Kansas did not have, to observe American farmers and adopt the commercial farming system that was becoming standard for that part of the Corn Belt. It would be wrong to overemphasize this point by suggesting that the French Canadians and Swedes had a significant advantage over their Mennonite counterparts. Although few contemporary observers may have been aware of the fact, the Mennonite farming experience in southern Russia, where the problems of drought and moisture supply were very similar to those of Kansas, was a much better preparation for farming in Kansas than several decades of farming in Illinois. The Swedish and French-Canadian farmers were in one respect like the American farmers who came to Kansas: it took them several decades to realize that major adjustments in the Corn Belt system of farming were required for successful farming in central Kansas.

The success of any group of farmers might well have been determined by the quality of the land that they obtained, the price they paid for it, and their proximity to a market outlet. The Mennonites obtained the best farmland of the three groups, but they also paid the most dearly for it. There was virtually no homesteading in the Mennonite settlement, and land costs ranged from $2.50 to $7.50 per acre. The Swedes did somewhat better—most of the land they obtained was of good quality except in the northern reaches of Union Township, and there was a substantial degree of homesteading. When the Swedes purchased land from the railroad companies, they bargained as a group and paid from $1.25 to $2.15 per acre. The land that the French-Canadian farmers took up was somewhat rough, especially in southern Shirley and in Aurora townships. But most of the French-Canadian farms were homesteaded, and where land purchases occurred, costs were low. In terms of proximity to markets all three groups were equally well off by the early 1880s, as branch line railroads were constructed within ten miles through adjacent townships.

During the first decade of settlement all three groups adjusted to the rectangular survey system. The Mennonites did try briefly to recreate their agricultural villages, but the experiment was short-lived. The French Canadians appeared to have juggled small units of land within the rectangular survey system so that they could avoid undesirable forty-acre lots and obtain better-quality land in amassing their quarter section. But no attempt was made to duplicate settlement patterns from the lower St. Lawrence valley. The rectangular survey was an important and still unacknowledged force in the Americanization of immigrants. In more than a literal sense it acted as a powerful mold creating a rational pattern of landscape to which immigrants had no option but to adjust. The survey precluded the duplication of field patterns and settlement systems from the old country, which in turn limited the duplication of social behavior or farming patterns by the newly arrived settlers. The rectangular survey system with its "dispersed homestead" pattern of settlement quietly underscored the ethos of economic individualism that lay at the heart of Jefferson's concept of the yeoman farmer and the family farm. Within this rectangular framework farmers acquired property and developed the territorial base for a community.

In developing a territorial base, the Mennonites were by far the most successful. Not only in the heart of their settlement but also along its fringes they bought out non-Mennonite neighbors with an unrelenting drive. Swedes were also fairly successful before 1900 in building up a solid territorial base in their community, but thereafter as new, American-born Swedes came of age the desire weakened and non-Swedes purchased formerly Swedish farms. French Canadians were the least territorial of the three groups. This may have been because in coming to Kansas they were not tightly organized as a group by church leaders and agricultural associations or colonization societies. The weak territorial ambition among French Canadians may have been another sign that they were already moving into the American mainstream and adopting American ways.

In terms of social life and political behavior, French Canadians evidenced signs of Americanization in other ways. They embraced the Republican party with rapidity and were readily admitted to local fraternal organizations. Although they supported branches of the expatriate St. Jean Baptiste Society, the ties with Quebec were never as strong as those with the community in Kankakee. Swedes also aligned themselves with the Republican party and followed the lead of their pastors, who encouraged the adoption of English in day-to-day transactions but reserved Swedish for church services and as a second language for school children. Rural Swedes, however, bucked the advice of their leaders during hard times by bolting the Republican party and supporting the Grange and Populist movements in their day. Mennonites were the slowest to adopt American political institutions and the English language. They were slow to join any political party at first, but when they did, they remained rock-bed Republicans, even during the depression years of the mid-1890s. Mennonites were very conservative on issues such as women's suffrage. But their pacifist belief remained intact, and so in 1916 they voted Republican on the local candidates and Democratic on the national candidates who vowed to keep America out of the European war. Strict community discipline and adherence to old religious beliefs inevitably slowed Mennonite entry into the American mainstream, even when the rate of farmer turnover was high in their communities.

The development of a core of experienced farmers in the Kansas communities was impeded by the high rate of farmer turnover among all three ethnic groups. The rate of farmer mobility among the immigrants was as high as among the native-born American farmers, so much so that it calls into question the traditional viewpoint that the European peasant, with his stubborn attachment to the soil, was more stable on the farming frontier than his American neighbors. Although the French Canadians were somewhat more mobile than the Mennonites and the Swedes the most stable of the three groups, the rate of turnover for all of them was unexpectedly high. By 1915, when second-generation, Kansas-born farmers were taking over the operation of their parents' farms, there was some sign of increasing stability within the farm populations. Even in the later years of farming, however, no significant differences are found between the three ethnic groups in terms of the number of farmers who had farmed for ten, wenty, thirty, or even forty years within each township. Consequently no single group built up a larger core of experienced farmers as time went on.

There is no way of knowing at present to what extent the high rate of farm turnover was the result of failure of those who left to make a go of their Kansas farms. Because of the increased hazards of farming in Kansas, the losses resulting from failure must have been greater than in the more humid eastern prairies and Mississippi lowlands. Likewise, losses during years of hardship, whether caused by drought or economic recession, must have been greater than in the favorable years. In the sample of French-Canadian farmers in Aurora Township, there is evidence of this higher rate of failure during bad years. The losses from 1895 to 1905 were very high; this was the group that registered the highest rate of farm foreclosure over the same period.

Consequently, this study has been concerned with survivors—those who were successful to some degree on their Kansas farms. The degree to which success was achieved varied from one group to another, and although no evidence shows that anyone lapsed back into a peasant subsistence (for even that system could not survive in central Kansas), no strong evidence supports the Turnerian thesis in its entirety. The three ethnic groups did not become more and more alike with each passing decade, although there is some evidence for such a trend among Swedes and French Canadians. In the early years of settlement the French Canadians and Mennonites were alike in terms of the value of farms, farming implements, and real estate and of farm size; the Swedes were the anomalous group. In later years, particularly after 1905, further similarities existed between the French Canadians and Swedes and a widening gap between both groups and the Mennonites. Furthermore, since the French Canadians were the most similar to their control group of mostly American farmers, they seem to have adopted the characteristics of the American farmer the most rapidly. The Swedes followed, but more slowly than the French Canadians. Mennonites, on the other hand, continued to affirm their own distinctive characteristics in 1905, 1915, and 1925.

One of the distinguishing features of the Swedish, Mennonite, and French-Canadian farms was the difference in agricultural investment practices. The study dispels the notion that French Canadians were adverse to innovation and that their investment in farm equipment and machinery was laggard. By 1905 the average value of equipment on French-Canadian farms was higher than on Mennonite or Swedish farms. The Swedes managed to acquire even larger farms than the French Canadians by 1925. Mennonites also increased the size of their farms, but not to the same degree as the Swedes and French Canadians. Rather than subscribing to the theory that bigger is better, the Mennonites acquired more valuable land than the others. With higher values of real estate than either the Swedes or the French Canadians, the Mennonites seemed to have invested their capital in improving the quality of their existing farms rather than in buying up additional tracts of land to increase the size of their holdings. In addition, the Mennonites owned more of the land they farmed and rented fewer farms than the Swedes and French Canadians.

Differences among the approaches to farming of the three ethnic groups become sharply etched when farming patterns are analyzed. The long-term trend for all three groups was to increase the number of major farm activities, thereby diversifying farm operations. But within that general trend, substantial differences existed among the three groups. Swedes tended to duplicate the eastern Corn Belt system of farming, emphasizing on their farms corn and also broomcorn for a cash crop in the early decades of settlement. Gradually they increased the number of farm enterprises, but with a good deal of caution and uncertainty in their approach to farming decisions. Mennonites were also cautious in the early years of farming, but after 1895 their system, with its twin goals of profit maximization and risk minimization, seemed a more assured, better-balanced one than that developed by the other two groups. French Canadians demonstrated the greatest flexibility in making their farming decisions, not hesitating to switch their farming emphasis from corn to wheat as the market dictated, and in this respect they were the most like native-born American farmers. Despite these fluctuations, the French Canadians, who were closest to the Mennonites in farming practices in 1875, had become closest to the Swedes in 1925, while the Mennonites had become the anomalous group.

The uniformity of decision making varies from group to group. The range of responses in farming was greatest among French Canadians, smallest among Mennonites. It is tempting to argue that this represents evidence of greater individualism among French Canadians than among Swedes, and that the Mennonites retained much of the old European pattern of conformity to a communal norm, and perhaps of individual submission to the interests of the community. Variations in the internal homogeneity of farming decisions also coincided with the spatial solidarity of each ethnic settlement. Mennonites were particularly successful in developing a solid territorial base for their community, which in itself reinforced the likelihood of cooperation in farming and like-minded decision making. For the Swedes and especially the French Canadians, the opportunity for cooperation and community cohesion was considerably less.

Notwithstanding the territorial differences among the three groups, the impact of segregation on the success and adaptation of the immigrant farmers *within* each group seems to have been quite small. Although the immigrant farmers living in homogeneous townships had slightly smaller farms, a higher value of real estate, and a greater degree of renting than those who lived along the edges of the major settlements in mixed townships, none of the differences are statistically significant. The greatest differences in farming patterns are found in 1875 and 1885 between the Swedes in Union Township and the Swedes in Rockville Township. The Rockville Swedes were overwhelmingly from the Illinois communities and had developed a more varied pattern of farming during the first decades than their counterparts in Union Township, who came from Sweden. By 1915 and 1925 the differences in farming patterns between the segregated and nonsegregated samples were small.

The implication should not be drawn from these comments that segregation was totally irrelevant to the rate of Americanization among rural immigrants. Segregation, as examined in this study, refers to a very localized aspect of the phenomenon—whether farmers on the fringe of an ethnic settlement behaved differently from those who lived near the center. No attempt has been made to determine if farmers living in isolation or at some distance from their fellow ethnics yielded to the pressures of Americanization more rapidly than those within a community. The nature and importance of connections among scattered ethnic settlements has not been examined, nor have the questions of settlement size or threshold levels for the survival of ethnic settlements. These are but a few of the untouched issues that are important in determining the relationship between segregation and rates of Americanization.

Much of the discussion on the Americanization of European immigrants is couched in sociological terms—the manner in which different cultural groups intermarried, participated in the electoral process, and adjusted their speech and social behavior as they adapted to a society created by earlier immigrants. A consistent undercurrent in the assimilation literature has been that the new arrivals would improve their economic well-being and social status with time. At the core of the American Dream lay the idea that the immigrant by dint of his own initiative and enterprise would attain greater heights of success in North America than he could ever have hoped to attain back home. In sum, he would become a man of much wider horizons than the European peasant, blinkered by the parochialism and localism of his European past. In the process he would become more and more similar to the immigrants who preceded him.

The making of an American farmer, however, was not simply a matter of transforming immigrants by having them adjust their social behavior, conform to political norms, or raise their economic expectations. It was also a matter of coping with the physical environment, which was unlike anything they had ever encountered. Turner argued that the encounter with the environment played a powerful role in molding the new American, but he too was blindsided by an assimilationist model that focused on the adaptation of the immigrant. Not only immigrants but also the American born were constantly adjusting to new physical environments as the frontier moved westward from the heavily wooded flanks of the Appalachians to the tall grass prairies of the western Mississippi lowlands, and eventually to the short grass prairies of the high plains. As the frontier moved westward, old patterns of farming were cast aside and new farming strategies formulated. In the assimilationist viewpoint it was assumed that American-born farmers led the way in developing these new strategies and the immigrants followed their lead.

In this survey of the development of farming communities in the prairie-plains transition zone, the superiority of American farmers and their influence on immigrants has not been confirmed. On the contrary, evidence convincingly suggests that the influence of immigrants on their American-born neighbors may have been stronger than vice versa. Of the three ethnic groups examined in this study two, the Swedes and French Canadians, showed a tendency to adopt a common pattern of behavior, or norm. In short, they were becoming more and more like their American neighbors. The Mennonite group showed the least tendency to adopt the behavioral patterns of the American born. This was also the most successful group in developing farming strategies suited to the special problems of moisture supply in central Kansas and to the uncertainties of market fluctuations. American farmers who lived adjacent to them also appear to have developed a more successful, similar system of farming than those who lived adjacent to the Swedes or French Canadians.

If a truly pluralist model of immigrant adaptation to American life is proposed, then it should be drawn up to include, in addition to the common assimilationist viewpoint of American-born influence on immigrant adjustment, the process of ethnogenesis and the influence ethnic communities exercised over their American-born neighbors. Immigrants coalesced around leaders and created communities. They established a new identity within those communities and reinforced it by forming a network of ties with communities of their own kind scattered across the continent. But in the Midwest they created a new way of life in response to local environmental challenges, as did their American neighbors.

Consequently, pluralist models should perhaps be cast within the framework of emerging regional cultures built within a distinctive environmental milieu. One of the most distinctive features of the winter wheat belt on the western grasslands was an abiding conservatism, which pervaded the economic, social, and religious lives of rural communities. The social philosophy that emerged within the region over the past century is most vividly expressed in a political conservatism and religious fundamentalism that echoes the old Russian Mennonite values. (It contrasts sharply with the spring wheat belt of the northern grasslands, the so-called Red Belt, where a liberal social activism and even radicalism emerged among the second- and third-generation farmers.) When pluralist models are cast within the framework of emerging regional cultures, an environmental component provides a useful datum line against which to measure change and adjustment. In doing so one may come closer to answering the question: "What then is an American, this new man?"

## Selection of the Sample Townships

Understandably, for the purposes of this study the first problem is the selection of adequate samples from the Swedish, Mennonite, and French-Canadian populations. Three major arguments can be made for using an areal sampling method over any other approach. First, the farm population was in a constant state of flux, particularly during the first years of settlement. The rate of farm turnover was high, and communities were continuously augmented by a flow of newly arrived immigrants. Any statement on the behavior patterns of the three ethnic groups must include the newly arrived with the earliest immigrants. It also has to include those farmers who stayed only a short time in the community as well as those who persisted over several decades. The problem is to devise an appropriate method for catching these different individuals as they moved into and out of the study area in Kansas. Its solution is to select an area within which the immigrant farmers had settled and farmed at one time or another and monitor their behavior within that area.

The second major reason for selecting an areal sample is that comparisons are to be made between the members of each ethnic group and a control group representative of the remainder of the farm population. It is important that the control-group farmers have faced the same limitations in farming as the ethnic-group farmers in terms of soil quality, terrain, local climate, and accessibility to market outlets. Therefore the control group must be selected in the vicinity of the ethnic-group settlement, perhaps even intermingled with its members. That aim also can be achieved most readily by using an areal sampling approach.

An important goal in this study is an examination of variations in the patterns of behavior between segregated and nonsegregated members of each ethnic group. This implies a stratification of the populations by location before the samples can be drawn. The members of each ethnic group must be stratified according to whether they lived in a segregated community or a mixed, heterogeneous community. In this case the necessity for an areal sampling approach is even more evident.

The township represents an ideal areal unit from which the samples could be drawn. The townships in central Kansas are almost all survey townships (i.e., thirty-six section blocks), and the township boundary lines provide an almost completely rectangular grid. Consequently the townships are fairly uniform in size and shape. Furthermore, each township contained from ninety to 130 farmers on average, which seems a manageable number of farms for each sample: the sample size is large enough for statistical testing without being unwieldy.

The published censuses of Kansas do not give a breakdown of the distribution of ethnic groups by townships, which is a distinct disadvantage. Data are aggregated at the county level only, and so it is not possible to use this source for selecting the samples. Fortunately, however, Carman had compiled his own township aggregations from the 1895 census manuscripts in preparing his study *Foreign Language Units in Kansas, Historical Atlas and Statistics.*[1] The results of that painstaking research were made available to me by Carman, and they are the source from which the sample townships were selected. It is also fortunate that Carman had selected the 1895 Kansas state census for his research; 1895 was close to the midway mark in the period to be covered in this study (1875–1925), and so it is an appropriate year for sample selection.

Carman's *Atlas* provides many maps showing the distribution of various foreign-language groups in 1895, and they are an excellent starting point for determining sampling procedures. However, the purpose of his maps is to show language groups rather than ethnic groups, and so a new set of maps have been constructed, giving the complete ethnic composition of the study area. The new maps show the relative importance of various immigrant groups in each township within the thirty-two-county study area— a total of 625 townships. Data are also available for some 157 incorporated towns and villages, but these were excluded since the aim of the exercise is to develop a map primarily of the farm population. The technique used in developing the maps is a modified version of Weaver's crop-combinations method.[2]

Weaver suggested the use of a theoretical curve to determine which combination of crop acreages best characterized land use in a given county. For example, if one crop accounted for 100 percent of all cropland, then land use in the country was described as monoculture when the theoretical curve was drawn up. If two crops each accounted for 50 percent of the cropland, that county was designated as a two-crop combination; if three crops in another county each had 33⅓ percent, it was designated a three-crop combination, and so on. This theoretical curve represented the "expected" distribution of cropland by categories. Weaver then measured the standard deviation between observed crop percentages in different midwestern counties and the expected distributions outlined above. As an example he used Keokuk County, Iowa, which had 54 percent of its cropland in corn, 24 percent in oats, 13 percent in hay, 5 percent in soybeans, and 2 percent in wheat. Table 25 demonstrates the steps taken to obtain the standard deviation for several combinations. The combination that produced the smallest standard deviation described most accurately the relative importance of the crop acreages, in Keokuk County, a three-crop combination.

A basic weakness in Weaver's method is that this use of the standard deviation requires that the percentage figures be normally distributed about the mean. However, in some counties a large number of crops occupied very small percentages of the total cropland. With a skewed distribution smaller and smaller standard deviations are obtained as additional minor crops are added to the combination. Weaver overcame this difficulty by removing the smaller percentages from consideration and ascribing these minor crops to a new category, "specialty crops."

Since normal distributions cannot be assumed for the distribution of ethnic groups in all the townships, it was decided to use an abbreviated version of Weaver's method that would yield the same results. The first step was to obtain the differences between the observed percentages in each township and the theoretical curve for each of nine different categories, ranging from one-group dominance to a nine-group combination. The next step was to select the largest difference within each of the categories. Finally, whichever of the maximum values are smallest indicates the combination that best characterizes the distribution within the township. In no township is there a group combination larger than a four-group one. The advantage of this method is that it requires fewer calculations, does not require the assumption that data be normally distributed, and provides the same result as Weaver's original method.

The ethnic combinations for each of the 625 townships were calculated and mapped. The maps indicate that over a very large part of the

TABLE 25 Standard Deviation Analysis for Keokuk County, Iowa

| | Monoculture | 2 Crops | | 3 Crops | | | 4 Crops | | | | 5 Crops | | | | |
|---|---|---|---|---|---|---|---|---|---|---|---|---|---|---|---|
| | C | C | O | C | O | H | C | O | H | S | C | O | H | S | W |
| % occupied cropland | 54 | 54 | 24 | 54 | 24 | 13 | 54 | 24 | 13 | 5 | 54 | 24 | 13 | 5 | 2 |
| Theoretical %, base curve | 100 | 50 | 50 | 33⅓ | 33⅓ | 33⅓ | 25 | 25 | 25 | 25 | 20 | 20 | 20 | 20 | 20 |
| Difference | 46 | 4 | 26 | 20⅔ | 9⅓ | 20⅓ | 29 | 1 | 12 | 20 | 34 | 4 | 7 | 15 | 18 |
| Difference squared | 2,116 | 16 | 676 | 427 | 87 | 413 | 841 | 1 | 144 | 400 | 1,156 | 16 | 49 | 225 | 324 |
| Sum of squared differences | 2,116 | 692 | | 927 | | | 1,386 | | | | 1,770 | | | | |
| Sum divided by number of crops | 2,116 | 346 | | 309 | | | 347 | | | | 354 | | | | |

SOURCE: J. C. Weaver, *Geographical Review*, vol. 44, 1954, p. 181.

C = corn
O = oats
H = hay
S = soybeans
W = wheat

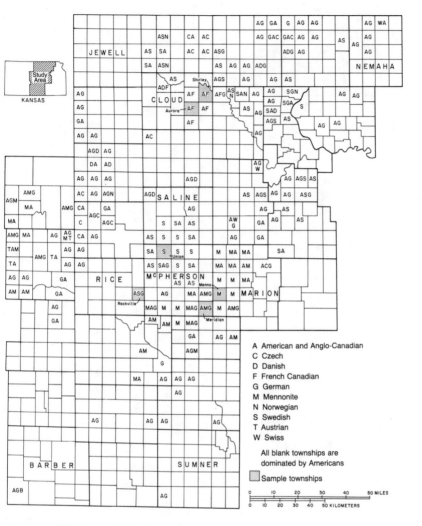

FIG. 34. **Ethnic combinations in central Kansas**

study area, American born were dominant (fig. 34). However, the areas of maximum concentration of the Swedish, Mennonite, and French-Canadian populations clearly stand out, along with their respective diaspora (fig. 35). The Swedes were concentrated in southern Saline and northern McPherson counties with smaller settlements scattered over a much wider area.

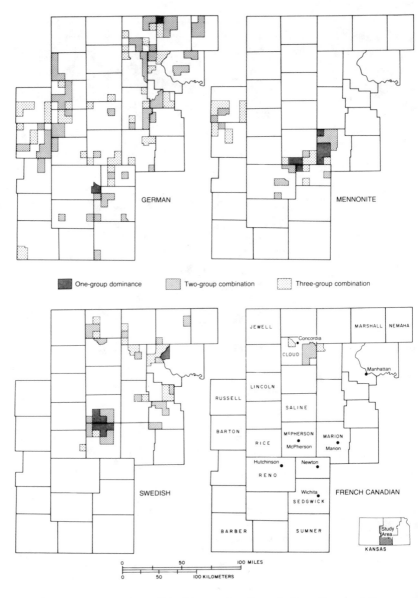

GERMAN

MENNONITE

■ One-group dominance    ▨ Two-group combination    ▨ Three-group combination

SWEDISH

JEWELL    MARSHALL    NEMAHA

Concordia

CLOUD

Manhattan

LINCOLN

RUSSELL    SALINE

BARTON    McPHERSON    MARION

RICE    McPherson    Marion

Hutchinson    Newton

RENO

Wichita    FRENCH CANADIAN

SEDGWICK

Study
Area

BARBER    SUMNER    KANSAS

0    50    100 MILES
0    50    100 KILOMETERS

FIG. 35. Location of Swedish, Mennonite, French-Canadian, and German settlements in central Kansas

The major Mennonite concentration was clearly in Marion and southeastern McPherson counties; the diaspora was much less scattered than for the Swedish. The French-Canadian population, on the other hand, was quite small (much smaller than the German population) and was concentrated in the north of the study area in eastern Cloud County and the western parts of Clay County. These maps provide a much more detailed description of the distribution of each ethnic group than Carman's maps, and they proved very useful in the next steps of selecting two sample townships for each ethnic group.

The selection of a township that represents a segregated part of the population was fairly straightforward: those townships were chosen that contained the highest percentage of Swedes, Mennonites, and French Canadians. They included Union in McPherson County for the Swedes, Menno in Marion County for the Mennonites, and Shirley Township in Cloud County for the French Canadians.

The selection of a second township to represent a heterogeneous community required several steps. Although the same procedure was used to select the second township for all three groups, it is easier to demonstrate the procedure by taking one group as an example—the Mennonites. The first step was to list all townships in which any Mennonites resided. Then those townships in which any group accounted for more than 75 percent of the population were removed from the list, since this was assumed to represent single-group dominance. The average percentage distribution of each ethnic group was calculated for the remaining townships, thereby indicating the nature of the Mennonite diaspora—the average community in which any Mennonite might be found who lived outside the core area. The results of these calculations are shown for all three groups in Table 26. With the ethnic composition of the ideal township, representative of the diaspora, established, the next step was to find the actual township that most closely approximated the ideal, not only in terms of the percentage of Mennonites but of the total ethnic matrix. Two further constraints were added to the selection procedure. Any township having less than one hundred Mennonites was eliminated in order to ensure a large enough sample size. In addition, any township that shared a boundary line with the segregated township (in this case Menno Township) was eliminated since it might be no more than a spillover from the core area. This last constraint resulted in a second choice being made for both Mennonites and French Canadians. Spring Valley Township (McPherson County) was passed over in favor of Meridian and Mulberry Township (Clay County) was rejected in

TABLE 26   Ethnic Composition by Percentage of the Swedish, Mennonite, and French-Canadian Diaspora

|  | Swedish | Mennonite | French Canadian |
|---|---|---|---|
| North Americans* | 56.92 | 50.08 | 57.11 |
| British † | 2.26 | 1.75 | 1.61 |
| Germans | 15.34 | 18.18 | 13.38 |
| Austrian | 0.20 | 2.50 | 0.23 |
| Swiss | 1.13 | 0.70 | 1.11 |
| Mennonites | 3.23 | 14.95 | 1.19 |
| Swedes | 12.06 | 3.59 | 8.03 |
| Norwegians | 0.90 | 0.27 | 0.23 |
| Danes | 2.02 | 0.65 | 2.84 |
| Flemings | 0.11 | 0.14 | 0.34 |
| French | 0.14 | 0.12 | 0.50 |
| Belgians | 0.06 | 0.01 | 0.65 |
| French Canadians | 0.91 | 0.10 | 7.42 |
| Italians | 0.01 | 0.01 | 0.04 |
| Czechs | 2.36 | 3.61 | 3.19 |
| Poles | 0.08 | 0.01 | 0.00 |
| Others | 2.27 | 4.33 | 2.13 |
| Total | 100.00 | 100.00 | 100.00 |
| Number of townships | 135 | 84 | 26 |

*North Americans included those born in English-speaking Canada and the United States.
†British included English, Scottish, Welsh, and Irish.

favor of Aurora. The final selection of heterogeneous, or mixed, townships was Rockville in Rice County for the Mennonites and Aurora in Cloud County for the French Canadians.

A further problem appeared in that the boundaries for two of the selected townships were not consistent with the 1895 boundaries. In 1875, Rockville Township had not yet been created, and it lay astride two larger townships in Rice County—Washington and Union townships. In 1875, township 20 south, range 1, east of the 6th prime meridian (which later became Menno Township), was part of a very large, 144-section township known as Risley. By 1885 this large township had been split in two, and Menno belonged in the northern half, known as Lehigh. In 1895 Lehigh Township was split in two and Menno Township created out of the western half of the older seventy-two-section township (fig. 36). Since the manu-

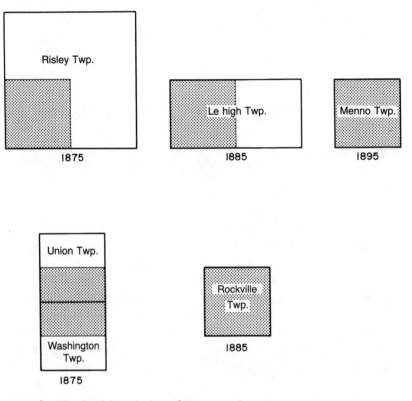

FIG. 36.  Territorial evolution of Menno and Rockville townships

scripts of the state census did not record the location of individual farms within a township, it was impossible to distinguish which farmers lived in the northwestern corner of Risley Township in 1875. The problem was resolved by using the total population of these large townships in 1875 and 1885 as surrogates for Rockville and Menno townships. In all the statistical tests in this study the total population of Washington and Union townships was used in place of Rockville in 1875; the populations of Risley and Lehigh in 1875 and 1885, respectively, were used in lieu of Menno Township.

## Analysis of Persistence Curves

A series of analysis of variance tests were applied to the "cumulative" persistence curves (i.e., the curves that were developed using Malin's method) in order to determine if the differences among the three ethnic groups were significant at the .05 confidence level (table 27). Comparisons were made between (1) the combined pairs of townships representing each ethnic group and (2) the homogenous and mixed townships. With 2 and 24 degrees of freedom, the value of the $F$ ratio for the combined samples of each ethnic group was 4.32. When the homogenous and mixed townships were considered separately, the value of the $F$ ratio was 4.18. The results of both tests indicated that the differences were indeed significant at the .05 confidence level.

The results of the two-way analysis of variance tests also indicated that the Mennonites had a significantly higher persistence rate (57.5 percent) than either the Swedes or French Canadians. In large measure this was due to the high persistence rate of the Mennonites in Meridian township (64.7 percent). In general, the three mixed townships had higher persistence records than the homogenous townships. In other words, the ethnic groups were much more mobile in those communities where they represented a majority of the population than in the townships where they were in the minority.

In order to identify the source of these differences more closely, the second measure of "cohort" persistence was used (i.e., each group beginning in a given census year was treated separately). The variation in persistence rates of the cohorts first appearing in the censuses of 1875, 1885, 1895,

TABLE 27    Cumulative Persistence for Ethnic Group Means and
Standard Deviations from Two-Way Analysis of Variance

| Township | | Swedish | Mennonite | French Canadian | Across Ethnicity |
|---|---|---|---|---|---|
| Homogeneous | M | 47.86 | 50.29 | 39.59 | 45.91 |
| | SD | 4.10 | 16.22 | 6.63 | 10.72 |
| Mixed | M | 53.79 | 64.74 | 45.11 | 54.55 |
| | SD | 10.44 | 12.79 | 14.33 | 14.34 |
| Across | M | 50.83 | 57.51 | 42.35 | 50.23 |
| segregation | SD | 8.10 | 15.74 | 10.92 | 13.19 |

M  = mean
SD = standard deviation

1905, and 1915 were measured: first within each ethnic group, between
those living in mixed townships and those living in homogeneous townships; second between the ethnic groups and control groups; and finally
between the three ethnic groups themselves.

## Segregated and Nonsegregated Communities

The stability of the Swedish farmers who appeared in the 1875 census was
somewhat higher than for farmers who appeared in the later decades. The
rate of persistence was markedly higher in the mixed township of Rockville
than in Union township. It should be remembered, however, that the total
size of the Swedish cohorts in Rockville was always small, so that although
only two Swedish farmers out of the eleven who first appeared in the census
of 1875 were still farming in 1915 (one of them survived to 1925), they
accounted for persistence rates of 18 and 9 percent respectively. Consequently, the small size of the original cohort explained the high persistence
rate for the 1875 census group. Although the rate of persistence was high in
Rockville, the analysis of variance test shows that the differences between
the Swedes in homogeneous and mixed townships were not significant at
the .05 level.

The curves of cohort persistence for the Mennonite townships showed
that the 1875 cohort in Menno had greater "staying power" than later
cohorts. This was true to a very marked degree in Meridian Township,
where 75 percent of the 1875 cohort was still farming in 1885 and 1895.

However, by 1915 this group had disappeared entirely. Apart from the somewhat anomalous pattern for the 1875 cohorts in both townships the persistence curves of the later cohorts were very similar, and in all cases the differences between the two township samples were not significant at the .05 level.

The patterns of farm turnover among the French Canadians in Shirley and Aurora townships did not differ greatly from those of the other ethnic groups in mixed and homogeneous townships. The 1875 cohort had a higher record of persistence than the later cohorts. It should be remembered that the 1875 cohorts for all townships were made up not only of farmers who had recently arrived in the township but also of farmers who may have been in the township in 1865, a decade before this study began. That explains why the 1875 cohorts in every township approximated the Malin curves more closely than did the cohorts of 1885 and succeeding decades. The major anomaly among the French-Canadian persistence curves was the 1895 cohort—of the twenty-six French Canadians who began farming in Aurora in 1895, only three remained in 1905. This represented an unusually high dropout rate. Nevertheless, a comparison of French Canadians living in homogeneous and mixed townships revealed no major differences that were significant at the .05 level.

*Ethnic Groups and Control Groups*

The farmers who lived in the mixed townships of Meridian, Rockville, and Aurora and were not members of the local ethnic group were considered representative of the remainder of the rural population in Kansas with whom the Swedes, Mennonites, and French Canadians came in contact. The majority of these other farmers were American, except for a few Germans, in all three townships. Although the 1875 cohorts for the control groups had a slightly higher rate of persistence than the later cohorts, the 1885 cohort in particular had a lower rate of persistence. In fact, the 1885 group suffered very heavy losses for the first two decades in Aurora and Rockville townships. Of the forty-seven non-French-Canadian farmers who began in Aurora in 1885, only one remained in 1905, and of the sixty non-Swedes who started out in Rockville in 1885, only two had survived twenty years later. The results of the analysis of variance test indicate that the differences were not significant, and so the null hypothesis was rejected and it was assumed that the three control groups were drawn from the same population.

The next test was carried out to determine whether the ethnic group

TABLE 28   Differences between Ethnic-Group and Control-Group Persistence for 1875 Cohort

|  |  | Meridian | Rockville | Aurora | Across Townships |
|---|---|---|---|---|---|
| Ethnic group | M | 43.3 | 32.7 | 25.7 | 33.9 |
|  | SD | 36.5 | 18.8 | 23.9 | 26.5 |
| Control group | M | 13.7 | 12.7 | 11.8 | 12.7 |
|  | SD | 18.6 | 12.9 | 13.7 | 14.2 |
| Across group | M | 28.5 | 22.7 | 18.7 | 23.3 |
|  | SD | 31.4 | 18.5 | 19.8 | 23.5 |

M  = mean
SD = standard deviation

varied significantly from its control group in terms of persistence rates (table 28). The performance of each pair of cohorts was compared, and the only significant differences were found for the ethnic groups in the mixed township and local control groups for the 1875 cohorts. In all other cases the cohort curves were not significantly different. The values of the $F$ ratio for significance of differences between townships was 0.49, but for differences between the ethnic group and control group it was 6.80. The average rate of persistence for other farmers of 12.7 percent was significantly lower than the ethnic persistence level of 33.9 percent, within the .05 confidence limits.

## Analysis across Decadal Curves

The analysis of persistence patterns up to this point has focused on the curves of individual cohorts. This involved taking the persistence levels of those who started in a given year and using the average figure of all the persistence levels in succeeding years. For example, the measure for the 1875 cohort was obtained by taking the values of that group for 1885, 1895, 1905, 1915, and 1925 and obtaining the average rate of persistence. Thus, if there was a high persistence value for the first decade and a sharp drop during the third decade, the irregularities were "smoothed out" in the averages obtained. As a result it was decided to investigate the persistence of each group by decades from the time of first appearance in the census. This involved a transect across the individual cohort curves.

Two-way analysis of variance tests were performed between ethnic

TABLE 29   Differences in Persistence into the Third Decade

|  |  | Mennonites | Swedes | French Canadians | Across Ethnicity |
|---|---|---|---|---|---|
| Homogeneous | M | 23.6 | 12.4 | 7.4 | 14.5 |
| townships | SD | 11.7 | 5.9 | 4.5 | 9.9 |
| Mixed | M | 38.4 | 22.3 | 10.7 | 23.8 |
| townships | SD | 17.2 | 12.4 | 11.3 | 17.0 |
| Across | M | 31.0 | 17.4 | 9.1 | 19.1 |
| segregation | SD | 15.4 | 10.2 | 7.9 | 14.3 |

M  = mean
SD = standard deviation

groups and among segregated and mixed townships for persistence patterns into the first decade, then the second, the third, and finally the fourth. Although first-decade persistence dropped sharply in Rockville Township from 1885 to 1895, the effect was largely eliminated in the overall average figure, and it was found that the difference in decadal curves was not significant for any period except one, which was persistence into the third decade (table 29). The use of 2 and 12 degrees of freedom and the F-ratio value of 5.71 resulted in the rejection of the null hypothesis that no significant differences existed in all the samples of ethnic groups. While the differences in persistence levels into the third decade were not significant between segregated and nonsegregated communities, the generally low persistence levels of French Canadians (9.1 percent) and high levels of Mennonites (31.0 percent) explain why the differences between the three groups were significant within the .05 confidence limits.

One of the major reasons for examining the population persistence rates of the various ethnic groups was to determine whether the rates could have affected the accumulation of agricultural experience within the various groups. If any group, segregated or nonsegregated, had a higher rate of farmer turnover throughout the years and a higher proportion of more recent arrivals in the township, that is, newer farmers in the community, then the effect on local farming decisions might have been considerable. Hence a final test was performed on the representation of farmers from preceding decades in the overall farming population of the township for each census year. It was found that the representation of older farmers did not differ significantly among all six townships in any of the census years, and so differing rates of population turnover did not produce variations in the accumulation of farming experience for any group.

## Crop Yields and Climate

The relation between crop yields and climatic variables is an extremely complex one that has attracted the attention of agricultural economists and botanists.[1] Nevertheless, the correlation of several simple climatic variables such as monthly precipitation values gives a rough indication of the critical periods in moisture supply for some of the major crops. In central Kansas the average county yields were correlated with the monthly precipitation figures recorded at the oldest weather station within that county (table 30). These included Concordia in Cloud County, Marion Center in Marion County, and McPherson in McPherson County; for Rice County the nearest station was at Ellsworth in neighboring Barton County.[2] The results of the simple linear correlations are given first between crop yields and the rainfall for each month, exclusive of the months from September to March. Precipitation in the fall and winter months, before the crop was harvested, was included in preseason precipitation.

The results of the simple linear correlation analysis demonstrate how little of the variation in crop yields can be explained directly by fluctuations in monthly precipitation. The method is simply too crude for such a complex relation. Obviously there is an optimum value of moisture required by plants at different stages of their growth, and that value is determined by a number of other physical variables—evaporation rate, air temperature, wind strength, and amount of sunshine—data that were not available in the late nineteenth century from weather stations in central Kansas. With only monthly precipitation and temperature data, however, an index of effective precipitation can be determined, using the formula suggested by H. P. Bailey:[3]

$$EP = P/1.025^T$$

TABLE 30    Simple Linear Correlation Coefficients of Monthly
Precipitation with Crop Yields in Four Kansas Counties

| | Wheat | Corn | Barley | Oats | Potatoes | Millet |
|---|---|---|---|---|---|---|
| Cloud County, 1886–1926 | | | | | | |
| Preseason | 0.56 | 0.04 | 0.37 | 0.43 | 0.02 | 0.05 |
| April | 0.22 | 0.07 | 0.10 | 0.04 | −0.01 | 0.02 |
| May | −0.01 | 0.46 | 0.29 | 0.38 | 0.38 | 0.17 |
| June | −0.28 | 0.13 | 0.19 | −0.10 | 0.24 | 0.24 |
| July | 0.06 | 0.64 | 0.11 | 0.02 | 0.50 | 0.44 |
| August | −0.01 | 0.29 | 0.26 | 0.23 | 0.23 | 0.13 |
| Marion County, 1893–1926 | | | | | | |
| Preseason | 0.14 | −0.32 | 0.17 | 0.21 | 0.10 | −0.24 |
| April | 0.06 | −0.12 | 0.08 | −0.04 | −0.19 | −0.13 |
| May | −0.32 | 0.26 | 0.32 | 0.29 | 0.41 | 0.13 |
| June | −0.43 | −0.03 | 0.01 | −0.11 | 0.32 | 0.04 |
| July | −0.33 | 0.44 | −0.16 | −0.07 | 0.24 | 0.36 |
| August | −0.13 | 0.41 | 0.12 | 0.35 | 0.16 | 0.24 |
| McPherson County, 1887–1926 | | | | | | |
| Preseason | 0.46 | 0.23 | 0.49 | 0.45 | 0.28 | 0.21 |
| April | 0.26 | −0.27 | 0.13 | −0.09 | −0.04 | −0.35 |
| May | −0.12 | 0.37 | 0.49 | 0.41 | 0.36 | 0.25 |
| June | −0.19 | 0.32 | 0.08 | 0.17 | 0.49 | 0.33 |
| July | −0.08 | 0.55 | −0.06 | −0.03 | 0.26 | 0.59 |
| August | −0.23 | 0.21 | 0.21 | 0.23 | 0.13 | 0.42 |
| Rice County, 1876–1926 | | | | | | |
| Preseason | 0.24 | 0.22 | 0.25 | 0.32 | 0.14 | 0.14 |
| April | 0.17 | −0.07 | 0.11 | −0.02 | −0.04 | −0.11 |
| May | 0.28 | 0.30 | 0.29 | 0.35 | 0.36 | 0.28 |
| June | −0.09 | 0.22 | 0.10 | 0.04 | 0.35 | 0.20 |
| July | −0.06 | 0.59 | 0.07 | 0.18 | 0.26 | 0.44 |
| August | −0.18 | 0.11 | 0.19 | −0.01 | 0.32 | 0.12 |

where $P$ = precipitation in inches and $T$ = temperature in degrees Fahrenheit.

This measure of effective precipitation was correlated with the county crop yields in a stepwise regression analysis with an inclusion and exclusion level for variables of 0.10. The coefficients of multiple correlation ($R$) and coefficient of determination ($R^2$) are given for the effective precipitation

TABLE 31 **Results of a Stepwise Multiple Correlation of Crop Yields with Monthly Effective Precipitation in Four Kansas Counties**

| Wheat | R | R² | Corn | R | R² | Barley | R | R² | Oats | R | R² | Potatoes | R | R² |
|---|---|---|---|---|---|---|---|---|---|---|---|---|---|---|
| | | | | | | Cloud County, 1886–1926 | | | | | | | | |
| Preseason | 0.59 | 0.35 | July | 0.67 | 0.45 | Preseason | 0.37 | 0.14 | Preseason | 0.49 | 0.24 | July | 0.54 | 0.29 |
| | | | May | 0.75 | 0.56 | August | 0.48 | 0.23 | August | 0.56 | 0.32 | May | 0.58 | 0.34 |
| | | | | | | June | 0.55 | 0.30 | | | | | | |
| | | | | | | Harvey County, 1889–1926 | | | | | | | | |
| June | 0.37 | 0.14 | July | 0.41 | 0.16 | May | 0.30 | 0.09 | Preseason | 0.40 | 0.16 | —* | — | — |
| | | | August | 0.54 | 0.30 | | | | | | | | | |
| | | | April | 0.61 | 0.37 | | | | | | | | | |
| | | | | | | McPherson County, 1893–1926 | | | | | | | | |
| June | 0.43 | 0.19 | July | 0.64 | 0.41 | May | 0.47 | 0.23 | August | 0.39 | 0.16 | June | 0.51 | 0.26 |
| April | 0.56 | 0.32 | August | 0.73 | 0.54 | Preseason | 0.59 | 0.34 | May | 0.48 | 0.23 | Preseason | 0.66 | 0.44 |
| May | 0.63 | 0.40 | | | | | | | | | | | | |
| | | | | | | Saline County, 1884–1926 | | | | | | | | |
| June | 0.36 | 0.12 | July | 0.72 | 0.51 | Preseason | 0.33 | 0.11 | Preseason | 0.34 | 0.12 | June | 0.45 | 0.20 |
| Preseason | 0.46 | 0.21 | August | 0.76 | 0.58 | June | 0.52 | 0.27 | | | | July | 0.54 | 0.29 |
| | | | Preseason | 0.79 | 0.63 | July | 0.55 | 0.31 | | | | | | |

*No variables were selected for inclusion in the model.

index of each month, in the order in which they were introduced to the model, in table 31. Because of the paucity of temperature records for the 1880s and 1890s at weather stations in Marion and Rice counties, two other adjacent counties were substituted for which records are available—Harvey and Saline counties.

The use of the effective precipitation index confirms some of the accepted views of critical periods for moisture supply, not only in terms of periods of deficiency but also of excess. In the case of winter wheat, excessive amounts of moisture in the spring months were more damaging than the moisture deficiency of the preseason months, when the crop was germinating.

The relation between corn and effective precipitation is much stronger than for wheat and effective precipitation. The critical months for corn were July and August. Deficient moisture during those months had the most adverse effect on corn yields.

For other small-grain crops, such as barley and oats, the danger periods in terms of moisture supply were similar to those for wheat. In the two northern counties of Cloud and Saline low amounts of moisture during the preseason had an adverse effect on yields, followed in importance by deficient moisture supply in the early growing months of May and June. In the southern counties of McPherson and Harvey the same danger periods are observed, but the rank ordering within the model is reversed. In the case of potatoes, a moisture deficiency in any of the summer months reduced yields; the actual months during which such deficiencies occurred varied from county to county.

The low correlation coefficients for monthly effective precipitation with wheat yields and the generally higher correlation coefficients for corn yields is not unexpected. Central Kansas is the more ideal ecological region for growing imported varieties of winter wheat, so that within the core of this ecological region, variations in climate generally have a smaller effect on the wheat yield. Central Kansas, however, is on the southwestern extremity of the ecological region best suited for corn production—the Corn Belt —so that minor fluctuations in the monthly effective precipitation have a substantial impact on corn yields.

## Estimating Variability of Farm Income

Each decade, when the state of Kansas took an agricultural census, it recorded the acreages in all field crops, the numbers of livestock on each farm, and other information. These data represent the decision of each farm operator on how to organize the resources of his farm. But the data are not directly comparable, nor do they reveal at first glance whether the farmer had made a high-risk or a low-risk decision. The issue then was to convert the field acreages and livestock numbers into labor units that are comparable, estimate farm enterprise combinations that indicate the truly important activities on the farm, and derive coefficients of variation that take into account parallel fluctuations in crop yields and market prices for different commodities produced on the farm.

## Derivation of Labor Units

In estimating the labor requirements for each crop and livestock enterprise, several difficulties were encountered because of variations in technology over time. For example, the amount of labor required per acre of corn in the eastern United States is quite different from that farther west in Kansas and Nebraska and differs sharply from the amount for the corn-growing areas in the South.[1] Beginning in the 1950s, however, the U.S. Department of Agriculture carried out a survey of labor requirements for the major crop and livestock enterprises in each state for the preceding decades. This information was the basis for the derivation of labor units in this study. For example, in 1950 the estimated number of man-hours required per acre of wheat was 3.4; per acre of corn it was 9.0.[2]

Estimates of the time required to work on each acre of crop include time spent on plowing and harrowing the land in preparation for seeding, time spent on manuring and fertilizing the soil, plus spraying and dusting with weed and pest controls. This is the preharvest work. In addition the harvest work includes gathering the crop from the fields and hauling it to storage, the local market, the grain elevator, or the processing plant. The estimates of the time required to care for livestock are similarly comprehensive. They include time spent on such operations as feeding, hauling feed and bedding for the animals, cleaning pens and barns, moving the animals from one pasture to another, and finally selling the animals and their products. The USDA survey is very comprehensive and detailed and of considerable value in determining the effort that went into the various farm enterprises in different parts of the United States.[3]

The estimates were then combined with an index of changing labor requirements for farm enterprises that takes into consideration changes in farming technology over time. The index was constructed for major geographical regions within the United States—Kansas is in the West North Central division—and for the major categories of crop and livestock enterprises.[4] These enterprise categories include feed grains, hay and forage, food grains, vegetables, and meat animals. The index determines the rate of change in labor requirements for each category of farm activity to the others over the period from 1919 to 1957. A trend is fitted to the index for each category in order to extrapolate backward in time to 1875. The equations derived for the trend lines are

| | |
|---|---|
| Feed grains: | $Y = 8503.72 - (4.31)$ |
| Hay and forage: | $Y = 5550.15 - (2.79)$ |
| Food grains: | $Y = 8103.91 - (4.11)$ |
| Vegetables: | $Y = 3716.43 - (1.85)$ |
| Meat animals: | $Y = (0.78) (\times) - 1,408.85$ |

By means of these equations it is possible to estimate the value of the labor index for the census years from 1875 to 1925 (table 32). The general trend is a decline in the number of man-hours required for all farming activities with the exception of meat production (beef cattle, sheep, lambs, and hogs). The amount of labor required to produce meat animals increased as the quality of feeds improved, along with methods of breeding, housing, and the general care of livestock. In other words, the

TABLE 32　Estimated Index Values for Farm Labor Per Acre and
Per Head of Livestock, 1875–1925 and 1950*

|  | 1875 | 1885 | 1895 | 1905 | 1915 | 1925 | 1950 |
|---|---|---|---|---|---|---|---|
| Feed grains | 418.7 | 375.6 | 332.5 | 289.4 | 246.2 | 203.1 | 84.0 |
| Hay and forage | 320.8 | 292.9 | 265.0 | 237.1 | 209.2 | 181.3 | 90.0 |
| Food grains | 399.5 | 358.4 | 317.3 | 276.3 | 235.2 | 194.1 | 77.0 |
| Vegetables | 231.7 | 317.3 | 194.6 | 176.0 | 157.4 | 138.8 | 88.0 |
| Meat animals | 49.7 | 57.5 | 65.3 | 73.0 | 80.8 | 88.6 | 107.0 |

*Base year, 1947–49 = 100

production of meat animals became increasingly labor-intensive with each
passing decade. Similarly, improvements in feeding, breeding, and housing
dairy cattle caused their care to become increasingly labor-intensive over
time. Estimates of the labor demands for dairy cows were obtained from
F. Bateman.[5]

The final step in deriving the labor units for each farm enterprise in the
census years involved the use of the index values in table 32 along with the
data provided by R. W. Hecht on labor demands in Kansas for 1950.[6] The
results are shown in table 33. With these data it is possible to determine
the total labor units required for each farm and the percentage of that total
which goes into wheat production, corn growing, dairying, and so on.
The percentages thus derived are used to determine the significant farm
activities in the farm combination.

The use of labor units in this case provides a means of standardizing crop
acreages and livestock numbers. It is not suggested that the number of
man-hours per acre of wheat or corn was the same for Swedes as for Mennonites or French Canadians. There are indeed some indications (chapter 5)
that the Swedes and Mennonites farmed more extensively than the French
Canadians. Consequently, differences in the intensity of farming practices
between the ethnic groups could result in different values of man-hours
per acre or per head of livestock being obtained for each ethnic group. The
figures in table 33 do not represent the *actual* man-hours required for each
group but rather an *average* measure of the labor requirements for all farms
in central Kansas.

TABLE 33    Estimated Labor Requirements in Man-Hours for Crops and Livestock in Kansas, 1875–1925

| Enterprise | 1875 | 1885 | 1895 | 1905 | 1915 | 1925 |
|---|---|---|---|---|---|---|
| Corn | 44.86 | 40.24 | 35.62 | 31.00 | 31.00 | 26.38 |
| Oats | 21.93 | 19.67 | 17.41 | 15.15 | 12.89 | 10.60 |
| Barley | 15.95 | 14.30 | 12.64 | 11.00 | 9.37 | 7.71 |
| Sorghum* | 26.91 | 24.13 | 21.33 | 18.57 | 15.80 | 13.01 |
| Wheat | 17.61 | 15.81 | 14.00 | 12.17 | 10.37 | 8.56 |
| Rye | 19.68 | 17.67 | 15.65 | 13.60 | 11.59 | 9.57 |
| Buckwheat | 34.70 | 31.15 | 27.60 | 23.98 | 20.43 | 16.88 |
| Alfalfa | 32.04 | 28.92 | 26.16 | 23.40 | 20.64 | 17.88 |
| Clover and timothy | 17.44 | 15.92 | 14.40 | 12.88 | 11.36 | 9.84 |
| Wild hay | 9.25 | 8.45 | 7.64 | 6.83 | 6.03 | 5.22 |
| Sorghum† | 35.60 | 32.50 | 29.40 | 26.30 | 23.20 | 20.10 |
| Potatoes | 99.94 | 94.62 | 83.98 | 75.62 | 67.64 | 59.66 |
| Sweet potatoes | 299.82 | 283.86 | 251.94 | 226.86 | 202.92 | 178.98 |
| Broomcorn | 72.98 | 66.62 | 60.27 | 53.91 | 47.56 | 41.20 |
| Beans | 71.26 | 67.47 | 59.89 | 53.92 | 48.23 | 42.54 |
| Milk cows‡ | 105.00 | 116.25 | 127.00 | 138.00 | 149.00 | 154.75 |
| Beef cattle | 5.06 | 5.83 | 6.71 | 7.48 | 8.25 | 9.13 |
| Hogs | 2.58 | 2.97 | 3.42 | 3.81 | 4.20 | 4.65 |
| Sheep¶ | 1.61 | 1.85 | 2.13 | 2.38 | 2.62 | 2.90 |

*Grain sorghum
†Sorghum for forage
‡Estimates derived from F. Bateman, "Labor Inputs and Productivity in American Dairy Agriculture, 1850–1910, *Journal of Economic History* 29(196): 206–29.
¶Farm flocks
NOTE: The estimated labor requirements for hogs were based on the average weight of hogs in Kansas of 244 pounds in 1958.

## Determination of the Farm Enterprise Combination

J. C. Weaver proposed the method of determining which farming activities most accurately described the system of farming in a given area. Using crop acreages from published census data, he determined which combination of crops most accurately described the system of land use in selected counties in the Midwest.[7] In another study he used livestock numbers to determine the appropriate livestock combinations for the same areas.[8] There are two problems with this method of describing agricultural systems. One is that Weaver did not consider crops and livestock together in his analysis of

TABLE 34    Derivation of the Coefficient of Variation for
Combinations of Wheat, Corn, and Barley in Cloud County,
1875–1925

| Crops | Variance | Standard Deviation | Correlation Coefficient | Coefficient of Variation |
|---|---|---|---|---|
| Wheat | 30.364 | 5.51 | | 37.92 |
| Corn | 173.056 | 13.15 | | 56.10 |
| Barley | 34.853 | 5.90 | | 29.07 |
| Wheat + corn | | | 0.38 | 42.35 |
| Wheat + barley | | | 0.52 | 28.59 |
| Corn + barley | | | 0.57 | 39.31 |
| Wheat + corn + barley | | | | 42.83 |

farming systems, and the second is that in some counties, where there were a large number of minor cropping patterns, he had to create a new category of specialty crops in order to obtain a satisfactory crop combination.[9]

For the purposes of the present study a modified version of the Weaver crop-combination technique was used (appendix C) to obtain the major enterprise combinations for each farm, in each township, in each census year. The results are given in tables 34 through 39. Thus it was possible to begin to ascertain the degree of variability in farm income and the degree of risk involved in the farmer's decision on how to allocate his farm's resources. For example, if a farmer decided to spread his risks, he would have four, or perhaps even five or six, major enterprises in his combination. With only one or two major enterprises in the combination, the risk of failure was much higher. Hence, the number of enterprises in the combination is one measure of the risk involved in the farming decision. The second measure involves the actual combination itself. Since the moisture demands of different crops varied from one time of the year to another, some crops yielded good results when others failed because of the months in which drought occurred. Similarly fluctuations in farm prices did not always coincide—the prices of corn and hogs fluctuated in a cyclical pattern. Various combinations of crop and livestock enterprises, therefore, could lower the variability of farm income.[10] The measurement of that variability is the subject of the next section.

TABLE 35    Percentage Distribution of Farm Enterprises on Swedish, Mennonite, French-Canadian and Control-Group Farms, 1875

<br>

### Swedes, Union Township

| | |
|---|---|
| Enterprise combinations | Single (89), two (9), three (1), four (–), five (0), six (0) |
| 1st enterprise | Dairy (70), beef (13), bcorn (7), corn (6), wheat (4) |
| 2d enterprise | Wheat (5), corn (5), pot (1) |

### Swedes, Rockville Township

| | |
|---|---|
| Enterprise combinations | Single (1), two (10), three (60), four (20), five (0), six (0) |
| 1st enterprise | Corn (100) |
| 2d enterprise | Dairy (40), wheat (20), oats (20), swht (10), corn (10) |
| 3d enterprise | Wheat (30), swht (20), rye (10), barl (10), oats (10) |

### Mennonites, Menno Township

| | |
|---|---|
| Enterprise combinations | Single (28), two (47), three (17), four (7), five (0), six (0) |
| 1st enterprise | Corn (62), dairy (21), wheat (9), swht (4), bwht (4) |
| 2d enterprise | Corn (23), dairy (19), wheat (19), spot (6) |
| 3d enterprise | Swht (9), wheat (6), spot (4) |

### Mennonites, Meridian Township

| | |
|---|---|
| Enterprise combinations | Single (8), two (50), three (25), four (0), five (8), six (8) |
| 1st enterprise | Dairy (58), corn (33), wheat (8) |
| 2d enterprise | Corn (50), dairy (25), oats (17) |
| 3d enterprise | Wheat (17), corn (8), dairy (8), barl (8) |

### French Canadians, Shirley Township

| | |
|---|---|
| Enterprise combinations | Single (20), two (20), three (48), four (3), five (9), six (0) |
| 1st enterprise | Corn (88), wheat (4), rye (4), swht (5) |
| 2d enterprise | Swht (48), oats (14), wheat (7), corn (4), barl (4) |
| 3d enterprise | Oats (27), wheat (16), swht (9), rye (4), barl (4) |

### French Canadians, Aurora Township

| | |
|---|---|
| Enterprise combinations | Single (5), two (19), three (48), four (14), five (14), six (–) |
| 1st enterprise | Corn (71), swht (14), dairy (9), oats (5) |
| 2d enterprise | Dairy (52), swht (33), barl (10) |
| 3d enterprise | Swht (24), dairy (24), barl (10) |
| 4th enterprise | Oats (14), wheat (5), corn (5), pot (5) |

TABLE 35    Continued

|  | Control Group, Rockville Township |
|---|---|
| Enterprise combinations | Single (32), two (22), three (29), four (12), five (4), six (1) |
| 1st enterprise | Corn (67), dairy (23) |
| 2d enterprise | Dairy (28), corn (16), wheat (4), oats (4), swht (3) |
| 3d enterprise | Wheat (19), oats (10), swht (6), dairy (3), rye (3) |
| 4th enterprise | Oats (6), wheat (4), rye (2), pot (2) |

|  | Control Group, Meridian Township |
|---|---|
| Enterprise combinations | Single (9), two (27), three (39), four (15), five (9), six (–) |
| 1st enterprise | Corn (48), dairy (32), wheat (9), oats (7) |
| 2d enterprise | Wheat (29), dairy (27), corn (22),oats (5) |
| 3d enterprise | Wheat (25), dairy (14), oats (8), corn (7) |
| 4th enterprise | Oats (12), wheat (5) |

|  | Control Group, Aurora Township |
|---|---|
| Enterprise combinations | Single (20), two (22), three (34), four (14), five (10), six (–) |
| 1st enterprise | Corn (58), dairy (23), swht (13) |
| 2d enterprise | Dairy (32), corn (20), swht (18) |
| 3d enterprise | Dairy (12), oats (8), barl (6), pot (6) |
| 4th enterprise | Swht (8), wheat (8), oats (4) |

| | | |
|---|---|---|
| dairy = dairying | bcorn = broomcorn | barl = barley |
| pot = potatoes | swht = spring wheat | wheat = winter wheat |
| sorg = sorghum | p. hay = prairie hay | grass = tame grasses |
| mill = millet | alfa = alfalfa | |

## Measurement of the Coefficient of Variation

The farmer faced with the decision of whether to diversify his farming system or specialize it is placed in the position of a gambler who must define his goals. If he wishes to have a stable income with as little variability as possible, then the solution is to diversify the farm operation. If, on the other hand, his view is a short-term one and he wishes to maximize his income regardless of the risk of failure, then the solution is to specialize his farm production. After all, there are cost benefits to monoculture. A diversified farm economy usually costs more money than a specialized one because of the capital costs for a variety of machines, equipment, and livestock. Furthermore, capital could be a limiting factor in the development

TABLE 36  Percentage Distribution of Farm Enterprises on Swedish, Mennonite, French-Canadian, and Control-Group Farms, 1885

### Swedes, Union Township

| | |
|---|---|
| Enterprise combinations | Single (13), two (45), three (35), four (6), five (1), six (0) |
| 1st enterprise | Corn (65), bcorn (18), wheat (10) |
| 2d enterprise | Wheat (40), corn (27), bcorn (11), p. hay (6) |
| 3d enterprise | Wheat (19), oats (11), p. hay (7) |

### Swedes, Rockville Township

| | |
|---|---|
| Enterprise combinations | Single (7), two (28), three (43), four (21), five (0), six (0) |
| 1st enterprise | Corn (64), dairy (21), bcorn (14) |
| 2d enterprise | Corn (36), dairy (36), bcorn (14) |
| 3d enterprise | Wheat (21), p. hay (21), dairy (14) |
| 4th enterprise | P. hay (14), wheat (7) |

### Mennonites, Menno Township

| | |
|---|---|
| Enterprise combinations | Single (7), two (18), three (57), four (14), five (3), six (1) |
| 1st enterprise | Wheat (49), corn (35), dairy (15) |
| 2d enterprise | Wheat (33), dairy (32), corn (27), oats (4) |
| 3d enterprise | Dairy (34), corn (25), wheat (11), oats (3), flax (1) |
| 4th enterprise | Oats (13), corn (1), pot (1), flax (1) |

### Mennonites, Meridian Township

| | |
|---|---|
| Enterprise combinations | Single (4), two (44), three (36), four (8), five (8), six (0) |
| 1st enterprise | Corn (50), wheat (39), dairy (8) |
| 2d enterprise | Wheat (40), dairy (16), corn (9), oats (4) |
| 3d enterprise | Dairy (24), wheat (8), corn (8), barl (8) |
| 4th enterprise | P. hay (12), oats (4) |

### French Canadians, Shirley Township

| | |
|---|---|
| Enterprise combinations | Single (33), two (37), three (24), four (4), five (1), six (0) |
| 1st enterprise | Corn (92), dairy (5) |
| 2d enterprise | Dairy (56), corn (4), wheat (3), oats (3) |
| 3d enterprise | Oats (11), p. hay (10), dairy (95), wheat (3) |

### French Canadians, Aurora Township

| | |
|---|---|
| Enterprise combinations | Single (39), two (32), three (28), four (1), five (0), six (0) |

TABLE 36    Continued

| 1st enterprise | Corn (93), dairy (7) |
| 2d enterprise | Dairy (49), corn (7), wheat (4), oats (2) |
| 3d enterprise | P. hay (12), oats (11), dairy (5), wheat (2) |

Control Group, Rockville Township

| Enterprise combinations | Single (19), two (35), three (36), four (10), five (0), six (0) |
| 1st enterprise | Corn (73), dairy (17), bcorn (7), wheat (92), sorg (1) |
| 2d enterprise | Dairy (41), corn (17), p. hay (13), wheat (6), bcorn (4) |
| 3d enterprise | P. hay (17), dairy (14), wheat (11), bcorn (3) |
| 4th enterprise | Wheat (6), p. hay (3), dairy (1) |

Control Group, Meridian Township

| Enterprise combinations | Single (8), two (36), three (38), four (13), five (4), six (1) |
| 1st enterprise | Corn (67), wheat (24), dairy (9) |
| 2d enterprise | Wheat (48), corn (24), dairy (15), p. hay (4), oats (1) |
| 3d enterprise | Dairy (18), wheat (15), oats (4), mill (3), corn (2) |
| 4th enterprise | Oats (7), p. hay (4), mill (3), dairy (2), wheat (2) |

Control Group, Aurora Township

| Enterprise combinations | Single (43), two (28), three (15), four (9), five (5), six (0) |
| 1st enterprise | Corn (91), dairy (9) |
| 2d enterprise | Dairy (40), corn (8), wheat (5), p. hay (3), mill (1) |
| 3d enterprise | Oats (9), dairy (6), p. hay (5), wheat (3), rye (3), mill (3) |
| 4th enterprise | Wheat (4), oats (4), p. hay (3), dairy (1) |

| dairy = dairying | bcorn = broomcorn | barl = barley |
| pot = potatoes | swht = spring wheat | wheat = winter wheat |
| sorg = sorghum | p. hay = prairie hay | grass = tame grasses |
| mill = millet | alfa = alfalfa | |

of a diversified farm operation, as one contributor to the *Kansas Gazette* explained in 1877.[11]

I have already shown that there are two sources of variability in farm income: the weather and the market stability for farm produce. I have also shown that crop yields do not always fluctuate together from year to year: some years were good years for the wheat crop while the corn crop may have failed and vice versa. Thus the problem is to develop a method of determining the variability of crop yields and the degree to which yields coincided. A method is required that combines the *variance* of crop yields

TABLE 37    Percentage Distribution of Farm Enterprises on
Swedish, Mennonite, French Canadian, and Control-Group
Farms, 1895

---

Swedes, Union Township

| Enterprise combinations | Single (6), two (14), three (38), four (22), five (16), six (4) |
|---|---|
| 1st enterprise | Corn (60), bcorn (18), dairy (11), wheat (7), p. hay (2) |
| 2d enterprise | Wheat (25), corn (24), bcorn (17), dairy (16), p. hay (13) |
| 3d enterprise | Wheat (36), dairy (28), p. hay (8), corn (7) |
| 4th enterprise | P. hay (15), dairy (12), wheat (6) |

Swedes, Rockville Township

| Enterprise combinations | Single (0), two (26), three (42), four (16), five (16), six (0) |
|---|---|
| 1st enterprise | Corn (79), dairy (16), bcorn (5) |
| 2d enterprise | Dairy (42), bcorn (26), wheat (11) |
| 3d enterprise | P. hay (26), wheat (16), dairy (16) |
| 4th enterprise | Wheat (21), p. hay (5), oats (5) |

Mennonites, Menno Township

| Enterprise combinations | Single (3), two (8), three (29), four (32), five (26), six (2) |
|---|---|
| 1st enterprise | Dairy (39), wheat (37), corn (23) |
| 2d enterprise | Wheat (39), corn (27), dairy (22), p. hay (5), oats (2) |
| 3d enterprise | Corn (35), dairy (25), wheat (15), oats (6), p. hay (5) |
| 4th enterprise | Oats (29), p. hay (19), dairy (6), corn (5) |
| 5th enterprise | P. hay (13), oats (11), swht (2), sorg (2) |

Mennonites, Meridian Township

| Enterprise combinations | Single (0), two (14), three (32), four (30), five (20), six (4) |
|---|---|
| 1st enterprise | Corn (48), dairy (32), wheat (20) |
| 2d enterprise | Dairy (40), wheat (30), corn (28) |
| 3d enterprise | Wheat (34), dairy (18), corn (12), oats (10), p. hay (8) |
| 4th enterprise | Oats (22), p. hay (14), dairy (4), wheat (4) |
| 5th enterprise | P. hay (12), oats (4), wheat (2), rye (2), sorg (2) |

French Canadians, Shirley Township

| Enterprise combinations | Single (11), two (14), three (68), four (6), five (1), six (–) |
|---|---|
| 1st enterprise | Corn (91), oats (5), dairy (3) |
| 2d enterprise | Oats (45), dairy (41), corn (2) |
| 3d enterprise | Oats (30), dairy (26), p. hay (10), corn (5), mill (4) |
| 4th enterprise | P. hay (5) |

TABLE 37   **Continued**

---

French Canadians, Aurora Township

| | |
|---|---|
| Enterprise combinations | Single (16), two (28), three (54), four (–), five (2), six (–) |
| 1st enterprise | Corn (87), dairy (7), oats (2) |
| 2d enterprise | Dairy (44), oats (26), corn (9), p. hay (5) |
| 3d enterprise | Oats (26), dairy (16), p. hay (14) |

Control Group, Rockville Township

| | |
|---|---|
| Enterprise combinations | Single (15), two (30), three (36), four (12), five (5), six (–) seven (2) |
| 1st enterprise | Corn (76), bcorn (15), dairy (5) |
| 2d enterprise | Dairy (26), wheat (22), corn (17), bcorn (10), p. hay (9) |
| 3d enterprise | Dairy (22), wheat (14), corn (9), p. hay (5) |
| 4th enterprise | Wheat (5), p. hay (5), oats (3), beef (3) |

Control Group, Meridian Township

| | |
|---|---|
| Enterprise combinations | Single (3), two (16), three (34), four (27), five (19), six (1) |
| 1st enterprise | Corn (76), dairy (20), wheat (4) |
| 2d enterprise | Dairy (47), wheat (27), corn (21) |
| 3d enterprise | Wheat (37), oats (17), dairy (11), p. hay (9) |
| 4th enterprise | P. hay (13), oats (11), mill (9), wheat (6), dairy (4) |
| 5th enterprise | Oats (6), mill (6) |

Control Group, Aurora Township

| | |
|---|---|
| Enterprise combinations | Single (19), two (19), three (52), four (8), five (1), six (1) |
| 1st enterprise | Corn (85), dairy (11), p. hay (2) |
| 2d enterprise | Dairy (41), oats (27), p. hay (8), corn (5) |
| 3d enterprise | Oats (17), dairy (11), p. hay (9) |

---

| | | |
|---|---|---|
| dairy = dairying | bcorn = broomcorn | barl = barley |
| pot = potatoes | swht = spring wheat | wheat = winter wheat |
| sorg = sorghum | p. hay = prairie hay | grass = tame grasses |
| mill = millet | alfa = alfalfa | |

while taking into account the *correlation* between crop yields. The method for achieving this was suggested by E. N. Castle in the following model for enterprises $x$ and $y$:

$$V_{x+y} = \frac{V_{x+y}V + 2rs_x s_y}{\bar{x} + \bar{y}} \times \frac{100}{1}$$

TABLE 38 Percentage Distribution of Farm Enterprises on Swedish, Mennonite, French Canadian, and Control-Group Farms, 1905

---

### Swedes, Union Township

| Enterprise combinations | Single (3), two (11), three (40), four (29), five (13), six (3) |
|---|---|
| 1st enterprise | Corn (46), dairy (16), wheat (14), p. hay (12), bcorn (11) |
| 2d enterprise | Wheat (33), corn (30), dairy (16), p. hay (11), bcorn (3) |
| 3d enterprise | Dairy (29), wheat (17), corn (17), p. hay (13), beef (5) |
| 4th enterprise | Wheat (15), dairy (9), sorg (5), beef (3) |
| 5th enterprise | Wheat (3), oats (2), sorg (2), beef (2), p. hay (2) |

### Swedes, Rockville Township

| Enterprise combinations | Single (0), two (12), three (29), four (53), five (6), six (0) |
|---|---|
| 1st enterprise | Corn (82), dairy (12), wheat (6) |
| 2d enterprise | P. hay (35), dairy (24), corn (12), bcorn (6) |
| 3d enterprise | Dairy (29), wheat (29), p. hay (18), oats (6), beef (6) |
| 4th enterprise | Beef (18), wheat (12), p. hay (12), dairy (12) |

### Mennonites, Menno Township

| Enterprise combinations | Single (7), two (10), three (42), four (23), five (16), six (2) |
|---|---|
| 1st enterprise | Dairy (36), corn (33), wheat (28) |
| 2d enterprise | Wheat (36), corn (24), dairy (24), p. hay (8) |
| 3d enterprise | Dairy (28), corn (27), wheat (19), oats (6), p. hay (3) |
| 4th enterprise | Oats (26), p. hay (7), dairy (4) |

### Mennonites, Meridian Township

| Enterprise combinations | Single (7), two (5), three (47), four (20), five (18), six (3) |
|---|---|
| 1st enterprise | Corn (37), dairy (35), wheat (27) |
| 2d enterprise | Corn (35), wheat (32), dairy (18), p. hay (5) |
| 3d enterprise | Dairy (35), wheat (18), corn (12), oats (12), p. hay (8) |
| 4th enterprise | Oats (17), p. hay (10), corn (3), sorg (3), grass (3) |

### French Canadians, Shirley Township

| Enterprise combinations | Single (14), two (11), three (35), four (31), five (9), six (0) |
|---|---|
| 1st enterprise | Corn (63), dairy (33) |
| 2d enterprise | Dairy (36), corn (23), oats (14), wheat (10) |
| 3d enterprise | Oats (32), wheat (20), p. hay (6), dairy (6), grass (5) |
| 4th enterprise | Oats (12), wheat (16), p. hay (7), hogs (2) |

TABLE 38 Continued

| | French Canadians, Aurora Township |
|---|---|
| Enterprise | |
| combinations | Single (2), two (18), three (25), four (41), five (14), six (0) |
| 1st enterprise | Corn (64), dairy (30), oats (4), wheat (2) |
| 2d enterprise | Dairy (43), corn (30), oats (9), p. hay (9), wheat (7) |
| 3d enterprise | Oats (25), dairy (18), p. hay (16), wheat (11) |
| 4th enterprise | Oats (25), p. hay (18), wheat (7) |
| | Control Group, Rockville Township |
| Enterprise | |
| combinations | Single (9), two (23), three (40), four (14), five (12), six (2) |
| 1st enterprise | Corn (79), dairy (19), bcorn (2) |
| 2d enterprise | Dairy (30), wheat (28), p. hay (16), corn (16) |
| 3d enterprise | P. hay (9), beef (5), grass (5) |
| 4th enterprise | P. hay (7), beef (7), hogs (5), dairy (5) |
| | Control Group, Meridian Township |
| Enterprise | |
| combinations | Single (6), two (16), three (45), four (18), five (8), six (5) |
| 1st enterprise | Corn (53), dairy (24), wheat (16), p. hay (4) |
| 2d enterprise | Wheat (31), dairy (22), corn (22), p. hay (12) |
| 3d enterprise | Wheat (24), dairy (16), corn (12), p. hay (8), oats (8) |
| 4th enterprise | Oats (10), p. hay (6), dairy (6), grass (4) |
| | Control Group, Aurora Township |
| Enterprise | |
| combinations | Single (4), two (27), three (38), four (24), five (7), six (0) |
| 1st enterprise | Corn (51), dairy (42), p. hay (4), oats (2) |
| 2d enterprise | Corn (41), dairy (37), p. hay (7), wheat (6), oats (4) |
| 3d enterprise | P. hay (24), oats (24), wheat (7), dairy (6) |
| 4th enterprise | P. hay (11), oats (11), wheat (4), sorg (3) |

| | | |
|---|---|---|
| dairy = dairying | bcorn = broomcorn | barl = barley |
| pot = potatoes | swht = spring wheat | wheat = winter wheat |
| sorg = sorghum | p. hay = prairie hay | grass = tame grasses |
| mill = millet | alfa = alfalfa | |

where $V$ = variance, $s$ = standard deviation, and $r$ = correlation coefficient.
Castle explained the method as follows:

> If two enterprises have equal variance and the correlation coefficient is zero,
> the combined variance will be one-half of either alone. If a third enterprise
> were added having equal variance and the correlation coefficient is zero,

TABLE 39  Percentage Distribution of Farm Enterprises on Swedish, Mennonite, French Canadian, and Control-Group Farms, 1915

### Swedes, Union Township

| Enterprise | |
|---|---|
| combinations | Single (8), two (4), three (19), four (31), five (26), six (9) |
| 1st enterprise | Corn (53), dairy (18), wheat (18) |
| 2d enterprise | Wheat (27), corn (22), dairy (14), p. hay (8), grass (8), beef (7) |
| 3d enterprise | Wheat (27), dairy (19), grass (14), corn (11), p. hay (8), beef (5) |
| 4th enterprise | Grass (15), dairy (13), sorg (9), p. hay (8), beef (8), wheat (5) |
| 5th enterprise | Hogs (11), grass (8), p. hay (5), sorg (5), beef (4), wheat (4) |

### Swedes, Rockville Township

| Enterprise | |
|---|---|
| combinations | Single (–), two (6), three (44), four (25), five (25), six (0) |
| 1st enterprise | Corn (69), dairy (19), wheat (12) |
| 2d enterprise | Dairy (38), wheat (31), corn (25), beef (6) |
| 3d enterprise | Wheat (31), p. hay (31), dairy (19) |
| 4th enterprise | Grass (19), p. hay (12), beef (12) |
| 5th enterprise | Oats (19), grass (6) |

### Mennonites, Menno Township

| Enterprise | |
|---|---|
| combinations | Single (8), two (6), three (28), four (28), five (27), six (2) |
| 1st enterprise | Wheat (52), dairy (35), corn (8), p. hay (1) |
| 2d enterprise | Corn (36), wheat (26), dairy (24), p. hay (4) |
| 3d enterprise | Corn (31), dairy (29), p. hay (10), wheat (7), oats (6) |
| 4th enterprise | Oats (29), p. hay (21) |
| 5th enterprise | Oats (15), p. hay (14) |

### Mennonites, Meridian Township

| Enterprise | |
|---|---|
| combinations | Single (3), two (7), three (25), four (49), five (5), six (0) |
| 1st enterprise | Wheat (75), corn (15), dairy (8), p. hay (2) |
| 2d enterprise | Corn (54), wheat (18), dairy (11), oats (7) |
| 3d enterprise | Dairy (49), oats (16), corn (10), p. hay (10) |
| 4th enterprise | Oats (31), dairy (13), p. hay (10), corn (7), sorg (3) |
| 5th enterprise | P. hay (7), oats (5), dairy (3), wheat (2) |

### French Canadians, Shirley Township

| Enterprise | |
|---|---|
| combinations | Single (6), two (11), three (26), four (33), five (19), six (3) |
| 1st enterprise | Wheat (42), dairy (36), corn (21) |
| 2d enterprise | Dairy (36), wheat (34), corn (18), oats (2) |

TABLE 39 **Continued**

| | |
|---|---|
| 3d enterprise | Corn (20), wheat (16), oats (15), p. hay (11), dairy (11), beef (5) |
| 4th enterprise | Oats (22), p. hay (16), corn (10), grass (3), beef (3) |
| 5th enterprise | P. hay (13), grass (3), oats (3), sorg (2) |

### French Canadians, Aurora Township

| | |
|---|---|
| Enterprise combinations | Single (3), two (8), three (34), four (31), five (22), six (2) |
| 1st enterprise | Dairy (46), wheat (45), p. hay (3), sorg (3) |
| 2d enterprise | Wheat (38), dairy (36), p. hay (16), corn (6) |
| 3d enterprise | P. hay (39), corn (17), oats (14), wheat (9), dairy (8) |
| 4th enterprise | Oats (23), p. hay (19), corn (9) |
| 5th enterprise | Oats (8), corn (6), grass (3) |

### Control Group, Rockville Township

| | |
|---|---|
| Enterprise combinations | Single (6), two (19), three (37), four (20), five (13), six (3) |
| 1st enterprise | Corn (83), wheat (7), dairy (6), p. hay (2), beef (2) |
| 2d enterprise | Wheat (37), dairy (24), corn (10), p. hay (10), grass (5), beef (3) |
| 3d enterprise | P. hay (21), dairy (18), wheat (13), grass (6), mill (3), beef (3) |
| 4th enterprise | Wheat (11), grass (5), dairy (5), p. hay (3), hogs (3) |
| 5th enterprise | Beef (5), hogs (5) |

### Control Group, Meridian Township

| | |
|---|---|
| Enterprise combinations | Single (7), two (5), three (27), four (37), five (22), six (1) |
| 1st enterprise | Wheat (61), corn (19), dairy (12), p. hay (5), beef (2) |
| 2d enterprise | Corn (34), wheat (20), dairy (24), p. hay (10) |
| 3d enterprise | Oats (34), dairy (24), corn (12), wheat (5), p. hay (5) |
| 4th enterprise | Oats (17), dairy (15), p. hay (10), grass (5), beef (5) |
| 5th enterprise | P. hay (10), beef (5) |

### Control Group, Aurora Township

| | |
|---|---|
| Enterprise combinations | Single (5), two (7), three (36), four (27), five (21), six (4) |
| 1st enterprise | Wheat (40), dairy (35), corn (14), p. hay (5) |
| 2d enterprise | P. hay (32), dairy (27), wheat (18), corn (7), oats (5) |
| 3d enterprise | P. hay (27), corn (20), wheat (18), oats (11), dairy (11) |
| 4th enterprise | P. hay (14), oats (11), corn (7), wheat (7), grass (5) |
| 5th enterprise | Oats (7), wheat (5), sorg (5), corn (4) |

| | | |
|---|---|---|
| dairy = dairying | bcorn = broomcorn | barl = barley |
| pot = potatoes | swht = spring wheat | wheat = winter wheat |
| sorg = sorghum | p. hay = prairie hay | grass = tame grasses |
| mill = millet | alfa = alfalfa | |

the combined variance would be one-third of either alone. Whether or not the addition of an enterprise will reduce variability will depend upon the variance of the original enterprise as compared with the variance of the added enterprise, and upon the degree of association or correlation of the returns of the two enterprises.[12]

Since the variances of crop yields were being added together and the average value of yields from one crop to another, Castle decided to standardize these values by dividing by the arithmetic means, thereby creating a coefficient of variation, comparable to the coefficient of variability.

The derivation of the coefficient of variation is illustrated with the example of wheat, corn, and barley yields in Cloud County over the fifty-year period from 1875 to 1925 (table 34). The average yields of wheat, corn, and barley are 14.53, 23.45, and 19.14 bushels per acre respectively. Several points can be made for the Cloud County example. The coefficient of variation for barley is quite low. The reason farmers did not grow this crop exclusively is that barley did not have a market advantage over other crops. Consequently, the coefficient of variation is only a measure of the variability of return from crops, indicating nothing about the competitive market position. Second, in the example above the combination of wheat and barley gives the lowest coefficient of variation—certainly much lower than the three-crop combination of wheat with corn and barley. The reason is that corn yields are much more variable than those of wheat or barley, so that the addition of corn to this particular combination does not reduce the variability of returns but increases it. The crop combinations that produced the lowest variability in yields for the sample counties (Cloud, Marion, McPherson, and Rice) in central Kansas were wheat-barley-millet–Hungarian grass and wheat–prairie grass.

The use of crop-yield data to determine the variability of farm income has several limitations. There is no way to include livestock enterprises in the analysis of farming systems; also, crop and livestock prices, an important element in income variability, did not fluctuate together. These two problems are overcome by introducing the "return per man-hour" of labor to the model. The labor units for each crop and livestock enterprise have been combined with farm prices according to the equation

$$\$ \text{ Return} = \frac{A \times B\,(C)}{Df'} + \frac{E\,(C)}{Df''}$$

where $A$ = crop yield in bushels per acre
$B$ = market value per bushel

$C$ = wholesale price index divided by 100
$D$ = man-hours required per acre per head of livestock
$E$ = price per head of livestock
$f'$ = proportion of farm activity given to crops
$f''$ = proportion of farm activity given to livestock

In these calculations, it is important to use prices that were representative of the prices for crops and livestock being received by Kansas farmers. Local farm prices are preferable to the national average on farm prices. The most obvious sources are the data published by the Kansas State Board of Agriculture in the Annual and Biennial reports—the same source from which crop yields are obtained. Here the county officials reported the acreage, yield, and value of crops as well as the numbers and value of livestock every year. J. C. Malin raised some doubts about the accuracy of the county data for the early years of farming, explaining that the market price of No. 1 wheat was often used to estimate the value of the wheat crop, whereas much of the crop was actually of No. 2 or even No. 3 quality.[13] However, a comparison of the county data with crop prices quoted in Chicago reveals only minor differences, and it was decided to employ the Kansas prices as quoted by the state board of agriculture. A further assumption was made that fluctuations in the values of beef cattle, hogs, and sheep reflect variations in the prices of beef, pork, and mutton or wool. All of these market prices were standardized, utilizing the Warren and Pearson wholesale price index, to discount inflationary trends over the fifty-year period.[14]

The "return per man-hour" value was developed for ten different farm enterprises—the production of wheat, corn, barley, oats, potatoes, millet and Hungarian grass, dairy cows, beef cattle, sheep, and hogs—over the fifty-year period from 1875 to 1925. The coefficients of variation for crop and livestock combinations were then obtained for each of the four counties —Cloud, Marion, McPherson, and Rice—and in all four the results are very similar. A combination of wheat-potatoes-sheep-hogs gives the lowest coefficient of variation, although other combinations such as oats-potatoes-hogs or barley-millet-sheep-hogs are also quite low. The reduction in the size of the coefficient of variation by addition of a fourth enterprise to a three-enterprise combination is quite small. Among the three-enterprise combinations, the oats-sheep-hogs group produced the smallest coefficient of variation. The addition of small grains such as barley or rye to a combination that already included oats and/or winter wheat does not greatly reduce the variability of farm income. The coefficients of variability for these combinations are given in tables 41 and 42.

TABLE 40   Percentage Distribution of Farm Enterprises on
Swedish, Mennonite, French Canadian, and Control-Group
Farms, 1925

Swedes, Union Township

| Enterprise | |
|---|---|
| combinations | Single (5), two (15), three (36), four (20), five (19), six (4) |
| 1st enterprise | Corn (50), dairy (24), wheat (9), pot (6), oats (3), sorg (5) |
| 2d enterprise | Wheat (21), corn (21), dairy (19), beef (11), barl (6), alfa (3) |
| 3d enterprise | Wheat (29), dairy (21), corn (8), alfa (8), beef (8), misc (6) |
| 4th enterprise | Beef (12), sorg (7), dairy (7), alfa (5), wheat (4), oats (4) |
| 5th enterprise | Sorg (8), alfa (5) |

Swedes, Rockville Township

| Enterprise | |
|---|---|
| combinations | Single (11), two (11), three (33), four (22), five (17), six (0) |
| 1st enterprise | Corn (50), wheat (28), dairy (22) |
| 2d enterprise | Dairy (50), corn (22), beef (11), wheat (6) |
| 3d enterprise | Wheat (39), corn (17), dairy (11), barl (6), alfa (6) |
| 4th enterprise | Beef (17), oats (11), alfa (11), wheat (6) |
| 5th enterprise | Barl (6), alfa (6), dairy (6), beef (6) |

Mennonites, Menno Township

| Enterprise | |
|---|---|
| combinations | Single (9), two (6), three (16), four (47), five (18), six (3) |
| 1st enterprise | Dairy (50), wheat (44), corn (4) |
| 2d enterprise | Wheat (40), dairy (38), corn (11), oats (5) |
| 3d enterprise | Corn (47), oats (23), dairy (7), wheat (4), sorg (3) |
| 4th enterprise | Oats (41), corn (14), sorg (8), alfa (3) |
| 5th enterprise | Sorg (10), alfa (4), oats (3), corn (1) |

Mennonites, Meridian Township

| Enterprise | |
|---|---|
| combinations | Single (12), two (18), three (30), four (19), five (19), six (2) |
| 1st enterprise | Wheat (58), dairy (39), corn (2), oats (2) |
| 2d enterprise | Dairy (46), wheat (27), corn (7), alfa (4) |
| 3d enterprise | Corn (43), oats (13), wheat (4), dairy (4) |
| 4th enterprise | Oats (22), sorg (16), corn (4), alfa (4) |
| 5th enterprise | Oats (6), sorg (7), alfa (3) |

French Canadians, Shirley Township

| Enterprise | |
|---|---|
| combinations | Single (4), two (24), three (37), four (27), five (7), six (1) |
| 1st enterprise | Corn (51), dairy (36), wheat (11), beef (1) |
| 2d enterprise | Dairy (36), corn (27), wheat (26), oats (5), beef (1), hogs (1) |

TABLE 40  **Continued**

| | |
|---|---|
| 3d enterprise | Wheat (26), oats (18), dairy (14), corn (11), beef (1), hogs (1) |
| 4th enterprise | Oats (9), wheat (6), sorg (6), alfa (5), dairy (4), beef (4) |
| 5th enterprise | Sorg (3), oats (1), alfa (1), beef (1), hogs (1) |

### French Canadians, Aurora Township

| | |
|---|---|
| Enterprise combinations | Single (9), two (26), three (49), four (11), five (4), six (–) |
| 1st enterprise | Dairy (72), corn (28) |
| 2d enterprise | Corn (40), dairy (23), oats (17), wheat (11) |
| 3d enterprise | Oats (25), corn (19), wheat (15), sorg (2), alfa (2), dairy (2) |
| 4th enterprise | Oats (6), sorg (4), wheat (2), alfa (2), p. hay (2) |
| 5th enterprise | Wheat (2), oats (2) |

### Control Group, Rockville Township

| | |
|---|---|
| Enterprise combinations | Single (11), two (20), three (46), four (16), five (7), six (0) |
| 1st enterprise | Corn (57), dairy (27), wheat (11) |
| 2d enterprise | Wheat (38), dairy (25), corn (21), oats (2), alfa (2), beef (2) |
| 3d enterprise | Wheat (27), dairy (23), corn (7), beef (7), oats (5) |
| 4th enterprise | Beef (5), corn (4), oats (4), alfa (4) |
| 5th enterprise | Oats (4), wheat (2), alfa (2) |

### Control Group, Meridian Township

| | |
|---|---|
| Enterprise combinations | Single (3), two (16), three (37), four (22), five (16), six (6) |
| 1st enterprise | Wheat (56), dairy (34), corn (9) |
| 2d enterprise | Wheat (34), dairy (31), corn (19), alfa (9), oats (3) |
| 3d enterprise | Corn (44), dairy (19), oats (16), wheat (3) |
| 4th enterprise | Oats (19), alfa (9), dairy (6), rye (3), sorg (3) |
| 5th enterprise | Alfa (6), sorg (6), beef (6), oats (3) |

### Control Group, Aurora Township

| | |
|---|---|
| Enterprise combinations | Single (13), two (27), three (35), four (18), five (6), six (2) |
| 1st enterprise | Dairy (53), corn (42) |
| 2d enterprise | Corn (44), dairy (27), oats (5), wheat (4), alfa (4) |
| 3d enterprise | Oats (20), wheat (9), alfa (9), dairy (7), beef (5) |
| 4th enterprise | Sorg (15), oats (7), alfa (2), hogs (2) |
| 5th enterprise | Alfa (4), sorg (2), p. hay (2) |

| | | |
|---|---|---|
| dairy = dairying | bcorn = broomcorn | barl = barley |
| pot = potatoes | swht = spring wheat | wheat = winter wheat |
| sorg = sorghum | p. hay = prairie hay | grass = tame grasses |
| mill = millet | alfa = alfalfa | |

## Coefficients of Variation for Crop Yields and Return Per Man-Hour

In the tables that follow, the abbreviations used for crops and livestock are W=wheat, C=corn, B=barley, O=oats, P=potatoes, M=millet and Hungarian grass, G=wild prairie grass, D=dairy cows, E=beef cattle, S=sheep, and H=hogs.

TABLE 41   Coefficients of Variation for Crop Yields

| | | | | | | | |
|---|---|---|---|---|---|---|---|
| | | | Cloud County | | | | |
| W | 37.90 | WC | 52.35 | CO | 41.16 | BG | 28.52 |
| C | 56.09 | WB | 28.59 | CP | 46.31 | OP | 40.66 |
| B | 29.06 | WO | 32.62 | CM | 53.28 | OM | 34.44 |
| O | 35.87 | WP | 41.64 | CG | 51.78 | OG | 33.79 |
| P | 48.01 | WM | 34.25 | BO | 29.55 | PM | 47.07 |
| M | 29.38 | WG | 34.30 | BP | 40.32 | PG | 46.82 |
| G | 50.37 | CB | 39.31 | BM | 27.76 | MG | 31.46 |
| WCB | 42.83 | WOP | 37.31 | BPM | 39.79 | COG | 39.66 |
| WCO | 36.94 | WOM | 31.73 | BPG | 39.63 | CPM | 45.71 |
| WCP | 41.84 | WOG | 31.38 | BMG | 27.36 | CPG | 45.41 |
| WCM | 41.17 | WPM | 41.03 | CBO | 35.22 | CMG | 49.50 |
| WCG | 40.30 | WPG | 40.81 | CBP | 40.86 | OPM | 40.16 |
| WBO | 28.88 | WMG | 31.51 | CBM | 38.47 | OPG | 39.93 |
| WBP | 36.64 | BOP | 36.42 | CBG | 37.91 | OMG | 32.61 |
| WBM | 27.71 | BOM | 29.01 | COP | 41.24 | PMG | 45.94 |
| WBG | 27.89 | BOG | 28.83 | COM | 40.34 | | |
| | | | Marion County | | | | |
| W | 30.33 | WC | 30.16 | CO | 31.28 | BG | 23.94 |
| C | 45.43 | WB | 22.88 | CP | 34.95 | OP | 29.80 |
| B | 24.70 | WO | 25.76 | CM | 43.12 | OM | 29.58 |
| O | 31.20 | WP | 29.16 | CG | 40.41 | OG | 29.13 |
| P | 35.02 | WM | 26.62 | BO | 25.00 | PM | 34.21 |
| M | 23.93 | WG | 26.51 | BP | 28.48 | PG | 33.49 |
| G | 40.06 | CB | 28.22 | BM | 22.67 | MG | 19.62 |
| WCB | 23.72 | WOP | 24.39 | BPM | 28.05 | COG | 29.63 |
| WCO | 26.22 | WOM | 24.82 | BPG | 27.64 | CPM | 34.86 |
| WCP | 34.90 | WOG | 24.52 | BMG | 22.03 | CPG | 33.79 |
| WCM | 29.43 | WPM | 28.38 | CBO | 25.82 | CMG | 38.63 |
| WCG | 27.79 | WPG | 28.10 | CBP | 29.67 | OPM | 29.40 |
| WBO | 23.01 | WMG | 23.45 | CBM | 27.60 | OPG | 28.94 |

TABLE 41 Continued

| | | | | | | | |
|---|---|---|---|---|---|---|---|
| WBP | 25.30 | BOP | 26.37 | CBG | 26.61 | OMG | 27.59 |
| WBM | 21.65 | BOM | 24.22 | COP | 30.67 | PMG | 32.80 |
| WBG | 22.07 | BOG | 24.26 | COM | 30.64 | | |

McPherson County

| | | | | | | | |
|---|---|---|---|---|---|---|---|
| W | 35.17 | WC | 37.70 | CO | 39.55 | BG | 28.34 |
| C | 54.56 | WB | 26.85 | CP | 41.31 | OP | 36.36 |
| B | 29.76 | WO | 31.83 | CM | 52.05 | OM | 35.80 |
| O | 37.22 | WP | 36.10 | CG | 49.24 | OG | 34.85 |
| P | 42.21 | WM | 31.40 | BO | 30.75 | PM | 41.39 |
| M | 28.15 | WG | 30.70 | BP | 35.70 | PG | 40.84 |
| G | 33.12 | CB | 32.27 | BM | 27.88 | MG | 18.95 |
| WCB | 28.20 | WOP | 33.07 | BPM | 35.23 | COG | 38.84 |
| WCO | 34.13 | WOM | 30.98 | BPG | 34.86 | CPM | 40.82 |
| WCP | 36.63 | WOG | 30.39 | BMG | 26.70 | CPG | 40.24 |
| WCM | 36.85 | WPM | 35.56 | CBO | 32.07 | CMG | 47.29 |
| WCG | 35.23 | WPG | 35.14 | CBP | 35.75 | OPM | 35.95 |
| WBO | 28.48 | WMG | 27.72 | CBM | 31.89 | OPG | 35.54 |
| WBP | 32.07 | BOP | 32.96 | CBG | 30.68 | OMG | 33.63 |
| WBM | 25.89 | BOM | 30.10 | COP | 37.11 | PMG | 40.10 |
| WBG | 25.77 | BOG | 29.78 | COM | 38.89 | | |

Rice County

| | | | | | | | |
|---|---|---|---|---|---|---|---|
| W | 38.11 | WC | 37.23 | CO | 39.46 | BG | 22.21 |
| C | 50.64 | WB | 26.40 | CP | 38.91 | OP | 36.02 |
| B | 24.39 | WO | 34.62 | CM | 48.02 | OM | 37.73 |
| O | 39.40 | WP | 35.41 | CG | 45.41 | OG | 37.11 |
| P | 40.58 | WM | 33.49 | BO | 30.48 | PM | 39.69 |
| M | 26.59 | WG | 32.23 | BP | 26.36 | PG | 39.14 |
| G | 36.85 | CB | 32.43 | BM | 23.41 | MG | 20.73 |
| WCB | 29.41 | WOP | 33.26 | BPM | 26.10 | COG | 37.34 |
| WCO | 35.07 | WOM | 33.58 | BPG | 25.78 | CPM | 38.37 |
| WCP | 35.14 | WOG | 32.37 | BMG | 21.43 | CPG | 36.52 |
| WCM | 36.16 | WPM | 34.80 | CBO | 32.51 | CMG | 43.41 |
| WCG | 34.58 | WPG | 34.32 | CBP | 33.27 | OPM | 35.54 |
| WBO | 29.45 | WMG | 28.73 | CBM | 31.89 | OPG | 35.04 |
| WBP | 31.47 | BOP | 32.51 | CBG | 30.57 | OMG | 34.43 |
| WBM | 25.43 | BOM | 29.88 | COP | 35.16 | PMG | 38.32 |
| WBG | 24.61 | BOG | 28.85 | COM | 38.68 | | |

## TABLE 42  Coefficients of Variation for Return Per Man-Hour

### Cloud County

| | | | | | | | | | |
|---|---|---|---|---|---|---|---|---|---|
| W | 41.89 | M | 27.75 | WC | 39.05 | CO | 41.71 | OE | 24.74 |
| C | 56.53 | D | 30.88 | WO | 37.92 | CD | 29.04 | OH | 13.79 |
| B | 44.53 | E | 29.20 | WD | 28.45 | CE | 26.30 | DE | 23.52 |
| O | 42.03 | S | 17.48 | WE | 23.66 | CH | 14.53 | DH | 12.97 |
| P | 51.68 | H | 17.14 | WH | 14.11 | OD | 29.17 | EH | 21.80 |
| WCO | 37.08 | WOD | 28.51 | WDH | 13.46 | COH | 13.16 | ODE | 21.39 |
| WCD | 27.95 | WOE | 21.31 | WEH | 18.54 | CDE | 21.95 | ODH | 13.03 |
| WCE | 21.95 | WOH | 14.44 | COD | 28.65 | CDH | 12.28 | OEH | 19.30 |
| WCH | 13.69 | WDE | 20.89 | COE | 22.69 | CEH | 20.14 | DEH | 18.43 |
| WCOD | 28.36 | WCDH | 13.44 | WODH | 14.39 | CODE | 20.25 | CDEH | 17.35 |
| WCOE | 20.13 | WCEH | 17.40 | WOEH | 17.01 | CODH | 12.99 | ODEH | 17.01 |
| WCDE | 19.90 | WODE | 19.76 | WDEH | 16.61 | COEH | 18.00 | | |

### Marion County

| | | | | | | | | | |
|---|---|---|---|---|---|---|---|---|---|
| W | 46.87 | M | 24.89 | WC | 37.95 | CO | 32.73 | OE | 24.65 |
| C | 40.55 | D | 30.88 | WO | 37.13 | CD | 28.39 | OH | 12.77 |
| B | 40.54 | E | 29.20 | WD | 28.12 | CE | 26.46 | DE | 23.51 |
| O | 37.21 | S | 17.48 | WE | 21.51 | CH | 14.47 | DH | 12.97 |
| P | 30.16 | H | 17.14 | WH | 15.70 | OD | 29.03 | EH | 21.80 |
| WCO | 33.06 | WOD | 27.46 | WDH | 13.49 | COH | 11.61 | ODE | 21.44 |
| WCD | 26.41 | WOE | 19.10 | WEH | 17.35 | CDE | 22.07 | ODH | 12.83 |
| WCE | 19.69 | WOH | 14.40 | COD | 27.57 | CDH | 12.29 | OEH | 19.18 |
| WCH | 14.10 | WDE | 19.21 | COE | 22.65 | CEH | 20.28 | DEH | 18.43 |
| WCOD | 26.25 | WCDH | 12.93 | WODH | 13.88 | CODE | 20.32 | CDEH | 17.47 |
| WCOE | 17.73 | WCEH | 16.17 | WOEH | 15.65 | CODH | 12.54 | ODEH | 16.98 |
| WCDE | 18.16 | WODE | 18.13 | WDEH | 15.52 | COEH | 17.95 | | |

### McPherson County

| | | | | | | | | | |
|---|---|---|---|---|---|---|---|---|---|
| W | 37.42 | M | 22.76 | WC | 32.03 | CO | 36.18 | OE | 25.15 |
| C | 46.51 | D | 30.86 | WO | 31.61 | CD | 29.14 | OH | 13.38 |
| B | 42.24 | E | 29.20 | WD | 26.92 | CE | 27.01 | DE | 23.51 |
| O | 38.86 | S | 17.48 | WE | 22.88 | CH | 14.88 | DH | 12.97 |
| P | 39.82 | H | 17.14 | WH | 13.97 | OD | 28.87 | EH | 21.82 |
| WCO | 29.78 | WOD | 26.32 | WDH | 13.00 | COH | 12.68 | ODE | 21.69 |
| WCD | 25.92 | WOE | 20.58 | WEH | 18.27 | CDE | 22.44 | ODH | 12.95 |
| WCE | 21.46 | WOH | 12.91 | COD | 28.15 | CDH | 12.60 | OEH | 19.51 |
| WCH | 12.78 | WDE | 20.24 | COE | 23.65 | CEH | 20.60 | DEH | 18.43 |
| WCOD | 25.78 | WCDH | 12.76 | WODH | 13.40 | CODE | 20.93 | CDEH | 17.72 |
| WCOE | 19.60 | WCEH | 17.35 | WOEH | 16.71 | CODH | 12.99 | ODEH | 17.19 |
| WCDE | 19.49 | WODE | 19.19 | WDEH | 16.30 | COEH | 18.58 | | |

TABLE 42  **Continued**

| | | | | | | Rice County | | | | |
|---|---|---|---|---|---|---|---|---|---|
| W | 38.95 | M | 29.67 | WC | 35.00 | CO | 38.24 | OE | 24.73 |
| C | 48.99 | D | 30.88 | WO | 34.69 | CD | 28.11 | OH | 13.54 |
| B | 45.39 | E | 29.20 | WD | 26.87 | CE | 26.33 | DE | 23.52 |
| O | 39.94 | S | 17.48 | WE | 22.18 | CH | 14.83 | DH | 12.97 |
| P | 41.41 | H | 17.14 | WH | 12.98 | OD | 27.41 | EH | 21.80 |
| WCO | 33.40 | WOD | 26.07 | WDH | 12.30 | COH | 12.96 | ODE | 21.15 |
| WCD | 25.76 | WOE | 19.72 | WEH | 17.70 | CDE | 21.87 | ODH | 12.20 |
| WCE | 20.32 | WOH | 12.86 | COD | 26.44 | CDH | 12.12 | OEH | 19.29 |
| WCH | 12.33 | WDE | 19.71 | COE | 22.67 | CEH | 20.22 | DEH | 18.43 |
| WCOD | 25.58 | WCDH | 12.02 | WODH | 12.66 | CODE | 19.91 | CDEH | 17.35 |
| WCOE | 18.40 | WCEH | 16.52 | WOEH | 16.06 | CODH | 12.02 | ODEH | 16.85 |
| WCDE | 18.56 | WODE | 18.34 | WDEH | 15.81 | COEH | 18.04 | | |

# Notes

## Chapter 1

1. J. H. St. John Crèvecoeur, *Letters from an American Farmer* (New York: Fox, Suffield and Co., 1904), 54, 55.
2. In 1963 Glazer and Moyihan, in their study of ethnic groups in New York City, concluded that ethnic identity was finally on the wane and that "religion and race define the next stage in the evolution of the American peoples." However, an assessment of progress during the 1960s led them to conclude in 1970 that "religion as a major line of division in the city is for the moment in eclipse. Ethnicity and race dominate the city more than ever seemed possible in 1963." N. Glazer and D. P. Moynihan, *Beyond the Melting Pot: The Negroes, Puerto Ricans, Jews, Italians, and Irish of New York City,* 2d ed (Cambridge: MIT Press, 1970), ix.
3. M. A. Jones, *American Immigration* (Chicago: University of Chicago Press, 1960), pp. 157–61. Hansen also argues that the effect of these movements was to produce a backlash that further strengthened the separate identity of the immigrant group rather than facilitated its assimilation into American society. M. L. Hansen, *The Immigrant in American History* (New York: Harper & Row, 1940), 136.
4. F. J. Turner, "The Significance of the Frontier in American History," *Annual Report,* American Historical Association, 1893, pp. 17–18.
5. Zaslow warns that among the many flaws of Turner's statement on the importance of the Midwest is an expression of "local patriotism and interest of a native midwesterner conscious of his region's influence on the history of the nation. It exemplified national patriotism in its insistence in the claim that American democracy was an indigenous growth. It followed prevailing American political philosophy in its assumption that the character of individuals and societies may be modified by the environment and the evolutionary interest of the period in the attention which it paid to processes of

the growth and development of societies and institutions." M. Zaslow, "The Frontier Thesis in Canadian Historiography," *Canadian Historical Review* 29 (1948): 153.

6. Turner, "The Significance," 153.

7. M. M. Gordon, *Assimilation in American Life: The Role of Race, Religion, and National Origins* (New York: Oxford University Press, 1964), 139–42.

8. E. K. Francis, "The Nature of the Ethnic Group," *American Journal of Sociology* 52 (1947): 393–400.

9. An exception is J. A. Fishman et al., *Language Loyalty in the United States: The Maintenance and Perpetuation of Non-English Mother Tongues by American Ethnic Groups* (The Hague: Mouton, 1966).

10. J. N. Carman, *Foreign Language Units of Kansas: Historical Atlas and Statistics* (Lawrence: University of Kansas Press, 1962).

11. There is a very large bibliography on rates of intermarriage, particularly in the sociological papers. For example, D. H. Bouma, "Religiously Mixed Marriages: Denominational Consequences in the Christian Reformed Church," *Marriage and Family Living* 25 (1963): 428–532; J. Drachsler, *Intermarriage in New York City* (New York: Columbia University Press, 1921); A. B. Hollingshead, "Cultural Factors in the Selection of Marriage Mates," *American Sociological Review* 15 (1950): 624; H. B. Johnson, "Intermarriages between German Pioneers and Other Nationalities in 1860 and 1870," *American Journal of Sociology* 51 (1946): 299–304; R. J. R. Kennedy, "Single or Triple Melting Pot? Intermarriage Trends in New Haven, 1870–1950," *American Journal of Sociology* 58 (1952): 56–59; J. I. Kolehmainen, "A Study of Marriage in a Finnish Community," *American Journal of Sociology* 42 (1936): 371–82; L. Nelson, "Intermarriage among Nationality Groups in a Rural Area of Minnesota," *American Journal of Sociology* 48 (1943): 585–92.

12. E. van Cleef, "Finnish Settlements in Canada," *Geographical Review* 42 (1952): 253–66.

13. R. H. Shyrock, "British versus German Traditions in Colonial Agriculture," *Mississippi Valley Historical Review* 26 (1939): 47; W. H. Gehrke, "The Ante-Bellum Agriculture of the Germans in North Carolina," *Agricultural History* 9 (1935): 143. These interpretations have been criticized by J. T. Lemon in *The Best Poor Man's Country* (Baltimore: Johns Hopkins Press, 1972); B. H. Hibbard, *History of Agriculture in Dane County* (Madison, Wis.: University Bulletin 101, Economic and Political Science Series, vol. 1, no. 2, 1904), 108.

14. J. T. Lemon, "Agricultural Practices of National Groups in Eighteenth-Century Southeastern Pennsylvania," *Geographical Review* 56 (1966): 470–71; J. Schafer, *Four Wisconsin Counties* (Madison, Wis.: Domesday Book, General Studies, vol. II, 1927), 92; H. B. Johnson, "Factors Influencing the Distri-

bution of the German Pioneer Population in Minnesota," *Agricultural History* 19 (1945): 39–57; and "The Location of German Immigrants in the Middle West," *Annals of the Association of American Geographers* 41 (1951): 1–41.

15. P. W. Gates, "Charles Lewis Fleischmann: German-American Agricultural Authority," *Agricultural History* 35 (1961): 13; A. B. Cozzens, "Conservation in German Settlements of the Missouri Ozarks," *Geographical Review* 33 (1943): 286–98. See also Shyrock, "British," 39–54, and Gehrke, "The Ante-Bellum," 143–60. W. M. Kollmorgen, "A Reconaissance of Some Cultural-Agricultural Islands in the South," *Economic Geography* 17 (1941): 409–30; "Agricultural-Cultural Islands in the South, part II," *Economic Geography* 19 (1943): 109–17; A. J. Tower and W. Wolf, "Ethnic Groups in Cullman County, Alabama," *Geographical Review* 33 (1943): 276–85.

16. W. M. Kollmorgen, "Immigrant Settlements in Southern Agriculture: A Commentary on the Significance of Cultural Islands in Agricultural History," *Agricultural History* 19 (1945): 69–78; W. D. Pattison, *Beginnings of the American Rectangular Land Survey, 1784–1800* (Chicago: University of Chicago, Dept. of Geography Research Paper no. 50, 1957); G. T. Trewartha, "Some Regional Characteristics of American Farmsteads," *Annals of the Association of American Geographers* 38 (1948): 196–225; J. Warkentin, "Manitoba Settlement Patterns," Historical and Scientific Society of Manitoba, *Papers,* series III, no. 16 (1961), 62–77.

17. F. Kniffen, "Folk Housing: Key to Diffusion," *Annals of the Association of American Geographers* 55 (1965): 549–77; L. Durand, "Dairy Barns in Southeastern Wisconsin," *Economic Geography* 19 (1943): 37–44; C. Mather and M. Kaups, "The Finnish Sauna: A Cultural Index to Settlement," *Annals of the Association of American Geographers* 53 (1963): 494–504; M. Kaups, "Finnish Placenames in Minnesota: A Study in Cultural Transfer," *Geographical Review* 56 (1966): 377–97. A particularly interesting study is that of J. Mannion, *Irish Settlements in Eastern Canada: A Study of Cultural Transfer and Adaption* (Toronto: University of Toronto, Dept. of Geography Research Publications, 1974). Mannion relates the rates of attrition of material culture within Irish settlements in Newfoundland, New Brunswick, and Ontario to the assimilation of Irish immigrants into Canadian society in the nineteenth century.

18. Two exceptions are J. T. Lemon, *The Best Poor Man's Country*. There is also a short discussion on adaptation in J. W. Bennett, *Northern Plainsmen: Adaptive Strategy and Agrarian Life* (Chicago: Aldine Press, 1969). See also Lemon's discussion, "Household Consumption in Eighteenth-Century America and Its Relationship to Production and Trade: The Situation Among Farmers in Southeastern Pennsylvania," *Agricultural History* 41 (1967): 59–70.

19. I have suggested some of these ideas in an essay on ethnic territoriality. See D. Aidan McQuillan, "Territory and Ethnic Identity: Some New Measures

of an Old Theme in the Cultural Geography of North America," in *Essays in Memory and Honour of Andrew Hill Clark*, edited by J. Gibson (Toronto: University of Toronto Press, 1978).

20. N. Glazer, "Ethnic Groups in America: From National Culture to Ideology," in *Freedom and Control in Modern Society*, M. Berger, T. Abel, and C. H. Page, eds. (New York: D. Van Nostrand, 1954), 158–73.

21. Hansen, *The Immigrant*, 132.

22. N. Glazer, "Ethnic Groups," 161; Turner, "The Significance," 15.

23. The 1865 census was not used in this study because the thirty-two county area was very sparsely settled prior to 1870. The manuscripts of the Federal Census for 1880 (which were the only federal materials available for research within the time span of the study) were not used because it was felt they would add but slightly to knowledge of the early years of settlement, and the investment in time required to gather the data would not be sufficiently rewarded.

# Chapter 2

1. R. Ostergren, *A Community Transplanted: The Trans-Atlantic Experience of a Swedish Immigrant Settlement in the Upper Middle West, 1835–1915* (Madison: University of Wisconsin Press, 1988); J. Gjerde, *From Peasants to Farmers: The Migration from Balestrand, Norway, to the Upper Middle West* (Cambridge: Cambridge University Press, 1985); W. D. Kamphoefner, *The Westfalians: From Germany to Missouri* (Princeton: Princeton University Press, 1987); K. N. Conzen, "Peasant Pioneers: Generational Succession among German Farmers in Frontier Minnesota," in *The Countryside in the Age of Capitalist Transformation*, S. Hahn and J. Prude, eds. (Chapel Hill: University of North Carolina Press, 1985), 259–92.

2. "The farmsteads are concentrated in one or several groups and the sown fields are situated in large, coherent blocks, surrounded by fences; the same is true of the meadows. No marking of individual properties is to be found, and there seems every reason to suppose that some form of open field system or at least a system of intermingled parcels is practised." G. Bodvall, "Periodic Settlement, Land-Clearing and Cultivation, with Special Reference to the Boothlands of North Halsingland," *Geografisker Annaler* 39 (1957): 235.

3. S. Helmfrid, "The *Storskifte*, *Enskifte* and *Laga Skifte* in Sweden—General Features," *Geografisker Annaler* 53 (1961): 117. Helmfrid noted that "Sweden was the first country apart from England where agricultural reform was introduced in the form of enclosure legislation. . . . Its aim was radical: dissolution of village communities and the total redistribution of the highly parcelled

land property. Nothing was said about decentralization from the clustered settlements, however" (p. 115).

4. J. S. Lindberg, *The Background of Swedish Emigration to the United States* (Minneapolis: University of Minnesota Press, 1930), 100.

5. O. F. Ander, "The Agricultural Revolution and Swedish Emigration," American Swedish Historical Foundation, *Yearbook* (1945): 53.

6. "The inclination to emigrate and the subsequent organization of the movement was . . . limited to the lower classes, especially the agrarian, while the educated and wealthy and the greater part of the middle class remained aloof, emigrating only under certain unusual conditions, such as social and financial failure. It is against this pattern that the later emigration must be viewed." Ibid., 64.

7. "Prior to 1860 the cultivated area increases one hectare for every person added to the population; thereafter, this relation decreases rapidly. During the seventies the increase in persons is about four times as great as the increase in hectares of cultivated land, and during the period 1890–1900 not quite one-fifth of a hectare is added for each new person." Lindberg, *The Background*, 108.

8. G. M. Stephenson, "The Background of the Beginnings of Swedish Immigration, 1850–1875," *American Historical Review* 31 (1926): 720.

9. C. A. Dawson, *Group Settlement: Ethnic Communities in Western Canada* (Toronto: Macmillan and Co., 1936), 98.

10. J. Driedger, "Family Among the Mennonites in East and West Prussia," *Mennonite Quarterly Review* 31 (1957): 17–20.

11. D. G. Remple, "The Mennonite Colonies in New Russia: A Study of Their Settlement and Economic Development from 1784 to 1914," unpublished Ph.D. thesis, Stanford University, 1933.

12. One of the Russian state counsellors reported to the Russian Senate on the condition of the Khortitsa colony: "Nearly all the Mennonites are orderly and clean in their domestic life, sober and honest in their moral life, and diligent and industrious in their economic life. In spite of their industry, however, those at Khortitsa will hardly ever achieve a prosperous condition. It is a predominantly rolling country on which, due to the dryness of the soil and the lack of rain, the grasses usually burn out and the grains grow poorly. Thus the plowman often tills and plants his field in vain. And few are those who harvest enough to provide for themselves for the entire year. Stock raising alone is of some profit to them. This branch of farming they make great use of, having bought a sufficient number of foreign breeds of horses and cattle. But this branch of economy too they are unable to develop to a degree they desire and are accustomed to on account of pasture and hay and the losses that the severe winters cause." Quoted by Rempel, "The Mennonite," 80–81.

13. The large landowners, however, reacted more slowly to new market opportunities than the smaller farmers in the newly established colonies. "The switch to arable farming was much slower on the Mennonite estates than in the colonies. Nor did it reach here [on the large farms] such a preponderant degree of small-grain production. On the contrary, many estate owners, by the introduction of forage and root crops, resorted much sooner to a more balanced system of farming." Rempel, "The Mennonite," 247.

14. Cornies realized that soil aridity rather than fertility was the major problem for crop production. After continued experimentation and observation he developed two methods for increasing the supply of soil moisture. One approach was to plow the fallow land in the fall, and the second was to harvest the cropland by cutting the grain high on the stalk. Both methods trapped the snow and kept it from blowing on the surface in winter, thereby increasing the supply of moisture to the soil during the spring melt.

15. Rempel, "The Mennonite," 184.

16. Rempel, "The Mennonite," 180–98.

17. "The original poverty of the Mennonite colonies gradually changed to wealth, and the change went still further for in many cases the old patriarchal farm and farm home became 'capitalist big business.'" C. Krahn, "Some Social Attitudes of the Mennonites in Prussia," *Mennonite Quarterly Review* 9 (1935): 170.

18. E. K. Francis, *In Search of Utopia: The Mennonites of Manitoba* (Glencoe, Ill.: Free Press, 1955), 25.

19. "These included in the main the more conservative groups, such as the daughter colonies of the Chortitz settlement, Bergthal and Fuerstenland, Alexanderwohl, the Swiss of Volhynia, the Hutterites, and the Kleine Gemeinde colony of Borsenko. These [colonies] emigrated bodily; but from every settlement and from almost every village there were some who preferred emigration to compromise." C. H. Smith, *The Coming of the Russian Mennonites* (Berne, Ind.: Mennonite Book Concern, 1927), 96.

20. G. Leibbrandt, "The Emigration of the German Mennonites from Russia to the United States and Canada, 1873–1880," part II, *Mennonite Quarterly Review* 7 (1933): 6.

21. Chief among the opponents was Senator Carpenter of Wisconsin, who declared: "We do not desire to have a town or a county settled by any foreign nationality, speaking their own language, having their own natural amusements, and in all things separated and different from Americans. The idea is and should be, and it should never be departed from, that in inviting foreigners to settle in this country they should take their place with our citizens, they should come here not to be Germans or Frenchmen or Italians, but to be Americans, to become American citizens, to speak our language, to support our institutions, to be of us in all things." Quoted by Leibbrandt, "The Emi-

gration," 20. In this speech Carpenter reiterated a federal policy established fifty years earlier whereby no government assistance would be given to any group seeking to establish solidly ethnic settlements.

22. For a full discussion of the growth in population and settlement see R. C. Harris, *The Seigneurial System in Early Canada* (Madison: University of Wisconsin Press, 1968), 89–105.

23. P. Garigue, "Change and Continuity in Rural French Canada," in *French Canadian Society,* Marcel Rioux and Yves Martin, eds. (Toronto: McClelland and Stewart, 1964), 127.

24. The existence of some common lands was acknowledged by Rodolphe deKoninck and J-A. Soltesz in "Geographie, Culture, Language aux Cent-Iles du Lac Saint-Pierre: Les Bases d'Une Etude," *Canadian Geographer* 17 (1973): 220–34. However, these occurrences were somewhat exceptional. "The evidence about settlement patterns, about the relationship of the seigneurie to roads, parishes, judicial, and economic functions, added to that which has already been presented about the seigneurs, leaves little doubt that the generalized picture of the seigneuries as a social unit is incorrect at least for the preconquest period. Not only had few seigneurs any interest in leading; most habitants did not want to be led." Harris, *Seigneurial System,* 191–92; A. Greer, *Peasant, Lord, and Merchant: Rural Society in Three Quebec Parishes, 1740–1840* (Toronto: University of Toronto Press, 1985), 135–38.

25. M. Séguin, *La "Nation Canadienne" et l'agriculture, 1760–1850* (Trois Rivieres: Editions boreal express, 1970), 192–211.

26. That importance of the family is central in any understanding of French-Canadian society has been attested to by most sociologists. "Many of the old culture traits are so closely allied to the thrifty, close family economy that they have resisted change to a remarkable degree." H. Miner, "Changes in Rural French-Canadian Culture," in *French Canadian Society,* M. Rioux and Y. Martin, eds. 64. "Even more than the rang, the family constituted the social unit par excellence. Due to its comparative isolation, even within the rang, the family was the real unit of subsistence and it was supposed to meet all the needs of the individual. Its functions were therefore very numerous." G. Fortin, "Socio-Cultural Changes in an Agricultural Parish," in *French-Canadian Society,* Rioux and Martin, eds. 94. In the preface to Horace Miner's book on the parish of St. Denis, Robert Redfield wrote: "The fabric of society is woven of threads of consanguineous and connubial connection; the family system is strong, pervasive, and certain in its effects." In H. Miner, *St. Denis: A French-Canadian Parish* (Chicago: University of Chicago Press, 1939).

27. Séguin has pointed out that the average export of wheat per farm from lower Canada was low in the early years of the nineteenth century and that it dropped even lower after 1817. Séguin, *"Nation Canadienne,"* 100–102.

28. M. McInnis, "A Reconsideration of the State of Agriculture in Lower Canada

in the First Half of the Nineteenth Century," *Canadian Papers in Rural History,* D. H. Akenson, ed. (Gananoque, Ontario: Langdale Press, 1982), 9–49; F. Ouellet, *Economic and Social History of Quebec, 1760–1850* (Ottawa: Gage Publishing, Carleton Library no. 120, 1980); J. McCallum, *Unequal Beginnings: Agriculture and Economic Development in Quebec and Ontario Until 1870* (Toronto: University of Toronto Press, 1980).

29. "Dedicated as they were to the preservation of their laws, their language, and their religion, they resisted any change, however small, in their mode of life. It was this aversion to innovation which rendered the distress in the seigneuries [in the 1840s] so acute and made it so difficult to ameliorate." R. L. Jones, "French-Canadian Agriculture in the St. Lawrence Valley, 1815–1850," *Agricultural History* 15 (1952): 148.

30. R. D. Vicero, "Immigration of French-Canadians to New England, 1840–1900: A Geographical Analysis," unpublished Ph.D. diss., University of Wisconsin, Madison, 1968, 61.

31. W. H. Parker, "A Revolution in the Agricultural Geography of Lower Canada, 1833–1838," *Revue Canadienne de geographie* 11 (1957): 189–94.

32. Jones, "French-Canadian," 144.

33. Province of Canada, Report of the Special Committee on the State of Agriculture in Lower Canada, *Journals of the Legislative Assembly* 9 (1830), appendix TT.

34. Jones, "French-Canadian," 144.

35. R. L. Jones, "The Agricultural Development of Lower Canada, 1850–1867," *Agricultural History* 19 (1945): 212–24.

36. For a full account of this migration see chapter 2 in R. D. Vicero, "Immigration," 89–133.

37. Ibid., 104.

38. D. A. McQuillan, "French-Canadian Communities in the American Upper Midwest during the Nineteenth Century," *Cahiers de geographie de Québec* 23 (1979): 53–72.

# Chapter 3

1. The dissolution of Indian reservations and the political rivalries in Kansas during the territorial period are discussed by Paul W. Gates, *Fifty Million Acres: Conflicts over Kansas Land Policy, 1854–1890* (New York: Atherton Press, 1966).

2. William F. Zornow, *Kansas: A History of the Jayhawk State* (Norman: University of Oklahoma Press, 1957), 135–37.

3. Bogue noted that land clearing needed capital. Subsistence farming would not support the family for a long time, and in order to pay off loans and mort-

gages crops had to be sold within the first few years. Allan G. Bogue, *Money at Interest: The Farm Mortgage on the Middle Border* (Ithaca: Cornell University Press, 1955) 274–75. Malin also commented on the inadequacy of subsistence farming: "A traditional subsistence agriculture was not possible as a regular system, and in years of cash crop failures, when subsistence was critical, these crops had usually already failed. They were conspicuously less drought-resistant than field crops. A subsistence agriculture was not even available under these circumstances as a crop insurance." James C. Malin, *Winter Wheat in the Golden Belt of Kansas* (Lawrence: University of Kansas Press, 1944), 105.

4. Peter Henry Pearson, *Prairie Vikings* (East Orange, N.J.: Karl J. Olson, 1927), 13–14; E. K. Lindquist, *Smoky Valley People: A History of Lindsborg, Kansas* (Lindsborg: Bethany College, 1953), 120.

5. "After having visited the valley they bargained with the Kansas Pacific Railroad Company for twenty-two sections of land in Saline and McPherson counties, and then brought the railroad company's land agent home to Galesburg. Here each member bought his own piece of land and the company was at once dissolved, but it had served its purpose and brought hundreds of thrifty and industrious young Swedes to the plains of Kansas." Alfred Bergin, "The Swedish Settlements in Central Kansas," *Collections*, Kansas State Historical Society, 12 (1909–10): 30.

6. Ibid., 23. The pattern of residential segregation was also a function of kinship and neighborly ties. "Relatives and friends who wished to live on adjoining farms banded together in groups of four to eight, depending on their desire for eighty or 160 acres, and one person represented them in drawing their land. The section was then parceled out by agreement or by lot among these individuals." Lindquist, *Smoky Valley*, 170–71.

7. The Bureau of Land Management records show that Stromquist, Rodell, Hawkinson, and Cederholm filed for homesteads in 1871 and 1872. There is clear evidence that these men arrived in the township in 1868, but there is no explanation for the delay in filing. Clearly the date of filing for homestead cannot be taken to indicate the year of initial settlement.

8. Exceptions existed in sections 2 and 12, where Swedes homesteaded on eighty-acre lots in 1869 and 1870.

9. G. I. Adams, "Physiographic Divisions of Kansas," *Transactions Kansas Academy of Science* 18 (1903): 121. One of the attractions for cattle raising in the northern part of Union Township was the large number of springs that issue from the base of the sandstone.

10. Adams, "Physiographic," 116–17.

11. Alfred Bergin, *Pioneer Swedish-American Culture in Central Kansas*, translated by Ruth Billdt (Lindsborg, Kan.: Lindsborg News Record, 1965), p. 38.

12. Indian attacks in 1867, 1868, and 1869 to the north and west of Salina frightened some settlers. The Rev. Olsson and his group, who were en route from

New York to Kansas in 1869, halted their journey in Missouri to reconsider their plans after receiving news of the attacks. E. K. Lindquist, *Vision for a Valley: Olof Olsson and the Early History of Lindsborg* (Rock Island, Ill.: Augustana Historical Society Publications, no. 22, 1970), 104; Pearson, *Prairie*, 30, 33–34.

13. Lindquist, *Smoky Valley*, 70.

14. Ibid., 84–86.

15. Pearson, *Prairie*, 85.

16. Lindquist, *Smoky Valley*, 60.

17. In April 1874, Carlson and twenty-six others withdrew from Olsson's congregation to establish a new church. One year later John Ferm and Anders Johan Nilson, also founders of the First Swedish Agricultural Company, were excommunicated by Olsson. Ibid., 41.

18. Ibid., 57.

19. Ibid., 78.

20. Lindquist, *Smoky Valley*, 39. Lindquist, *Vision*, 78.

21. Pearson, *Prairie*, 25.

22. Lindquist, *Smoky Valley*, 40.

23. Lindquist, *Vision*, 74.

24. C. C. Janzen, "A Study of the Mennonite Settlement in the Counties of Marion McPherson, Harvey, Reno, and Butler, Kansas," unpublished Ph.D. diss., University of Chicago, 1926, 27; D. A. Haury, *Prairie People: A History of the Western District Conference* (Newton, Kan.: Faith and Life Press, 1981), p. 37.

25. A. Pantle, "Settlement of the Krimmer Mennonite Brethren at Gnadenau, Marion County," *Kansas Historical Quarterly* 13 (1945): 266.

26. Janzen, "A Study," 27–34. See also C. C. Janzen, "Americanization of the Russian Mennonites in central Kansas," unpublished M.A. thesis, University of Kansas, 1914, 60; Writers Program, *A Guide to Hillsboro, Kansas* (Hillsboro, Kans.: Mennonite Brethren Publishing House), 1940, 16; A. Albrecht, "Mennonite Settlements in Kansas," unpublished M.A. thesis, University of Kansas, 1925, 37–40; also Haury, *Prairie People*, 34–35. Mennonite villages did not survive more than a decade in the United States, although in Canada they did continue for several decades before breaking up. J. Warkentin, "Mennonite Agricultural Settlements of Southern Manitoba," *Geographical Review* 49 (1959): 342–68.

27. N. L. Prentis, *South-Western Letters* (Topeka: Kansas Publishing House, 1982), 14. See also *Mennonite Life* 25 (April 1970): 59–62; J. D. Butler, "The Mennonite Stove," *Mennonite Life* 4 (October 1949): 16–17; Janzen, "Americanization," 63; Albrecht, "Mennonite," 37; Writers Program, *A Guide*, 20; M. Gingerich, "Russian Mennonites React to Their New Environment," *Mennonite Life* 15 (1960): 176.

28. Prentis, *South-Western*, 27; Janzen, "A Study," 35; Albrecht, "Mennonite," 49.

29. Janzen, "Americanization," 74.

30. Albrecht, "Mennonite," 10–17; Haury, *Prairie People,* 29–55; Janzen, "Americanization," 102.

31. Janzen, "A Study," 35.

32. Writers Program, *A Guide,* 19. Albrecht, "Mennonite," 41. Haury corrects this mistake, as did Malin, and explains how Bernhard Warkentin worked with officials of the Department of Agriculture in importing hard red winter wheat in 1885 for cultivation. D. A. Haury, "Bernhard Warkentin and the Kansas Mennonite Pioneers," *Mennonite Life,* 29, no. 4 (1974): 75; Prentis, *South-Western,* 14.

33. N. Prentis, *Kansas Miscellaneous* (Topeka: Kansas Publishing House, 1889), 165.

34. E. W. Hoch, "All About Marion County Kansas," *Marion County Record,* 1876, 17; C. B. Schmidt, "Reminiscences of Foreign Immigration Work for Kansas," *Collections,* Kansas State Historical Society, 9 (1905–06): 495. Bishop Wiebe wrote of the immigrants to Marion County, "We were all poor people, many families owed their travelling expenses. They had to go in debt for the land, oxen plow, farmer's wagon, and even the sod house; they had to have provisions for a year; there was little or no chance of earning something so they had to go into debt for that too." (Quoted in Writers Program, *A Guide,* 17–18). The case of Heinrich Richert may well be typical of the Mennonites' reputed wealth. He arrived in Marion County in 1874 with $1,000 and a family of ten, but before his farm was operational he had incurred a debt of $1,300. Nevertheless, by 1879 he was out of debt and owned 266 acres of land, six horses, good farm implements, a flourishing orchard, and a sturdy home (ibid., 20).

35. C. H. Smith, *The Coming of the Russian Mennonites* (Berne, Ind.: Mennonite Book Concern), 1927, 157.

36. Smith, *The Coming,* 115.

37. Janzen, "A Study," 34. "Only one thing was lacking—a convenient market. The western part of Marion County then had no railroad and produce must be hauled ten to twenty-five miles to Peabody, or Newton, or some other point on the Santa Fe Main line. But the situation was soon remedied [in 1879] and in the process Hillsboro was born." (Writers Program, *A Guide,* 20).

38. Writers Program, *A Guide,* 21–22.

39. E. F. Hollibaugh, *Biographical History of Cloud County, Kansas* (no publisher or date of publication), 118; W. E. Reid, *Edwards' Atlas of Cloud County, Kansas* (Quincy, Ill.: John P. Edwards, 1885), 6–7.

40. Hollibaugh, *Biographical,* 39–52; Reid, *Edwards' Atlas,* 8.

41. J. M. Hagaman, *Blade Annual and History of Cloud County* (Concordia, Kans.: Blade Steam Printing House, 1884), 14.

42. W. E. Reid wrote vividly a decade later of the grasshopper invasion of 1874:

"Not only did they devour the growing crop, but they prevented the sewing of winter wheat, eating the kernel when sowed, and the young sprout as soon as it appeared above the ground. The suffering caused by the devastation was very great, but, by the kindly assistance of friends in the east, the majority stayed on their claims, and were rewarded by an excellent crop in 1875" (Reid, *Edwards' Atlas*, 10; Hollibaugh, *Biographical*, 109, 166).

43. Hollibaugh, *Biographical*, 110. See also the Concordia *Empire*, December 20, 1901, which remembered a serious prairie fire in October rather than in August of 1871. A few French Canadians did not persevere but returned to Illinois after the grasshopper invasion. Norma Meier, "Link with the Past," Concordia *Blade Empire*, March 31, 1981.

44. P. Beckman, "The Catholic Church on the Kansas Frontier," unpublished Ph.D. thesis, Catholic University, 1943, 134.

45. L. Mattas, *St. Joseph Church, Centennial Edition 1868–1968* (Concordia, Kans.: St. Joseph Church, 1968), 10.

46. Beckman, "The Catholic Church," 115.

47. Reid, *Edwards' Atlas*, 9; Hollibaugh, *Biographical*, 158.

48. Hollibaugh, ibid., 127.

49. Hollibaugh, ibid., 880; Reid, *Edwards' Atlas*, 11.

50. Reid, ibid., 10; Hollibaugh, *Biographical*, 409–10; Reid, *Edwards' Atlas*, 10–11.

51. Hollibaugh, *Biographical*, 158; Hagaman, *Blade Annual*, 27. Much of this material is drawn from brief biographies of the early settlers in Concordia provided by E. F. Hollibaugh in *Biographical*, 271–335.

52. Ibid., 520.

53. H. B. Johnson, "Rational and Ecological Aspects of the Quarter Section," *Geographical Review* 47 (1957): 330–48. See also *Order Upon the Land* (New York: Oxford University Press, 1976), 135–40.

## Chapter 4

1. Walter T. K. Nugent, *The Tolerant Populists: Kansas Populism and Nativism* (Chicago: University of Chicago Press, 1963), 43; E. K. Lindquist, *Smoky Valley People: A History of Lindsborg, Kansas* (Lindsborg: Bethany College, 1953), 200. Juhnke points out that the Swedish vote for Republicans was often twenty points higher than the average for Kansas in the decades before 1900. J. C. Juhnke, *A People of Two Kingdoms: The Political Acculturation of The Kansas Mennonites* (Newton, Kans.: Faith and Life Press, 1975), 6, 42.

2. Nugent, *The Tolerant*, 43; E. K. Lindquist, *Vision for a Valley: Olof Olsson and the Early History of Lindsborg* (Rock Island: Augustana Historical Society, 1974), 58.

3. E. K. Lindquist, "The Scandinavian Element in Kansas," in *Kansas: The First*

*Century*, vol. 1, John D. Bright, ed. (New York: Lewis Historical Publishing Company), 323; Lindquist, *Smoky Valley*, 200–201.

4. Lindquist, *Vision*, 72; Lindquist, *Smoky Valley*, 185.
5. Lindquist, "The Scandinavian Element," 313.
6. Lindquist, *Vision*, 72; Lindquist, *Smoky Valley*, 183, 185; Lindquist, "The Scandinavian Element," 313.
7. Lindquist, *Smoky Valley*, 44, 73, 167.
8. Lindquist, "The Scandinavian Element," 314.
9. C. T. Pihlblad, "The Kansas Swedes," *Southwestern Social Sciences Quarterly*, 13 (1932): 47.
10. Lindquist, "The Scandinavian Element," 316.
11. Pihlblad, "The Kansas Swedes," 47.
12. Nugent, *The Tolerant*, 39.
13. C. C. Janzen, "Americanization of the Russian Mennonites in central Kansas," unpublished M.A. thesis, University of Kansas, 1914, 110; C. C. Janzen, "A Study of the Mennonite Settlement in the Counties of Marion, McPherson, Harvey, Reno, and Butler, Kansas," unpublished Ph.D. thesis, University of Chicago, 1926, 53.
14. Nugent, *The Tolerant*, 40.
15. Juhnke, *A People*, 51.
16. Janzen, "Americanization," 114.
17. Juhnke, *A People*, 61.
18. Janzen, "A Study," 97, 101, 102.
19. D. A. Haury, *Prairie People: A History of the Western Conference*. (Newton: Faith and Life Press, 1981), 177.
20. Janzen, "Americanization," 129–30; Writers' Program, *A Guide to Hillsboro, Kansas* (Hillsboro: Mennonite Brethren Publishing House, 1940), 22; Janzen, "A Study," 136; J. N. Carman, "Foreign Language Units of Kansas," unpublished manuscript, Kansas State Historical Society, n.d., 164.
21. Janzen offered several explanations for the schisms. "First, the Mennonite faith fosters an extreme individualism, which makes for strength of character but lack of uniformity. Second, the congregational form of church government and the absence of unifying conferences in the past permitted slight differences to develop in the scattered congregations. Third, being a rural people, unlearned, they have not been trained to subordinate non-essentials to the broader and more important interests of life. Fourth, in some instances stubborn, self-willed, quarrelsom [sic] individuals have made use of these characteristics and fostered schisms." Janzen, "A Study," 69.
22. Ibid., 151. Janzen, "Americanization," 89.
23. Janzen, "Americanization," 81, 135.
24. Janzen, "A Study," 150, 142.
25. Ibid., 147.
26. Janzen, "Americanization," 69, 105; Janzen, "A Study," 43, 44.

27. Janzen, "Americanization," 80.

28. E. F. Hollibaugh, *Biographical History of Cloud County, Kansas* (no publisher or date of publication), 9.

29. Ibid., 18–19.

30. Nugent, *The Tolerant*, 44.

31. *The Visitor*, 11 September 1884.

32. *The Visitor*, July 7, 1887.

33. E. Thomas, *Footprints on the Frontier: A History of the Sisters of St. Joseph, Concordia, Kansas*. (Westminster, Md.: Newman Press, 1948), 142–50; L. Mattas, *St. Joseph Church, Centennial Edition 1868–1968* (Concordia, Kans.: St. Joseph Church, 1968), 12.

34. Thomas, *Footprints*, 173, 175, 180, 182, 194, 197, 223, 237. Mattas, *St. Joseph*, 12.

35. *The Visitor*, 11 September 1884; Thomas, *Footprints*, 158.

36. N. Prentis, "Through Northern Kansas" in the Atchison *Weekly Champion*, 6 August 1881.

37. Topeka, *Capital Journal*, 5 March 1961.

38. Kansas City, *Star*, 10 December 1911.

39. Carman, *Foreign*, 214.

40. Ibid., 214.

41. Prentis, "Through," op. cit.

42. Kansas Presbyterian Synod, *Minutes*, vol. 1, 1879–93 (Topeka: Geo. W. Martin, Kansas Publishing House, 1893).

43. Concordia, *Empire*, 31 January 1884 and 7 February 1884.

44. Hollibaugh, *Biographical*, 16. C. Paulsen, "Trivial History of Concordia and Environs," unpublished manuscript, Cloud County Historical Society, Concordia, December 1984, 5.

45. J. C. Malin, "The Turnover of Farm Population in Kansas," *Kansas Historical Quarterly* 4 (1935): 341.

46. Malin demonstrated that "the economic development of the farm communities was not promoted by the high rate of turnover of farmers." Malin, "Turnover," 355. I have investigated this issue at length elsewhere. See D. A. McQuillan, "The Mobility of Immigrants and Americans: A Comparison of Farmers on the Kansas Frontier," *Agricultural History* 53, no. 3 (1979): 576–96.

47. J. C. Malin, *Winter Wheat in the Golden Belt of Kansas* (Lawrence: University of Kansas Press, 1944), 133; M. Curti, *The Making of an American Community* (Stanford: Stanford University Press, 1959), 65. See also A. B. Hollingshead, "Changes in Land Ownership as an Index of Succession in Rural Communities," *American Journal of Sociology* 43 (March 1938): 775.

48. In the much earlier study "Farm Population Turnover," Malin deliberately excluded the foreign born from his selection of sample townships, but even then he had some reservations about the traditional view of immigrant mo-

bility. "The foreign population was usually more stable than the native born, but not so much as is usually supposed. The second and later generations seemed to take on rather quickly much of the characteristics of the native born." Malin, "The Turnover," 352.

49. D. A. McQuillan, "Territory and Ethnic Identity: Some New Measures of an Old Theme in the Cultural Geography of the United States," in *European Settlement and Development in North America: Essays on Geographical Change in Honour and Memory of Andrew Hill Clark*, J. R. Gibson, ed. (Toronto: University of Toronto Press), 1978, 136–69.

50. G. D. Suttles, *The Social Construction of Communities* (Chicago: University of Chicago Press), 162; D. Ward, "The Emergence of Central Immigrant Ghettoes," *Annals of the Association of American Geographers* 58 (1968): 343–59.

51. Hollingshead, "Changes," 772.

52. McQuillan, "Territory," 146.

53. Family size in this context refers to "census family size," which includes the number of children residing with their parents at the time of the census. The census family size often underestimates actual family size because children over sixteen years may have left home to work elsewhere.

# Chapter 5

1. The problems of hunger and persecution were very real in the nineteenth century; that is not denied. But their significance for the vast majority of emigrants has probably been overstated. The exceptional circumstances of government oppression and famine were more important in setting emigration in motion than in sustaining the flood of emigration that followed. The number of individuals who felt sufficiently threatened to take the drastic step of searching out a new home thousands of miles across the ocean was probably quite small. However, once the first emigrants had made the journey and were established in the New World, the decision to emigrate was made much easier for the thousands who followed. And for them the motivation was not fear of hunger or threat of persecution but the prospect of improving their material well-being. This was true both in the United States and in Canada. See R. Ostergren, *A Community Transplanted: The Trans-Atlantic Experience of a Swedish Immigrant Settlement in the Upper Middle West, 1835–1915* (Madison: University of Wisconsin Press, 1988); J. Gjerde, *From Peasants to Farmers: The Migration from Balestrand, Norway, to the Upper Middle West* (Cambridge: Cambridge University Press, 1985); H. Brotz, "Multiculturalism in Canada: A Muddle," *Canadian Public Policy*, 6, no. 1, (1980): 41–46.

2. M. Curti, *The Making of an American Community* (Stanford: Stanford University Press, 1959), 192.

3. Some of these themes are developed in D. A. McQuillan, "Farm Size and the

Work Ethic: Measuring the Success of Immigrant Farmers on the American Grasslands, 1875–1925," *Journal of Historical Geography* 4 (1977): 57–76.

4. Ibid., 58.

5. J. C. Malin, *Winter Wheat in the Golden Belt of Kansas* (Lawrence: University of Kansas Press, 1944), 128. See also p. 90.

6. J. C. Malin, *The Grassland of North America: Prolegomena to Its History with Addenda and Postscript* (Gloucester, Mass.: Peter Smith, 1967), 294.

7. Ibid., 294–95. A similar pattern of speculation was identified by A. G. Bogue, *From Prairie to Corn Belt* (Chicago: University of Chicago Press, 1963), 52; and by M. P. Conzen, *Frontier Farming in an Urban Shadow* (Madison: State Historical Society of Wisconsin, 1971), 66.

8. See J. W. Watson, "Rural Depopulation in South-Western Ontario," *Annals of the Association of American Geographers* 37 (1947): 145–54.

9. R. M. Finley, "A Budgeting Approach to the Question of Homestead Size on the Plains," *Agricultural History* 42 (1968): 114.

10. In a study of mortgaging patterns in Kinsley Township, Edwards County, Kansas, Bogue found that there were three peak years of mortgaging: 1879, 1886, and 1905. The 1879 peak coincided with the first spate of title granting in Kinsley Township, whereby many farmers obtained outright ownership of their farms. Thus, the farm was used as security for a loan to buy more farm implements and machinery. A. G. Bogue, *Money at Interest: The Farm Mortgage on the Middle Border* (Ithaca: Cornell University Press, 1955), 247.

11. Malin, *The Grassland*, 294–95; also Malin, *Winter*, 127, 299.

12. A. G. Bogue, "Farming in the Prairie Peninsula, 1830–1870," *Journal of Economic History* 23 (1963): 5.

13. M. B. Bogue, *Patterns from the Sod: Land Use and Tenure in the Grand Prairie, 1850–1900* (Springfield: Illinois State Historical Library, Collections, vol. 34, 1959).

14. Ibid., 150.

15. The difference of means tests for differences in farm size demonstrated some variability between the members of each ethnic group and the control group:

|  |  | 1885 | 1895 | 1905 | 1915 | 1925 |
|---|---|---|---|---|---|---|
| Swedes/others | t | 1.0168 | 2.2801* | 0.1616 | 0.6931 | 0.3658 |
|  | df | 208 | 165 | 166 | 159 | 147 |
| Mennonites/others | t | 2.4351* | 3.8075* | 1.9584* | 1.5873 | 2.0525* |
|  | df | 252 | 246 | 248 | 229 | 218 |
| French Canadians/others | t | 1.8509* | 1.1856 | 0.5449 | 0.9084 | 1.4154 |
|  | df | 206 | 189 | 197 | 208 | 185 |

df = degrees of freedom
*Significant at the .05 confidence level.

16. The results for difference of means tests in farm size between the segregated
and nonsegregated samples were:

|  |  | 1885 | 1895 | 1905 | 1915 | 1925 |
|---|---|---|---|---|---|---|
| Swedes | $t$ | 0.8042 | 0.1564 | 1.6405 | 1.0893 | 0.1077 |
|  | df | 110 | 107 | 109 | 99 | 93 |
| Mennonites | $t$ | 1.7828* | 1.5708 | 2.5428* | 0.7240 | 1.2946 |
|  | df | 172 | 177 | 200 | 188 | 186 |
| French Canadians | $t$ | 1.3114 | 0.7280 | 0.7794 | 2.4017* | 1.8730* |
|  | df | 142 | 123 | 125 | 151 | 131 |

df = degrees of freedom
*Significant at the .05 confidence level

17. McQuillan, "Farm Size," 66.
18. H. M. Blalock, *Social Statistics* (New York: McGraw-Hill, 1960), 73–74.
19. For the moment it is noted that this observation simply reflects the fact that
Swedes had larger farms than Mennonites or French Canadians.

|  | 1885 | 1895 | 1905 | 1915 | 1925 |
|---|---|---|---|---|---|
| $F$ ratio | 5.03* | 0.02 | 4.51* | 5.17* | 2.50* |
| Degrees of freedom | 2/263 | 2/241 | 2/247 | 2/237 | 2/221 |

*Significant at the .05 confidence level

20. The problem of inequities in tax assessment was common throughout the
Midwest. Bogue described some attempts to overcome these variations from
county to county and from township to township in Illinois and Iowa: "Early
in the history of Illinois, appraisal procedures specified simply that lands
should be categorized as first, second, and third class in quality and that a
specified uniform valuation be given to all lands in each classification. Illinois
legislators abandoned this procedure and decided that property should be ap-
praised at its true value, a procedure approved in Iowa as well. So strong were
local pressures, however, that the assessors never obeyed the law. Local classification systems were common; underassessment was general." A. G. Bogue,
*From Prairie to Corn Belt* (Chicago: University of Chicago Press, 1963), 191.
21. Finley, "A Budgeting," 109–14.
22. The following table shows differences in the mean value of real estate and
results of difference of means tests between segregated and nonsegregated
samples for Swedes, Mennonites, and French Canadians.

| Sample | | 1885 | 1895 | 1905 | 1915 | 1925 |
|---|---|---|---|---|---|---|
| Union-Rockville | | 390 | 347 | −65 | −2,492 | −2,012 |
| Menno-Meridian | | −447 | −318 | −165 | −2,879 | −7,043 |
| Shirley-Aurora | | 198 | 72 | −34 | −1,755 | −3,195 |
| Swedes | t | 1.917* | 0.916 | 0.403 | 1.876* | 1.002 |
| | df | 79 | 78 | 63 | 45 | 40 |
| Mennonites | t | 4.097* | 2.321* | 1.218 | 2.817* | 4.112* |
| | df | 94 | 98 | 116 | 121 | 112 |
| French Canadians | t | 0.430 | 3.034* | 0.552 | 0.193 | 1.611* |
| | df | 18 | 84 | 71 | 64 | 65 |

df = degrees of freedom
*Significant at .05 level

In 1905 the differences in mean value of real estate were not significant for any of the three groups; before and after 1905 the differences were indeed significant, as the *t* values indicate.

23. Gray has expressed some reservations about the validity of the assumption of the agricultural ladder theory that each step on the ladder always represents progress: "Moreover, progress in independence does not always mean progress in well-being. Many a tenant who is subject to the supervision of a capable and honest landlord may be better off than a farm owner who has not sufficient experience or capital to operate his farm efficiently." Furthermore, "a mortgaged owned farmer may have a smaller equity in the farm capital than a tenant or part owner free of mortgage." L. C. Gray et al., "Farm Ownership and Tenancy," *Agriculture Yearbook,* USDA (Washington: Government Printing Office, 1924), 548.

24. In his study of immigrant farmers Brunner asserted that "the primary goal of the new and old immigrant alike has been and is land and home ownership." E. deS. Brunner, *Immigrant Farmers and Their Children* (Garden City, New York: Doubleday, Doran and Co., 1925), 115.

25. A. G. Bogue estimated that in 1850 between 7 and 11 percent of the farms in Clarion Township, Bureau County, Illinois, were rented and between 10 and 22 percent of the farms in Union Township, Davis County, Iowa. By 1900 the rate of tenancy was as high as 50 percent and even 60 percent. Bogue, "Farming," 25–26. Cogswell estimated that farm tenancy increased from almost 18 percent in 1850 to 27 percent in 1880 for a six-county area in eastern Iowa. S. Cogswell, *Tenure, Nativity, and Age as Factors in Iowa Agriculture, 1850–1880* (Ames: Iowa University Press, 1975), 22. M. B. Bogue also discovered that in parts of central Illinois the rate of tenancy was 38 percent in 1880, over 41 percent in 1890, and almost 46 percent in 1900. Bogue, *Patterns,* 156.

26. Gray et al., "Farm Ownership," 507–600; E. A. Goldenweiser and Leon E.

Truesdell, *Farm Tenancy in the United States* (U.S. Bureau of the Census, Washington: Government Printing Office, 1924).

27. Curti, *The Making*, 144; Cogswell, *Tenure*, 29–30; Goldenweiser and Truesdell, *Farm Tenancy*, 272.

28. Bogue, *From Prairie*, 65.

29. Paul W. Gates, "Frontier Landlords and Pioneer Tenants," *Landlords and Tenants on the Prairie Frontier: Studies in American Land Policy* (Ithaca: Cornell University Press, 1973), 238–302.

30. Curti observed: "For many people the very word has about it the flavor of misfortune, but for large numbers of those who came into Tremplealeau almost penniless it was a farm mortgage which enabled them really to make a farm. In the 1850's and early 1860's especially, it was relatively easy to get land. Even if there were not the $50 one needed to buy a forty in 1860, the money could be earned by farm labor for others, perhaps in a single year. But it took money to turn this real property into a farm, money at least for a plow, a horse, and a cow, and for pigs to furnish meat for the winter." Curti, *The Making*, 156. A major contribution in this area is that of Robert P. Swierenga, *Pioneers and Profits: Land Speculation on the Iowa Frontier* (Ames: Iowa State University Press, 1968).

31. A. G. Bogue, *Money at Interest: The Farm Mortgage on the Middle Border* (Ithaca: Cornell University Press, 1955), 249, 271.

32. Swedes may have been avoiding farm mortgaging, preferring to rent additional land to increase the size of their farms. See McQuillan, "Farm Size," 72.

33. Brunner, *Immigrant*, 51.

34. Brunner, *Immigrant*, 115; Bogue, *Patterns*, 161; Bogue, *From Prairie*, 66.

35. Brunner, *Immigrant*, 41.

36. Malin, *The Grassland*, 312–15.

# Chapter 6

1. J. C. Malin, *Winter Wheat in the Golden Belt of Kansas* (Lawrence: University of Kansas Press, 1944), 80. "The first reaction to the distress of the seventies was a clamor for diversification, but the relative success with winter wheat during the mid-seventies brought 'the wheat fever,' which threatened 'to spread all over the state to the great detriment of other interests and of the commonwealth.'" Ibid., 51.

2. The editor of the same newspaper also wrote in January 1880: "Were it not for the hogs and cattle that our farmers are now selling, there would be very little money in this country to do business with. Our friends in the country can now realize that there are other sources of wealth than the growing of wheat. Corn put into hogs always commands a fair price and is never a complete fail-

ure. This year will be referred to by those advocating mixed farming." Ibid., 80, 86.

3. "In social science use of the term *risk* assumes that decision makers have an estimate of some future value or event, but that their estimate is subject to some error. If the probable error is small, we say that the risk is slight; if the error is large, the situation is said to be quite 'risky.' . . . This is in direct contrast to the situation where a farmer has no estimate of the probability of a future event, which is referred to as a condition of *uncertainty*." W. Found, *A Theoretical Approach to Rural Land-Use Patterns* (Toronto: Macmillan and Co., 1971), 106.

4. Malin, *Winter Wheat,* 130. "It was one thing to argue theoretically on how farming should be done, but it was quite another to do it at a profit with the facilities at hand. The adjustment to crop and tillage had not been fully accomplished; the type of managerial ability necessary to efficient farming was scarce in the type of migrant pioneer settler who constituted the rank and file of operators; and capital available to most was not adequate to finance land and machinery. There was no reasonable course open even to the best farmers but to spend as little cash as possible under the uncertainties of pioneer agriculture and of climatic hazards." Ibid., 135–36.

5. J. C. Malin, *The Grassland of North America: Prolegomena to its History with Addenda and Postscript* (Gloucester, Mass.: Peter Smith, 1967), 307. Castle argued that "economic logic and simple arithmetic would indicate that the highly variable production function together with considerable variation in prices would tend to cause extreme variations in gross income. Historically this variability has been accentuated by the fact that low prices and low yields and high prices and high yields have tended to coincide." E. N. Castle, "Adapting Western Kansas Farms to Uncertain Prices and Yields," Kansas Agricultural Experimental Station, *Technical Bulletin,* no. 75 (February 1954): 6.

6. C. L. Bernays, "Among the Mennonites of Kansas in 1878," *Mennonite Life* 4 (October 1949): 20.

7. Malin, *Winter Wheat,* 167.

8. E. K. Lindquist, *Smoky Valley People: A History of Lindsborg Kansas* (Lindsborg: Bethany College, 1953), 39.

9. The discriminant analysis model used was developed by John Schlater at the Madison Academic Computing Center, University of Wisconsin, Madison, April 1974. For a full explanation of the derivation and use of the $D^2$ statistic see R. L. Miller and J. S. Kahn, *Statistical Analysis in the Geological Sciences* (New York: John Wiley and Sons, 1962), 258–84.

# Appendix A

1. J. N. Carman, *Foreign Language Units in Kansas, Historical Atlas and Statistics* (Lawrence: University of Kansas Press, 1962).
2. J. C. Weaver, "Crop Combination Regions in the Middle West," *Geographical Review* 44(1954): 175–200.

# Appendix C

1. Many studies have been done on the relation between crop yields and climate; e.g., chapters in *Climate and Man* (Washington, D.C.: USDA Yearbook, 1941); W. A. Hendricks and J. C. Scholl, *The Joint Effects of Temperature and Rainfall on Corn Yields,* North Carolina Agricultural Experimental Station, Research Bulletin no. 74, 1943; J. A. Hodges, "The Effect of Rainfall and Temperature on Corn Yields in Kansas," *Journal of Farm Economics* 13 (1931): 305–18; A. D. Robb, "The Critical Period of Corn in Northeastern Kansas," *Monthly Weather Review* 62 (1934): 286–89; J. K. Rose, "Corn Yield and Climate in the Corn Belt," *Geographical Review* 26 (1936): 88–102; L. M. Thompson, *An Evaluation of Weather Factors in the Production of Corn* (Ames, Iowa: Iowa State University, Center for Agricultural and Economic Adjustment, Report 12T, 1962); L. M. Thompson, "Evaluation of Weather Factors in the Production of Wheat," *Journal of Soil and Water Conservation* 17 (1962): 149–56; L. M. Thompson, "Multiple Regression Techniques in the Evaluation of Weather and Technology in Crop Production," in *Weather and Our Food Supply,* CAED Report no. 20 (Ames, Iowa: State University of Iowa, 1963), 75–91; J. C. Weaver, "Climate Relations of American Barley Production," *Geographical Review* 33 (1943): 569–88.
2. The climatic data used in this analysis were obtained from summaries published by the USDA Weather Bureau. U.S. Weather Bureau, *Climatic Survey of the United States,* Section 40 Eastern Kansas, Section 41, Western Kansas (Washington, D.C.: 1930). Additional temperature and rainfall data were obtained from primary records kept in the offices of the U.S. Weather Service, Kansas City, Missouri. These included temperature and rainfall data for Conway, Marion County, 1889–90; precipitation for Marion, Marion County, 1893–1908; and temperature records for Halstead, Harvey County, 1889–98. Further data were obtained from the *Monthly Weather Review:* temperature records for Marion, Marion County, 1900–25, and for Ellinwood, Barton County, from 1895–1925.
3. H. P. Bailey, "A Simple Moisture Index Based upon a Primary Law of Evaporation," *Geografiska Annaler* 40 (1958): 196–215.

## Appendix D

1. "In general more labor was required per acre, on farms surveyed, when the corn was harvested by cutting and shocking and later husking from the shock than when picked from the stalk for grain. The former practice was followed most commonly in eastern sections, where small acreages of corn were grown and where the stover was carefully conserved for forage. Least labor was used where the crop was harvested for fodder and the ears were fed with the stalk. This latter practice was followed most often in the small-grain area, where yields are light. The greater part of the crop, however, was harvested by grain for husking from the standing stalk, the practice commonly followed in the corn area and the cotton area. Where the corn was husked from the stalks labor varied from approximately 6 hours an acre in the southern small-grain area to more than 33 in the delta cotton area. As between sections of the corn area, however, even when the corn was all harvested by this same method, labor varied from 11 to 17 hours." J. A. Hopkins, *Technology and Employment in Agriculture* (Washington, D.C.: USDA Bureau of Agricultural Economics, Works Project Administration, 1940), 115.

2. R. W. Hecht and K. R. Vice, *Labor Used for Field Crops* (Washington, D.C.: USDA Agricultural Research Service, Statistical Bulletin no. 144, June 1954). The estimates for livestock production were based on 1959 figures, which were later standardized to 1950 estimates. R. W. Hecht, *Labor Used to Produce Livestock: Estimates by States, 1959* (Washington, D.C.: USDA Economic Research Service, September 1963).

3. In an introduction to this series of estimated labor demands for farm activities it was explained that "the series of man-hours of farm labor are used to establish the amount of, and to measure changes in, the labor input in agriculture. They are useful in measuring historical changes and geographical differences in farm labor productivity. They are of help in determining the effects of technological advances, such as mechanization and new hybrids or varieties of crops and animals, on the quantity of farm labor used." J. R. Anderson et al., *Major Statistical Series of the U.S.D.A.: How They Are Constructed and Used* (Washington, D.C.: USDA Agricultural Handbook no. 118, 1957), 13.

4. USDA, *Changes in Farm Production and Efficiency* (Washington, D.C.: Statistical Bulletin no. 233, supplement II, August 1958), 12–13.

5. F. Bateman, "Improvement in American Dairy Farming, 1850–1910: A Quantitative Analysis," *Journal of Economic History* 28 (1968): 255–73; also "Labor Inputs and Productivity in American Dairy Agriculture, 1850–1910," *Journal of Economic History* 29 (1969): 206–29.

6. Hecht and Vice, *Labor Used for Field Crops*, 11–37; Hecht, *Labor Used to Produce*, 8–14.

7. J. C. Weaver, "Crop Combination Regions in the Middle West," *Geographical Review* 44 (1954): 175–200.

8. J. C. Weaver, L. P. Hoag, and B. L. Fenton, "Livestock Units and Combination Regions in the Middle West," *Economic Geography* 32 (1956): 237–59.

9. Weaver, "Crop Combination," 182.

10. Found warned that the inferences that can be drawn from evidence of farm diversification are multiple and often interrelated. "Problems can arise in analysing land-use patterns when risk-inducing procedures are similar to those related to other concepts. Diversification, for example, may represent an attempt to reduce risk, an example of complementary production, or a long-run rotation system. Or it may represent all three. This overlap makes the problem of identifying a land-use pattern as related to one specific motive very difficult. The situation is complicated even further if production costs per acre per crop are partially dependent on the degree of diversification. If costs increase with diversification, a farmer might have to decide between the risk benefits of diversification and the cost benefits of monoculture." W. Found, *A Theoretical Approach to Rural Land-Use Patterns* (Toronto: Macmillan and Co., 1971), 108–9.

11. The contributor to the *Kansas Gazette* declared that "a diversified agriculture was slow but sure; and that a man who could not buy stock and wait for maturity could not buy land, teams, seed, and machinery, and wait to raise a crop; the real difficulty was trying to farm without capital—it was not the country or the farmer—farming on credit and speculation on a single crop to pay obligations meant ruin." J. C. Malin, *Winter Wheat in the Golden Belt of Kansas* (Lawrence: University of Kansas Press, 1944), 74.

12. E. N. Castle, "Adapting Western Kansas Farms to Uncertain Prices and Yields," Kansas Agricultural Experimental Station, *Technical Bulletin,* no. 75 (February 1954): 19.

13. Malin, *Winter Wheat,* 48.

14. G. F. Warren and F. A. Pearson, *Prices* (New York: John Wiley and Sons, 1933), 25–27.

# BIBLIOGRAPHY

## Manuscript Documents

Atchison, Topeka, and Santa Fe Railroad Company, Topeka, Kansas
  Land Records
Cloud County Courthouse, Concordia, Kansas
  Personal Property Taxation Records, Cloud County
  Real Estate Taxation Records, Cloud County
Kansas State Historical Society, Topeka, Kansas
  Foreign Language Units of Kansas, J. Neale Carman, vol. 2
  State Agricultural Census, Cloud County, 1875, 1885, 1895, 1905, 1915, and
    1925
  State Agricultural Census, McPherson County, 1875, 1885, 1895, 1905, 1915,
    and 1925
  State Agricultural Census, Marion County, 1875, 1885, 1895, 1905, 1915, and
    1925
  State Agricultural Census, Rice County, 1875, 1885, 1895, 1905, 1915, and
    1925
  State Population Census, Cloud County, 1875, 1885, 1895, 1905, 1915, and
    1925
  State Population Census, McPherson County, 1875, 1885, 1895, 1905, 1915,
    and 1925
  State Population Census, Marion County, 1875, 1885, 1895, 1905, 1915, and
    1925
  State Population Census, Rice County, 1875, 1885, 1895, 1905, 1915, and
    1925
Lindsborg Historical Society, Lindsborg, Kansas
  Personal Property Taxation Records, McPherson County
  Real Estate Taxation Records, McPherson County

Marion County Courthouse, Marion Center, Kansas
  Personal Property Taxation Records, Marion County
  Real Estate Taxation Records, Marion County
National Archives and Records Administration, Washington, D.C.
  Bureau of Land Management, Homestead Records
Rice County Courthouse, Lyons, Kansas
  Personal Property Taxation Records, Rice County
  Real Estate Taxation Records, Rice County


## Published Documents

Kansas State Board of Agriculture. *Annual Reports* and *Biennial Reports.* Topeka, Kans.: 1875–1925.

Sweden, *Emigrationsutredningen.* Stockholm: Boktryckeriet, P. A. Norstedt and Söner, 1909.

United States Census Office. *Twelfth Census of the United States,* vol. 5, Agriculture, part I. Washington, D.C.: 1902.

———, *Thirteenth Census of the United States,* vol. 6, Agriculture, Part I. Washington, D.C.: 1913.

———, *Fourteenth Census of the United States,* vol. 6, Agriculture, part I. Washington, D.C.: 1922.

United States Census Bureau. *Historical Statistics of the United States from Colonial Times to 1957.* Washington, D.C.: 1960.

United States Dept. of Agriculture. *Changes in Farm Production and Efficiency: A Summary Report.* Washington, D.C.: Agricultural Research Service, Statistical Bulletin no. 233, 1958.

United States Weather Bureau. *Climatic Survey of the United States: Climatic Data from the Establishment of Stations to 1930.* Washington, D.C.: 1930. Section 40 of this report was given to records for western Kansas and Section 41 to records for eastern Kansas.

In addition temperature data were obtained from manuscript originals in the U.S. Weather Bureau Office, Kansas City, Missouri, for the following weather stations: Conway, Marion County, 1889–90; Halstead, Harvey County, 1889–98; Salina, Saline County, 1883–85. Additional climatic data were obtained from summaries printed in the *Monthly Weather Review.*

# Books and Articles

*Weather and Crops*

Borchert, John R. "The Climate of the Central North American Grassland." *Annals of the Association of American Geographers* 40 (1950): 1–39.

————. "The Dust Bowl in the 1970's." *Annals of the Association of American Geographers* 61 (1971): 1–22.

Bryam, J. W. "The Drought of 1913 at Concordia, Kans." *Monthly Weather Review* 41 (1913): 1436–37.

Castle, Emery N. "Adapting Western Kansas Farms to Uncertain Prices and Yields." Topeka, Kans.: Kansas Agricultural Experiment Station, *Technical Bulletin*, no. 75, 1954.

Flora, S. D. *The Climate of Kansas*. Topeka, Kans.: Report of Kansas State Board of Agriculture, June 1948.

Found, William C. *A Theoretical Approach to Rural Land-Use Patterns*. Toronto: Macmillan and Co., 1971.

Frisby, E. M. "Weather-Crop Relationships: Forecasting Spring-Wheat Yield in in the Northern Great Plains of the United States." *Transactions, Institute for British Geographers* 17 (1951): 77–96.

Hayes, M. W. "Climatological Data for August 1913, District No. 6, Missouri Valley," *Monthly Weather Review* 41 (August 1913): 1193.

Hecht, Reuben W. *Labor Used to Produce Livestock: Estimates by States, 1959*. Washington, D.C.: USDA Economic Research Service, 1963.

Hecht, Reuben W., and K. R. Vice. *Labor Used for Field Crops*. Washington, D.C.: USDA Agricultural Research Service, Statistical Bulletin no. 144, 1954.

Hodges, J. A. "The Effect of Rainfall and Temperature on Corn Yields in Kansas." *Journal of Farm Economics* 13 (1931): 305–18.

Hopkins, John A. *Changing Technology and Employment in Agriculture*. Washington, D.C.: USDA Bureau of Agricultural Economics, Works Project Administration, 1940.

Jenkins, M. T. "Influence of Climate and Weather on Growth of Corn." In *Climate and Man* (Washington, D.C.: USDA Yearbook, 1941, 308–20.

Kansas Experiment Station. "Relation of Rainfall to the Corn Crop." *First Annual Report*. Topeka: 1889, 99–116.

Kansas State Agricultural College. "Experiments with Wheat." *Second Annual Report*, 1889, 29–42.

————. *Experiences with Cultivated Grasses and Clovers in Kansas*. Bulletin no. 2, 1890.

————. *Experiments with Wheat*. Bulletin no. 11, 1890.

Kansas State Agricultural College. *Experiments with Oats*. Bulletin no. 13, 1890.

————. *Experiments with Sorghum.* Bulletin no. 16, 1890.

————. *Experiments with Forage Plants.* Bulletin no. 18, 1890.

————. *Experiments with Wheat.* Bulletin no. 20, 1891.

————. *Experiments with Sorghum.* Bulletin no. 25, 1891.

————. *Experiments with Oats.* Bulletin no. 29, 1891.

————. *Experiments with Corn.* Bulletin no. 30, 1891.

————. *Experiments with Wheat.* Bulletin no. 33, 1892.

————. *Experiments with Potatoes.* Bulletin no. 37, 1892.

————. *Experiments with Wheat.* Bulletin no. 40, 1893.

————. *Experiments with Oats.* Bulletin no. 42, 1893.

————. *Experiments with Sorghum.* Bulletin no. 43, 1893.

————. *Experiments with Corn.* Bulletin no. 45, 1893.

————. *Experiments with Wheat.* Bulletin no. 47, 1894.

————. *Experiments with Oats.* Bulletin no. 54, 1895.

————. *Experiments with Corn and Kaffir Corn.* Bulletin no. 56, 1895.

————. *Experiments with Wheat.* Bulletin no. 59, 1896.

————. *Experiments with Oats.* Bulletin no. 63, 1896.

————. *Experiments with Corn.* Bulletin no. 64, 1897.

————. *Soil Moisture.* Bulletin no. 68, 1897.

————. *Experiments with Wheat.* Bulletin no. 71, 1897.

————. *Experiments with Oats.* Bulletin no. 74, 1897.

————. *Investigations of the Growth of Alfalfa in Kansas.* Bulletin no. 85, 1899.

————. *The Native Agricultural Grasses of Kansas.* Bulletin no. 87, 1899.

————. *Alfalfa in Eastern Kansas.* Bulletin no. 90, 1900.

————. *A New Drouth-Resisting Crop—Soy Beans.* Bulletin no. 92, 1900.

————. *Kafir Corn.* Bulletin no. 93, 1900.

————. *Soy Beans in Kansas 1900.* Bulletin no. 100, 1901.

————. *Fall Seeding of Alfalfa.* Bulletin no. 104, 1901.

————. *Growing Alfalfa in Kansas.* Bulletin no. 114, 1902.

————. *Crop Experiments in 1903.* Bulletin no. 123, 1904.

————. *The Study of Corn.* Bulletin no. 139, 1906.

Kincer, Joseph B. "The Climate of the Great Plains as a Factor in Their Utilization." *Annals of the Association of American Geographers* 13 (1923): 67–80.

Martin, J. H. "Climate and Sorghum." *Climate and Man.* Washington, D.C.: USDA Yearbook, 1941, 343–47.

Mitchell, J. M. "A Critical Appraisal of Periodicities in Climate." *Weather and Food Supply.* Ames, Iowa: Center for Agricultural and Economic Development, Report no. 20, 189–227.

————. "Recent Secular Changes of Global Temperature." *Annals of the New York Academy of Science* 95 (1961): 235–50.

Palmer, Wayne C. *Meteorological Drought.* Washington, D.C.: U.S. Weather Bureau, Research Paper no. 45, 1965.

Robb, A. D. "The Critical Period of Corn in Northeastern Kansas." *Monthly Weather Review* 62 (1934): 286–89.

————. "Rains in Kansas." *Monthly Weather Review* 66 (1938): 277–79.

Rose, John K. "Corn Yield and Climate in the Corn Belt." *Geographical Review* 26 (1936): 88–102.

Saarinen, Thomas F. *Perception of the Drought Hazard on the Great Plains*. Chicago: University of Chicago, Dept. of Geography, Research Paper no. 106, 1966.

Salmon, S. C. "Climate and Small Grains." *Climate and Man*. Washington, D.C.: USDA Yearbook, 1941, 321–42.

Shantz, H. L. "The Natural Vegetation of the Great Plains Region." *Annals of the Association of American Geographers* 13 (1923): 81–107.

Snow, Frank H. "Climate of Kansas." *Transactions of the Kansas State Board of Agriculture*, 1874, 397–407.

Thompson, Louis M. *An Evaluation of Weather Factors in the Production of Corn*. Ames, Iowa: Iowa State University, Center for Agricultural and Economic Adjustment, Report 12T, 1962.

————. "Evaluation of Weather Factors in the Production of Grain Sorghum." *Agronomics Journal* 52 (1963): 182–85.

————. "Evaluation of Weather Factors in the Production of Wheat." *Journal of Soil and Water Conservation* 17 (1962): 149–56.

————. "Multiple Regression Techniques in the Evaluation of Weather and Technology in Crop Production." *Weather and Our Food Supply*. Ames: State University of Iowa, CAED Report 20, 1963, 75–91.

————. *Weather and Technology in the Production of Corn and Soybeans*. Ames, Iowa: State University of Iowa, CAED Report 17, 1963.

Thornwaite, C. Warren. "An Approach Toward a Rational Classification of Climate." *Geographical Review* 38 (1948): 55–94.

————. "Climate and Settlement in the Great Plains." *Climate and Man*. Washington, D.C.: USDA Yearbook, 1941, 177–87.

————. "The Great Plains." In *Migration and Economic Opportunity*, edited by Carter Goodrich. Philadelphia: University of Pennsylvania Press, 1936, 202–50.

Trewartha, Glenn T. "Climate and Settlement in the Subhumid Lands." *Climate and Man*. Washington, D.C.: USDA Yearbook, 1941, 167–76.

Wahl, E. W., and T. L. Lawson. "The Climate of the Midnineteenth Century United States Compared to the Current Normals." *Monthly Weather Review* 98 (1970): 259–65.

Weaver, John C. "Climatic Relations of American Barley Production." *Geographical Review* 33 (1943): 569–88.

————. "Crop Combination Regions in the Middle West." *Geographical Review* 44 (1954): 175–200.

Weaver, John C., L. P. Hoag, and B. L. Fenton. "Livestock Units and Combination Regions in the Middle West." *Economic Geography* 32 (1956): 237–59.

*Studies on Emigration, Immigration, and Agricultural History*

Ander, O. Fritiof. "The Agricultural Revolution and Swedish Emigration." *Yearbook*. Philadelphia: American-Swedish Historical Foundation, 1945, 48–54.

————. *The Cultural Heritage of the Swedish Immigrant: Selected References*. Rock Island, Ill.: Augustana College Library, 1956.

————. "Some Factors in the Americanization of the Swedish Immigrant." *Journal of the Illinoist State Historical Society* 26 (1933): 136–50.

————. "The Swedish American Press and the Election of 1892." *Mississippi Valley Historical Review* 33 (March 1937): 533–54.

Anderson, Charles H. *White Protestant Americans: From National Origins to Religious Group*. Englewood Cliffs: Prentice-Hall, 1970.

Beijbom, Olf. *Swedes in Chicago: A Demographic and Social Study of the 1846–1880 Immigration*, Donald Brown, trans. Stockholm: Läromedelsförlaget, 1971.

Benson, Adolph B., and Naboth Hedin. *Americans from Sweden*. New York: J. P. Lippincott, 1950.

Bergin, Alfred. *Pioneer Swedish-American Culture in Central Kansas*. Lindsborg, Kans.: Lindsborg News Record, 1965.

————. "The Swedish Settlements in Central Kansas." *Collections*, Kansas State Historical Society 11 (1909–10): 19–46.

Berkhofer, Robert. "Space, Time, Culture and the New Frontier." *Agricultural History* 38 (1964): 21–30.

Bernays, C. "Among the Mennonites of Kansas in 1878." *Mennonite Life* 4 (October 1949): 20–39.

Beshers, J. M., et al. "Ethnic Congregation-Segregation, Assimilation and Stratification." *Social Forces* 42 (May 1964): 482–89.

Billington, Ray A. *America's Frontier Heritage*. New York: Holt, Rinehart and Winston, 1966.

————, ed. *The Frontier Thesis: Valid Interpretations of American History?* New York: Holt, Rinehart and Winston, 1966.

————. *Westward Expansion: A History of the American Frontier*, 3d ed., New York: The Macmillan Co., 1967.

Bodvall, Gunnar. "Periodic Settlement, Land Clearing and Cultivation, with Special Reference to the Boothlands of North Hälsingland." *Geografisker Annaler* 39 (1957): 213–56.

Bogue, Allan G. "Farming in the Prairie Peninsula, 1830–1890." *Journal of Economic History* 23 (1963): 3–29.

————. "Foreclosure Tenancy on the Northern Plains." *Agricultural History* 39 (January 1965): 3–16.

————. *From Prairie to Corn Belt: Farming on the Illinois and Iowa Prairies in the Nineteenth Century*. Chicago: University of Chicago Press, 1963.

————. "The Land Mortgage Company in the Early Plains States." *Agricultural History* 25 (1951): 20–33.

————. *Money at Interest: The Farm Mortgage on the Middle Border*. Ithaca: Cornell University Press, 1955.

Bogue, Allan G., and M. B. Bogue. "Profits and the Frontier Land Speculator." *Journal of Economic History* 17 (1957): 1–24.

Bogue, Margaret B. *Patterns from the Sod: Land Use and Tenure in the Grand Prairie, 1850–1900*. Springfield: Illinois State Historical Library, *Collections*, vol. 34, 1959.

Bowden, Martyn J. "The Perception of the Western Interior of the United States, 1800–1870: A Problem in Historical Geography." *Proceedings of the Association of American Geographers* 1 (1969): 16–21.

Bowers, W. L. "Crawford Township, 1850–1870: A Population Study of a Pioneer Community." *Iowa Journal of History* 58 (1960): 1–30.

Brotz, Howard. "Multiculturalism in Canada: A Muddle." *Canadian Public Policy* 6 (1980): 41–46.

Brunner, Edmund deS. *Immigrant Farmers and their Children*. New York: Doubleday, Doran and Co., 1929.

Carman, J. Neale. *Foreign Language Units of Kansas, Historical Atlas and Statistics*. Lawrence: University of Kansas Press, 1962.

Clark, Andrew H. "Geographical Change: A Theme for Economic History." *Journal of Economic History* 20 (1960): 607–13.

Cogswell, Seddie. *Tenure, Nativity, and Age as Factors in Iowa Agriculture, 1850–1880*. Ames: Iowa University Press, 1975.

Conzen, Kathleen Neils. "Historical Approaches to the Study of Rural Ethnic Communities." In *Ethnicity on the Great Plains*, edited by F. C. Luebke. Lincoln: University of Nebraska Press, 1980, 1–18.

————. *Immigrant Milwaukee, 1836–1860: Accommodation and Community in a Frontier City*. Cambridge, Mass.: Harvard University Press, 1976.

————. "Peasant Pioneers: Generational Succession Among German Farmers in Frontier Minnesota." In *The Countryside in the Age of Capitalist Transformation*, edited by S. Halm and J. Prude. Chapel Hill: University of North Carolina Press, 1985, 259–92.

Conzen, Michael P. *Frontier Farming in an Urban Shadow: The Influence of Madison's Proximity on the Agricultural Development of Blooming Grove*. Madison: State Historical Society of Wisconsin, 1971.

Correll, Ernst. "The Sociological and Economic Significance of the Mennonites as a Culture Group in History." *Mennonite Quarterly Review* 41 (1942): 161–66.

Coulter, Hugh P. "The Introduction and Development of Hard Red Winter Wheat in Kansas." Kansas State Board of Agriculture, *Biennial Report*, no. 15 (1905–6), 945–48.

Cox, Lawanda F. "Tenancy in the United States, 1865–1900: A Consideration of the Validity of the Agricultural Ladder Hypothesis." *Agricultural History* 18 (1944): 97–105.

Cozzens, Arthur B. "Conservation in German Settlements of the Missouri Ozarks." *Geographical Review* 33 (1943): 286–98.

Crèvecoeur, J. H. St. J. *Letters from an American Farmer.* New York: Fox, Duffield and Co., 1904.

Curti, Merle. *The Making of an American Community: A Case Study of Democracy in a Frontier County.* Stanford: Stanford University Press, 1959.

Dawson, C. A. *Group Settlement: Ethnic Communities in Western Canada.* Toronto: Macmillan and Co., 1936.

deKoninck, R., and J-A. Soltesz. "Geographie, Culture, Language aux Cent-Iles du Lac Saint-Pierre: Les Bases d'Une Etude." *Canadian Geographer* 17 (1973): 220–34.

Driedger, Johann. "Farming Among the Mennonites in West and East Prussia, 1534–1945." *Mennonite Quarterly Review* 31 (1957) 16–21.

Dumont, Fernand, and Guy Rocher. "An Introduction to the Sociology of French-Canada." *French-Canadian Society,* edited by M. Rioux and Y. Martin. Ottawa: McClelland and Stewart, Carleton Library, 1964, 178–200.

Duncan, O. D., and S. Lieberson. "Ethnic Segregation and Assimilation." *American Journal of Sociology* 64 (1959): 364–74.

Farmer, Hallie. "The Economic Background of Frontier Populism." *Mississippi Valley Historical Review* 10 (1923): 406–27.

Finley, Robert M. "A Budgeting Approach to the Question of Homestead Size on the Plains." *Agricultural History* 42 (April 1968): 109–14.

Fowke, V. C. "An Introduction to Canadian Agricultural History." *Agricultural History* 16 (1942): 79–90.

Francis, E. K. "The Adjustment of a Peasant Group to a Capitalistic Economy: The Mennonites of Manitoba." *Rural Sociology* 17 (1952): 218–28.

———. "Mennonite Institutions in Early Manitoba: A Study of Their Origins." *Agricultural History* 22 (1948): 144–55.

———. "The Nature of the Ethnic Group." *American Journal of Sociology* 52 (1947): 393–400.

———. "The Russian Mennonites: From Religious to Ethnic Group." *American Journal of Sociology* 44 (1948): 101–7.

———. *In Search of Utopia: The Mennonites of Manitoba.* Glencoe, Ill.: The Free Press, 1955.

———. "Tradition and Progress among the Mennonites in Manitoba." *Mennonite Quarterly Review* 24 (1950): 312–28.

Fretz, J. Winfield. "Factors Contributing to the Success and Failure in Mennonite Colonization." *Mennonite Quarterly Review* 24 (1950): 130–35.

————. "Mennonites and Their Economic Problems." *Mennonite Quarterly Review* 14 (1940): 195–213.

————. "Mutual Aid among Mennonites." *Mennonite Quarterly Review* 13 (1939): 28–58.

Garigue, Philip. "Change and Continuity in Rural French Canada." *French-Canadian Society,* edited by M. Rioux and Y. Martin. Ottawa: McClelland and Stewart, Carleton Library, 1964, 123–37.

Gates, Paul W. "Charles Lewis Fleischmann: German-American Agricultural Authority." *Agricultural History* 35 (1961): 13–23.

————. *Fifty Million Acres: Conflicts over Kansas Land Policy 1854–1890.* Ithaca: Cornell University Press, 1954.

————. *Landlords and Tenants on the Prairie Frontier: Studies in American Land Policy.* Ithaca: Cornell University Press, 1973.

Gehrke, William H. "The Ante-Bellum Agriculture of the Germans in North Carolina." *Agricultural History* 9 (1935): 143–60.

Gerin, Leon. "The French-Canadian Family—Its Strengths and Weaknesses." *French-Canadian Society,* edited by M. Rioux and Y. Martin. Ottawa: McClelland and Stewart, Carleton Library, 1964, 32–57.

Gerlach, Russell L. *Immigrants in the Ozarks.* Columbia: University of Missouri Press, 1977.

Gingerich, Melvin. *The Mennonites in Iowa.* Iowa City: State Historical Society of Iowa, 1939.

————. "Rural Life Problems and the Mennonites." *Mennonite Quarterly Review* 16 (1942): 167–73.

Gjerde, John. *From Peasants to Farmers: The Migration from Balestrand, Norway, to the Upper Middle West.* Cambridge: Cambridge University Press, 1985.

Glazer, Nathan. "Ethnic Groups in America: From National Culture to Ideology." In *Freedom and Control in Modern Society,* edited by M. Berger, T. Abel, and C.H. Page. New York: Van Nostrand, 1954, 158–73.

Glazer, Nathan, and D. P. Moynihan. *Beyond the Melting Pot: The Negroes, Puerto Ricans, Jews, Italians and Irish of New York City.* Cambridge, Mass.: MIT Press and Harvard University Press, 1963.

Goldenweiser, E. A., and Leon E. Truesdell. *Farm Tenancy in the United States.* United States Bureau of the Census, Washington: Government Printing Office, 1924.

Gordon, M. M. *Assimilation in American Life: The Role of Race, Religion and National Origins.* New York: Oxford University Press, 1964.

Gray, L. C. et al. "Farm Ownership and Tenancy." USDA Agricultural Yearbook. Washington: Government Printing Office, 1924.

Greeley, Andrew M. *Ethnicity in the United States: A Preliminary Reconnaissance.* New York: John Wiley, 1974.

————. *Why Can't They Be Like Us?* New York: Institute of Human Relations Press, 1969.

Greer, Alan. *Peasant, Lord, and Merchant: Rural Society in Three Quebec Parishes, 1740–1840.* Toronto: University of Toronto Press, 1985.

Guindon, Hubert. "The Social Evolution of Quebec Reconsidered." In *French-Canadian Society*, edited by M. Rioux and Y. Martin. Ottawa: McClelland and Stewart, Carleton Library, 1964, 137–61.

Hansen, Marcus Lee. *The Immigrant in American History.* New York: Harper & Row, 1940.

Harris, R. C. *The Seigneurial System in Early Canada: A Geographical Study.* Madison: University of Wisconsin Press, 1968, 247.

Helmfrid, Staffan. "The *Storskifte, Enskifte* and *Laga Skifte* in Sweden—General Features." *Geografisker Annaler* 53 (1961): 114–29.

Henripin, Jacques. "From Acceptance of Nature to Control: The Demography of the French-Canadians Since the Seventeenth Century." In *French-Canadian Society*, edited by M. Rioux and Y. Martin. Ottawa: McClelland and Stewart, Carleton Library, 1964, 204–216.

Hewes, Leslie. "Cultural Fault Line in the Cherokee County." *Economic Geography* 19 (1943): 136–42.

Hicks, John D. "The Western Middle West, 1900–1914." *Agricultural History* 20 (1946): 65–77.

Hill, George W. "The Use of the Culture Area Concept in Social Research." *American Journal of Sociology* 47 (1941): 39–47.

Hoch, E. W. *All About Marion County, Kansas.* Marion Center: Marion Co. Record, 1876.

Hofstadter, Richard. "Turner and the Frontier Myth." *The American Scholar* 18 (1948–49): 433–43.

Hollibaugh, E. F. *Biographical History of Cloud County, Kansas.* Loganport, Ind.: Wilson, Humphry and Co., 1903.

Hollingshead, A. B. "Changes in Land Ownership as an Index of Succession in Rural Communities." *American Journal of Sociology* 53 (1938): 764–77.

————. "Cultural Factors in the Selection of Marriage Mates." *American Sociological Review* 15 (1950): 624.

Ianni, F. A. "Time and Place as Variables in Acculturation Research." *American Anthropologist* 60 (1958): 39–46.

Janson, Florence E. *The Background of Swedish Immigration, 1840–1930.* New York: Arno Press, 1970.

Johnson, Hildegard B. "Factors Affecting the Distribution of the German Pioneer Population in Minnesota." *Agricultural History* 19 (1945): 39–57.

————. "Intermarriages Between German Pioneers and Other Nationalities in Minnesota in 1860 and 1870." *American Journal of Sociology* 51 (1945): 299–304.

————. "Rational and Ecological Aspects of the Quarter Section." *Geographical Review* 47 (1957): 330–48.

Jonassen, C. T. "Cultural Variables in the Ecology of an Ethnic Group." *American Sociological Review* 14 (1949): 32–41.

Jones, M. A. *American Immigration*. Chicago: University of Chicago Press, 1960.

Jones, Robert L. "French-Canadian Agriculture in the St. Lawrence Valley, 1815–1850." *Agricultural History* 16 (1942): 137–48.

Jordan, Terry G. "Between the Forest and the Prairie." *Agricultural History* 38 (1964): 205–16.

————. *German Seed in Texas Soil: Immigrant Farmers in Nineteenth-Century Texas*. Austin: University of Texas Press, 1966.

Juhnke, James C. "The Political Acculturation of the Kansas Mennonites, 1870–1940." *Mennonite Quarterly Review* 43 (1969): 247–48.

Kamphoefner, W. D. *The Westfalians: From Germany to Missouri*. Princeton: Princeton University Press, 1987.

Kaups, M. "Finnish Placenames in Minnesota: A Study in Cultural Transfer." *Geographical Review* 56 (1966): 377–97.

Kennedy, R. J. R. "Single or Triple Melting Pot? Intermarriage Trends in New Haven, 1870–1950." *American Journal of Sociology* 58 (1952): 56–59.

Kollmorgen, Walter M. "Agricultural-Cultural Islands in the South, part II." *Economic Geography* 19 (1943): 109–17.

————. "The Agricultural Stability of the Old Order Amish and the Old Order Mennonites of Lancaster County, Pennsylvania." *American Journal of Sociology* 44 (1943): 233–41.

————. *Culture of a Contemporary Rural Community: The Old Order Amish of Lancaster County, Pennsylvania*. USDA Rural Life Studies no. 4, September 1942.

————. "Immigrant Settlements in Southern Agriculture: A Commentary on the Significance of Cultural Islands in Agricultural History." *Agricultural History* 19 (1945): 69–78.

————. Personal communication, October 19, 1972.

————. "Rainmakers on the Plains." *Scientific Monthly* 40 (1935): 146–52.

————. "A Reconnaissance of Some Cultural-Agricultural Islands in the South." *Economic Geography* 17 (1941): 409–30.

————. "The Role of Mennonite Agriculture." *Mennonite Community* 1 (1947): 18–20.

Kollmorgen, Walter M., and David S. Simonett. "Grazing Operations in the Flint Hills–Bluestem Pastures of Chase County, Kansas." *Annals of the Association of American Geographers* 55 (1965): 260–90.

Krahn, Cornelius, ed. *From the Steppes to the Prairies*. Newton, Kans.: Mennonite Publication Office, 1949.

————. "Mennonite Community Life in Russia." *Mennonite Quarterly Review* 16 (1942): 174–77.

―――. "Some Social Attitudes of the Mennonites in Russia." *Mennonite Quarterly Review* 9 (1935): 165–77.

Le Duc, Thomas. "The Disposal of the Public Domain on the Trans-Mississippi Plains: Some Opportunities for Investigation." *Agricultural History* 24 (1950): 199–204.

Leibbrandt, Georg. "The Emigration of the German Mennonites from Russia to the United States and Canada in 1873–1880, part I." *Mennonite Quarterly Review* 6 (1932): 205–26.

―――. "The Emigration of the German Mennonites from Russia to the United States and Canada, 1873–1880, part II." *Mennonite Quarterly Review* 7 (1933): 5–41.

Lemon, James T. "The Agricultural Practices of National Groups in Eighteenth-Century Southeastern Pennsylvania." *Geographical Review* 56 (1966): 467–96.

―――. *The Best Poor Man's Country: A Geographical Study of Early Southeastern Pennsylvania.* Baltimore: Johns Hopkins Press, 1972.

―――. "Household Consumption in Eighteenth-Century America and Its Relationship to Production and Trade: The Situation Among Farmers in Southeastern Pennsylvania." *Agricultural History* 41 (January 1967): 59–70.

Lewis, G. M. "Changing Emphases in the Description of the Natural Environment of the American Great Plains Area." *Transactions, Institute for British Geographers* 30 (1962): 75–90.

―――. "Regional Ideas and Reality in the Cis-Rocky Mountain West." *Transactions, Institute for British Geographers* 38 (1966): 135–50.

―――. "Three Centuries of Desert Concepts of the Cis-Rocky Mountain West." *Journal of the West* 4 (1965): 457–68.

Lindberg, J. S. *The Background of Swedish Emigration to the United States.* Minneapolis: University of Minnesota Press, 1930.

Lindquist, Emory K. *Smoky Valley People: A History of Lindsborg, Kansas.* Lindsborg: Bethany College, 1953.

―――. *Vision for a Valley: Olof Olsson and the Early History of Lindsborg.* Rock Island, Ill.: Augustana Historical Society Publications, no. 22, 1970.

―――. "The Scandinavian Element in Kansas." *Kansas, The First Century,* edited by John D. Bright. New York: Lewis Historical Publishing Company, 1956.

Luebke, Frederick, ed. *Ethnicity on the Great Plains.* Lincoln: University of Nebraska Press, 1980.

Malin, James C. "The Adaptation of the Agricultural System to Sub-humid Environment." *Agricultural History* 10 (1936): 118–41.

―――. *The Grasslands of North America: Prolegomena to Its History with Addenda.* Gloucester, Mass.: P. Smith, 1967.

―――. Personal communication, October 19, 1972.

―――. "The Turnover of Farm Population in Kansas." *Kansas Historical Quarterly* 4 (1935): 339–72.

————. *Winter Wheat in the Golden Belt of Kansas: A Study in Adaptation to Subhumid Geographical Environment.* Lawrence: University of Kansas Press, 1944.

Mather, C., and M. Kaups. "The Finnish Sauna: A Cultural Index to Settlement." *Annals of the Association of American Geographers* 53 (1963): 494–504.

Mattas, L. *St. Joseph Church, Centennial Edition 1868–1968.* Concordia, Kans.: St. Joseph Church, 1968.

McArthur, N., and M. E. Gerland. "The Spread and Migration of French Canadians." *Tijdschrift voor Economische en Sociale Geografie* 52 (1961): 141–47.

McCallum, John. *Unequal Beginnings: Agriculture and Economic Development in Quebec and Ontario until 1870.* Toronto: University of Toronto Press, 1980.

McInnis, R. M. "A Reconsideration of the State of Agriculture in Lower Canada in the First Half of the Nineteenth Century." *Canadian Papers in Rural History,* vol. III, edited by D. H. Akenson. Gananoque, Ontario: Langdale Press, 1982, 9–49.

McQuillan, D. Aidan. "The Creation and Survival of French-Canadian Communities in the Upper Midwest During the Nineteenth Century." *Cahiers de geographie de Quebec* 23 (1979): 53–72.

————. "Farm Size and Work Ethic: Measuring the Success of Immigrant Farmers on the American Grasslands, 1875–1925." *Journal of Historical Geography* 4 (1978): 57–76.

————. "The Interface of Physical and Historical Geography: The Analysis of Farming Decisions in Response to Drought Hazards on the Margins of the Great Plains." *Period and Place: Research Methods in Historical Geography,* edited by A. R. H. Baker and M. Billinge. Cambridge: Cambridge University Press, 1982, 136–44.

————. "The Mobility of Immigrants and Americans: A Comparison of Farmers on the Kansas Frontier." *Agricultural History* 53 (1979): 576–96.

————. "Territory and Ethnic Identity: Some New Measures of an Old Theme in the Cultural Geography of North America." In *Geographical Change: Essays in Honour and Memory of Andrew Hill Clark,* edited by J. R. Gibson. Toronto: University of Toronto Press, 1978, 136–69.

Meinig, D. W. *On the Margins of the Good Earth.* Chicago: Association of American Geographers Monograph Series, Rand McNally, 1962.

Mikesell, Marvin. "Comparative Studies in Frontier History." *Annals of the Association of American Geographers* 50 (1960): 62–74.

Miner, Horace. *St. Denis: A French-Canadian Parish.* Chicago: University of Chicago Press, 1939.

Neatby, Hilda. *Quebec: The Revolutionary Age, 1760–1791.* Toronto: McClelland and Stewart, 1966.

Nelson, L. "Intermarriage among Nationality Groups in a Rural Area of Minnesota." *American Journal of Sociology* 48 (1943): 585–92.

North, Douglas C. *Growth and Welfare in the American Past: A New Economic History*. Englewood Cliffs: Prentice-Hall, 1966.

Nugent, Walter T. K. *The Tolerant Populists: Kansas Populism and Nativism*. Chicago: University of Chicago Press, 1963.

Ostergren, Robert. *A Community Transplanted: The Formative Experience of a Swedish Immigrant Community in the Upper Middle West, 1835–1915*. Madison: University of Wisconsin Press, 1988.

Parker, W. H. "A Revolution in the Agricultural Geography of Lower Canada, 1833–1838." *Revue canadienne de geographie* 11 (1957): 189–94.

Peachey, Paul. "Identity Crisis Among American Mennonites." *Mennonite Quarterly Review* 42 (1968): 243–59.

Pihlblad, C. T. "The Kansas Swedes." *Southwestern Social Science Quarterly* 13 (1932): 34–47.

Rasmussen, Wayne D. "The Impact of Technological Change on American Agriculture 1862–1962." *Journal of Economic History* 22 (1962): 578–91.

Redfield, Robert. "French-Canadian Culture in St. Denis." *French-Canadian Society*, edited by M. Rioux and Y. Martin. Ottawa: McClelland and Stewart, Carleton Library, 1964, 57–62.

Rempel, David G. "The Mennonite Migration to New Russia (1787–1870): I. The Colonization Policy of Catherine II and Alexander I." *Mennonite Quarterly Review* 9 (1935): 71–91.

————. "The Mennonite Migration to New Russia (1787–1870): II. The Emigration to Russia." *Mennonite Quarterly Review* 9 (1935): 109–28.

Rice, John G. *Patterns of Ethnicity in a Minnesota County, 1880–1905*. Umea, Sweden: University of Umea, Dept. of Geography, Geographical Report no. 4, 1973.

Rosenof, T. *Cultural Sensitivity to Environmental Change: The Case of Ellis County Kansas, 1870–1900*. Madison: University of Wisconsin, Institute for Environmental Studies, Report 5, 1973.

Ross, Earle D. *Iowa Agriculture: An Historical Survey*. Iowa State Historical Society, 1951.

Saloutos, Theodore. "The Immigrant Contribution to American Agriculture." *Agricultural History* 50 (1976): 45–67.

Saveth, Edward N. *American Historians and European Immigrants 1875–1925*. New York: Columbia University Press, 1948.

Schafer, Joseph. *Four Wisconsin Counties*. Madison: Wisconsin Domesday Book, General Studies, vol. II, 1927.

————. "The Wisconsin Domesday Book: A Method of Research for Agricultural Historians." *Agricultural History* 14 (1940): 23–32.

Schell, Herbert S. "Adjustment Problems in South Dakota." *Agricultural History* 14 (1940): 65–74.

Schmidt, C. B. "Reminiscences of Foreign Immigration Work for Kansas." *Collections of the Kansas State Historical Society* 9 (1905–6): 485–97.

Seguin, Maurice. *La "Nation Canadienne" et l'agriculture, 1760–1850.* Trois Rivieres: Editions boreal express, 1970.

Shannon, Fred A. *The Farmer's Last Frontier: Agriculture 1860–1897.* New York: Harper & Row, 1945.

Shyrock, Richard H. "British versus German Traditions in Colonial Agriculture." *Mississippi Valley Historical Review* 26 (June 1939): 39–54.

Smith, C. Henry. *The Coming of the Russian Mennonites: An Episode in the Settling of the Last Frontier, 1874–1884.* Berne, Ind.: Mennonite Book Concern, 1927.

Speek, Peter A. "The Meaning of Nationality and Americanization." *American Journal of Sociology* 32 (1926): 237–49.

Stephenson, G. M. "The Background of the Beginnings of Swedish Immigration, 1850–1875." *American Historical Review* 31 (1926): 708–23.

———. "The Mind of the Scandinavian Immigrant." *Studies and Records,* Norwegian-American Historical Association 6 (1929): 63–73.

Stonequist, Everett V. "The Problem of the Marginal Man." *American Journal of Sociology* 41 (1935): 1–12.

Suttles, Gerald D. *The Social Construction of Communities.* Chicago: University of Chicago Press, 1972.

———. *The Social Order of the Slum: Ethnicity and Territory in the Inner City.* Chicago: University of Chicago Press, 1968.

Swierenga, Robert P. *Pioneers and Profits: Land Speculation on the Iowa Frontier.* Ames: Iowa State University Press, 1968.

Thiessen, Irmgard. "Values and Personality Characteristics of Mennonites in Manitoba." *Mennonite Quarterly Review* 40 (1966): 48–61.

Throne, Mildred. "Southern Iowa Agriculture, 1839–1890: The Progress from Subsistence to Commercial Corn-Belt Farming." *Agricultural History* 23 (1949): 124–30.

Tower, J. Allen, and W. Wolf. "Ethnic Groups in Cullman County, Alabama." *Geographical Review* 33 (1943): 276–85.

Turner, F. J. "The Significance of the Frontier in American History." *Annual Report,* American Historical Association, 1893, 199–227.

Useem, J., and R. H. Useem. "Minority Group Pattern in Prairie Society." *American Journal of Sociology* 50 (1945): 377–85.

von Nardoff, Ellen. "The American Frontier as a Safety Valve—The Life, Death, Reincarnation, and Justification of a Theory." *Agricultural History* 36 (1962): 123–42.

Ward, David. *Cities and Immigrants: A Geography of Change in Nineteenth-Century America.* New York: Oxford University Press, 1971.

———. "The Emergence of Central Immigrant Ghettos." *Annals of the Association of American Geographers* 58 (1968): 343–59.

———. "The Internal Spatial Structure of Immigrant Residential Districts in the Late Nineteenth Century." *Geographical Analysis* 1 (1969): 337–53.

Warkentin, John. "Manitoba Settlement Patterns." Historical and Scientific Society of Manitoba, *Papers,* series III, no. 16 (1961): 62–77.

———. "Mennonite Agricultural Settlements of Southern Manitoba." *Geographical Review* 49 (1959): 342–68.

Webb, Walter P. *The Great Plains.* New York: Grosset and Dunlap, 1931.

Westin, Gunnar. "Background of the Swedish Pioneer Immigration, 1840–1850." American-Swedish Historical Foundation, *Yearbook,* 1948, 20–31.

White, Gerald T. "Economic Recovery and the Wheat Crop of 1897." *Agricultural History* 13 (1939): 13–21.

Wilson, M. L. "Cultural Patterns in Agricultural History." *Agricultural History* 12 (1938): 3–10.

Wirth, Louis. "The Problem of Minority Groups." *Theories of Society,* edited by P. Talcott et al. New York: Free Press of Glencoe, 1961, 309–15.

Woolston, H. "The Process of Assimilation." *Social Forces* 24 (1945): 415–24.

Writers Program, Kansas. *A Guide to Hillsboro, Kansas.* Hillsboro Chamber of Commerce, 1940.

Zelinsky, Wilbur. *The Cultural Geography of the United States.* Englewood Cliffs: Prentice-Hall, 1973.

Zimmerman, Carl C. "Rural Society." *Encyclopaedia of the Social Sciences* 13 (1935): 469.

Zornow, William F. *Kansas: A History of the Jayhawk State.* Norman: University of Oklahoma Press, 1957.

## Unpublished Theses and Dissertations

Albertson, H. Curtis. "The Relationship between Wheat Yields and Water Availability in Kansas." M.A. thesis, University of Kansas, 1959.

Albrecht, Abraham. "Mennonite Settlements in Kansas." M.A. thesis, University of Kansas, 1925.

Beckman, Peter. "The Catholic Church on the Kansas Frontier." Ph.D. diss. Catholic University, Washington, D.C., 1943.

Conzen, Kathleen Neils. " 'The German Athens': Milwaukee and the Accommodation of its Immigrants, 1836–1860." Ph.D. diss., University of Wisconsin, 1972.

Crothall, W. Robert. "French-Canadian Agriculture in Ontario, 1861–1872: A Study of Cultural Transfer." M.A. thesis, University of Toronto, 1968.

Gibson, James R. "A Comparison of Anglo-Saxon, Mennonite and Dutch Farms in the Lower Fraser Valley." M.A. thesis, University of Oregon, 1959.

Gregory, Kathryn A. "Population Settlement and Movement in the Great Plains Area of Kansas from 1870 to 1900," M.A. thesis, Penn State University, 1966.

Janzen, Cornelius C., "Americanization of the Russian Mennonites in Central Kansas." M.A. thesis, University of Kansas, 1914.

———. "A Study of the Mennonite Settlement in the Counties of Marion, McPherson, Harvey, Reno, and Butler, Kansas." Ph.D. diss., University of Chicago, 1926.

Rempel, D. G. "The Mennonite Colonies in New Russia: A Study of Their Settlement and Economic Development from 1789 to 1914." Ph.D. diss., Stanford University, 1934.

Siemans, Alfred H. "Mennonite Settlement in the Lower Fraser Valley." M.A. thesis, University of British Columbia, 1960.

Slocum, W. L. "Ethnic Stocks as Culture Types in Rural Wisconsin." Ph.D. thesis, University of Wisconsin, 1940.

Vicero, Ralph D. "Immigration of French-Canadians to New England, 1840–1900: A Geographical Analysis." Ph.D. diss., University of Wisconsin, 1968, 2 vols.

# Index

Grasshopper plagues, 13; among French Canadians, 73; among Mennonites, 61, 63–64;
among Swedes, 51, 52
Gravelin, Mrs. (hotel owner in Aurora), 96
Great Bend lowlands of Arkansas River valley,
61
Greer, A., 31

*Habitant*, 31, 193
Halland, dairy farming in, 19
Halstead, 63, 66, 69, 81, 92
Hard winter wheat, Mennonite use of, 164–65
Harms, P., 66
Harris, R. C., 31
Hecht, R. W., 223
Henry, T. C., 125, 159
Hespeler, W., 29
Higher education: among French Canadians, 98;
Mennonites, 91–92, 98; Swedes, 59, 88–89
Hillsboro, 69, 92, 93
Homestead abandonment among French Cana-
dians, 75, 77
Homestead Act, 54, 82, 122, 125
Homestead claims: among French Canadians,
75–77, 82–33; among Mennonites, 65–66;
among Swedes, 47, 54–55, 82–83
Houses built by first Mennonites in Kansas, 62

Indians: French-Canadian contacts with, 72;
Kaw Indian reservation, 63; Mennonite
contacts with, 63; removal of, 44; Swedish
contacts with, 50
Individualism, 39, 190, 198
Infant mortality, 51
Intermarriage, 6, 86; among Swedes, 88–89
Investment in farming, 135–44, 197
Irish immigrants, 7, 8
Iroquois County, Ill., 132
Islet County, Quebec, 35

Jackson, President Andrew, 2
Janzen, C. C., 63, 93, 94
Johnson, J. H., 58
Johnson County, Iowa, 146
John XXIII, Pope, 5
Juhnke, J. C., 91

Kallen, H., 4
Kamaska County, Quebec, 35
Kamphoefner, W. D., 16
Kankakee, Ill., chain migration from, 70; family
ties with, 81; first settlers in Kansas from, 72;
French-Canadian migrants to, 16; schism in,
38, 191
Kansas City, 45
Kansas State Board of Agriculture, 163, 237

Kanwaka Township, Kans., 127, 130
Kaw Indian reservation, 63
Kennedy, President John, 5
Kentucky, Kansas and Texas Cattle Company,
55
Keokuk County, Iowa, 205
Khortitsa, Mennonite colony in, 25
Kinsley Township, Kans., 148
Knights of Pythias, 96
Know-Nothing movement, 2, 5

Labor, female, 64, 94
Labor units: on farms, 223; estimates of, 163,
165, 221–24
Lafond, C., 79
Lagaskifte Act, 17
Land speculation, 55, 126
Land use, intensity of, 135
Lanoue, E., 80
La Rocque, F., 79, 80–81
Ledoux, C., 100
Lehigh, 69
Lemon, J. T., 7
Letourneau, G., 80
Letourneau, Mrs. (hotel owner in Aurora), 96
Lindberg, J. S., 21
Lindquist, E. K., 52, 88
Lindsborg, 47, 49, 50, 53, 58, 59, 81, 86, 87,
88, 89, 90, 192
Linguistic assimilation, 5, 85–86; among French
Canadians, 99, 119; among Mennonites,
91–92, 119; among Swedes, 87–88, 119
Livingston County, Ill., 132
Lutheran church in Sweden, 40, 121, 190–91
Lutheran state church, 21, 40
Lyons, 58

McLean County, Ill. 132
McPherson, town of, 58
Malin, J. C.: on early crop estimates, 237; farm
management skills, 160; farm size, 125, 127–
28, 130, 131–32; hard winter wheat, 165;
land speculation, 126; population, 100, 212;
rented farmland, 155–56; weather and market
hazards, 160–61
Marcotte, Dr. F. L., 80
Market price fluctuation, 160–61
Melting pot, 2, 4, 5
Mennonite Board Of Guardians, 30
Mennonite Brethren in Gnadenau, Kans., 64
Mennonites: and anti-German sentiment, 91;
cooperation among, 66, 94, 157, 198–99;
distribution of in Kansas, 59–61, 209; economic individualism of, 94; and farmland,
66, 194; and female farm labor, 64, 94;
gender differentiation among, 93, 94; grass-

The
American
West as
Living
Space

WALLACE
STEGNER

. . . . . . . . . . . . . . . . . .

# The
American
West as
Living
Space

The University of
Michigan Press
Ann Arbor

Copyright © by The University of Michigan 1987

All rights reserved

Published in the United States of America by

The University of Michigan Press

Manufactured in the United States of America

1990   1989   1988   1987     4   3   2   1

Library of Congress Cataloging-in-Publication Data

Stegner, Wallace Earle, 1909–
    The American West as living space.

    "Derives with only minor changes from a series of
three William W. Cook Lectures delivered at the Law
School of the University of Michigan in Ann Arbor
on October 28, 29, and 30, 1986"—Pref.
    Bibliography: p.
    1. West (U.S.)—Description and travel. 2. Natural
resources—West (U.S.) 3. Environmental protection—
West (U.S.) I. Title.
F591.S823   1987      917.8      87-19114
ISBN 0-472-09375-4 (alk. paper)
ISBN 0-472-06375-8 (pbk. : alk. paper)

Photographs courtesy of The Wilderness Society

# PREFACE

· · · · · · · · · · · · · · · ·

THIS book derives with only minor changes
from a series of three William W. Cook Lectures delivered at the Law School of the University of
Michigan in Ann Arbor on October 28, 29, and 30, 1986.

The subject to be discussed was the West. A sensible
way to discuss it would have been to select some manageable aspect of it and focus on that—to discuss the West
geographically as high plains, Rocky Mountains, southwestern plateaus, Great Basin deserts, the California lit-
toral, and the Pacific Northwest; or historically as the
romantic frontier of the fur trade, the wagon trains, the
mining rushes, and the sod house homesteads; or philo-
sophically as the dream of six-shooter freedom and
orange-grove bliss; or economically as the New West of
sunshine cities, the energy boom, and the grandiose,
costly, federally funded effort that has converted some
western valleys into gardens and most western rivers into
plumbing systems; or sociologically as an emergent sub-
species of the half-defined American culture.

That would have been orderly. It would also have been
the way the blind men approached the elephant. I decided
that I would rather risk superficiality and try to leave an
impression of the region in all its manifestations, to try a

holistic portrait, a look at the gestalt, the whole shebang, than settle for a clear impression of some treelike, spearlike, or ropelike part.

It used to be a boast among travelers in the West that they had "seen the elephant." I do not flatter myself that in three one-hour lectures I have been able to do more than sketch an outline. But I hope that it is at least an outline of the whole thing, the living region, with its country and its people, its splendors and its limitations, its facts and its fantasies, its opportunities and its problems, its romantic past and booming present and dubious future all suggested.

I have painted with a broad brush because there was no space to do more; and in the end I have concluded that the space limitation was salutary: it made me concentrate upon the essentials and kept me from getting tangled up in detail. And I have been personal because the West is not only a region but a state of mind, and both the region and the state of mind are my native habitat.

# CONTENTS

. . . . . . . .

The
American
West as
Living
Space

· · · · · · · · · · · · · · · · ·

# ONE

# Living Dry

THE West is a region of extraordinary variety within its abiding unity, and of an iron immutability beneath its surface of change. The most splendid part of the American habitat, it is also the most fragile. It has been misinterpreted and mistreated because, coming to it from earlier frontiers where conditions were not unlike those of northern Europe, we found it different, daunting, exhilarating, dangerous, and unpredictable, and we entered it carrying habits that were often inappropriate, and expectations that were surely excessive. The dreams we brought to it were recognizable American dreams—a new chance, a little gray home in the West, adventure, danger, bonanza, total freedom from constraint and law and obligation, the Big Rock Candy Mountain, the New Jerusalem. Those dreams had often paid off in earlier parts of America, and they paid off for some in the West. For the majority, no. The West has had a way of warping well-carpentered habits, and raising the grain on exposed dreams.

The fact is, it has been as notable for mirages as for the realization of dreams. Illusion and mirage have been built into it since Coronado came seeking the Seven Cities of Cíbola in 1540. Coronado's failure was an early, spectacular trial run for other and humbler failures. Witness the young men from all over the world who fill graveyards in California's Mother Lode country. There is one I remember: *Nato a Parma 1830, morto a Morfi 1850,* an inscription as significant for its revelation of the youth of many argonauts as for its misspelling of Murphy's, the camp where this boy died. Witness too the homesteaders who retreated eastward from the dry plains with signs on their covered wagons: "In God we trusted, in Kansas we busted." Yet we have not even yet fully lost our faith in Cíbola, or the nugget as big as a turnip, or even Kansas.

Anyone pretending to be a guide through wild and fabulous territory should know the territory. I wish I knew it better than I do. I am not Jed Smith. But Jed Smith was not available for this assignment, and I was. I accepted it eagerly, at least as much for what I myself might learn as for what I might be able to tell others. I can't come to even tentative conclusions about the West without coming to some conclusions about myself.

I have lived in the West, many parts of it, for the best part of seventy-seven years. I have found stories and novels in it, have studied its history and written some of it, have tried to know its landscapes and understand its people, have loved and lamented it, and sometimes rejected its most "western" opinions and prejudices, and pretty consistently despised its most powerful politicians and the general trend of their politics. I have been a lover but not much of a booster. Nevertheless, for better or worse, the West is in my computer, the biggest part of my software.

If there is such a thing as being conditioned by climate and geography, and I think there is, it is the West that has conditioned me. It has the forms and lights and colors that I respond to in nature and in art. If there is a western speech, I speak it; if there is a western character or personality, I am some variant of it; if there is a western culture in the small-*c*, anthropological sense, I have not escaped it. It has to have shaped me. I may even have contributed to it in minor ways, for culture is a pyramid to which each of us brings a stone.

Therefore I ask your indulgence if I sometimes speak in terms of my personal experience, feelings, and values, and put the anecdotal and normative ahead of the statistical, and emphasize personal judgments and trial syntheses rather than the analysis that necessarily preceded them. In doing so, I shall be trying to define myself as well as my native region.

Perhaps we will all know better what I think when we see what I say.

There are other ways of defining the West, but since Major John Wesley Powell's 1878 *Report on the Lands of the Arid Region* it has usually been said that it starts about the 98th meridian of west longitude and ends at the Pacific Ocean. Neither boundary has the Euclidean perfection of a fixed imaginary line, for on the west the Pacific plate is restless, constantly shoving Los Angeles northward where it is not wanted, and on the east the boundary between Middle West and West fluctuates a degree or two east or west depending on wet and dry cycles.

Actually it is not the arbitrary 98th meridian that marks the West's beginning, but a perceptible line of real import that roughly coincides with it, reaching southward about a third of the way across the Dakotas, Nebraska, and Kansas, and then swerving more southwestward across Oklahoma and Texas. This is the isohyetal line of twenty inches, beyond which the mean annual rainfall is less than the twenty inches normally necessary for unirrigated crops.

A very little deficiency, even a slight distortion of the season in which the rain falls, makes all the difference. My family homesteaded on the Montana-Saskatchewan border in 1915, and burned out by 1920, after laying the foundation for a little dust bowl by plowing up a lot of buffalo grass. If the rains had been kind, my father would have proved up on that land and become a naturalized Canadian. I estimate that I missed becoming Canadian by no more than an inch or two of rain; but that same deficiency confirmed me as a citizen of the West.

The West is defined, that is, by inadequate rainfall, which means a general deficiency of water. We have water only between the time of its falling as rain or snow and the time when it flows or percolates back into the sea or the deep subsurface reservoirs of the earth. We can't create water, or increase the supply. We can only hold back and redistribute what there is. If rainfall is inadequate, then streams will be inadequate, lakes will be few and sometimes saline, underground water will be slow to renew itself when it has been pumped down, the air will be very dry, and surface evaporation from lakes and reservoirs will be extreme. In desert parts of the West it is as much as ten feet a year.

The only exception to western aridity, apart from the mountains that provide the absolutely indispensable snowsheds, is the northwest corner, on the Pacific side of the Cascades. It is a narrow exception: everything east of the mountains, which means two-thirds to three-quarters of Washington and Oregon, is in the rain shadow.

California, which might seem to be an exception, is not.

*Utah, 1940*

Though from San Francisco northward the coast gets plenty of rain, that rain, like the lesser rains elsewhere in the state, falls not in the growing season but in winter. From April to November it just about can't rain. In spite of the mild coastal climate and an economy greater than that of all but a handful of nations, California fits Walter Webb's definition of the West as "a semi-desert with a desert heart." It took only the two-year drought of 1976–77, when my part of California got eight inches of rain each year instead of the normal eighteen, to bring the whole state to a panting pause. A five-year drought of the same severity would half depopulate the state.

So—the West that we are talking about comprises a dry core of eight public lands states—Arizona, Colorado, Idaho, Montana, Nevada, New Mexico, Utah, and Wyoming—plus two marginal areas. The first of these is the western part of the Dakotas, Nebraska, Kansas, Oklahoma, and Texas, authentically dry but with only minimal public lands. The second is the West Coast—Washington, Oregon, and California—with extensive arid lands but with well-watered coastal strips and with many rivers. Those marginal areas I do not intend to exclude, but they do complicate statistics. If I cite figures, they will often be for the states of the dry core.

A RIDITY, and aridity alone, makes the various Wests one. The distinctive western plants and animals, the hard clarity (before power plants and metropolitan traffic altered it) of the western air, the look and location of western towns, the empty spaces that separate them, the way farms and ranches are either densely concentrated where water is plentiful or widely scattered where it is scarce, the pervasive presence of the federal government as landowner and land manager, the even more noticeable federal presence as dam builder and water broker, the snarling states'-rights and antifederal feelings whose burden Bernard DeVoto once characterized in a sentence—"Get out and give us more money"—those are all consequences, and by no means all the consequences, of aridity.

Aridity first brought settlement to a halt at the edge of the dry country and then forced changes in the patterns of settlement. The best guide to those changes is Walter Webb's seminal study, *The Great Plains* (1931). As Webb pointed out, it took a lot of industrial invention to conquer the plains: the Colt revolver, a horseman's weapon, to subdue the horse Indians; barbed wire to control cattle; windmills to fill stock tanks and irrigate little gardens and hayfields; railroads to open otherwise unlivable spaces and bring first buffalo hides and buffalo bones and then cattle and wheat to market; gang machinery to plow, plant, and harvest big fields.

As it altered farming methods, weapons, and tools, so the dry country bent water law and the structure of land ownership. Eastern water law, adopted with little change from English common law, was essentially riparian. The owner of a stream bank, say a miller, could divert water from the stream to run his mill, but must flow it back when it had done his work for him. But in the arid lands only a little of the water diverted from a stream for any purpose—gold mining, irrigation, municipal or domestic consumption—ever finds its way back. Much is evaporated and lost. Following the practice of Gold Rush miners who diverted streams for their rockers and monitors, all of the dry core states subscribe to the so-called Colorado Doctrine of prior appropriation. First come, first served. The three coastal states go by some version of the California Doctrine, which is modified riparian.

Because water is precious, and because either prior appropriation or riparian rights, ruthlessly exercised, could give monopolistic power to an upstream or riparian landowner, both doctrines, over time, have been hedged with safeguards. Not even yet have we fully adapted our water law to western conditions, as was demonstrated when the California Supreme Court in 1983 invoked the "Public Trust" principle to prevent a single user, in this case the Los Angeles Water and Power Authority, from ever again draining a total water supply, in this case the streams that once watered the Owens Valley and fed Mono Lake. The court did not question the validity of Los Angeles' water rights. It only said that those rights could not be exercised at the expense of the public's legitimate interest.

The conditions that modified water use and water law also changed the character of western agriculture. The open range cattle outfits working north from Texas after the Civil War had only a brief time of uninhibited freedom before they ran into nesters and barbed wire. But the homesteaders who began disputing the plains with cat-

tlemen quickly found that 160 acres of dry land were a
hand without even openers. Many threw in. Those who
stuck either found land on streams or installed windmills;
and they moved toward larger acreages and the stock farm,
just as the cattlemen eventually moved toward the same
adjustment from the other end.

Powell had advocated just such an adjustment in 1878.
In country where it took 20, 30, even 50 acres to feed one
steer, quarter-section homesteads were of no use to a stock
raiser. But 160 acres of intensively worked irrigated land
were more than one family needed or could handle. Furthermore, the rectangular cadastral surveys that had been
in use ever since the Northwest Ordinance of 1787 paid no
attention to water. Out on the plains, a single quarter or
half section might contain all the water within miles, and
all the adjacent range was dominated by whoever owned
that water.

Powell therefore recommended a new kind of survey
defining irrigable homesteads of 80 acres and grazing
homesteads of 2,560, four full sections. Every plot should
have access to water, and every water right should be tied
to land title. Obviously, that program would leave a lot of
dry land unsettled.

Unfortunately for homesteaders and the West, Powell's
report was buried under dead leaves by Congress. Ten
years later, his attempt to close the Public Domain until he
could get it surveyed and its irrigable lands identified was
defeated by Senator "Big Bill" Stewart of Nevada, the
first of a long line of incomparably bad Nevada senators.

In 1889 and 1890 the constitutional conventions of Montana, Idaho, and Wyoming territories would not listen when Powell urged them to lay out their political boundaries along drainage divides, so that watershed and timber lands, foothill grazing lands, and valley irrigated lands could be managed intelligently without conflict. The only place where a drainage divide does mark a political boundary is a stretch of the Continental Divide between Idaho and Montana. And to cap this history of old habits stubbornly clung to and hopes out of proportion to possibilities, when Powell addressed the boosters of the Irrigation Congress in Los Angeles in 1893 and warned them that they were laying up a heritage of litigation and failure because there was only enough water to irrigate a fifth of the western lands, the boosters didn't listen either. They booed him.

Powell understood the consequences of aridity, as the boosters did not, and still do not. Westerners who would like to return to the old days of free grab, people of the kind described as having made America great by their initiative and energy in committing mass trespass on the minerals, grass, timber, and water of the Public Domain, complain that no western state is master in its own house. Half its land is not its own. 85 percent of Nevada is not Nevada, but the United States; two-thirds of Utah and Idaho likewise; nearly half of California, Arizona, and Wyoming—48 percent of the eleven public lands states.

There are periodic movements, the latest of which was the so-called Sagebrush Rebellion of the 1970s, to get these lands "returned" to the states, which could then dispose of them at bargain-basement rates to favored stockmen, corporations, and entrepreneurs.

The fact is, the states never owned those lands, and gave up all claim to them when they became states. They were always federal lands, acquired by purchase, negotiation, or conquest before any western state existed. The original thirteen colonies created the first Public Domain when they relinquished to the federal government their several claims to what was then the West. The states between the Alleghanies and the Mississippi River were made out of it. All but one of the rest of the contiguous forty-eight were made out of the Louisiana and Florida purchases, the land acquired by the Oregon settlement with Great Britain, and the territory taken from Mexico in the Mexican War or obtained by purchase afterward. All of the western states except Texas, which entered the Union as an independent republic and never had any Public Domain, were created out of federal territory by formal acts of Congress, which then did everything it could to dispose of the public lands within them.

As far as a little beyond the Missouri, the system of disposal worked. Beyond the 98th meridian it did not, except in the spotty way that led Webb to call the West an "oasis civilization." Over time, large areas of forest land and the most spectacular scenery were reserved in the public interest, but much land was not considered worth reserving, and could not be settled or given away. The land laws—the Preemption Act, Homestead Act, Desert Land Act, Carey Act, Timber and Stone Act—produced more failure and fraud than family farms. Not even the Newlands Act of 1902, though it has transformed the West, has put into private hands more than a modest amount of the Public Domain.

Despite all efforts, the West remained substantially federal. In 1930 Herbert Hoover and his Secretary of the Interior Ray Lyman Wilbur tried to give a lot of abused dry land to the states, and the states just laughed. Then in 1934, in the worst Dust Bowl year, the Taylor Grazing Act acknowledged the federal government's reluctant decision to retain—and rescue and manage—the overgrazed, eroded Public Domain. In the 1940s the stockmen's associations tried to steal it, as well as the Forest Service's grazing lands, in a dry rehearsal of the later Sagebrush Rebellion. Bernard DeVoto, in the Easy Chair pages of *Harper's Magazine,* almost single-handedly frustrated that grab.

But by the 1940s more than stockmen were interested, and more than grass was at stake. During and after World War II the West had revealed treasures of oil, coal, uranium, molybdenum, phosphates, and much else. States whose extractive industries were prevented from unhampered exploitation of these resources again cried foul, demanding "back" the lands they had never owned, cared for, or really wanted, and complaining that the acreages of the Bureau of Land Management, national forests, national parks and monuments, wildlife refuges, military reservations, and dam sites, as well as the arid poor farms where we had filed away our Indian responsibilities, were off the state tax rolls and outside of state control and "locked up" from developers who, given a free hand, would make the West rich and prosperous.

Never mind that grazing fees and coal and oil lease fees and timber sale prices are so low that they amount to a fat subsidy to those who enjoy them. (The flat fee of $1.35 per Animal-Unit-Month set by the Reagan Administration as a grazing fee is about 20 percent of what leasers of private land must pay in most districts. Many timber sales are below cost). Never mind that half of the money that does come in from fees and leases is given to the states in lieu of taxes. Never mind that the feds spend the other half, and more, rescuing and rehabilitating the lands whose proper management would bankrupt the states in which they lie. Never mind the federal aid highways, and the federally financed dams, and the write-offs against flood control, and the irrigation water delivered at a few dollars an acre foot. Take for granted federal assistance, but damn federal control. Your presence as absentee landlord offends us, Uncle. Get out, and give us more money.

There are other objections, too, some of them more legitimate than those of stockmen, lumbermen, and miners greedy for even more than they are getting. There are real difficulties of management when the landscape is checkerboarded with private, state, and federal ownership. And federal space is tempting whenever the nation needs a bombing range, an atomic test site, missile silo locations, or places to dump nuclear waste or store nerve gas. Generally, the West protests that because of its public lands it gets all the garbage; but sometimes, so odd we are as a species, one or another western state will fight for the garbage, and lobby to become the home of a nuclear dump.

More by oversight than intention, the federal government allowed the states to assert ownership of the water within their boundaries, and that is actually an ownership far more valuable but more complicated than that of land. The feds own the watersheds, the stream and lake beds, the dam sites. Federal bureaus, with the enthusiastic concurrence of western chambers of commerce, have since 1902 done most of the costly impoundment and distribution of water. And federal law, in a pinch, can and does occasionally veto what states and irrigation districts do with that water. It is a good guess that it will have to do so more and more—that unless the states arrive at some relatively uniform set of rules, order will have to be imposed on western water by the federal government.

It will not be easy, and the federal government has created a nasty dilemma for itself by giving its blessing both to the legal fiction of state water ownership and to certain Native American rights to water. As early as 1908, in the so-called Winters Doctrine decision, the Supreme Court confirmed the Indians' rights in water originating within or flowing through their reservations. Though those rights have never been quantified or put to use (a beginning has been made by the tribes on the Fort Peck Reservation), Indian tribes all across the West have legitimate but unspecified claims to water already granted by the states to white individuals and corporations. Even without the Indian claims, many western streams—

for a prime example the Colorado—are already over-subscribed. The Colorado River Compact allocated 17.5 million acre feet annually among the upper basin, lower basin, and Mexico. The actual annual flow since 1930 has averaged about 12 million acre feet.

Aridity arranged all that complicated natural and human mess, too. In the view of some, it also helped to create a large, spacious, independent, sunburned, self-reliant western character, and a large, open, democratic western society. Of that, despite a wistful desire to believe, I am less than confident.

NINETEENTH-CENTURY America, overwhelm-ingly agricultural, assumed that settlement meant agricultural settlement. That assumption under-lies—some say it undermines—Frederick Jackson Tur-ner's famous hypothesis, expressed in his 1893 lecture "The Significance of the Frontier in American History," that both democratic institutions and the American char-acter have been largely shaped by the experience of suc-cessive frontiers, with their repeated dream of betterment, their repeated acceptance of primitive hardships, their re-peated hope and strenuousness and buoyancy, and their repeated fulfillment as smiling and productive common-wealths of agrarian democrats.

Turner was so intent upon the mass movement toward free land that he paid too little attention to a growing movement toward the industrial cities, and his version of the American character is therefore open to some qualifi-cations. He also paid too little attention to the drastic changes enforced by aridity beyond the 98th meridian, the changes that Powell before him and Webb after him concentrated upon.

The fact is, agriculture at first made little headway in the West, and when it was finally imposed upon the susceptible—and some unsusceptible—spots, it was established pretty much by brute force, and not entirely by agrarian democrats.

Until the Civil War and after, most of the West was not a goal but a barrier. Webb properly remarks that if it had turned out to be country adapted to the slave economy, the South would have fought for it, and its history would have been greatly different. He also points out that if the country beyond the Missouri had been wooded and well watered, there would have been no Oregon Trail.

E MIGRANTS bound up the Platte Valley on their way to Oregon, California, or Utah, the first targets of the westward migration, almost universally noted in their journals that a little beyond Grand Island their nostrils dried out and their lips cracked, their wagon wheels began to shrink and wobble, and their estimates of distance began to be ludicrously off the mark. They observed that green had ceased to be the prevailing color of the earth, and had given way to tans, grays, rusty reds, and toned white; that salt often crusted the bottoms of dry lakes (they used some of it, the sodium or potassium bicarbonate that they called saleratus, to leaven their bread); that the grass no longer made a turf, but grew in isolated clumps with bare earth between them; that there was now no timber except on the islands in the Platte; that un-familiar animals had appeared: horned toads and prairie dogs that seemed to require no water at all, and buffalo, antelope, jackrabbits, and coyotes that could travel long distances for it.

They were at the border of strangeness. Only a few miles into the West, they felt the difference; and as Webb says, the degree of strangeness can be measured by the fact that almost all the new animals they saw they misnamed. The prairie dog is not a dog, the horned toad is not a toad, the jackrabbit is not a rabbit, the buffalo is not a buffalo, and the pronghorn antelope is more goat than antelope. But they could not mistake the aridity. They just didn't know how much their habits would have to change if they wanted to live beyond the 98th meridian. None of them in that generation would have denied aridity to its face, as William Gilpin, the first territorial governor of Colorado, would do a generation later, asserting that it was a simple matter on the plains to *dig* for wood and water, that irriga-tion was as easy as fencing, which it supplanted, and that the dry plains and the Rockies could handily support a population of two hundred million. That kind of fantasy, like Cyrus Thomas's theory that cultivation increases rain-fall, that "rain follows the plow," would have to wait for the boosters.

Two lessons all western travelers had to learn: mobility and sparseness. Mobility was the condition of life beyond the Missouri. Once they acquired the horse, the Plains Indians were as migrant as the buffalo they lived by. The mountain men working the beaver streams were no more fixed than the clouds. And when the change in hat fashions killed the fur trade, and mountain men turned to guiding wagon trains, the whole intention of those trains was to get an early start, as soon as the grass greened up, and then get *through* the West as fast as possible. The Mormons were an exception, a special breed headed for sanctuary in the heart of the desert, a people with a uniquely cohesive social order and a theocratic discipline that made them better able to survive.

But even the Mormons were villages on the march, as mobile as the rest until, like Moses from Pisgah's top, they looked upon Zion. Once there, they quickly made themselves into the West's stablest society. But notice: Now, a hundred and forty years after their hegira, they have managed to put only about 3 percent of Utah's land under cultivation; and because they took seriously the Lord's command to be fruitful and multiply, Zion has been overpopulated, and exporting manpower, for at least half a century. One of the bitterest conflicts in modern Utah is that between the environmentalists who want to see much of that superlative wilderness preserved roadless and wild, and the stubborn Mormon determination to make it support more Saints than it possibly can.

LIEUTENANT Zebulon Pike, sent out in 1806 to explore the country between the Missouri and Santa Fe, had called the high plains the Great American Desert. In 1819 the expedition of Major Stephen Long corroborated that finding, and for two generations no-

sage of life there, and the land will not be lived
its own fashion. The Shoshones live like their
great spaces between. . . ."
t have added, though I don't remember that
w often Shoshonean place names contain the
: Tonopah, Ivanpah, Pahrump, Paria. In the
language, *-pah* means water, or water hole.
es are the Water Utes, taking their name from
and most precious resource. They live mainly
Nevada, the two driest states in the Union,
regions water is safety, home, life, *place*. All
e precious watered places, forbidding and un-
ly space, what one must travel through be-
s of safety.
ly adapted, the Pah-Utes (Paiutes) were mi-
ween fixed points marked by seasonal food
by water. White Americans, once they began
the dry country from east, west, and south,
ablished their settlements on dependable
hose towns have a special shared quality, a
blance.
oment, forget the Pacific Coast, furiously bent
Conurbia from Portland to San Diego. For-
politan sprawl of Denver, Phoenix, Tucson,
, Dallas–Fort Worth, and Salt Lake City,
he limits of their water and beyond, like bac-
s overflowing the edges of their agar dishes
g to sicken on their own wastes. If we want
western towns we must look for them, para-
yond the West's prevailing urbanism, out in

body seriously questioned it. The plains were unfit for
settlement by a civilized, meaning an agricultural, people,
and the farther west you went, the worse things got. So
for the emigrants who in 1840 began to take wheels westward up the Platte Valley, the interior West was not a
place but a way, a trail to the Promised Land, an adventurous, dangerous rite of passage. In the beginning there
were only two *places* on its two-thousand-mile length:
Fort Laramie on the North Platte and Fort Hall on the
Snake. And those were less settlements than way stations,
refreshment and recruitment stops different only in style
from motel-and-gas-and-lunchroom turnouts on a modern interstate.

Insofar as the West was a civilization at all between the
time of Lewis and Clark's explorations and about 1870, it
was largely a civilization in motion, driven by dreams. The
people who composed and represented it were part of a
true Folk-Wandering, credulous, hopeful, hardy, largely
uninformed. The dreams are not dead even today, and the
habit of mobility has only been reinforced by time. If, as
Wendell Berry says, most Americans are not placed but
displaced persons, then western Americans are the most
displaced persons of all.

Ever since Daniel Boone took his first excursion over
Cumberland Gap, Americans have been wanderers. When
Charles Dickens, in the Mississippi Valley, met a full-sized
dwelling house coming down the road at a round trot, he
was looking at the American people head-on. With a continent to take over and Manifest Destiny to goad us, we

could not have avoided being footloose. The initial act of emigration from Europe, an act of extreme, deliberate disaffiliation, was the beginning of a national habit.

It should not be denied, either, that being footloose has always exhilarated us. It is associated in our minds with escape from history and oppression and law and irksome obligations, with absolute freedom, and the road has always led west. Our folk heroes and our archetypal literary figures accurately reflect that side of us. Leatherstocking, Huckleberry Finn, the narrator of *Moby Dick,* all are orphans and wanderers: any of them could say, "Call me Ishmael." The Lone Ranger has no dwelling place except the saddle. And when teenagers run away these days, in the belief that they are running toward freedom, they more often than not run west. Listen to the Haight-Ashbury dialogues in Joan Didion's *Slouching toward Bethlehem.* Examine the American character as it is self-described in *Habits of the Heart,* by Robert Bellah and others.

But the rootlessness that expresses energy and a thirst for the new and an aspiration toward freedom and personal fulfillment has just as often been a curse. Migrants deprive themselves of the physical and spiritual bonds that develop within a place and a society. Our migratoriness has hindered us from becoming a people of communities and traditions, especially in the West. It has robbed us of the gods who make places holy. It has cut off individuals and families and communities from memory and the continuum of time. It has left at least some of us with a kind of spiritual pellagra, a deficiency disease, a hungering for the ties of a rich and stable social order. Not only is the Ameri-

can home a launchir
American communit
night camp. Americ
and cherished, has de
tive, which is belongi
out to be airless and u
what we have instead
half memory, shared
long enough at one s

The principal inver
the motel, the princij
motive roadside. The
ism, which is not onl
might want to be, the
visitations or a trail to
ature, from *Roughing*
*Cowboy* to *Lonesome Do
tain* to *The Big Sky,* has
but of motion.

Trying to capture
Stein said, "Conceive
If she had been reared i
so plainly; but she was
few Westerners die wh
out their lives as a seri

ADAPTATION
organisms s
Austin, writing of the C
the Sierra, remarked t

makes the
in except i
trees, witl
She mi
she did, h
syllable -*t*
Shoshone
The Pah-
their rare
in Utah
and in th
around tl
livable, i
tween pl
Thoro
gratory
supplies
to edge
likewise
water, a
family r
For tl
on beco
get the
Albuqu
growin
terial c
and be;
charact
doxical

the boondocks where the interstates do not reach, mainline planes do not fly, and branch plants do not locate. The towns that are most western have had to strike a balance between mobility and stability, and the law of sparseness has kept them from growing too big. They are the places where the stickers stuck, and perhaps were stuck; the places where adaptation has gone furthest.

Whether they are winter wheat towns on the subhumid edge, whose elevators and bulbous silver water towers announce them miles away, or county towns in ranch country, or intensely green towns in irrigated desert valleys, they have a sort of forlorn, proud rightness. They look at once lost and self-sufficient, scruffy and indispensable. A road leads in out of wide emptiness, threads a fringe of service stations, taverns, and a motel or two, widens to a couple of blocks of commercial buildings, some still false-fronted, with glimpses of side streets and green lawns, narrows to another strip of automotive roadside, and disappears into more wide emptiness.

The loneliness and vulnerability of those towns always moves me, for I have lived in them. I know how the world of a child in one of them is bounded by weedy prairie, or the spine of the nearest dry range, or by flats where plugged tin cans lie rusting and the wind has pasted paper and plastic against the sagebrush. I know how precious is the safety of a few known streets and vacant lots and familiar houses. I know how the road in both directions both threatens and beckons. I know that most of the children in such a town will sooner or later take that road, and that only a few will take it back.

In mining country, vulnerability has already gone most or all of the way to death. In those ghosts or near ghosts where the placers have been gutted or the lodes played out, the shafts and drifts and tailings piles, the saloons and stores and hotels and houses, have been left to the lizards and a few survivors who have rejected the command of mobility. The deader the town, the more oppressive the emptiness that surrounds and will soon reclaim it. Unless, of course, the federal government has installed an atomic testing site, or new migrant entrepreneurs have come in to exploit the winter skiing or bring summer-festival culture. Then the ghost will have turned, at least temporarily, into a Searchlight, an Aspen, a Telluride, a Park City—a new way station for new kinds of migrants.

WE return to mobility and the space that enforces it. Consider the observations of William Least Heat Moon, touring the blue highways of America. "The true West," he says (and notice that he too finds the true West somewhere outside the cities where 75 percent of Westerners live),

> differs from the East in one great, pervasive, influential, and awesome way: space. The vast openness changes the roads, towns, houses, farms, crops, machinery, politics, economics, and, naturally, ways of thinking. . . . Space west of the line is perceptible and often palpable, especially when it appears empty, and it's that apparent emptiness which makes matter look alone, exiled, and uncon-

nected. . . . But as the space diminishes man and
his constructions in a material fashion it also—
paradoxically—makes them more noticeable.
*Things show up out here.* The terrible distances eat
up speed. Even dawn takes nearly an hour just to
cross Texas. (*Blue Highways,* p. 136)

Distance, space, affects people as surely as it has bred
keen eyesight into pronghorn antelope. And what makes
that western space and distance? The same condition that
enforces mobility on all adapted creatures, and tolerates
only small or temporary concentrations of human or
other life.

Aridity.

And what do you do about aridity, if you are a nation
inured to plenty and impatient of restrictions and led
westward by pillars of fire and cloud? You may deny it for
a while. Then you must either adapt to it or try to engineer
it out of existence.

. . . . . . . . . . . . . . . . . .

# TWO

# Striking
# the Rock

THE summer of 1948 my family and I spent on Struthers Burt's ranch in Jackson Hole. I was just beginning the biography of John Wesley Powell, and beginning to understand some things about the West that I had not understood before. But during that busy and instructive interval my wife and I were also acting as western editors and scouts for a publishing house, and now and then someone came by with a manuscript or the idea for a book. The most memorable of these was a famous architect contemplating his autobiography. One night he showed us slides of some of his houses, including a million-dollar palace in the California desert of which he was very proud. He said it demonstrated that with imagination, technical know-how, modern materials, and enough money, an architect could build anywhere without constraints, imposing his designed vision on any site, in any climate.

In that waterless pale desert spotted with shad scale and creosote bush and backed by barren, lion-colored mountains, another sort of architect, say Frank Lloyd Wright, might have designed something contextual, something low, broad-eaved, thick-walled, something that would mitigate the hot light, something half-underground so that people could retire like the lizards and rattlesnakes from the intolerable daytime temperatures, something made of native stone or adobe or tamped earth in the colors and shapes of the country, something no more visually intrusive than an outcrop.

Not our architect. He had built of cinderblock, in the form of Bauhaus cubes, the only right angles in that desert. He had painted them a dazzling white. Instead of softening the lines between building and site, he had accentuated them, surrounding his sugary cubes with acres of lawn and a tropical oasis of oleanders, hibiscus, and palms—not the native *Washingtonia* palms either, which are a little scraggly, but sugar and royal palms, with a classier, more Santa Barbara look. Water for this estancia, enough water to have sustained a whole tribe of desert Indians, he had brought by private pipeline from the mountains literally miles away.

The patio around the pool—who would live in the desert without a pool?—would have fried the feet of swimmers, three hundred days out of the year, and so he had designed canopies that could be extended and retracted by push button, and under the patio's concrete he had laid pipes through which cool water circulated by day. By night, after the desert chill came on, the circulating water was heated. He had created an artificial climate, inside and out.

Studying that luxurious, ingenious, beautiful, sterile incongruity, I told its creator, sincerely, that I thought he could build a comfortable house in hell. That pleased him; he thought so too. What I didn't tell him, what he would not have understood, was that we thought his desert house immoral. It exceeded limits, it offended our sense not of the possible but of the desirable. There was no economic or social reason for anyone's living on a barren flat, however beautiful, where every form of life sought shelter during the unbearable daylight hours. The only reasons for building there were to let mad dogs and rich men go out in the midday sun, and to let them own and dominate a view they admired. The house didn't fit the country, it challenged it. It asserted America's never-say-never spirit and America's ingenious know-how. It seemed to us an act of arrogance on the part of both owner and architect.

I felt like asking him, What if a super-rich Eskimo wanted a luxury house on Point Hope? Would you build it for him? Would you dam the Kobuk and bring megawatts of power across hundreds of miles of tundra, and set up batteries of blower-heaters to melt the snow and thaw the permafrost, and would you erect an international style house with picture windows through which the Eskimo family could look out across the lawn and strawberry bed and watch polar bears on the pack ice?

He might have taken on such a job, and he was good enough to make it work, too—until the power line blew down or shorted out. Then the Eskimos he had encouraged to forget igloo building and seal oil lamps would freeze into ice sculptures, monuments to human pride. But of course that is all fantasy. Eskimos, a highly adapted and adaptable people, would have more sense than to challenge their arctic habitat that way. Even if they had unlimited money. Which they don't.

That desert house seemed to me, and still seems to me, a paradigm—hardly a paradigm, more a caricature—of what we have been doing to the West in my lifetime. Instead of adapting, as we began to do, we have tried to make country and climate over to fit our existing habits and desires. Instead of listening to the silence, we have

*Arizona, 1940*

d industrial demands for water have greatly in-
, 80 to 90 percent of the water used in the West is
ften wastefully, on fields, to produce crops gener-
urplus elsewhere. After all the billions spent by the
of Reclamation, the total area irrigated by its pro-
about the size of Ohio, and the water impounded
tributed by the bureau is about 15 percent of all the
tilized in the West. What has been won is only a
ead, and a beachhead that is bound to shrink.

NE of the things Westerners should ponder,
but generally do not, is their relation to and
toward the federal presence. The bureaus admin-
all the empty space that gives Westerners much of
door pleasure and many of their special privileges
t of their pride and self-image are frequently re-
esisted, or manipulated by those who benefit eco-
y from them but would like to benefit more, and
rally taken for granted by the general public.
deral presence should be recognized as what it is:
against our former profligacy and wastefulness,
at adaptation and stewardship in the interest of
onment and the future. In contrast to the prin-
r agency, the Bureau of Reclamation, which was
of the boosters and remains their creature, and
ime purpose is technological conversion of the
, the land-managing bureaus all have as at least
eir purpose the preservation of the West in a
natural, healthy, and sustainable condition.
tone became the first national park in 1872 be-

shouted into the void. We have tried to make the arid West into what it was never meant to be and cannot remain, the Garden of the World and the home of multiple millions.

THAT does not mean either that the West should never have been settled or that water should never be managed. The West—the habitable parts of it—is a splendid habitat for a limited population living within the country's rules of sparseness and mobility. If the unrestrained engineering of western water was original sin, as I believe, it was essentially a sin of scale. Anyone who wants to live in the West has to manage water to some degree.

Ranchers learned early to turn creeks onto their hay land. Homesteaders not on a creek learned to dam a runoff coulee to create a "rezavoy" as we did in Saskatchewan in 1915. Kansas and Oklahoma farmers set windmills to pumping up the underground water. Towns brought their water, by ditch or siphon, from streams up on the watershed. Irrigation, developed first by the Southwestern Indians and the New Mexico Spanish, and reinvented by the Mormons—it was a necessity that came with the territory—was expanded in the 1870s and 1880s by such cooperative communities as Greeley, Colorado, and by small-to-medium corporate ventures such as the one I wrote about in *Angle of Repose*—the project on the Boise River that after its failure was taken over by the Bureau of Reclamation and called the Arrowrock Dam.

Early water engineers and irrigators bit off what they

and the local community coul
streams that they could mana
on larger rivers, as Arthur Fo
went broke at it. By and large
rate, and cooperative irrigat
they could go with water engi
were for local use and under
been better if the West had
through the 1890s the uns
federal aid to let the West r
they got the Newlands Ac
undertake water projects—r
owned, or at least state regul
of Reclamation.

Reclamation projects w
charged irrigation districts.
interest-free indebtedness b
that was upped to twenty,
much of the burden of repa
of water to the sale of hydr
eliminated entirely by the
ing, with write-offs for fl
other public goods. Once
ernment—which meant t
try, including taxpayers
reclamation because they
something that would c
farmers—absorbed or w
costs, accepting the fact t
subsidy to western agric

pal an
crease
used,
ally in
Bureau
jects is
and dis
water u
beachh

attitude
istering
their ou
and a l
sented,
nomical
are gene

The fe
a reactio
an effort
the envi
cipal wat
a creatio
whose p
arid land
part of t
relatively

Yellow

cause a party of Montana tourists around a campfire voted down a proposal to exploit it for profit, and pledged themselves to try to get it protected as a permanent pleasuring-ground for the whole country. The national forests began because the bad example of Michigan scared Congress about the future of the country's forests, and induced it in 1891 to authorize the reservation of public forest lands by presidential proclamation. Benjamin Harrison took large advantage of the opportunity. Later, Grover Cleveland did the same, and so did Theodore Roosevelt. The West, predictably, cried aloud at having that much plunder removed from circulation, and in 1907 western Congressmen put a rider on an agricultural appropriations bill that forbade any more presidential reservations without the prior consent of Congress. Roosevelt could have pocket vetoed it. Instead, he and Chief Forester Gifford Pinchot sat up all night over the maps and surveys of potential reserves, and by morning Roosevelt had signed into existence twenty-one new national forests, sixteen million acres of them. Then he signed the bill that would have stopped him.

It was Theodore Roosevelt, too, who created the first wildlife refuge in 1903, thus beginning a service whose territories, since passage of the Alaska National Interest Lands Conservation Act of 1980, now exceed those of the National Park Service by ten million acres.

As for the biggest land manager of all, the Bureau of Land Management (BLM), it is the inheritor of the old General Land Office whose job was to dispose of the Public Domain to homesteaders, and its lands are the leftovers once (erroneously) thought to be worthless. Worthless or not, they could not be indefinitely neglected and abused. The health of lands around them depended on their health.

They were assumed as a permanent federal responsibility by the Taylor Grazing Act of 1934, but the Grazing Service then created was a helpless and toothless bureau dominated by local councils packed by local stockmen— foxes set by other foxes to watch the henhouse, in a travesty of democratic local control. The Grazing Service was succeeded by the Bureau of Land Management, which was finally given some teeth by the Federal Land Policy and Management Act of 1976. No sooner did it get the teeth that would have let it do its job than the Sagebrush Rebels offered to knock them out. The Rebels didn't have to. Instead, President Reagan gave them James Watt as secretary of the interior, and James Watt gave them Robert Burford as head of the BLM. The rebels simmered down, their battle won for them by administrative appointment, and BLM remains a toothless bureau.

All of the bureaus walk a line somewhere between preservation and exploitation. The enabling act of the National Park Service in 1916 charged it to provide for the *use without impairment* of the parks. It is an impossible assignment, especially now that more than three hundred million people visit the national parks annually, but the Park Service tries.

The National Forest Service, born out of Pinchot's philosophy of "wise use," began with the primary purpose of halting unwise use, and as late as the 1940s so informed a critic as Bernard DeVoto thought it the very best of the federal bureaus. But it changed its spots during the first Eisenhower administration, under the Mormon patriarch Ezra Taft Benson as secretary of agriculture, and began aggressively to harvest board feet. Other legitimate uses— recreation, watershed and wildlife protection, the gene banking of wild plant and animal species, and especially wilderness preservation—it either neglected or resisted whenever they conflicted with logging.

By now, unhappily, environmental groups tend to see the Forest Service not as the protector of an invaluable public resource and the true champion of multiple use, but as one of the enemy, allied with the timber interests. The Forest Service, under attack, has reacted with a hostility bred of its conviction that it is unjustly criticized. As a consequence of that continuing confrontation, nearly every master plan prepared in obedience to the National Forest Management Act of 1976 has been challenged and will be fought, in the courts if necessary, by the Wilderness Society, the Sierra Club, the Natural Resources Defense Council, and other organizations. The usual charge: too many timber sales, too often at a loss in money as well as in other legitimate values, and far too much roading—roading being a preliminary to logging and a way of forestalling wilderness designation by spoiling the wilderness in advance.

What is taking place is that Congress has been responding to public pressures to use the national forests for newly perceived social goods; and the National Forest Service, for many years an almost autonomous bureau with a high morale and, from a forester's point of view, high principles, is resisting that imposition of control.

Not even the Fish and Wildlife Service, dedicated to the preservation of wild species and their habitats, escapes criticism, for under pressure from stockmen it has historically waged war on predators, especially coyotes, and the 1080 poison baits that it used to distribute destroyed not only coyotes but hawks, eagles, and other wildlife that the agency was created to protect. One result has been a good deal of public suspicion. Even the current device of 1080-poisoned collars for sheep and lambs, designed to affect only an attacking predator, is banned in thirty states.

The protection provided by these various agencies is of course imperfect. Every reserve is an island, and its boundaries are leaky. Nevertheless this is the best protection we have, and not to be disparaged. All Americans, but especially Westerners whose backyard is at stake, need to ask themselves whose bureaus these should be. Half of the West is in their hands. Do they exist to provide bargain-basement grass to favored stockmen whose grazing privileges have become all but hereditary, assumed and bought and sold along with the title to the home spread? Are they hired exterminators of wildlife? Is it their function to negotiate loss-leader coal leases with energy conglomerates, and to sell timber below cost to Louisiana Pacific? Or should they be serving the much larger public whose outdoor recreations of backpacking, camping, fishing, hunting, river running, mountain climbing, hang gliding, and, God help us, dirt biking are incompatible with clear-cut forests and overgrazed, poison-baited, and strip-mined grasslands? Or is there a still higher duty—to maintain the health and beauty of the lands they manage, protecting from everybody, including such destructive segments of the public as dirt bikers and pothunters, the watersheds and spawning streams, forests and grasslands, geological and scenic splendors, historical and archaeological remains, air and water and serene space, that once led me, in a reckless moment, to call the western public lands part of the geography of hope?

As I have known them, most of the field representatives of all the bureaus, including the BLM, do have a sense of responsibility about the resources they oversee, and a frequent frustration that they are not permitted to oversee them better. But that sense of duty is not visible in some, and at the moment is least visible in the political appointees who make or enunciate policy. Even when policy is intelligently made and well understood, it sometimes cannot be enforced because of local opposition. More than one Forest Service ranger or BLM man who tried to enforce the rules has had to be transferred out of a district to save him from violence.

There are many books on the Public Domain. One of the newest and best is *These American Lands,* by Dyan Zaslowsky and the Wilderness Society, published in 1986 by Henry Holt and Company. I recommend it, not only for its factual accuracy and clarity, but for its isolation of problems and its suggestions of solutions. Here and now, all I can do is repeat that the land bureaus have a strong, often disregarded influence on how life is lived in the West. They provide and protect the visible, available, unfenced space that surrounds almost all western cities and towns—surrounds them as water surrounds fish, and is their living element.

The bureaus need, and some would welcome, the kind of public attention that would force them to behave in the long-range public interest. Though I have been involved in controversies with some of them, the last thing I would want to see is their dissolution and a return to the policy of disposal, for that would be the end of the West as I have known and loved it. Neither state ownership nor private ownership—which state ownership would soon become—could offer anywhere near the disinterested stewardship that these imperfect and embattled federal bureaus do, while at the same time making western space available to millions. They have been the strongest impediment to the careless ruin of what remains of the Public Domain, and they will be necessary as far ahead as I, at least, can see.

The Bureau of Reclamation is something else. From the beginning, its aim has been not the preservation but the remaking—in effect the mining—of the West.

A principal justification for the Newlands Act was that fabled Jeffersonian yeoman, the small freehold farmer, who was supposed to benefit from the Homestead Act, the Desert Land Act, the Timber and Stone Act, and other land-disposal legislation, but rarely did so west of the 98th meridian. The publicized purpose of federal reclamation was the creation of family farms that would eventually feed the world and build prosperous rural commonwealths in deserts formerly fit for nothing but horned toads and rattlesnakes. To insure that these small farmers would not be done out of their rights by large landowners and water users, Congress wrote into the act a clause limiting the use of water under Reclamation Bureau dams to the amount that would serve a family farm of 160 acres.

Behind the pragmatic, manifest-destinarian purpose of pushing western settlement was another motive: the hard determination to dominate nature that historian Lynn White, in the essay "Historical Roots of Our Ecologic Crisis," identified as part of our Judeo-Christian heritage. Nobody implemented that impulse more uncomplicatedly than the Mormons, a chosen people who believed the Lord when He told them to make the desert blossom as the rose. Nobody expressed it more bluntly than a Mormon hierarch, John Widtsoe, in the middle of the irrigation campaigns: "The destiny of man is to possess the whole earth; the destiny of the earth is to be subject to man. There can be no full conquest of the earth, and no real satisfaction to humanity, if large portions of the earth remain beyond his highest control" (*Success on Irrigation Projects*, p. 138).

That doctrine offends me to the bottom of my not-very-Christian soul. It is related to the spirit that builds castles of incongruous luxury in the desert. It is the same spirit that between 1930 and the present has so dammed, diverted, used, and reused the Colorado River that its saline waters now never reach the Gulf of California, but die in the sand miles from the sea; that has set the Columbia, a far mightier river, to tamely turning turbines; that has reduced the Missouri, the greatest river on the continent, to a string of ponds; that has recklessly pumped down the water table of every western valley and threatens to dry up even so prolific a source as the Ogalalla Aquifer; that has made the Salt River Valley of Arizona, and the Imperial, Coachella, and great Central valleys of California into gardens of fabulous but deceptive richness; that has promoted a new rush to the West fated, like the beaver and grass and gold rushes, to recede after doing great environmental damage.

The Garden of the World has been a glittering dream, and many find its fulfillment exhilarating. I do not. I have already said that I think of the main-stem dams that made it possible as original sin, but there is neither a serpent nor a guilty first couple in the story. In Adam's fall we sinnéd all. Our very virtues as a pioneering people, the very genius of our industrial civilization, drove us to act as we did. God and Manifest Destiny spoke with one voice urging us to "conquer" or "win" the West; and there was no voice of comparable authority to remind us of Mary Austin's quiet but profound truth, that the manner of the country makes the usage of life there, and that the land will not be lived in except in its own fashion.

Obviously, reclamation is not the panacea it once seemed. Plenty of people in 1986 are opposed to more dams, and there is plenty of evidence against the long-range viability and the social and environmental desirability of large-scale irrigation agriculture. Nevertheless, millions of Americans continue to think of the water engineering in the West as one of our proudest achievements, a technology that we should export to backward Third World nations to help them become as we are. We go on praising apples as if eating them were an injunction of the Ten Commandments.

F O R its first thirty years, the Bureau of Reclamation struggled, plagued by money problems and unable to perform as its boosters had promised. It got a black eye for being involved, in shady ways, with William Mulholland's steal of the Owens Valley's water for the benefit of Los Angeles. The early dams it completed sometimes served not an acre of public land. It did increase homestead filings substantially, but not all those homesteads ended up in the hands of Jeffersonian yeomen: according to a 1922 survey, it had created few family farms; the 160-acre limitation was never enforced; three-quarters of the farmers in some reclamation districts were tenants.

Drought, the Great Depression, and the New Deal's effort to make public works jobs gave the bureau new life. It got quick appropriations for the building of the Boulder (Hoover) Dam, already authorized, and it took over from the state of California construction of the enormous complex of dams and ditches called the Central Valley Project, designed to harness all the rivers flowing westward out of the Sierra. It grew like a mushroom, like an exhalation. By the 1940s the bureau that only a few years before had been hanging on by a shoestring had built or was building the four greatest dams ever built on earth up to that time—Hoover, Shasta, Bonneville, and Grand Coulee—and was already the greatest force in the West. It had discovered where power was, and allied itself with it: with the growers and landowners, private and corporate, whose interests it served, and with the political delegations, often elected out of this same group, who carried the effort in Washington for more and more pork barrel projects. In matters of western water there are no political parties. You cannot tell Barry Goldwater from Moe Udall, or Orrin Hatch from Richard Lamm.

Nevertheless there was growing opposition to dams from nature lovers, from economists and cost counters, and from political representatives of areas that resented paying these costs in subsidy of their competition. Uniting behind the clause in the National Park Service Act that enjoined "use without impairment," environmental groups in 1955 blocked two dams in Dinosaur National Monument and stopped the whole Upper Colorado River Storage Project in its tracks. Later, in the 1960s, they also blocked a dam in Marble Canyon, on the Colorado, and another in Grand Canyon National Monument, at the foot of the Grand Canyon.

In the process they accumulated substantial evidence, economic, political, and environmental, against dams, the bureau that built them, and the principles that guided that bureau. President Jimmy Carter had a lot of public sympathy when he tried to stop nine water-project boondoggles, most of them in the West, in 1977. Though the hornet's nest he stirred up taught him something about western water politics, observers noted that no new water projects were authorized by Congress until the very last days of the 99th Congress, in October 1986.

The great days of dam building are clearly over, for the best dam sites are used up, most of the rivers are "tamed," costs have risen exponentially, and public support of reclamation has given way to widespread and searching criticism. It is not a bad time to assess what the big era of water engineering has done to the West.

The voices of reappraisal are already a chorus. Four books in particular, all published within the past four years, have examined western water developments and practices in detail. They are Philip Fradkin's *A River No More,* about the killing of the Colorado; William A. Kahrl's *Water and Power,* on the rape of the Owens Valley by Los Angeles; Donald Worster's *Rivers of Empire,* a dismaying survey of our irrigation society in the light of Karl Wittvogel's studies of the ancient hydraulic civilizations of Mesopotamia and China; and Marc Reisner's *Cadillac Desert,* a history that pays particular unfriendly attention to the Bureau of Reclamation and its most empire-building director, Floyd Dominy.

None of those books is calculated to please agribusiness or the politicians and bureaucrats who have served it. Their consensus is that reclamation dams and their little brother the centrifugal pump have made an impressive omelet but have broken many eggs, some of them golden, and are in the process of killing the goose that laid them.

B EGIN with some environmental consequences of "taming" rivers, if only because the first substantial opposition to dams was environmental.

First, dams do literally kill rivers, which means they kill not only living water and natural scenery but a whole congeries of values associated with them. The scenery they kill is often of the grandest, for most main-stem dams are in splendid canyons, which they drown. San Francisco drowned the Hetch Hetchy Valley, which many thought as beautiful as Yosemite itself, to ensure its future water supply. Los Angeles turned the Owens Valley into a desert by draining off its natural water supplies. The Bureau of Reclamation drowned Glen Canyon, the most serene and lovely rock funhouse in the West, to provide peaking power for Los Angeles and the Las Vegas Strip.

The lakes formed behind dams are sometimes cited as great additions to public recreation, and Floyd Dominy even published a book to prove that the Glen Canyon Dam had beautified Glen Canyon by drowning it. But drawdown reservoirs rarely live up to their billing. Nothing grows in the zone between low-water mark and high-water mark, and except when brimming full, any drawdown reservoir, even Glen Canyon, which escapes the worst effects because its walls are vertical, is not unlike a dirty bathtub with a ring of mud and mineral stain around it.

A dammed river is not only stoppered like a bathtub, but it is turned on and off like a tap, creating a fluctuation of flow that destroys the riverine and riparian wildlife and creates problems for recreational boatmen who have to adjust to times when the river is mainly boulders and times when it rises thirty feet and washes their tied boats off the beaches. And since dams prohibit the really high flows of the spring runoff, boulders, gravel, and detritus pile up into the channel at the mouths of side gulches, and never get washed away.

Fishing too suffers, and not merely today's fishing but the future of fishing. Despite their fish ladders, the dams on the Columbia seriously reduced the spawning runs of salmon and steelhead, and they also trapped and killed so many smolts on their way downriver that eventually the federal government had to regulate the river's flow. The reduction of fishing is felt not only by the offshore fishing fleets and by Indian tribes with traditional or treaty fishing rights, but by sports fishermen all the way upstream to the Salmon River Mountains in Idaho.

If impaired rafting and fishing and sight-seeing seem a trivial price to pay for all the economic benefits supposedly brought by dams, reflect that rafting and fishing and sight-seeing are not trivial economic activities. Tourism is the biggest industry in every western state. The national parks, which are mainly in the public lands states, saw over three hundred million visitors in 1984. The national forests saw even more. A generation ago, only five thousand people in all the United States had ever rafted a river; by 1985, thirty-five million had. Every western river from the Rogue and the Owyhee to the Yampa, Green, San Juan, and Colorado is booked solid through the running season. As the rest of the country grows more stressful as a dwelling place, the quiet, remoteness, and solitude of a week on a wild river become more and more precious to more and more people. It is a good question whether we may not need that silence, space, and solitude for the healing of our raw spirits more than we need surplus cotton and alfalfa, produced for private profit at great public expense.

The objections to reclamation go beyond the obvious fact that reservoirs in desert country lose a substantial amount of their impounded water through surface evaporation; and the equally obvious fact that all such reservoirs eventually silt up and become mud flats ending in concrete waterfalls; and the further fact that an occasional dam, because of faulty siting or construction, will go out, as the Teton Dam went out in 1976, bringing disaster to people, towns, and fields below. They go beyond the fact that underground water, recklessly pumped, is quickly depleted, and that some of it will only be renewed in geological time, and that the management of underground water and that of surface water are necessarily linked. The ultimate objection is that irrigation agriculture itself, in deserts where surface evaporation is extreme, has a limited though unpredictable life. Marc Reisner predicts that in the next half century as much irrigated land will go out of production as the Bureau of Reclamation has "reclaimed" in its whole history.

Over time, salts brought to the surface by constant flooding and evaporation poison the soil: the ultimate, natural end of an irrigated field in arid country is an alkali flat. That was the end of fields in every historic irrigation civilization except Egypt, where, until the Aswan Dam, the annual Nile flood leached away salts and renewed the soil with fresh silt.

Leaching can sometimes be managed if you have enough sweet water and a place to put the runoff. But there is rarely water enough—the water is already 125 percent allocated and 100 percent used—and what water is available is often itself saline from having run through other fields upstream and having brought their salts back to the river. Colorado River water near the headwaters at Grand Lake is 200 parts per million (ppm) salt. Below the Wellton-Mohawk District on the Gila it is 6,300 ppm salt. The 1.5 million acre feet that we are pledged to deliver to Mexico is so saline that we are having to build a desalinization plant to sweeten it before we send it across the border.

Furthermore, even if you have enough water for occasional leaching, you have to have somewhere to drain off the waste water, which is likely not only to be saline, but to be contaminated with fertilizers, pesticides, and poisonous trace minerals such as selenium. Kesterson Reservoir, in the Central Valley near Los Banos, is a recent notorious instance, whose two-headed, three-legged, or merely dead waterfowl publicized the dangers of draining waste water off into a slough. If it is drained off into a river, or out to sea, the results are not usually so dramatic. But the inedible fish of the New River draining into the Salton Sea, and the periodically polluted beaches of Monterey Bay near the mouth of the Salinas River, demonstrate that agricultural runoff is poison anywhere.

The West's irrigated bounty is not forever, not on the scale or at the rate we have been gathering it in. The part of it that is dependent on wells is even more precarious than that dependent on dams. In California's San Joaquin Valley, streams and dams supply only 60 percent of the demand for water; the rest is pumped from wells—hundreds and thousands of wells. Pumping exceeds replenishment by a half-trillion gallons a year. In places the water table has been pumped down three hundred feet; in places the ground itself has sunk thirty feet or more. But with those facts known, and an end clearly in sight, nobody is willing to stop, and there is as yet no state regulation of groundwater pumping.

In Arizona the situation is if anything worse. 90 percent of Arizona's irrigation depends on pumping. And in Nebraska and Kansas and Oklahoma, old Dust Bowl country, they prepare for the next dust bowl, which is as inevitable as sunrise though a little harder to time, by pumping away the groundwater through center-pivot sprinklers.

Add to the facts about irrigation the fact of the oversubscribing of rivers. The optimists say that when more water is needed, the engineers will find a way—"augmentation" from the Columbia or elsewhere for the Colorado's overdrawn reservoirs, or the implementation of cosmic schemes such as NAWAPA (North American Water and Power Alliance), which would dam all the Canadian rivers up against the east face of the Rockies, and from that Mediterranean-sized reservoir supply water to every needy district from Minneapolis to Yuma. I think that there are geological as well as political difficulties in the way of water redistribution on that scale. The solution of western problems does not lie in more grandiose engineering.

Throw into the fact barrel, finally, a 1983 report from the Council on Environmental Quality concluding that desertification—the process of converting a viable arid-lands ecology into a lifeless waste—proceeds faster in the western United States than in Africa. Some of that desertification is the result of overgrazing, but the salinization of fields does its bit. When the hydraulic society falls back from its outermost frontiers, it will have done its part in the creation of new deserts.

T HE hydraulic society. I borrow the term from Donald Worster, who borrowed it from Karl Wittvogel. Wittvogel's studies convinced him that every hydraulic society is by necessity an autocracy. Power, he thought, inevitably comes to reside in the elite that understands and exercises control over water. He quotes C. S. Lewis: "What we call man's power over nature turns out to be a power exercised by some men over other men with nature as its instrument" (*The Abolition of Man,* p. 35); and Andre Gorz: "The total domination of nature inevitably entails a domination of people by the techniques of domination" (*Ecology as Politics,* p. 20). Those quotations suggest a very different approach from the human domination advocated by such as John Widtsoe.

The hydraulic society involves the maximum domination of nature. And the American West, Worster insists, is the greatest hydraulic society the world ever saw, far surpassing in its techniques of domination the societies on the Indus, the Tigris-Euphrates, or the Yellow River. The West, which Walter Webb and Bernard DeVoto both feared might remain a colonial dependency of the East, has instead become an empire and gotten the East to pay most of the bills.

The case as Worster puts it is probably overstated. There are, one hopes, more democratic islands than he allows for, more areas outside the domination of the water managers and users. Few parts of the West are totally controlled by what Worster sees as a hydraulic elite. Nevertheless, no one is likely to call the agribusiness West, with most of its power concentrated in the Iron Triangle of growers, politicians, and bureaucratic experts and its work done by a permanent underclass of dispossessed, mainly alien migrants, the agrarian democracy that the Newlands Act was supposed to create.

John Wesley Powell understood that a degree of land monopoly could easily come about in the West through control of water. A thorough Populist, he advocated cooperative rather than federal waterworks, and he probably never conceived of anything on the imperial scale later realized by the Bureau of Reclamation. But if he were alive today he would have to agree at least partway with Worster: water experts ambitious to build and expand their bureau and perhaps honestly convinced of the worth of what they are doing have allied themselves with landowners and politicians, and by making land monopoly through water control immensely profitable for their backers, they have made it inevitable.

How profitable? Worster cites figures from one of the most recent of the mamoth projects, the Westlands, that brought water to the western side of the San Joaquin Valley. Including interest over forty years, the cost to the taxpayers was $3 billion. Water is delivered to the beneficiaries, mostly large landholders, at $7.50 an acre foot—far below actual cost, barely enough to pay operation and maintenance costs. According to a study conducted by economists Philip LaVeen and George Goldman, the subsidy amounted to $2,200 an acre, $352,000 per quarter section—and very few quarter-section family farmers were among the beneficiaries. Large landholders obliged by the 160-acre limitation to dispose of their excess lands disposed of them to family members and cronies, paper farmers, according to a pattern by now well established among water users.

So much for the Jeffersonian yeoman and the agrarian democracy. As for another problem that Powell foresaw, the difficulty that a family would have in handling even 160 acres of intensively farmed irrigated land, both the corporate and the family farmers solve it the same way: with migrant labor, much of it illegally recruited below the Rio Grande. It is anybody's guess what will happen now that Congress has passed the Immigration Reform and Control Act, but up to now the border has been a sieve, carefully kept open from this side. On a recent rafting trip through the Big Bend canyons of the Rio Grande, my son twice surprised sheepdog functionaries herding wetbacks to safety in America.

Those wetbacks are visible not merely in California and

Texas, but pretty much throughout the West. Visiting Rigby, Idaho, up in the farming country below the washed-out Teton Dam, I found a shantytown where the universal language was Spanish. Wherever there are jobs to do, especially laborious or dirty jobs—picking crops, killing turkeys—there have been wetbacks brought in to do them. Like drug running, the importation of illegals has resulted from a strong, continuing American demand, most of it from the factories in the fields of the hydraulic society. One has to wonder if penalties for such importations will inhibit growers any more than the 160-acre limitation historically did.

M ARC Reisner, in *Cadillac Desert,* is less concerned with the social consequences than with the costs and environmental losses and the plain absurdities of our long battle with aridity.

> Only a government that disposes of a billion
> dollars every few hours would still be selling water
> in deserts for less than a penny a ton. And only an
> agency as antediluvian as the Bureau of Reclama-
> tion, hiding in a government as elephantine as
> ours, could successfully camouflage the enormous
> losses the taxpayer has to bear for its generosity.
> (P. 500)

Charles P. Berkey of Columbia University, a hydrologist, wrote in 1946,

The United States has virtually set up an empire
on impounded and re-distributed water. The nation is encouraging development, on a scale never
before attempted, of lands that are almost worthless except for the water that can be delivered to
them by the works of man. There is building up,
through settlement and new population, a line of
industries foreign to the normal resources of the
region. . . . One can claim (and it is true) that
much has been added to the world; but the longer
range view in this field, as in many others, is
threatened by apparently incurable ailments and
this one of slowly choking to death with silt is the
most stubborn of all. There are no permanent
cures. (Letter quoted in Kazmann, *Modern Hydrology,* p. 124)

Raphael Kazmann himself agrees:

The reservoir construction program, objectively
considered, is really a program for the continued
and endless expenditure of ever-increasing sums of
public money to combat the effects of geologic
forces, as these forces strive to reach positions of
relative equilibrium in the region of rivers and the
flow of water. It may be that future research in the
field of modern hydrology will be primarily to find
a method of extricating ourselves from this unequal struggle with minimum loss to the nation.
(P. 125)

And Donald Worster pronounces the benediction: "The next stage after empire is decline." The West, aware of its own history, might phrase it differently: The next stage after boom is bust. Again.

WHAT should one make of facts as depressing as these? What do such facts do to the self-gratifying image of the West as the home of freedom, independence, largeness, spaciousness, and of the Westerner as total self-reliance on a white stallion? I confess they make this Westerner yearn for the old days on the Milk and the Missouri when those rivers ran free, and we were trying to learn how to live with the country, and the country seemed both hard and simple, and the world and I were young, when irrigation had not yet grown beyond its legitimate bounds and the West provided for its thin population a hard living but a wonderful life.

Sad to say, they make me admit, when I face them, that the West is no more the Eden that I once thought it than the Garden of the World that the boosters and engineers tried to make it; and that neither nostalgia nor boosterism can any longer make a case for it as the geography of hope.

. . . . . . . . . . . . . . . . . . . .

# THREE

# Variations on a Theme by Crèvecoeur

THERE are many kinds of wildernesses, Aldo Leopold wrote in *A Sand County Almanac,* and each kind forces on people a different set of adaptations and creates a different pattern of life, custom, and belief. These patterns we call cultures.

By that criterion, the West should have a different cultural look from other American regions, and within the regional culture there should be discernible a half dozen subcultures stemming from our adaptations to shortgrass plains, alpine mountains, slickrock canyons, volcanic scablands, and both high and low deserts.

But cultural differentiation takes a long time, and happens most completely in isolation and to homogeneous peoples, as it happened to the Paiutes. The West has had neither time nor isolation nor homogeneity of race and occupation. Change, both homegrown and imported, has overtaken time, time and again. We have to adapt not only to our changed physical environment but to our own adaptations, and sometimes we have to backtrack from our own mistakes.

Forming cultures involving heterogeneous populations do not grow steadily from definable quality to definable quality. Not only is their development complicated by class, caste, and social mobility, but they undergo simultaneous processes of erosion and deposition. They start from something, not from nothing. Habits and attitudes that have come to us embedded in our inherited culture, especially our inherited language, come incorporated in everything from nursery rhymes to laws and prayers, and they often have the durability of flint pebbles in puddingstone. No matter how completely their old matrix is dissolved, they remain intact, and are deposited almost unchanged in the strata of the new culture.

The population that for the eleven public lands states and territories was four million in 1900 was forty-five million in 1984, with at least a couple of million more, and perhaps twice that many, who weren't counted and didn't want to be. Many of those forty-five or forty-seven or forty-nine million came yesterday, since the end of World War II. They have not adapted, in the cultural sense, very far. Some of them are living anonymously in the Spanish-speaking barrios of San Diego, El Paso, Los Angeles, San Jose, where the Immigration Service can't find them. Some are experimenting with quick-change life-styles in the cultural confusion of western cities. Some are reading *Sunset Magazine* to find out what they should try to become. Some already know, from the movies and TV.

Being a Westerner is not simple. If you live, say, in Los Angeles, you live in the second largest city in the nation, urban as far as the eye can see in every direction except west. There is, or was in 1980—the chances would be somewhat greater now—a 6.6 percent chance that you are Asian, a 16.7 percent chance that you are black, and a 27 percent chance that you are Hispanic. You have only a 48 percent chance of being a non-Hispanic white.

This means that instead of being suitable for casting in the cowboy and pioneer roles familiar from the mythic and movie West, you may be one of those Chinks or Spics or Greasers for whom the legendary West had a violent contempt. You'd like to be a hero, and you may adopt the costume and attitudes you admire, but your color or language or the slant of your eyes tells you that you are one of the kind scheduled to be a villain or a victim, and your current status as second-class citizen confirms that view. You're part of a subculture envious of or hostile to the dominant one.

This ethnic and cultural confusion exists not only in Los Angeles but in varying proportions in every western city and many western towns. Much of the adaptation that is going on is adaptation to a very uncertain reality or to a reality whose past and present do not match. The western culture and western character with which it is easiest to identify exist largely in the West of make-believe, where they can be kept simple.

As invaders, we were rarely, or only temporarily, dependent on the materials, foods, or ideas of the regions we pioneered. The champagne and oysters that cheered midnight suppers during San Francisco's Gold Rush period were not local, nor was the taste that demanded them. The dominant white culture was always aware of its origins; it brought its origins with it across the plains or around the Horn, and it kept in touch with them.

The Spanish of New Mexico, who also brought their origins with them, are in other ways an exception. Settled at the end of the sixteenth century, before Jamestown and Quebec and well before the Massachusetts Bay Colony, New Mexico existed in isolation, dependent largely on

*California, Central Valley Project, 1930s*

itself, until the Americans forcibly took it over in 1846; and during those two and a half centuries it had a high Indian culture close at hand to teach it how to live with the country. Culturally, the Spanish Southwest is an island, adapted in its own ways, in many ways alien.

By contrast, the Anglo-American West, barely breached until the middle of the nineteenth century, was opened during a time of rapid communication. It was linked with the world by ship, rail, and telegraph before the end of the 1860s, and the isolation of even its brief, explosive outposts, its Alder Gulches and Cripple Creeks, was anything but total. Excited travelers reported the West in words to match its mountains; it was viewed in Currier and Ives prints drawn by enthusiasts who had never been there except in imagination. The outside never got over its heightened and romantic notion of the West. The West never got over its heightened and romantic notion of itself.

The pronounced differences that some people see between the West and other parts of America need to be examined. Except as they involve Spanish or Indian cultures, they could be mainly illusory, the result of the tendency to see the West in its mythic enlargement rather than as it is, and of the corollary tendency to take our cues from myths in the effort to enhance our lives. Life does sometimes copy art. More than drugstore cowboys and street corner Kit Carsons succumb. Plenty of authentic ranch hands have read pulp Westerns in the shade of the bunkhouse and got up walking, talking, and thinking like Buck Duane or Hopalong Cassidy.

No matter what kind of wilderness it developed in, every part of the real West was a melting-pot mixture of people from everywhere, operating under the standard American drives of restlessness, aggressiveness, and great expectations, and with the standard American freedom that often crossed the line into violence. It was supposed to be a democracy, and at least in the sense that it was often every man for himself, it was. Though some of its phases—the fur trade, the gold rushes, the open range cattle industry—lasted hardly longer than the blink of an eye, other phases—logging, irrigation farming, the stock farm with cattle or sheep—have lasted by now for a century or more, and have formed the basis for relatively stable communities with some of the attributes of place, some identity as subcultures of the prevailing postfrontier culture of America. If Turner's thesis is applicable beyond the 98th meridian, then the West ought to be, with minor local variations, America only more so.

Actually it is and it isn't. It would take fast footwork to dance the society based on big reclamation projects into a democracy. Even the cattle kingdom from which we derive our most individualistic and independent folk hero was never a democracy as the Middle West, say, was a democracy. The real-life cattle baron was and is about as democratic as a feudal baron. The cowboy in practice was and is an overworked, underpaid hireling, almost as homeless and dispossessed as a modern crop worker, and his fabled independence was and is chiefly the privilege of quitting his job in order to go looking for another just as bad. That, or go outside the law, as some did. There is a discrepancy between the real conditions of the West, which even among outlaws enforced cooperation and group effort, and the folklore of the West, which celebrated the dissidence of dissent, the most outrageous independence. Bernard DeVoto once cynically guessed that the only true individualists in the West wound up on the end of a rope whose other end was in the hands of a bunch of cooperators.

The dynamics of contemporary adaptation work ambiguously. The best imitators of frontier individualism these days are probably Silicon Valley and conglomerate executives, whose entrepreneurial attributes are not greatly different from those of an old-time cattle baron. Little people must salve with daydreams and fantasy the wounds of living. Some may imagine themselves becoming captains of industry, garage inventors whose inventions grow into Fortune 500 companies overnight; but I think that more of them are likely to cuddle up to a culture hero independent of the system and even opposed to it—a culture hero given them by Owen Wister, an eastern snob who saw in the common cowherd the lineaments of Lancelot. Chivalry, or the daydream of it, is at least as common among daydreamers as among entrepreneurs.

P HYSICALLY, the West could only be itself. Its scale, its colors, its landforms, its plants and animals, tell a traveler what country he is in, and a native that he is at home. Even western cities owe most of their distinctiveness to their physical setting. Albuquerque with its mud-colored houses spreading like clay banks along the valley of the Rio Grande could only be New Mexico. Denver's ringworm suburbs on the apron of the Front Range could only be boom-time Colorado. Salt Lake City bracing back against the Wasatch and looking out toward the dead sea and the barren ranges could only be the Great Basin.

But is anything except their setting distinctive? The people in them live on streets named Main and State, Elm and Poplar, First and Second, like Americans elsewhere. They eat the same Wheaties and Wonder Bread and Big Macs, watch the same ball games and soaps and sitcoms on TV, work at the same industrial or service jobs, suffer from the same domestic crises and industrial blights, join the same health clubs and neighborhood protective associations, and in general behave and misbehave much as they would in Omaha or Chicago or East Orange. The homogenizing media have certainly been at work on them, perhaps with more effect than the arid spaciousness of the region itself, and while making them more like everybody else have also given them misleading clues about who they are.

"WHO is the American, this new man?" Crèvecoeur asked rhetorically in his *Letters from an American Farmer* more than two hundred years ago, and went on to idealize him as the American farmer—industrious, optimistic, upwardly mobile, family-oriented, socially responsible, a new man given new hope in the new world, a lover of both hearth and earth, a builder of communities. He defined him in the terms of a new freedom, emancipated from feudalism, oppression, and poverty, but with no wish to escape society or its responsibilities. Quite the contrary.

Crèvecoeur also sketched, with distaste, another kind of American, a kind he thought would fade away with the raw frontier that had created him. This kind lived alone or with a slattern woman and a litter of kids out in the woods. He had no fixed abode, tilled no ground or tilled it only fitfully, lived by killing, was footloose, uncouth, anti-social, impatient of responsibility and law. The eating of wild meat, Crèvecoeur said, made him ferocious and gloomy. Too much freedom promoted in him a coarse selfishness and a readiness to violence.

The pioneer farmer as Crèvecoeur conceived him has a place in western history, and as the Jeffersonian yeoman he had a prominent place in the mistaken effort to oversettle the West, first by homestead and later by reclamation. Traces of him are to be found in western literature, art, and myth. Sculptors have liked his sturdy figure plodding beside the covered wagon on which ride his poke-bonneted wife and his barefoot children. He strides through a lot of WPA murals. The Mormons, farmers in the beginning, idealize him. He has achieved more than life size in such novels of the migration as *The Covered Wagon* and *The Way West*.

But those, as I have already suggested, are novels more of motion than of place, and the emigrants in them are simply farmer-pioneers on their way to new farms. They have not adapted to the West in the slightest degree. They belong where the soil is deep, where the Homestead Act worked, where settlers planted potato peelings in their fireguards and adjourned to build a combination school–church–social hall almost before they had roofs on their shanties. The pioneer farmer is a midwestern, not a western, figure. He is a pedestrian, and in the West, horseman's country even for people who never got on a horse in their lives, pedestrians suffer from the horseman's contempt that seems as old as the Scythians. The farmer's very virtues as responsible husband, father, and home builder are against him as a figure of the imagination. To the fantasizing mind he is dull, the ancestor of the clodhopper, the hayseed, and the hick. I have heard Wyoming ranch hands jeer their relatives from Idaho, not because the relatives were Mormons—so were the ranch hands—but because they were farmers, potato diggers.

It was Crèvecoeur's wild man, the borderer emancipated into total freedom, first in eastern forests and then in the plains and mountains of the West, who really fired our imaginations, and still does. We have sanitized him somewhat, but our principal folk hero, in all his shapes good and bad, is essentially antisocial.

In real life, as Boone, Bridger, Jed Smith, Kit Carson, he appeals to us as having lived a life of heroic courage, skill, and self-reliance. Some of his manifestations such as Wild Bill Hickok and Buffalo Bill Cody are tainted with outlawry or showmanship, but they remain more than life-size. Even psychopathic killers such as Billy the Kid and Tom Horn throw a long shadow, and some outlaws such as Butch Cassidy and Harry Longabaugh have all the engaging imitability of Robin Hood. What charms us in them is partly their daring, skill, and invulnerability, partly their chivalry; but not to be overlooked is their impatience with all restraint, their freedom from the social responsibility that Crèvecoeur admired in his citizen farmer, and that on occasion bows the shoulders of every man born.

Why should I stand up for civilization? Thoreau asked a lecture audience. Any burgher or churchwarden would stand up for that. Thoreau chose instead to stand up for wildness and the savage heart.

We all know that impulse. When youths run away from home, they don't run away to become farmers. They run away to become romantic isolates, lone riders who slit their eyes against steely distance and loosen the carbine in its scabbard when they see law, or obligation, or even company, approaching.

Lawlessness, like wildness, is attractive, and we conceive the last remaining home of both to be the West. In a folklore predominantly masculine and macho, even women take on the look. Calamity Jane is more familiar to us than Dame Shirley, though Dame Shirley had it all over Jane in brains, and could have matched her in courage, and lived in mining camps every bit as rough as the cow towns and camps that Calamity Jane frequented.

The attraction of lawlessness did not die with the frontier, either. Look at the survivalist Claude Dallas, who a couple of years ago killed two Idaho game wardens when they caught him poaching—shot them and then finished them off with a bullet in the back of the head. In that act of unchivalrous violence Dallas was expressing more than an unwillingness to pay a little fine. For months, until he was captured early in 1987, he hid out in the deserts of Idaho and Nevada, protected by people all over the area. Why did they protect him? Because his belated frontiersman style, his total self-reliance and physical competence, his repudiation of any control, appealed to them more than murder repelled them or law enlisted their support.

All this may seem remote from the life of the average Westerner, who lives in a city and is more immediately concerned with taxes, schools, his job, drugs, the World Series, or even disarmament, than with archetypal figures out of folklore. But it is not so remote as it seems. Habits persist. The hoodlums who come to San Francisco to beat up gays are vigilantes, enforcing their prejudices with violence, just as surely as were the miners who used to hunt down Indians and hang Chinese in the Mother Lode, or the ranchers who rode out to exterminate the nesters in Wyoming's Johnson County War.

Habits persist. The hard, aggressive, single-minded energy that according to politicians made America great is demonstrated every day in resource raids and leveraged takeovers by entrepreneurs; and along with that competitive individualism and ruthlessness goes a rejection of any controlling past or tradition. What matters is here, now, the seizable opportunity. "We don't need any history," said one Silicon Valley executive when the Santa Clara County Historical Society tried to bring the electronics industry together with the few remaining farmers to discuss what was happening to the valley that only a decade or two ago was the fruit bowl of the world. "What we need is more attention to our computers and the moves of the competition."

We are not so far from our models, real and fictional, as we think. As on a wild river, the water passes, the waves remain. A high degree of mobility, a degree of ruthlessness, a large component of both self-sufficiency and self-righteousness mark the historical pioneer, the lone-riding folk hero, and the modern businessman intent on opening new industrial frontiers and getting his own in the process. The same qualities inform the extreme individualists who believe that they belong to nothing except what they choose to belong to, those who try on life-styles as some try on clothes, whose only communal association is with what Robert Bellah calls "life-style enclaves," casual and temporary groupings of the like-minded. One reason why it is so difficult to isolate any definitely western culture is that so many Westerners, like other Americans only more so, shy away from commitment. Mobility of every sort—physical, familial, social, corporate, occupational, religious, sexual—confirms and reinforces the illusion of independence.

Back to the freedom-loving loner, whom we might call Leatherstocking's descendant, as Henry Nash Smith taught us to, if all that tribe were not childless as well as orphaned. In the West this figure acquired an irresistible costume—the boots, spurs, chaps, and sombrero bequeathed to him by Mexican vaqueros, plus the copper-riveted canvas pants invented for California miners by a peddler named Levi Strauss—but he remained estranged from real time, real place, and any real society or occupation. In fact, it is often organized society, in the shape of a crooked sheriff and his cronies, that this loner confronts and confounds.

The notion of civilization's corruption, the notion that the conscience of an antisocial savage is less calloused than the conscience of society, is of course a bequest from Jean-Jacques Rousseau. The chivalry of the antisocial one, his protectiveness of the weak and oppressed, especially those whom James Fenimore Cooper customarily referred to as "females," is from Cooper with reinforcement from two later romantics, Frederic Remington and Owen Wister, collaborators in the creation of the knight-errant in chaps.

The hero of Wister's 1902 novel *The Virginian* is gentle-seeming, easygoing, humorous, but when the wicked force him into action he is the very gun of God, better at violence than the wicked are. He is a daydream of glory made flesh. But note that the Virginian not only defeats Trampas in a gunfight as formalized as a fourteenth-century joust, the first of a thousand literary and movie walk-downs, but he also joins the vigilantes and in the name of law and order acts as jury, judge, and hangman for his friend Shorty, who has gone bad and become a rustler.

The Virginian feels sorry about Shorty, but he never questions that the stealing of a few mavericks should be punished by death, any more than Wister questioned the motives of his Wyoming rancher host who led the Johnson County vigilantes against the homesteaders they despised and called rustlers. This culture hero is himself law. Law is whatever he and his companions (and employers) believe (which means law is his and their self-interest).

Whatever action he takes is law enforcement. Compare Larry McMurtry's two ex-Texas Rangers in *Lonesome Dove*. They kill more people than all the outlaws in that book put together do, but their killings are *right*. Their lawlessness is justified by the lack of any competing socialized law, and by a supreme confidence in themselves, as if every judgment of theirs could be checked back to Coke and Blackstone, if not to Leviticus.

Critics have noted that in *The Virginian* (and for that matter in most of its successors, though not in *Lonesome Dove*) there are no scenes involving cattle. There is no manure, no punching of postholes or stringing of barbed wire, none of the branding, castrating, dehorning, dipping, and horseshoeing that real cowboys, hired men on horseback, spend their laborious and unromantic lives at. The physical universe is simplified like the moral one. Time is stopped.

The Virginian is the standard American orphan, dislocated from family, church, and place of origin, with an uncertain past identified only by his nickname. With his knightly sense of honor and his capacity to outviolence the violent, he remains an irresistible model for romantic adolescents of any age, and he transfers readily from the cowboy setting to more modern ones. It is only a step from his "When you call me that, smile," to the remark made famous by the current mayor of Carmel and the fortieth president of the United States: "Go ahead, make my day."

There are thousands more federal employees in the West than there are cowboys—more bookkeepers, aircraft and electronics workers, auto mechanics, printers, fry cooks. There may be more writers. Nevertheless, when most Americans east of the Missouri hear the word "West" they think "cowboy." Recently a documentary filmmaker asked me to be a consultant on a film that would finally reveal the true West, without romanticizing or adornment. It was to be done by chronicling the life of a single real-life individual. Guess who he was. A cowboy, and a rodeo cowboy at that—a man who had run away from his home in Indiana at the age of seventeen, worked for a year on a Texas ranch, found the work hard, made his way onto the rodeo circuit, and finally retired with a lot of his vertebrae out of line to an Oklahoma town where he made silver-mounted saddles and bridles suitable for the Sheriff's Posse in a Frontier Days parade, and spun yarns for the wide-eyed local young.

Apart from the fantasy involved in it, which is absolutely authentic, that show business life is about as typically western as a bullfighter's is typically Spanish. The critics will probably praise the film for its realism.

I spend this much time on a mythic figure who has irritated me all my life because I would obviously like to bury him. But I know I can't. He is a faster gun than I am. He is too attractive to the daydreaming imagination. It gets me nowhere to object to the self-righteous, limited, violent code that governs him, or to disparage the novels of Louis L'Amour because they are mass-produced with interchangeable parts. Mr. L'Amour sells in the millions, and has readers in the White House.

But what one can say, and be sure of, is that even while

the cowboy myth romanticizes and falsifies western life, it says something true about western, and hence about American, character.

Western culture and character, hard to define in the first place because they are only half-formed and constantly changing, are further clouded by the mythic stereotype. Why hasn't the stereotype faded away as real cowboys became less and less typical of western life? Because we can't or won't do without it, obviously. But also there is the visible, pervasive fact of western space, which acts as a preservative. Space, itself the product of incorrigible aridity and hence more or less permanent, continues to suggest unrestricted freedom, unlimited opportunity for testings and heroisms, a continuing need for self-reliance and physical competence. The untrammeled individualist persists partly as a residue of the real and romantic frontiers, but also partly because runaways from more restricted regions keep reimporting him. The stereotype continues to affect romantic Westerners and non-Westerners in romantic ways, but if I am right it also affects real Westerners in real ways.

In the West it is impossible to be unconscious of or indifferent to space. At every city's edge it confronts us as federal lands kept open by aridity and the custodial bureaus; out in the boondocks it engulfs us. And it does contribute to individualism, if only because in that much emptiness people have the dignity of rareness and must do much of what they do without help, and because self-reliance becomes a social imperative, part of a code. Witness the crudely violent code that governed a young Westerner like Norman Maclean, as he reported it in the stories of *A River Runs through It.* Witness the way in which space haunts the poetry of such western poets as William Stafford, Richard Hugo, Gary Snyder. Witness the lonely, half-attached childhood of a writer such as Ivan Doig. I feel the childhood reported in his *This House of Sky* because it is so much like my own.

Even in the cities, even among the dispossessed migrants of the factories in the fields, space exerts a diluted influence as illusion and reprieve. Westerners live outdoors more than people elsewhere, because outdoors is mainly what they've got. For clerks and students, factory workers and mechanics, the outdoors is freedom, just as surely as it is for the folkloric and mythic figures. They don't have to own the outdoors, or get permission, or cut fences, in order to use it. It is public land, partly theirs, and that space is a continuing influence on their minds and senses. It encourages a fatal carelessness and destructiveness because it seems so limitless and because what is everybody's is nobody's responsibility. It also encourages, in some, an impassioned protectiveness: the battlegrounds of the environmental movement lie in the western public lands. Finally, it promotes certain needs, tastes, attitudes, skills. It is those tastes, attitudes, and skills, as well as the prevailing destructiveness and its corrective, love of the land, that relate real Westerners to the myth.

David Rains Wallace, in *The Wilder Shore,* has traced the effect of the California landscape—the several California landscapes from the Pacific shore to the inner deserts—on

California writers. From Dana to Didion, the influence has been varied and powerful. It is there in John Muir ecstatically riding a storm in the top of a two-hundred-foot sugar pine; in Mary Austin quietly absorbing wisdom from a Paiute basketmaker; in Jack London's Nietzschean supermen pitting themselves not only against society but against the universe; in Frank Norris's atavistic McTeague, shackled to a corpse that he drags through the 130-degree heat of Death Valley; and in Robinson Jeffers on his stone platform between the stars and the sea, falling in love outward toward space. It is also there in the work of western photographers, notably Ansel Adams, whose grand, manless images are full of the awe men feel in the face of majestic nature. Awe is common in that California tradition. Humility is not.

Similar studies could be made, and undoubtedly will be, of the literature of other parts of the West, and of special groups of writers such as Native Americans who are mainly western. The country lives, still holy, in Scott Momaday's *Way to Rainy Mountain*. It is there like a half-forgotten promise in Leslie Marmon Silko's *Ceremony*, and like a homeland lost to invaders in James Welch's *Winter in the Blood* and Louise Erdrich's *Love Medicine*. It is a dominating presence, as I have already said, in the work of Northwest writers.

Western writing turns out, not surprisingly, to be largely about things that happen outdoors. It often involves characters who show a family resemblance of energetic individualism, great physical competence, stoicism, determination, recklessness, endurance, toughness, rebelliousness, resistance to control. It has, that is, residual qualities of the heroic, as the country in which it takes place has residual qualities of the wilderness frontier.

Those characteristics are not the self-conscious creation of regional patriotism, or the result of imitation of older by younger, or greater by lesser, writers. They are inescapable; western life and space generate them; they are what the faithful mirror shows. When I wrote *The Big Rock Candy Mountain* I was ignorant of almost everything except what I myself had lived, and I had no context for that. By the time I wrote *Wolf Willow,* a dozen years later, and dealt with some of the same experience from another stance, I began to realize that my Bo Mason was a character with relatives throughout western fiction. I could see in him resemblance to Ole Rölvaag's Per Hansa, to Mari Sandoz's Old Jules, to A. B. Guthrie's Boone Caudill, even to the hard-jawed and invulnerable heroes of the myth. But I had not been copying other writers. I had been trying to paint a portrait of my father, and it happened that my father, an observed and particular individual, was also a type—a very western type.

Nothing suggests the separateness of western experience so clearly as the response to it of critics nourished in the Europe-oriented, politicized, sophisticated, and anti-heroic tradition of between-the-wars and postwar New York. Edmund Wilson, commenting on Hollywood writers, thought of them as wreathed in sunshine and bougainvillea, "spelling cat for the unlettered"; or as sentimental toughs, the boys in the back room; or as easterners of talent (Scott Fitzgerald was his prime example) lost to significant achievement and drowning in the La Brea tar pits.

Leslie Fiedler, an exponent of the *Partisan Review* subculture, came west to teach in Missoula in the 1950s and discovered "the Montana face"—strong, grave, silent, bland, untroubled by thought, the face of a man playing a role invented for him two centuries earlier and a continent-and-ocean away by a French romantic philosopher.

Bernard Malamud, making a similar pilgrimage to teach at Oregon State University in Corvallis, found the life of that little college town intolerable, and retreated from it to write it up in the novel *A New Life*. His Gogolian antihero S. Levin, a Jewish intellectual, heir to a thousand years of caution, deviousness, spiritual subtlety, and airless city living, was never at home in Corvallis. The faculty he was thrown among were suspiciously open, overfriendly, overhearty, outdoorish. Instead of a commerce in abstract ideas, Levin found among his colleagues a devotion to the art of fly-fishing that simply bewildered him. Grown men!

If he had waited to write his novel until Norman Maclean had written the stories of *A River Runs through It,* Malamud would have discovered that fly-fishing is not simply an art but a religion, a code of conduct and language, a way of telling the real from the phony. And if Ivan Doig had written before Leslie Fiedler shook up Missoula by the ears, Fiedler would have had another view of the Montana face. It looks different, depending on whether you encounter it as a bizarre cultural artifact on a Montana railroad platform, or whether you see it as young Ivan Doig saw the face of his dependable, skilled, likable, rootless sheepherder father. Whether, that is, you see it from outside the culture, or from inside.

In spite of the testimony of Fiedler and Malamud, if I were advising a documentary filmmaker where he might get the most quintessential West in a fifty-six-minute can, I would steer him away from broken-down rodeo riders, away from the towns of the energy boom, away from the cities, and send him to just such a little city as Missoula or Corvallis, some settlement that has managed against difficulty to make itself into a place and is likely to remain one. It wouldn't hurt at all if this little city had a university in it to keep it in touch with its cultural origins and conscious of its changing cultural present. It would do no harm if an occasional Leslie Fiedler came through to stir up its provincialism and set it to some self-questioning. It wouldn't hurt if some native-born writer, some Doig or Hugo or Maclean or Welch or Kittredge or Raymond Carver, were around to serve as culture hero—the individual who transcends his culture without abandoning it, who leaves for a while in search of opportunity and enlargement but never forgets where he left his heart.

It is in places like these, and through individuals like these, that the West will realize itself, if it ever does: these towns and cities still close to the earth, intimate and interdependent in their shared community, shared optimism, and shared memory. These are the seedbeds of an emergent western culture. They are likely to be there when the agribusiness fields have turned to alkali flats and the dams have silted up, when the waves of overpopulation that have been destroying the West have receded, leaving the stickers to get on with the business of adaptation.

# BIBLIOGRAPHY

. . . . . . . . . . . . . . . . .

The titles listed here are only those that were most immediately useful in the preparation of these lectures. They do not constitute more than the minutest fraction of a comprehensive bibliography of the West, but all of them would belong on such a comprehensive list, and most of them would be indispensable.

Austin, Mary. *The Land of Little Rain*. Boston and New York, 1903.

Bellah, Robert; Madsen, Richard; Sullivan, William M.; Swidler, Ann; and Tipton, Steven M. *Habits of the Heart*. Berkeley, 1985.

Crèvecoeur, Hector St. John. *Letters from an American Farmer,* edited with a preface by William P. Trent and an introduction by Ludwig Lewisohn. New York, 1925.

DeVoto, Bernard. *The Uneasy Chair*. Boston, 1955.

Doig, Ivan. *This House of Sky*. New York, 1978.

Fradkin, Philip L. *A River No More: The Colorado River and the West*. New York, 1981.

Gilpin, William. *The Mission of the North American People —Geographical, Social, and Political*. Philadelphia, 1873.

Kahrl, William A. *Water and Power*. Berkeley, 1982.

Kazmann, Raphael. *Modern Hydrology*. 2d ed. New York, 1972.

Leopold, Aldo. *A Sand County Almanac and Sketches Here and There*. New York, 1949.

Maclean, Norman. *A River Runs through It*. Chicago and London, 1976.

Moon, William Least Heat. *Blue Highways*. New York, 1984.

Powell, J. W. *Report on the Lands of the Arid Region of the United States, with a More Detailed Account of the Lands of Utah*. 45th Cong., 2d sess., 1878. H.R. Exec. Doc. 73.

Reisner, Marc. *Cadillac Desert: The American West and Its Disappearing Water*. New York, 1986.

Smith, Henry Nash. *Virgin Land*. Cambridge, 1950.

Stegner, Wallace. *Beyond the Hundredth Meridian: John Wesley Powell and the Second Opening of the West*. Boston, 1954.

———. *Wolf Willow: A History, a Story, and a Memory of the Last Plains Frontier*. New York, 1962.

Turner, Frederick Jackson. *The Frontier in American History*. New York, 1920.

Wallace, David Rains. *The Wilder Shore*. San Francisco, 1985.

Webb, Walter Prescott. *The Great Plains*. New York, 1931.

White, Lynn. "Historical Roots of Our Ecologic Crisis." *Science* 155(March 10, 1967):1203–7.

Widtsoe, John. *Success on Irrigation Projects*. New York, 1928.

Wister, Owen. *The Virginian*. New York, 1902.
Worster, Donald. *Rivers of Empire: Water, Aridity, and the Growth of the American West*. New York, 1985.
Zaslowsky, Dyan, and the Wilderness Society. *These American Lands*. New York, 1986.